HARVARD ORIENTAL SERIES

Edited by MICHAEL WITZEL

VOLUME SIXTY-FIVE

Kaṭha Āraṇyaka

Critical edition
with
a translation into German
and an introduction

by

Michael Witzel

PUBLISHED BY
THE DEPARTMENT
OF SANSKRIT AND INDIAN STUDIES,
HARVARD UNIVERSITY

DISTRIBUTED BY
HARVARD UNIVERSITY PRESS
CAMBRIDGE, MASSACHUSETTS
AND LONDON, ENGLAND

2004

For information write to Editor, Harvard Oriental Series,
Department of Sanskrit and Indian Studies,
1 Bow Street, Cambridge MA 02138, USA
617-496 2990; email: witzel@fas.harvard.edu
http://www.fas.harvard.edu/~witzel/mwpage.htm

Library of Congress Cataloguing in Publication Data

Kaṭha Araṇyaka. Critical edition with a translation into German and an introduction (Harvard Oriental Series; v. 65)
ISBN 0-674-01806-0
I. Witzel, M. 1943- II. Title
III. Series: Harvard Oriental Series; 65

CIP

uxori optissimae

For Yayoi

on

our 35th anniversary

on revient toujours
à ses premiers amours
HULTZSCH, BDhS

PREFACE

The present edition and translation of the Kaṭha Āraṇyaka (KaṭhĀ) is a diplomatic reprint of the partial printing (*Teildruck*, Erlangen/Kathmandu 1974) of my thesis (Erlangen 1972), required as a part of the *Inauguraldissertation*. No changes have been made in the text of the *Teildruck*, except for obvious spelling mistakes and small oversights corrected without further indication.

For several reasons, I have decided to make the text available in the present format. The original *Teildruck* (printed in offset from a typewritten MS) had been available only in certain libraries and with some of my friends and colleagues. However, I have been receiving frequent inquiries about the availability of the text from libraries and colleagues.[i]

Furthermore, *not one* new MS of this text, preserved in just one Kashmir birch bark MS, kept at Tübingen University Library since 1895, has turned up over the past thirty years. The Tübingen MS seems to be the only remaining continuous text.[ii]

In addition, the text is a significant part of the fragmentary corpus of the important Kaṭha School of the Black Yajurveda. However, the KaṭhĀ has been neglected even after L. von Schroeder published a hastily compiled print in 1898. Scholars have hardly taken notice or paid scant attention to it. The KaṭhĀ has not even figured in works dealing with its main topic, the Pravargya ritual. Such is, inexplicably, the case of van Buitenen's *Pravargya*; it has been used only in the recent book on the Pravargya in TĀ IV-V by J. Houben. In short, it is high time that the KaṭhĀ is made easily available to Vedic scholars.

---

[i] One recent initiative (C. Setzer, Maharishi University of Management, Fairfield, Iowa) has resulted in a Devanāgarī version of the Sanskrit text (on CD) that has not, however, been seen by me before its 'publication'. A specimen has been added at the end of the present book.

[ii] A small portion appears in a Paris MS dév. 230 (see below, III 199) and I have once seen a small section overlapping with KaṭhĀ II 115, but I can no longer find my relevant, decades-old note now; cf. however the Tübingen manuscript MaI 400 (T_5 in Schroeder 1998: 39-42) which reads *oṁ dhenúr vā eṣā́ satī ná duhe ... yáthaivá sá śríyaṃ prāpnóty evá enaṁ śríyaṃ prā́payati*; cf. also MaI 396, section 10b, fol. 335a, line 2 sqq. with 6(!) vocatives addressing the *dhenu*.

Earlier, in 1976/7, while working at Kathmandu, I had planned an edition in Nāgarī characters, to be printed as part of the new series of the Nepal Research Centre (see plates in the appendix). However, after taking up a teaching position at Leiden in 1978, this undertaking was terminated one or two years after I left. A small section of this edition is reproduced in the appendix.

A very slightly revised version of the original *Teildruck* is now presented here, some thirty years later, due to a coincidence of circumstances. In Fall 2003, while convalescing from an operation, I used the opportunity to scan the whole text and convert it by OCR into a (more or less) readable text. This version has gradually been corrected and checked during the Winter of 2003 and the Spring of 2004.

In addition, the original German *Introduction* has been translated into English as closely as possible, to provide the general background of the KaṭhĀ and its peculiarities. A more extensive introduction dealing with the the world view of the text, written at Kathmandu in 1977 for the planned NRC edition, has been added as well. Its text, too, has been left unchanged; however, I have supplied a few additions and updates, clearly marked by brackets [...].

Furthermore, I have added a new facsimile of the only extant MS at Tübingen University Library. It has been restored some 20 years ago, thanks to the perceptiveness and initiative of the then-South Asian librarian, Dr. Dorothea Blieske and her colleagues Dr. Seck and Dr. H.O. Feistel.[iii] In the film that I could make of the MS in 1969 and that I used for my dissertation, many small passages were not visible due to the original "restoration" by R. von Roth. He had done so with semi-transparent strips of paper, pasted on the fragmentary MS that Marc Aurel Stein had sent him from Kashmir in 1895 (see Schroeder 1898: 3). The new and more better readable facsimile added in the present edition was made possible by a high quality scan, carried out by Gunthard Mueller for his e-ternal company (http://www.e-ternals.com). My warm thanks go to him and to Dr. Gabriele Zeller, South Asian librarian, Universitätsbibliothek Tübingen, for making this new version of the Tübingen MS available.

I hope that by providing the original MS of the KaṭhĀ in easily accessible form, this will enable future scholars to make additional corrections and incidental restorations of the many damaged passages of the text preserved only with scanty remnants of letters and accent marks. However, as major parts of the final leaves of the MS had been lost before it reached Tübingen, large gaps will inevitably remain. That is, unless a lucky find produces another MS among the MSS of Kashmiri Brahmins who have left the Valley over the past 300 years, or among the collections

[iii] My friend Albrecht Wezler and I visited the Staatsbibliothek in Munich in November 1969 to investigate the possibility of restoring birch bark MSS without causing further damage to them. As a test, some leaves of MaI 396 were restored from the sections (MaI 396 1c, 2a, 3, 5b, 9, 10a, 10b) taken there by us and, subsequently in February 1971, by Dr. Hartmut Ortwin Feistel. It was also tested to enclose and seal some fragile birchbark leaves with plastic sheets, but it was then decided to avoid this, as the long term effects of such sealing were unknown. Instead, layers of thin Japanese paper were used and sealed by high pressure. The Tübingen Kaṭha MSS were restored over the coming years, until 1983. The result is visible in the appended tables that make certain sections readable for the first time.

of Ṛcakas in various public libraries. So far, luck has escaped us.

I have personally seen and gone through most of the contents of such public libraries in Europe and India, and also some private collections in Kashmir (1973, 1979). They include those at the University of Kashmir (Srinagar, formerly at the Dept. of Archaeology: Archives, Libraries Research and Museums); Pt. Dīnanāth Yech Śāstri, Srinagar; Pt. Shyam Lal Jatoo, Srinagar; Jammu (Raghunath Temple Library/Ranbir Research Institute); Hoshiarpur (VVRI & VISIS Library, Panjab University), New Delhi (National Museum and National Archives), Dr. Lokesh Chandra's private collection (J 22 Hauz Khas Enclave, New Delhi), Panjab University Library (Lahore); some Uttar Pradesh libraries (Akhila Bharatiya Sanskrit Parishad, Lucknow; State Archives of U.P., Allahabad, see Saletore 1970), Benares (Skt. University); Calcutta (Asiatic Society of Bengal); Calcutta (Library of the Asiatic Society), Baroda (Oriental Institute), Pune (Bhandarkar Oriental Research Institute: Bühler's Kashmir collection, formerly kept at Deccan College); and in Europe: Vienna (National Library and University Library, see now Slaje 1990), Berlin (Prussian State Library: Chambers, Hultzsch and later additions); Göttingen (University Library: Kielhorn coll. and later additions); Utrecht (University Library, Caland coll.); collections made by M.A. Stein in Kashmir at the end of the 19th century (presented to the Vienna, Paris, Berlin, Oxford, Tübingen libraries).

In addition, one must look for the c. 900 Mss that existed about a hundred years ago in private collections of Kashmiri Pandits in Uttar Pradesh and neighboring states (Devi Prasad 1883-93). Many seem to have since been acquired by local libraries (Lucknow; Allahabad, see Saletore 1970). Other, somewhat unexpected, locations may be added, such as the Osmania University Library at Hyderabad. Then, there are uncatalogued and continously inaccessible collections, such as a large additional one at the Benares Sanskrit University,[iv] and special cases: at Kathmandu, a Kashmiri birch bark MS was destroyed by the politically-inspired burning of the Singha Darbar Govt. palace in the Summer of 1973, one day before I had the chance to inspect it.

I thank the authorities of all these institutions for having helped me in my search for Kashmiri and other Vedic MSS in India, a project carried out during the years 1973-1977. I pointedly refrain from giving individual names of living scholars, as this may lead, these days, to unwanted and even violent consequences for them and their institutions, such as witnessed at Pune in December 2003 and January 2004. Instead of 'compromising' my friendly and helpful Indian colleagues in the eyes of some current, misguided, political movements, I ask them to accept this generally phrased, but sincerely-felt expression of my gratitude. They will know.

However, I can single out these late scholars: Vishva Bandhu at Hoshiarpur, R.N. Dandekar at Pune, V. Raghavan at Chennai, and Sreekrishna Sarma at Tirupati for their generous assistance. I remain deeply indebted and grateful to

[iv] I have visited that institution three times in 1973/74, paid up all fees for microfilming, deposited a film and even the chemicals, to no avail. I am still waiting for delivery, thirty years later, even after the current director had contacted me last year for unrelated reasons and I had then appealed to him for help.

them.

Finally, I warmly thank our Ph.D. cand. Makoto Fushimi and Neil Krishan Aggarwal for carefully reading the proofs of this book. Any remaining mistakes are mine. Last, but not least, I thank my wife, Yayoi Witzel-Yoshida, for all of her help and encouragement extended when I was engaged in writing my thesis, some 35 years ago, and ever since.

M. Witzel
Cambridge
August 23, 2004

INTRODUCTION

On the Kaṭha School and its Texts

The Kaṭha-Āraṇyaka is presented here in a critical edition for the first time. It belongs to the many texts of the Kāṭha School of the Black Yajurveda preserved only in a fragmentary state and not yet published completely, or only in perfunctory fashion. Among the texts normally constituting the canon of a YV school, in this Śākhā only the following ones have been preserved and edited completely: the Saṁhitā,[1] the famous but late Upaniṣad,[2] the Gṛhyasūtra,[3] the Cārāyaṇīya-Mantrārṣādhyāya,[4] and the Viṣṇu-Smṛti,[5] revised at a late date but adhering, in its nucleus, to the Kaṭha school. In the so-called Ṛcakas,[6] the ritual

[1] Kāṭhakam (or Kāṭhaka-Saṁhitā), ed. L. v. Schroeder, Leipzig 1900-1912; ed. Satvalekar, Aundh 1943; -- for the relevant literature, see Renou, *Ecoles védiques*, p.144sq, 150sqq. and especially the complete account of secondary literature by Tsuji, *Genzon Yajurveda Bunken* (*Existent Yajurveda Literature*), Toyo Bunko Ronso, Ser. A, Vol. LII, Tokyo 1970, p. 51, 151, n. 476. -- The Kapiṣṭhala-(Kaṭha)-Saṁhitā, that deviates only in a few points from the text of KS has been edited by Raghu Vira, Lahore 1932, reprint Delhi 1968 (with new pagination!); for literature, see Renou, *op. cit.* p. 154 f., Tsuji, *op. cit.*, p. 54, 159, n. 519.

[2] Kaṭhopaniṣad, which can be traced back, as is well known, to one of the Kaṭha sections, TB III 10 (cf. n. 7), s. Renou, *op.cit.*, p. 197 with lit.; Tsuji *op.cit.*, p. 52, 154 n. 491 on the many editions and translations.

[3] Kāṭhaka-Gṛhyasūtra, ed. Caland, Lahore 1925; the same text was edited as Laugākṣi-GS, by M.S. Kaul, Bombay 1928-34; see Tsuji, *op.cit.* p. 53, 157.

[4] Viśvabandhu Śāstri, Lahore 1935; important for checking on the text of KS, extant only in one complete manuscript (cf. Renou, *op.cit.*, p. 151); another large ms. of KS is found at VVRI, Hoshiarpur; -- for literature, see TSUJI, *op.cit.*, p. 51, 153 n. 487.

[5] Ed. Jolly, Bibl. Ind. 1881, repr. Chowkhamba; translated by Jolly, SBE VII; on the relationship between Viṣṇu-Smṛti and the Kaṭha school, see Renou, *op.cit.*, p. 194 with literature, Tsuji, *op.cit.*, p. 158sq.

[6] An impression of a Ṛcaka can be gained from the *Vaidikamantrakalpalatā*, ed. Pt. Viśvanāth, Srinagar 1913, admittedly difficult to obtain, though its various parts appear in quite arbitrary ordering. More is found with von Schroeder, especially in *Sitzungsberichte der Kaiserlichen Akademie der Wissenschaften* Wien 1898: *Die Tübinger Kaṭha-Handschriften und ihre Beziehung zum Taittirīya Āraṇyaka*. [See now also Lokesh Chandra 1982-.] Apparently, the character of the Ṛcakas has been misunderstood, in part, by Renou, *op.cit.*, p. 15sq., 141, 153; see also Tsuji, *op.cit.*, p. 154, n. 488. -- So far, I know of Ṛcakas in: Berlin, Preußische Staatsbibliothek (in part lost during the war), Universitätsbibliothek Tübingen, Nationalbibliothek in Wien (where filming was not permitted), Bibliothèque Nationale in Paris, Oxford (Collection Stein: Indian Institute Library),

handbooks of the Kashmiri Brahmins, there are also found -- with random admixture of hymns from RV, RVKh, and KS, later commentaries and Paddhatis -- parts of the [following]: the Brāhmaṇa (apparently lost as a complete text),[7] the Āraṇyaka,[8] the Śikṣā-Upaniṣad[9] (a text not been recognized so far; it apparently formed the end of Veda study in this Śākhā and has to be regarded as the old Upaniṣad of the Kaṭhas); further, the lost Śrautasūtra,[10] the Gṛhyasūtra-Mantrapāṭha,[11] and perhaps, also parts of the Pitṛmedha-Sūtra,[12] the Śulba-

---

Vishveshvaranad Vedic Research Institute (VVRI) in Hoshiarpur (where the administration, of gratefully acknowledged openmindeness, allowed me to take microfilms), Deccan College in Poona (now deposited in: BORI, Poona), Akhila Bharatiya Sanskrit Parishad in Lucknow. In the Province of Audh, c. one thousand mss. of this type existed just 120 years ago, see Catalogue of Sanskrit Manuscripts for the year 1882-90 by Pt. Devi Prasad, Allahabad 1883-93; some of then must have been acquired by libraries in Uttar Pradesh (e.g., in Lucknow, but not in Allahabad). More Ṛcakas were found in Lahore, Panjab University Library. I will be grateful for more information (cf. n. 15a); [see above, *Foreword*]. On the Ṛcakas, cf. also Tsuji, *op.cit.*, p.154 n. 488.

[7] It is already known to Indian tradition that parts of KaṭhB (in part, more correctly: of KapB!) have been taken over into TB (3.10-12) and TĀ (1-2), the so-called *aṣṭau kāṭhakāni*; on the accuracy of this tradition see Schroeder, *Sitzungsberichte* Wien 1898, cf. also *Sitzungsberichte* Wien 1895, *Zeitschrift der Deutschen Morgenländischen Gesellschaft* 49, 145-171; cf. Renou, *op. cit.* p. 146, 174 (BaudhŚS), 177 and Tsuji *op.cit.*, p. 52, 154 n. 488, 490. On the fragment (= TB 3. 12) of the KaṭhB (KapB) in the ms. of KpS, see ed. KpS [by Raghu Vira], repr. p. XIX. -- Parts of KaṭhB have been printed by Schroeder, *SB Wien* 1898, *SB Wien* 1895; more is found in Caland, *Verslagen en mededeelingen der koninklijke Akademie van Wetenschappen*, Amsterdam 1920; some new texts also in Suryakanta, *Kāṭhakasaṃkalanam*, Lahore 1943 (where, however, Caland has been reprinted to a large degree).

[8] An uncritical, frequently incomplete and unfortunately quite hasty printing by L. V. Schroeder, due to his preoccupation with his work on KS, in *Sitzungsberichte Wien* 1898, p. 92-120, where KaṭhĀ is found among a multitude of fragments of KaṭhB.

[9] Preserved in Ṛcakas, e.g., in ms. Paris, dév. 230, Tübingen MaI 396; already printed in Laugākṣi-GS, Vol. II, p. 92sqq. with the commentary of Devapāla (also on the Mantras; the commentary has not been printed by Caland). By and large, these fragments correspond to TU 1.1,4,11,12. Therefore, I propose to call this Upaniṣad the Kaṭha-Śikṣā- Up., in parallel with the designations in some MSS and TU I. The Up. has been transmitted without accents; however, it is vouched for by Devapāla's commentary.

[10] A text of 39 Adhyāyas still available to Devayajñika; quotations from his Paddhati, collected in handwritten form already by Weber; it is edited by Raghu Vira, *Oriental College Patrika*, Lahore 1928; reprinted and completed by Sūryakānta, *Kāṭhakasaṃkalanam*; further fragments of the Sūtra were edited by Raghu Vira, *Journal of Vedic Studies* 2, p. 104sqq., Caland, *Indischer Ahnencult*, p. 212, cf. p. 65sqq.; cf. also Caland's frequent references in his edition of KGS and the reconstructions of N. Tsuji (*a.k.a.* N. Fukushima) in *Comm. Volume of the Science of Religion*, Tokyo, Imperial Univ. 1934, and *Brāhmaṇa to Śrautasūtra to no kankei* (*On the relation between Brāhmaṇas and Śrautasūtras*) Tokyo 1952 (English summary p.185sqq.); see also Tsuji, *Existent Yajurveda-Literature* (*op. cit.*) p. 156.

[11] Partly edited by Caland, KGS, appendix; the marriage song preserved there (Sarasvatyanuvāka) is prescribed by the Vādhūlas, see *AO* VI 158 f., *AO* VII 305 f.

[12] See already Caland on the Piṇḍapitṛyajña, *Altindischer Ahnencult*, p. 212; Kashikar, *Survey of Śrautrasūtras*, p. 108.

Sūtra,[13] the Pravara-Sūtra and the Paribhāṣā-Sūtra,[14] various Pariśiṣṭas, and the Dharma-Sūtra. [In the meantime, the Kaṭha Śikṣā Upaniṣad has been added].

The present edition of the KaṭhĀ,[15] therefore, constitutes only a small part of the complete edition, in progress,[15a] of fragments of the Kaṭha school preserved in many Ṛcakas and, in part, also in a few printed ritual handbooks of the Kashmiri Sārasvata Brahmins.

This Śākhā apparently represents, together with the Maitrāyaṇī school that differs only slightly from it, the earliest formulation < II> of the YV traditions.[16] Therefore, the fragmentary nature of the canon of both schools is even more deplorable. As far as the Kaṭhas are concerned, this was apparently due to the lack of care taken of this Veda in the medieval habitat of this school in western North India and in Kashmir. It was, in part, due to Islamic conquests and, in part, due to advances made by the White Yajurveda[17]. In the preceding period, the Kaṭha school was widespread in all of North India, since the end of the Vedic period. The actual area of origin was confined to the eastern Panjab.[18] In this area, the Kaṭhas, and especially one of their branches, the

---

[13] See Tsuji, *op. cit.* p. 52, 157 n. 500.

[14] See Caland, KGS, p. 272; Tsuji, *op.cit.* p. 157 n. 499; - for the Paribhāṣā-Sūtra, see Caland, ed. KGS, p. 61 and cf. *Baroda Alphabetical List,* 1942, Vol. I, p.158sq. no. 148.

[15] In order to distinguish KaṭhĀ from the Kauṣītaki-Āraṇyaka (KĀ), I propose this somewhat cumbersome abbreviation.

[15a] At first, an edition of all Brāhmaṇa fragments had been envisioned (that exceed what has been compiled by Sūryakānta) [now in progress, see the Harvard PhD, 2004, by S. Rosenfield]; to be followed by fragments of the Śrautasūtra, other ritual works, and also by important commentaries [in part carried out by C. Dreyer 1986; The Kaṭha Śikṣā Up. has been identified, edited and translated, see Witzel, *JNRC* I, 1977, *WZKS* 20/21: 1979/1980]. Therefore, I would be grateful to learn of other Kaṭha mss. (cf. n. 6), and also of quotations in other texts (especially in Pūrvamīmāṁsā texts!).

[16] For the group MS/KS (*Caraka-Saṁhitā) cf. Renou, *Ecoles védiques,* p.144, Tsuji, *Existent YV-Literature,* p. 4sq., 36sq. - TS has some linguistically younger traits (differently, Keith, Introduction to his translation of TS, 1914, p. xciii, but cf. p. xcv; Renou, *Ecoles védiques,* p.144 voices some doubts but speaks positively about the Mantras of MS/KS, p. 152 n.1). Furthermore, TS is already much more systematic and concise: the long stories of MS/KS have been reduced to a few sentences, a relationship also seen between JB and PB. Even a fairly superficial comparison of the contents of MS, apparently the oldest YV-Saṁhitā, and of KS indicates that both schools must have had a long period of common development (cf. also Pāṇini: *kaṭhakalāpa-*), before they finally started to developed separately in various ways. [For details see Witzel, Veda in Kashmir, in prep., ch. IX]

[17] Some epigraphical instances in Renou, *Ecoles védiques,* p. 203, and in greater detail, in *Festschrift S. Varma*; cf. Yajurvedavṛkṣa, *Journal of Vedic Studies* 2. Mādhyandinīyas are already attested to in Gujarāt, the homeland of the Maitr. during the past few millennia, in 641 CE (*Indian Antiquary,* 1886, p. 343). Apparently, their quick expansion was, in part, due to the protection of the Guptas, as is the case in many other similar instances.

[18] KS 33.8: 54,12 *tasmād āpaḥ pratīcīr bhūyiṣṭhā dhāvanti* "Therefore, the waters run westwards most copiously." In northern India, this applies only to the upper courses of the Satlej (*Śutudrī*), some confluent rivers (Bein, with confluents), and to the lower course of the Ghaggar (in its upper course = Sarsuti, Ved. *Sarasvatī*), along with its left confluent Chautang (*Dṛṣadvatī*). This is the area

Kapiṣṭhalas, were in contact with the Kauthuma school of the Sāmaveda,[19] due to cooperation in ritual an geographical neighborhood. The close connection of both schools now also appears in the only quotation of the KaṭhĀ in another Vedic text, the Anupada Sūtra.[20] The ĀpŚS is a special case: it quotes many injunctions of the Kaṭhas, especially in its Pravargya Praśna, without naming the source.[21]

Contents and Age of the KaṭhĀ

In the Kaṭha Āraṇyaka, the discussion of the Pravargya ritual is the nucleus of the text, just as in the other Āraṇyakas of the Yajurveda. Currently, it is not certain if the explanation of the Mantras and corresponding expositions of the Mahāvrata viz. the Pravargya, was followed, as in the related texts (especially so in the Āraṇyakas of the RV), by other heterogeneous sections of texts. For, the only extant manuscript of the KaṭhĀ is incomplete in its last portions. Perhaps the Śikṣā Upaniṣad had been added as the text constituting the conclusion of Veda study.[22] As long as a complete manuscript has not been found, only the following is

---

between, in the North, the lower Himalayas; in the West, the Beās (*Vipāś*), or the Black Bein, flowing parallel to it; in the South, the desert (*maru*); and in the East, the watershed of the *Yamunā*. This area also includes *kurukṣetra,* the "Holy Land" of the Saṁhitās. The town Kaiṭhal is to be found here, which Raghu Vira and Suryakanta have already traced back to **kapiṣṭhala*. This is one of the not infrequent cases of place names that go back to names of Vedic schools, cf., e.g., Vārāhī in North Gujarāt (the Vārāha school was settled, according to the Yajurvedavṛkṣa, in the desert, *marudeśe*), and Pip(pi)lī in Orissa, where Paippalādins are indeed found even today. As is well known, the Kaṭhas and Kapiṣṭhalas (Καθαιοι, Καμβισθολοι) are localized by classical authors in eastern and southern Panjab. (For the present state of research, see *Paulys Realencyclopädie der classischen Altertumswisschenschaft* [vol. 20, col. 2512-13]. Cf. perhaps also Kaṭhāna, a place c. 30 km south of Kaiṭhal and Kāṭhúā, on the upper Ravī, east of Jammū.

[19] See now Parpola, translation of LŚS, Vol. I, p.91; to be added is the *śārga*-Sāman (KaṭhĀ III 233), whose name is the form used by the Kauthumas while the Rāṇāyanīyas and the Jaiminīyas use *śārṅga*.

[20] See Parpola, *loc.cit.* Vol. I.2, p.106sqq. He could not verify this quotation in the edition of v. Schroeder that is incomplete here as well. KaṭhĀ III 234 is found in a split line that therefore has been left out by Schroeder.

[21] See Caland's frequent references in his translation of ĀpŚS; the Kaṭhas are quoted only twice by name (see Garbe, ed. ĀpŚS, Vol. III p. XVIII sq. For the second case, i.e. the Kāṭhaka-Cāturmāsyas (Caland, ĀpŚS transl., 19.15.7, note 3) which Caland could not verify in KS, see now the injunctions in KaṭhĀ III 233, fol. 355b, beginning. Cf. Renou, *Ecoles védiques*, p. 177.

[22] Caland, *Verslagen en mededelingen* 1920, attributes some Brāhmaṇa sections published by him to the Āraṇyaka. Cf. further his many references in the edition of KGS, e.g., p. 256. Some further expansion of the present text can probably be expected by closely scrutinizing all Ṛcakas. By chance, I found a section of KaṭhĀ III 199 in the ms. Paris dév. 230, whose position was confirmed by overlaps with the existent text of Tüb. MaI 396. - Perhaps the box IV ("Kasten IV", see Schroeder 1898: 3, 30) of fragments of the Tübingen Ms. MaI 396 still contains materials that belong here: A check was not possible [in 1972/74] due to limitations on time and location.

reasonably certain. The KaṭhĀ must have consisted of three parts: [23] <III>

KaṭhĀ I, a collection of the *Mantras* of the Pravargya ritual (preserved only in fragments),

KaṭhĀ II, the *Yuñjate-Brāhmaṇa*, that explains, in 'theological fashion', the actual Pravargya Ritual, and

KaṭhĀ III, the *Gharmājaṭharā-Brāhmaṇa*,[24] with extensive appendixes and special injunctions.

This ordering does not completely correspond to what one would expect from the related texts (TĀ 4-5, ŚB 14, MS 4.9). For, in TĀ and ŚB, the Pravargya ritual has been validated and explained "theologically," by and large, following the order of the ritual. This explanation is based on the magical identification [or, correlation] technique[25] found in the YV Saṁhitās, Brāhmaṇas and Āraṇyakas. In the present text, however, at first only the complete Pravargya ritual is dealt with in the same fashion: from the manufacturing of the *gharma* vessel up to the Agnihotra, putting together the *gharma* vessel, and deposition of the utensils belonging to the Pravargya, -- [all] without mentioning [even] once that the Pravargya ritual is part of the Soma ritual.[26] This is a clear indication of the frequently assumed independence of the old milk offering to the Aśvins already alluded to in the RV; -- especially so, if this part of the KaṭhĀ could lay claim to an older age than the corresponding sections of TĀ and ŚB. In the case of ŚB, the question can be answered positively and with certainty.[27] However, the Pravargya Brāhmaṇa of the

---

[23] The Mantra section is presupposed by the designation of the section beginning with *yuñjate manaḥ* as *prathama-anuvāka-* in MS Paris dév. 230. Thus, the Kaṭhas did not begin their Āraṇyaka (or, at least, the Mantra chapter of the Pravargya) with the Pūrvakā Śāntiḥ as TĀ IV does; rather, they are closer to the tradition of the Maitrāyaṇīyas, who place the Śāntis at the end of the Mantra chapter. - As the Mantra chapter currently cannot be reconstructed in its entirety, only such sections are given in the present edition found in the Paddhatis of the Śukriya-Vrata; cf. the opening notes before the Mantra section (KaṭhĀ I).

[24] This designation is not found in the manuscript as a colophon has not been preserved. It has been inserted here based ondesignations given for KaṭhĀ II and many designations of sections of KS found in the Ṛcakas that use the initial word(s) of a section (both in the case of Mantra as well as Brāhmaṇa sections); cf. e.g., KS 1.1 *iṣetvorjetveti-brāhmaṇa*(!), 10.5 *pāṭhikṛtam*, 37.11 *rāṣṭrabhṛd-brāhmaṇa*, etc.

[25] See S. Schayer, Die Struktur der magischen Weltanschauung nach dem Atharvaveda und den Brāhmaṇatexten, *Zeitschrift für Buddhismus* 1925, and Die Weltanschauung der Brāhmaṇatexte, *Rocznik Orientalistyczny* 2, 1924.

[26] Even in the Sūtras (except for the late VaikhŚS), the Pravargya is still treated as a separate unit, though it was meant to be part of the Soma ritual, as the very same Sūtras teach. However, in KaṭhĀ, all of the complicated discussion of TĀ 5.2.2 (ĀpŚS 15.1.2, etc.) is missing. This discussion had perhaps been added at the end of the preserved text (III 239a, und fragment f. 357b). Even the Udvāsana is not described and explained in KaṭhĀ II, only after various insertions (III 146-73), in KaṭhĀ III, Anuvāka 3, in close agreement with the Soma ritual. (However, a hint of the relationship with the Soma ritual is perhaps found in the Mantra itself at KaṭhĀ II 137: *sunvate* 'for the one who presses (Soma)'.

[27] One just has to think of the use of the Perfect as the tense of narration. [See now Witzel 1989:

TĀ exhibits clear signs of late composition, for example, frequent schematic identifications[28] and also thoughtless copying of TS VI 4,9 in TĀ V 1,1-7.[29] The exposition of mythological legends, excerpted [from KS], invented or varied *ad hoc*, strengthen this hypothesis. In quite a systematic fashion, TĀ as well as ŚB report, already at the beginning of the exposition of the Pravargya, <IV> the whole tale from the acquisition of the secret of Dadhyañc by the Aśvins and their subsequent re-attachment of the head of the sacrifice, in order to magically validate the complete Pravargya ritual as part of the Soma ritual. However, in KaṭhĀ, only parts of the legend[30] are used, just in instances appropriate for explanation. These stories are varied individually as needed, and KaṭhĀ is much more independent than TĀ, though from time to time, it closely relies on the Saṁhitā, too.[31] It is also symptomatic that complicated theological aims are not found in this Brāhmaṇa section (KaṭhĀ II). Next to the usual wishes uttered in rituals, only obtaining rain[32] is mentioned, and in a somewhat unclear passage[33] the 'heavenly form' that the sponsor of the ritual shall obtain by the performance of the Pravargya. Further, speculations about the meaning and effect of the Pravargya

---

139sqq]. As far as I know, this has penetrated the Kaṭha school only in a few sections of the KaṭhB, e.g., in the Kaṭha section that corresponds to TB 3.10.11 (Nāciketas tale), or in the Kūṣmāṇḍa-Br. (*Sitzungsberichte Wien* 1898, p. 77sqq.). However, the age of some sections of KaṭhB is uncertain, cf. note 37.

28 In this case, the redactor, viz. the author of the text, has frequently not / no longer thought it necessary to place the commonly found reinforcing particle *vái*; cf. further the Brāhmaṇa style identifications in TĀ 5 with corresponding ones in KaṭhĀ II. [For the age of KaṭhĀ and TĀ cf. now Houben 1991: 39.]

29 This is a word-by word copy from the Saṁhitā, in spite of a different context of (meaning and) ritual. In both cases, the Aśvin cup appears instead of the Gharma drink to be expected in TĀ; the latter (Gharma cup) is correctly treated in KaṭhĀ II 115.

30 E.g., the legend at II 100 that is otherwise not found in this form; a short cut version at III 225; compare II 115 with KS 27.4 : 143,8 (and contrast TĀ/TS in note 29!)

31 For example, II 115 is used to explain the Mantra = KS 24.4:43,20; the explanation of the ritualists' question *prāśyā3 ná prāśyā3* at II 143 = KS 29.2; III 177 and 233 *upagāyanam* ... up to ... *hnuvate* = KS 34.2:37,2; III 198 *daśākṣarā* ... up to the end of the section = KS 21.10 (beginning) : 49,23sqq.; III 198 *kiṃ* ... up to ... *•dīkṣayā* = KS 24.9, end; for the *araṇye 'nuvākyo gaṇaḥ* cf. KS 21.10. -- KaṭhĀ III 207 shows close connection with another Kaṭha text, i.e. the Kaṭha section preserved in TĀ 1.5.2, where KaṭhĀ obviously depends on KaṭhB; compare also III 207 with TĀ 5.10; -- further III 219 (beginning) *araṇyam paretya* ... = KaṭhB (Svādhyāya-Br.) *Sitzungsberichte Wien* 1898, p. 64; -- interdependence within KaṭhĀ itself is seen in III 170 : II 128; compare also the formulation and style of the tale at III 229 with that at II 76 and 79.

32 II 123; cf. the allusion to the Pravargya in connection with the rainy season, already seen in the 'frog hymn' of the RV (7.103).

33 *svargākṛti-* in II 143. Unfortunately, *saṁsthiti-*, too, is not very clear, cf. e.g., also Caland on *saṁsthā* in AO VI, p. 184, No.69 (where one has to read: ĀpŚS 7.23.7). Is the meaning 'strict injunction' in both cases? -- Cf. the use of *sthiti-*, *sthita-* in VādhS, AO II, p. 155; these indicate the Siddhānta at the end of a discussion, a usage that is found already in ŚBK and KB [in correspondence with TĀ 5.8.2, to be edited as **svagákṛti*?].

ritual are only found in KaṭhĀ III, the Gharmājaṭharā Brāhmaṇa.[34]

KaṭhĀ II, the Yuñjate Brāhmaṇa, therefore represents an older section of the canon of the Kaṭhas, one that could only be learned on open ground, in the wilderness (*araṇya*)[35] as it belonged to the most magically dangerous rituals.[36] In fact, this section could be as old as the Saṁhitā,[36a] specially as it describes and explains an old ritual, and as the exact order of individual sections of the canon was not absolutely fixed for a long time. However, this section was been exposed for a longer period to modernization and additions than the relatively early fixed Saṃhitā, due to its position in the memorization of texts --just before the end of Veda study-- and also as it was, in the end, not taken over into the Saṁhitā (differently from MaitrS), a feature certainly due to the optionality of the ritual. This situation should also explain the earliest[37] <V> mention in a Vedic text of *four* Vedas at KaṭhĀ II 117, while the trinity of the holy texts appears several times in KaṭhĀ as well. Leaving apart the latter case, KaṭhĀ stands out several times from the related texts by its greater antiquity. However, at KaṭhĀ III, the Pravargya ritual is fully integrated into the celebration of the Soma ritual. Furthermore, this section offers much new material otherwise known only from the Sūtras. Mantras III 146-149, for example, are attested in identical form only in ĀpŚS, where they are one of the frequent borrowings from the ritual of the Kaṭhas.[38] That these Mantras have their old place in the Pravargya ritual is proved

---

[34] Where quite apparently the Pravargya (text) is already spoken of as an Upaniṣad [III 229]. (On this, the more ritualistic meaning of Upaniṣad, cf. VādhS, AO VI p. 153, No.41: *upaniṣadādānam anvākhyānam*, and the instance in ŚB 10, the Agnirahasya). -- III 167, too, points to the character of the 'Pravargya-Upaniṣad' as secret teaching; a more 'philosophic' aspect of the term is indicated by III 219: [*ápa punarm*]*ṛtyúm jayati, yá eváṃ véda.*

[35] Thus, the frequent warning about the glowing vessel that is identified with the sun and Rudra.

[36] See Oldenberg, *araṇyaka* (1915); cf. III 219 and III 155: *araṇye 'nuvākyo gaṇaḥ* (KS 21.10); cf. I 4.

[36a] Differently, Renou, *Ecoles védiques*, p. 140sq., about the Pravargya ritual as such; on the other hand, on p. 149, he assumes the composition of a *single*, original Āraṇyaka for all of the YV (which then should have been of a relatively early date!). Apparently he did so as he thought that TĀ and KaṭhĀ are very similar (which is quite doubtful for KaṭhĀ II, and certainly incorrect for KaṭhĀ III). -- A Maitrāyaṇī-Ār., inferred in *Ecoles védiques* p. 149, n. 1, is presented on p.157 as existent (for its Brāhmaṇa section). However, it has not been found, as far as I know. (It is not to be confused with the Maitr.Up. sometimes called thus, for example by Satvalekar 1942). [There is, however, one quote from a Maitr. Br., see Caland, ed. BŚS, vol. III, vol 3, 401: 10-11 *samacaturaśrābhir agniṃ cinute daivyasya ca mānuṣasya ca vyāvṛttyai iti maitrāyṇīyabrāhmaṇaṃ bhavati.*]

[37] As long as it is unclear whether some fragments of KaṭhB collected by v. Schroeder (*Sitzungsberichte Wien* 1898, e.g., p. 57, top) and Caland (*Verslagen* 1920) also mentioning *four* Vedas do in fact belong to the Brāhmaṇa; or, whether they have been interpolated at a late stage; or, whether parts of, or all known sections of KaṭhB, in fact, are texts that can be compared with the Brāhmaṇa sections of ŚŚS, BŚS, and especially the Anvākhyānas of the VādhS; in other words, whether they perhaps belonged to the lost KaṭhŚS. Perhaps the *upagranthas* that appear in the tradition as subschools of the Kaṭha, are to be placed in this context? (cf. Renou, *Ecoles védiques*, p. 130). [See, however, Witzel 1979b, 1980.]

[38] See Caland on ĀpŚS 6.21; Renou, *op. cit.*, p. 177, Tsuji, *Existent YV-Literature*, p. 160, n. 519, Garbe,

by an injunction of the VādhS, according to which the *gharma* vessel must be gripped and lifted by the pincers with them.[39] While these Mantras relate to a detail of the ritual that should already have been treated at KaṭhĀ II, M. 74 sqq.,[40] the rest of KaṭhĀ III also contains clearly additional materials:

III 150	Agnihotra (?)	
151-154	Udvāsana and depositing (in shape of the sun) [41] of the utensils used during the Pravargya	
155-156	Avāntaradīkṣā, the so-called 'intermediate consecration'	
157-158	Rauhiṇa cakes used at the morning viz. evening Pravargya	
159-168	Uttaraśānti (with clear reference to teaching of the text in 167-168)	
169-170	Vārṣāhara Sāman	
170 end -172	Dadhigharma	
175	general atonement offerings (?)[42]	
174-198	Udvāsana (with depositing the utensils in the shape of a man, in 183a)	
198 end - 226	Avāntaradīkṣā, including:	<VI>
	199a-207	beginning of the Uttaraśānti
	207 end	deliberations, when the Pravargya is to be carried out,
	208a-214	beginning of the Pūrvakaśānti
	215-219	four sections of the Uttaraśānti
	219 beg.	special observances at the Avāntaradīkṣā
	219 mid	injunctions about the learning of the Pravargya text
	219 end	depositing (?) of the Pravargya Utensils in the shape of a head
	219m-226	a part of the Pūrvakaśānti
226-229	Avakāśa Mantras	
229 end-231	Sāman of the Adhvaryu	
232-233	special injunctions about the Pravargya celebrated on pressing days and during the Cāturmāsyas	

ed. ĀpŚS, vol. III, p. XVIII, n.1 .

39 AO IV, p. 162sq.

40 If one cannot assume either use at the Agnihotra (III 150, where, however, the ritual use is not very clear as well); or whether one wants to reconstruct a new Dadhigharma according to the Mantras III 146sqq. and III 170, end - 172. -- As long as KaṭhŚS is not available, a decision can be made only with difficulty, due to the frequently imprecise character of the Mantras (see already Lindner quoted by Renou, *Ecoles védiques*, p. 138, n. 1).

41 III 154 is also used at the Dadhigharma! What has been said in note 40, is valid here as well. A further use is seen in KS 21.10.

42 Thus, BŚS 9.12:282,7 before putting together the utensils used at the Pravargya, cf. Caland [1921-28] on ĀpŚS 15.17.4.

233 end-234 Solos of the Prastotar[43] (*parisāmāni*)
233-239 Prāyaścittas for disruptions during the Pravargya ritual
239a-240 deliberations about collecting the utensils necessary for a Pravargya ritual,

and about the start of the actual ritual, at the very end of the text, where it is only very fragmentarily preserved. The various types of depositions of utensils used in the Pravargya, the intermediate consecration, the Sāman of the Adhvaryu, the Parisāmāni and some of the Prāyaścittas are preserved, or rather treated at length for the first time in a Brāhmaṇa text. The exposition of these ritual details seems to have formed the last, large appendix to the treatment of the Pravargya. It is distinguished from the first appendices (III 146-172) in a formal way as well, in that it begins the third (and perhaps subsequent)[44] Anuvākas. In style, too, KaṭhĀ III, Anuvāka 3 (sqq.) is distinguished from the preceding sections by a frequently more extensive exposition that approaches that of the style of the Anubrāhmaṇas of the Vādhūla school.[45] <VII>

The KaṭhĀ is an important source for the Vedic ritual, but for other subjects as well.[46] It is to be regretted even more that the text is preserved only quite fragmentarily, and that its uncritical and often incomplete printing by L. von Schroeder has, in addition, taken place at a location out of general view[47] so that it

[43] Or, according to the Akṣara remnants of the MS, perhaps sung by the Udgātar. However, *udgātar* may have been used here as a generic designation of the priests singing Sāmans. This would not be unusual for a YV text, cf. for example *adhvaryū* 'both Adhvaryus' (i.e. Adhvaryu and Pratiprasthātar) in the RV Brāhmaṇas dealing with the Pravargya.

[44] According to the contents, not much text is actually to be assumed after III 240. The expiations have already been discussed. Further, a section about the collection of the utensils that are used in addition to the Pravargya vessel has been added, a feature that has not been dealt with at the beginning of KaṭhĀ. And, at the very end, a reference is made to the start of the actual Pravargya ceremony. However, the text division before the last preserved words indicates that a shorter or longer section followed. According to the appearance of the ms., one (or even more) leaves could have followed (apparently including the fragment containing the two lines of f.357b viz., 358), as their left half, containing the first folios of fascicle 10b of Mal 396 is still preserved. The last folios may just as well contained, as is generally common in Ṛcakas, various disparate items, such as one of the frequent excerpts from Purāṇas or even poems, or, as it also occurs, they could have been left empty.

[45] Between both schools there exists a number of other points of contact, see above, n. 11, 39. Further, note perhaps the position of KaṭhB and the Brāhmaṇa sections (Anvākhyānas) of the Vādhūlas within the development of the ritual prose texts of both schools; cf. also n. 34.

[46] Next to linguistic details (such as unattested Mantras, new words such as *ādhi-*, unattested verb forms such as *ṛghyāsam*, new compounds such as in seen in III 146-149, phonetic peculiarities such as 'Ṛgvedic' *-ḷ-* and special Sandhi forms), note especially the not infrequent identifications of macrocosm and microcosm, and the concurrent transition to the Upaniṣads, cf. also *pravargyopaniṣad-* in III 229, *punarmṛtyu-* in III 219.

[47] A text, designated as 'Kaṭha Āraṇyaka', does not occur in the bibliographies; in v. Schroeder's edition it is hidden, along with the fragments of the KaṭhB, long tables of contents of Ṛcakas, etc., under the title "Die Tübinger Kaṭha-Handschriften und ihre Beziehung zum Taittirīya-Āraṇyaka"

has remained, by and large, unknown.[48]

The Manuscripts; phonetic peculiarities of the text.

The major part of KaṭhĀ is preserved in just one[49] very damaged, though quite old, manuscript that is incomplete at the end. It consists of the last preserved leaves of a birch bark Ṛcaka written in Śāradā script bought by Sir M. Aurel Stein at Srinagar in 1894. It was presented to the University Library of Tübingen, where it was catalogued as Mal 396, fascicle 10 a and b. The leaves containing the KaṭhĀ are numbered by the original, indigenous folio number in the left lower corner of the recto side, under the abbreviation of the title,[50] as fol. 337b- 357b. Only the first three folios are fairly well preserved. The rest, that is fascicle 10b, consists only of fragments, of which the upper third of each leaf has broken off. The last three folios are even more damaged, and at the end, at least one folio is missing.[51]

[The Tübingen Kaṭha manuscripts and their relationship with the Taittirīya-Āraṇyaka].

48 In spite of Caland's frequent references in his translation of ĀpŚS (and, *nota bene*, exactly in the Pravargya Praśna!) as well as that of PB, and e.g., Renou's clear reference in *Ecoles védiques*, p. 152, §141. The KaṭhĀ has *not* been included in Suryakanta's *Kāṭhakasaṃkalanam*. It has not been made use of in Bloomfield-Edgerton's *Vedic Variants* (see Renou, *Ecoles védiques* p. 152), and not included in Bloomfieldös *Vedic Concordance* (1910). Also, it has not been mentioned at all in the lone exposition of the Pravargya, in spite of the importance of the *vidhi* elements in the Brāhmaṇas for an explanation of the Sūtras (see Caland, transl. of ĀpŚS, Vol. I, p. 3sq., Tsuji, *On the Relation*, p. 193, Renou, *Ecoles védiques*, p.142): J.A.B. van Buitenen, *The Pravargya*, Poona 1968, anyhow relies, by and large, on the Sūtras. Only in the introduction, the Brāhmaṇas dealing with the Pravargya (of course, with the exception of KaṭhĀ) have been adduced for an interpretation of the nature of the Pravargya ritual. [However, see now Houben 1991].

49 Nothing is found in the *New Catalogus Catalogorum* of Raghavan and Raja and in the Ṛcakas and Kaṭha mss. known to me. The assertion of Bhagavad Datta made in his *History of Vedic Literature* (*Vaidik vāṅmay kā itihās*), Lahore 1927, p. 26, that there was as MS (no. 175) containing this text, in the Dayanand Anglo-Indian College, is erroneous, as I was told to at VVRI, Hoshiarpur: the MSS of the DAV College were carried [in backpacks] to Hoshiarpur after the division of India, and the MS designated as no. 175 (now no. 6445) merely contains the Kāṭhaka section of TĀ. Incidentally, this one of the quite frequent confusions made between KaṭhĀ and the *aṣṭau kāṭhakāni* that are, in part, still counted as a separate text in South India (cf.. also Aufrecht, *Catalogus Catalogorum*, p. 89 b [and see Staal, Nambudiri Veda Recitation , 1961: 56, Keith, TS transl., introduction p. xxvii sqq.].

50 That is, *oṁ śu[kriya]brā[hmaṇam]*, apparently the designation of the whole Brāhmaṇa section explaining the Pravargya, as well as that of the Mantra chapter, cf. the beginning of KaṭhĀ I and of the Śāntis, with *oṁ śukriyaṃ rudrasya*. The Veda-Vrata, during which the Āraṇyaka is learnt, is called *śukriyavrata* as well by the Kaṭhas [See Witzel, An unknown Upaniṣad of the Kṛṣṇa Yajurveda, 1977]. The abbreviation mark on the margin of the fol. is broken off in the last three folios.

51 In spite of the missing pagination of the last three folios, their order is ascertained by their content.

Due to the lack of a colophon, the age of the Ms. is not easily determined. A relatively old age is indicated by the very fact that the text has been written on birch bark. According to Bühler, paper was introduced into Kashmir only around 1600. [But, as we now know from the later Rājataraṅgiṇīs, this change was made already under King Zain ul Abidin, 1419-1470]. However, a Ṛcaka of the Vienna National Library,[52] brought to Vienna by Baron von Hügel already in 1836, is dated as late as 1675/76 CE. -- Some peculiarities of the script of the Tübingen manuscript, <VIII>
for example the designation of vowels,[53] however, indicate that this Ṛcaka was copied during the period of transition to the recent Śāradā script. Therefore, as is also the case for the Kashmirian Atharvaveda of the Paippalāda school dated at (15)19,[54] a date of copying around 1500 CE. has to be assumed.[55]

Next to the Tübingen Ṛcaka (T) that mainly contains KaṭhĀ I and III, the following manuscripts were available for text constitution, though they only contain parts of the mantra section (KaṭhĀ I).

Ms. Tübingen MaI 396, fols. 274a-284b (**t_1**), a part of the Ṛcaka (**T**) just mentioned and unfortunately damaged in almost the same fashion, accented (but not in all Mantras); - Paris, National Library (Bibliothèque Nationale), Ms. dév.

---

[52] This Ṛcaka came to Europe as the first of its kind, but it has hardly been available for research until today. This is even more regrettable, as this is a nearly completely preserved, quite old MS that still has its old leather cover, as is common in Kashmir for Bhūrja texts. First announced by Rieu in *Indische Studien* I, p. 70, it was *not* made available to Weber for thirty years (see *Monatsberichte der Preußischen Akademie*, Berlin 1879, p. 201, n. 1). Then, it was at least briefly described by Bühler (*loc.cit.*, p. 200-202) and closely investigated by v. Schroeder for the accentuation system of KS 35, contained in this MS (*Zeitschrift der Deutschen Morgenländischen Gesellschaft* 45, p. 432-438), and used for his edition of KS (but *only* for KS 35). The rest of this MS of c. 500 fols. has never been investigated. During a stay at Vienna years ago [in the spring of 1969], I could only take a few notes. The preparation of a microfilm, regretfully, was "interdicted" by the administration of the manuscript division of the National Library [*Nationalbibliothek*] "because of the fragile state of the writing material." Caland seems to have had a similar experience in the Twenties (see ed., KGS p. IV, second paragraph). In the same vein, and for the same reasons, a film could not be made of the manuscript described as W_1 by L. v. Schroeder, *Sitzungsberichte Wien* 1895: this concerns a well preserved paper manuscript. [See now the catalogue by W. Slaje 1990.]

[53] The writing of *-o-* and *-au-*, by a combination of a horizontal stroke above the line and a perpendicular stroke of half length on the right side of the Akṣara, is relatively common. In the MS only 112 of the 571 cases of *-o/au-* have been written in the form that became regular later on, a swallow-like sign above the Akṣara (*o* / *au*), about a fifth (19,61%) of all existent cases. The rest however has the older form described above (*o* , *au*). It is striking that in the first Brāhmaṇa section, the Yuñjate Br., only 39 of 258 cases appear in swallow-form (i.e., 15,12%), while in the Gharmājaṭharā Br. already 73 of 313 (i.e., 23,32%) do so.

[54] In Kashmir, the two numbers indicating the century of the Saptarṣi (or Laukika-) Era are not written, see for example the v. Hügel Ṛcaka in Bühler (see above, n. 52).

[55] As has been confirmed to me by Dr. B.K. Deambi, who has written a Palaeography of Śāradā script, due to appear soon; this is based on many manuscripts and inscriptions. [See now Kaul Deambi 1984].

230, p. 304-317 (**P**), written in modern Śāradā on paper, no accents, dated (17)80 C.E. (or perhaps 1880); - Paris, Ms. dév. 227b, fols. 10 sqq. (**P2**), written in younger Śāradā script, on rough 'country paper', accent rests; - edition of the Laugākṣi Gṛhyasūtra (**L**) by M.S. Kaul, vol. II, p. 52-91 (unfortunately without variant readings, but with Devapāla's commentary on the Mantras). The similarity of certain Akṣaras or ligatures in Śāradā script caused many copying mistakes and misreadings, especially in the younger manuscripts. Some of the more common ones include the following:

> *m* interchanges with *s*, *ta* with u, *rdh/rv/b*, *bhv/ty*, *br/vr*, *nt/tt/rt/tu*, *nv/rv*, *b/v*, *d/c*, *ru/t/ḍ*, *kt/ku*, *rth/u-*, *ṣṭh/ṣṭ/ṣy,yu/a-*, *tha/ṣa*, *bdh/bv*, *r*+cons./*n*+cons., *nn/tr*; *ṣṭh* and *ṣṭ* have the same sign.

Other mistakes are due to the local pronunciation of Kashmir. Thus, *e* is interchanged with *i/ī*, *o* with *u/ū*, consonant + *va* with consonant + *u*, and vice versa. Consonants found before *-r-* are frequently doubled.[56] Many of the other, apparently orthographic peculiarities of this and other older Kashmir <IX>
Veda MSS represent an older pronunciation, when compared to most Veda MSS from the last few centuries, and especially so when compared to the standard editions that have been normalized according to these late mss., or according to the orthographic habits of classical Sanskrit. Thus, just like in the Kashmirian Ṛgveda and Paippalāda MS, Anunāsika *(ṁ)*, not Anusvāra *(ṃ)*, is quite commonly written before *ś*, *ṣ*, *s*, and *ḥ*, and sometimes also before *y*, *r*, and *v*. This is to be regarded as authentic for the Kaṭha school.[57] It cannot yet be determined with certainty if the clusters *ṁyy*, *ṁvv* are original.[58]

Also, the still frequent occurence of homorganic nasal before stops is antiquated. It is found instead of the more convenient one with Anusvāra that nevertheless occurs quite frequently in this MS. However, instead of Visarga usually substituted in standard editions, the respective phonetic variant required by the

[56] On writing mistakes and 'dialect influence', see especially Scheftelowitz, *Wiener Zeitschrift zur Kunde des Morgenlandes* 21. [See now Witzel 1994.].

[57] Cf. Schroeder's preface to his edition of KS. (He doubts the justification for *ṁy*, *ṁv*). In the present MS such cases do exist : II 11 *yajñiyaṁ yad*, III 219 *rūpaṁ yajūṁṣi*, III 183a *enaṁ rudro*, III 207 (end) *nainaṁ rudro*. As far as I see, *ṁv* is not attested but known to me from other texts, such as the Kūṣmāṇḍa Br., a part of KaṭhB.

[58] This writing appears, simplified to *ṃyy*, *ṃvv*, for example, in the younger MS Paris dév. 230; cf. the notes on III 199. In contrast, the Kashmirian RV and the RVKh, both used by Scheftelowitz, still write *ṁyy*, *ṁvv*, while the sections of AĀ III that are appended to the Khilāni in this MS, already have *ṃyy*, *ṃvv* (see Scheftelowitz, edition of RVKh, p. 167). There is far-reaching agreement of the orthography in the Kashmir manuscripts of RV, RVKh, AĀ, AVP and the Kaṭha texts, and thus apparently also of the pronunciation at its basis. This is without a doubt caused by the fact that the Kashmiri Brahmins were Caturvedins (just like the Maitrāyaṇīya-Moḍhas), who transposed their pronunciation habits from the Yajurveda to all texts studied by them. Mutual influence in pronunciation (and depiction of accents) is found elsewhere, in schools of various Vedas that live in the same area. -- The Sandhi of *-m l-* is only attested as *ṃl* viz. *ṃll*, thus, e.g., in II 103, 108a, 109, III 179, 199.

following sound is written consistently: Jihvāmūlīya *ẖ* [*x*] before voiceless velars, Upadhmānīya *ḫ* [ɸ] before voiceless labials; *ś* before voiceless 'palatals'; the respective assimilated sibilant before *ś, ṣ, s*; *s* before voiceless dentals, and *ṣ* before voiceless 'cerebrals'. Visarga *ḥ* is found only in final position.[59]

The importance of the constant writing of *śch* instead of classical Skt. *cch* has not been noticed so far. It is written as *ch* in RV and Maitr.S. manuscripts,[60] and it was pronounced -- as the metre indicates -- as a consonant *cluster*. The Kashmirian spelling *śch* cannot have been caused by recent local pronunciation, as *c* is now pronounced [*tˢ*] and *ch* as [*t ˢʰ*], i.e. aspirated [*tˢ*]. Since the cluster *śch* represents, in many cases, an Indo-European **sk'*, the usual explanation as writing mistake (*cch* > *śch*) seems to be excluded.[61] <X>
The appearance of Ṛgvedic *-ḷ-* instead of *-ḍ-* in texts of the Kaṭha school,[62] however, has gone completely unnoticed, though both letters are clearly distinguished in Śāradā by a diacritic mark. Since *-ḷ-*, instead of intervocalic *-ḍ-* does not only appear in RV quotations but also frequently in Brāhmaṇa sections, one has to assume, against the testimony of printed editions, the sounds *-ḷ-* and *-ḷh-*[63] in texts of the Kaṭha school. These sounds apparently were found well beyond the dialect of the RV diaskeuasts.[64] As far as this item is concerned, the spelling of the manuscript is not consistent either. Just as in the RV, uncontracted *ṛ-* frequently appears in KaṭhĀ after word-final *-a*; however, the younger form *-a r-* also appears, without any difference in distribution, both in Mantra and prose sections.[65]

---

[59] Apparently, Visarga is occasionally used as a sign for pause, for example in I 42-47. Frequently, Visarga or its variants (ḫ, ẖ) have been left out or mutually confused (II 108a, variant reading 3). Incidentally, in the manuscripts of Maitrāyaṇī Saṃhitā, the Sandhi *-ś ś-* , *-ṣ ṣ-*, *-s s-* is attested, but it has not been carried out by v. Schroeder in his edition (see preface to the edition of MS, vol. I p. XLII).

[60] See v. Schroeder, MS Vol. I, p. XLIII, n.2.

[61] Thus v. Schroeder in the preface of KS. For exceptions to writing *śch,* see Scheftelowitz, *WKZM* 21: 120 and note, e.g., the usage in the KaṭhĀ manuscripts at I.II 41-47. For literature on *śch* see Tsuji, *Existent Yajurveda Literature*, p. 153 n. 483. [Note further, Wackernagel 1896: 157 sqq. ; and cf. the writing as *cś* and (sometimes *ch*) in Kerala, Ikari 1995:14].

[62] Neither in v. Schroeder's or Satvalekar's editions; not in Schroeder's, Caland's or Suryakanta's collections of Kaṭha texts; also not in Caland's edition of the KGS. Only in the edition of the Laugākṣi-GS, *-ḷ* - is occasionally found.

[63] Though it has no longer been carried through consistently, just like many other phonetic peculiarities: *-ḷ-* is found in II 100, III 213, 215, 219, 233; *-ḍ-* in III 198; *-ḍh-* in III, 233 (end), 235; *-ḷh-* is not attested in KaṭhĀ and, curiously, it does not seem to have been differentiated from *-ḍh* by a diacritical mark, as could have been expected. On *-ḷ-* in KpS see the edition of Raghu Vira, reprint, p. XXIII.

[64] Found with the Kāṇvas, Jaiminīyas (where, mostly, Dravidian influence has been assumed), and apparently also with the Kāpiṣṭhalas (see note 63). [See now Witzel 1989: 165sqq and W. Rau 1983]

[65] For example, *-a ṛ-* in II 9, 71, 97, III 181, 195; *-a r-* in II 9, 75, etc. There does not seem to be a difference in the treatment of Sandhi between the Mantras and the Brāhmaṇa sections. The usual

The archaisms mentioned above have not yet been normalized in the present edition, according to Vedic or Classical norms; instead, they appear in the form met with in the manuscript. However, in addition to sentence punctuation, the Avagraha has been introduced as a reading aid. It appears only three times in this manuscript.

The accentuation system of the KaṭhĀ has not been reproduced in the edition, but normalized in the usual fashion. In the annotations and variant readings, however, every accent sign has been noted when necessary for understanding the passage. -- The designation of the accents in the manuscript corresponds exactly to those of accented sections of KS, found in the various Ṛcakas: Anudātta = ˌ a perpendicular stroke under the respective Akṣara, Udātta = ˈ a perpendicular stroke above the respective Akṣara, dependent Svarita = . a dot below the Akṣara, independent Svarita before accented syllable = a hook ‸ under the Akṣara; however, without exception, a hook ˜ on top of the Akṣara before an unaccented syllable.[66] <XI>

On the present edition

The fragmentary character of the only extant manuscript containing the major part of the text required an exact representation of destroyed passages as well as of lines or Akṣaras, of which only the upper or lower part, or even less, has been preserved.

In the **edition,** such passages (and uncertain readings in general) have been indicated by italics [originally, in the 1974 print, by = under the line]. The approximate number of broken off Akṣaras has been suggested by *x*, occasionally a missing vowel sign by ə, especially when the original accent was still discernible. Text in brackets [ ] has been restored according to parallel passages, or even freely so. However, restoration frequently results, with remarkable certainty, due to the

Sandhi of words ending in -*r* and beginning with *r*- is found once, at III 158, *ketū rātrī*.

[66] However, v. Schroeder also uses other signs in his edition; for the accent system of the Kaṭhas, cf. Schroeder, *Sitzungsberichte Wien* 1898 p. 3, etc.; the present manuscript distinguishes, without exception, between actual (independent) Svarita before unaccented syllable (mark: ˜) and that before accented syllable (mark: ‸). However, a possible exception is *tanvaṁ* at II 13 (cf. the variant readings). Furthermore, as noticed by v. Schroeder in the MS W_1 (see *Sitzungsberichte Wien* 1895, p. 29), a Devanāgarī number '2' (or a sign that has, by chance, the same form) is found three times (thus, not a '2' of Śāradā script). Twice it has been used to designate independent Svarita before accented syllable (II 101, n. 2: *pravargye saṅ•* ; at II 101, n. 3, however, above the line and together with a hook: *•gyaṁ saṅ•*). The third case is unclear, see III 207, variant reading 12 (perhaps it was just used to designate the dependent Svarita). - Once, a sign is found that looks like a Devanāgarī '3'. Here (II 133, variant reading 3), Abhinihita Sandhi is found, however, not Svarita, but Udātta; perhaps '3' is nothing but an Avagraha sign. -- The Śāradā number '3' is otherwise used as sign of Pluti, see II 143 *prāśyā3*, III 231 *jyotī3r*.

'inevitability' of Brāhmaṇa style.[67] For the first lines of a page of the manuscript that have mostly been broken off, [...] has always been inserted in order to indicate the amount of missing text. One line of the edition corresponds to about half a line of the original.

For reasons of expediency, Mantras and Praiṣas have been numbered, though no longer consistently, [e.g., the parapharases of Mantras have no longer been counted, done in the original numbering based on a provisional reading of the MS around 1970]. As the original numbering of sections of the text has been preserved only sporadically,[68] quoting the text according to Mantra number is the most expedient method. This includes the Brāhmaṇa passages following each Mantra, e.g., KaṭhĀ III 207. For more exact quotations, page number and line number may be suggested. In KaṭhĀ II and III the Mantras and Praiṣas have been emphasized by bold letters [originally, in the 1974 print, by underlining]. However, in the Mantra chapter KaṭhĀ I, bold characters indicate whether and how far the respective Mantra has been preserved in the Brāhmaṇas (KaṭhĀ II and III); these sections have to be compared in the respective cases. <XII>
In the appended list of variants, however, a more exact depiction of the damaged portions of the text has been attempted, which nevertheless, due to the ambiguity of (half) broken Akṣaras, cannot replace a facsimile. Italics [in the original, underlining __] indicate half or completely broken off Akṣaras whose reading is uncertain. The sign *x* is used for a completely destroyed Akṣara or for the upper half of a ligature whose lower part is represented by *z*. Text appearing in parentheses ( ) was not readable in the extant microfilm of the Tübingen manuscript. Soon after the arrival of the manuscript in 1895, these passages were pasted over by R. von Roth with a relatively nontransparent paper film in order to save the manuscript from further decay. In these cases, the readings of L. von Schroeder have been inserted (only within the parentheses). These readings were mostly found to be correct during a recheck of the manuscript itself in the summer of 1972. [Compare now the new fascsimile, included at the very end of this edition; it was made in 2004, and shows the state of the MS after restorations made in the

---

[67] The term has been coined by K. Hoffmann. Obviously, my restorations are only more or less certain. Those *only* been guessed have been included in the variants readings and should only be used as proposals for discussion. One example may suffice: in III 219 (beginning) I had at first inserted, though based on a passage from KaṭhŚS preserved in Paris dév. 230: *grā́mād adṛ́ṣṭo 'gním prájvalayati*. However, a parallel in KaṭhB (Svādhyāya-Br., *Sitzungsberichte Wien* 1898, p. 64) also begins: *áraṇyam parétya śúcau bhūmyāvakāśé grā́mād acchadírdarśe* (for this see Böhtlingk-Roth, St. Petersburg Dictionary, vol. II p. 286b) *svādhyāyám eváinam adhīyánn*. This would suggest a corresponding restoration. The reconstruction given first would have belonged to the context, however, the Brāhmaṇa uses a more terse expression, and the restoration would have been mistaken.

[68] Preserved are only the Anuvāka numbers 1, 2, 3 and 7 of the Yuñjate Br., and just 1 and 2 of the Gharmājāṭharā Br.; cf. also variant reading 2 in III 189. [See, however, the new facsimile of fol. 349b, in the appendix, where no *anuvāka* number is visible]. Furthermore, there are marks designating a large number of subsections that, in contradistinction to the Anuvākas, do not cause dissolution of Sandhi. A similar subdivision is also found in KS, likewise not numbered; it has been indicated by v. Schroeder by double Daṇḍa.

Seventies and Eighties.]

The symbol **T** indicates variant readings of the main manuscript Tüb. MaI 396, (KaṭhĀ II and III), **S** is the reading of L. v. Schroeder in his print of the text, in so far as it does not differ from the text constituted here or from *T*. Therefore, *S* is without any text-critical value, apart from a few instances where the MS has been further destroyed since 1898. The symbol **t1** indicates variant readings of the Mantra section (KaṭhĀ I) in the Tübingen Ms. MaI 396, fols. 274a-284b, **P** of the Ms. Paris dév. 230, **P2** of Ms. Paris 227b, and **L** of the Laugākṣi Gṛhyasūtra.

The **translation** follows the idiom of the original as closely as possible. Words that do not appear in the original Sanskrit text but that are important for its understanding, have been added within parentheses ( ). Undoubtedly, this is not to be understood as an explanation of all peculiarities of the text. This is something that has been reserved for my commentary, not published here. As before, brackets [ ] indicate, <XIII>
as far as possible, the state of preservation of the text.

As there is, essentially, only one continuous manuscript of the KaṭhĀ (T), some difficulties arose in the constitution of the text, even though manuscripts of the Mantra chapter offered some welcome control of T, where the text could be restored according to it.[69] Although, on the whole, T proved to be quite reliable,[70] the related texts had to be compared with increasing measure in the present situation. That is, for the Mantras, TĀ 4, MS 4.9, ŚB 14, and VS 37-39 respectively; TĀ 5 and ŚB 14 for the Brāhmaṇas, even though the greater originality of KaṭhĀ III set some limits. Furthermore, the Sūtras dealing with the Pravargya had to be compared.[71] A large number of destroyed passages could thus be restored[72] with the help of these texts; furthermore, with the help of aids now available, such as Bloomfield's *Vedic Concordance* and Vishva Bandhu's *Vedic Word Concordance*, and, frequently, due to the inevitability (*Zwangsläufigkeit*) of Brāhmaṇa style. I have tried to ascertain the *authentic* form [of the text],[73] especially for the Mantras, and to distinguish it, as far as possible, from the *original* one.

In conclusion, it is my duty and pleasure to thank the Bibliothèque

---

69 The difference in II 6 *á devy* : I 6 *prá devy* is remarkable. [Note that BŚS 9.2.3: 269: 20 and VādhS read *ā devy*].

70 Apart from the influence of local pronunciation (such as interchange of *e/ī*), most writing mistakes are due to writer's haplology: II 19,35; III 229, variant reading 5, is perhaps the most obvious case; further, inversion of syllables or sounds: II 133 variant reading 7; 134 *var. lect.* 2.

71 See above, n. 48, on the importance of a constant comparison of Brāhmaṇa and Sūtra texts.

72 Obviously, not *all* broken off passages could be restored, even where some remnants of letters still remained, especially at the beginning of a page. Frequently, the ritual intended is not discernible at the respective passage, most frequently in KaṭhĀ III, where, in most cases, the possibility of comparison with related texts does not exist. - It is therefore to be expected that not all restorations will hit the mark; cf. above, n. 67.

73 For the terms see K. Hoffmann, *Indo-Iranian Journal* 11, p.4.

Nationale in Paris and the Universitätsbibliothek Tübingen for the microfilms of manuscripts made available to me. I also would like to thank Dr. A. Parpola warmly; he has kindly written to me about two passages concerning the ritual of the Sāmaveda,[74] proposing several corrections that could be carried out in the present partial print (*Teildruck*).[75] I also thank Dr. B.K. Deambi who, during a stay at Hoshiarpur, gave me valuable hints based on his comprehensive knowledge of the paleography of Śāradā script. I especially thank my esteemed teacher, Prof. Dr. K. Hoffmann, who suggested working on the fragments of the Kaṭha school, for his extensively granted advice, and constant support, by which he has accompanied the work on the present dissertation.[76]

Svayaṃbhūnāth
Kāṭhmāṇḍū
July 17, 1973
[July 10, 2004]

---

[74] III 229c-231 and 233-234 (*parisāmāni*).

[75] I would have liked to check many other cases; however, this could not be carried out [then] due to the large gaps in technical literature, especially of European and American provenance, in local Kathmandu libraries.

[76] This also contains, in addition to the present 'partial print', a detailed introduction on the texts and history of the Kaṭha school, etc., and a commentary on the whole text. -- It was [then] planned to publish this in a second volume.

The Kaṭha Āraṇyaka : ritual and world view

§1. The* KaṭhĀ in Vedic literature

The Kaṭha Āraṇyaka is one of the texts of Vedic tradition that belongs, according to the traditional division[77] of the Vedas, to its third layer. It comes after the Saṃhitās and Brāhmaṇas, which are, in fact, presupposed and quoted by it.[78] The KaṭhĀ thus precedes the fourth stratum of Vedic texts, the Upaniṣads, but occasionally anticipates some of their ideas and as such, stands at the crossroads in the development of pre-Buddhist and early Hindu thought: from here, different paths lead to the establishment of Upaniṣadic philosophy, early Buddhist and Jaina thought, and to the continuous development of Brahmanical ritualism.

As an Āraṇyaka, it contains the secret doctrine of its particular Veda school (*śākhā*) and has to be studied in the wilderness (*araṇya*). In the present text, this is the Pravargya, a ritual in which a blazing clay vessel (*mahāvīra*) is identified with the sun and Rudra Mahāvīra.[79] The ritual also aims at giving the sponsor of the ritual (*yajamāna*) a new, heavenly body.[80] This is established by multiple Upaniṣad-like identifications between various entities of microcosm (man), ritual (*yajña*), and

---

* The text of this extended introduction dealing with the world view underlying the KaṭhĀ has been left as written at Kathmandu in 1977. Other aspects of the KaṭhĀ, the Kaṭha school, and its relationship with other texts can be found in the unpublished part of my thesis, Erlangen 1972. This introduction had therefore been intended for a South Asian audience. Sometimes this will show, for example, in mostly quoting easily available secondary sources written in English. Also, by now, the text may appear somewhat old-fashioned, a quarter century after its composition. However, a few corrections and some limited updating have been carried out while preparing the present publication. Such additions are indicated by brackets [ ]. -- All quotations without any further reference to a particular text are from KaṭhĀ, e.g., II 115.

[77] These do not coincide with the actual linguistic development of the texts, which indicate *five* layers of development: Ṛgveda, Mantra language (mantras of the YV, SV, AV, RV Khila), prose sections of the Black YV, Brāhmaṇas proper (which include the Āraṇyakas and the older Upaniṣads), Sūtras. [See now Witzel 1989, 1997. For an electronic version see: http://www.people.fas.harvard.edu/~witzel/canon.pdf].

[78] The Atharvaveda and Yajurveda contain Ṛgvedic mantras, often in slightly perseverated fashion; the Brāhmanas, too, and in addition they quote from the post-Ṛgvedic Saṃhitās; the Āraṇyakas and Upaniṣads quote the Brāhmaṇas, etc.; and the Sūtras quote from all of the above. [For the early Upaniṣads see now Fujii 1997].

[79] [Cf. now the discussion by Houben 1991 : 10 sqq.]

[80] Note, however, the insecure reading *svargākṛti*, II 143, see Introd. note 33, (and below n. 244, 259). [Cf. now Houben 1991: 124 n. 117 for the Taittirīya reading *svagā*-].

macrocosm (heaven, universe).

However, in the present text, the germs of such Upaniṣadic philosophical ideas are still represented in ritualistic fashion, inherited from the preceding Brāhmaṇa and Saṃhitā period. Understandably so, as the Kaṭha Āraṇyaka belongs to the tradition of the Yajurveda, the Veda directly concerned with ritual formulas (*mantra*), actual order of procedure of a particular ritual (*vidhi* portion of the Brāhmaṇas) and esoteric interpretation of all of these details (*arthavāda* sections of the Brāhmaṇa texts). As mentioned, the present Āraṇyaka tries to do so for one of the most secret ritual in the Yajurveda, the Pravargya.

§2. The ritual

Literally, Pravargya means 'the one to be turned towards (the fire)', i.e., 'the one to be heated.' This signifies the clay vessel and its contents used in this ritual. In the oldest Vedic text, the Ṛgveda, the Pravargya was an offering of milk to the Heavenly Twins, the Aśvin. Milk was put into a (metal) vessel that was then heated and made to boil over. This much is already alluded to in the so-called Frog Hymn[81] of the Ṛgveda. In post-Ṛgvedic times, this small rite was incorporated into the elaborate Soma ritual (*yajña*)[82]; it was placed shortly after the initiation ceremony (*dīkṣā*) of the sponsor of the ritual, the *yajamāna*. By its incorporation into the Soma ritual, it became the subject of elaborate Brahmanical speculation into origins of the rite, its secret meaning, the various ways and times to perform it, and the beneficial effects resulting from its performance. All of this is treated in the present text (see examples below, § 6).

In Yajurveda tradition,[83] however, there also existed another, less 'ritual-oriented' application of this rite: the Pravargya text was connected with learning, by heart, the sacred texts of this Veda. In particular, it served to prepare the Veda student for the study of the more secret texts of Vedic tradition: the Āraṇyaka itself and the Upaniṣad.[84] Thus, in both of its main functions, that is, as a prelude to the Soma ritual and as the starting point of secret study, the Pravargya acts as some kind of special initiation (*dīkṣā*). The interrelation of both kinds of initiation is an interesting theme that cannot be elaborated here, a subject of special study.[85]

---

[81] RV 7.103, see P. Thieme, *Gedichte aus dem Rig-Veda*. Stuttgart: Reclam 1964: 61 sqq. [For the age of the Pravargya ritual, see now Houben 1991: 28 sqq.; in addition, he finds a reference to the ritual in the difficult stanza, RV 1.164.43].

[82] I try to avoid the term 'sacrifice' whenever possible, as the Pravargya does not involve the killing and offering of animals. The same is true for the Soma ritual proper (though its classical Vedic form included a goat sacrifice, spread out throughout the ritual). I also prefer to use the indigenous term *yajña*, as a near-synonym of the rather broad English term 'ritual.' [For the Soma ritual and the Pravargya, see now Houben 1991: 16 sqq.]

[83] Preserved in the KaṭhĀ I-III, TĀ 4-5, ŚB 14.1-3. [For details see now Houben 1991: 5 sqq.]

[84] See Witzel 1977 [and add now Houben 1991: 28 sqq; cf. Witzel 1979b, 1980].

[85] See my forthcoming book, *The Veda in Kashmir*, ch. VI [largely written up in 1976/1989, but still not

The treatment of the texts relating to this ritual in the Āraṇyaka, i.e. at the beginning of the more esoteric and secret texts of the Vedas, carries its own meaning. An Āraṇyaka usually contains, as its nucleus, the most dangerous ritual held in highest esteem in a particular branch of the Veda.[86] In the Ṛgveda Āraṇyakas, it is the Mahāvrata ceremony, the culmination of the one year *gavām ayana* Sattra ritual. It is selected for separate treatment outside the Ṛgveda Brāhmaṇas proper. In the Yajurveda, however, it is the Pravargya ritual that is given this kind of special attention. The main reason for the particular care and secrecy attached to the Pravargya ceremony is its inherent danger: the blazing Pravargya vessel is identified with the sun and the ominous god Rudra Mahāvīra, and therefore regarded as highly dangerous. One can only perform it after a long and very special initiation.[87] This, and the actual ceremony, has to take place outside the settlement, in the wilderness (*araṇya*)[88], "from where on cannot see the roofs of the settlement."[89] Looking at the glowing Pravargya vessel would make a woman barren, and she therefore must be separated and shielded by a cloth.[90]

§3. Vedic thought: magical interpretation of the world

The preceding paragraphs have referred to some contemporary, indigenous *interpretations* of the ritual and its constituent parts, as mentioned in the present text. It is not the aim of the Āraṇyaka (as well as Brāhmaṇa and YV Saṃhitā) texts to *describe* a particular ritual but to give an exegetical commentary (*brāhmaṇa*) on the multitude of ritual Mantras and actions constituting it. Therefore, it is not a *handbook*[91] for the priests, indicating *how* to perform the ritual,[92] and in which

finalized and released]; cf. below §6.7.2. [See now Houben 1991: 21 sqq.].

86 Around this nucleus, other materials have gradually been added, often including the Upaniṣads of the Veda school in question, and various late, in the case of TĀ, even post-Vedic, sections (TĀ 1, 10). For the Āraṇyakas in general, see Witzel in *Kindlers Neues Literaturlexikon* 1972, 1992:134-5; [and now, Houben 1991: 32 with note 61, Fujii 1997].

87 The *avāntaradīkṣā*, the 'intermediate' or 'inserted (*ava-antara*)' consecration. See KaṭhĀ III 197, 219, ĀpŚS 15.20.21; van Buitenen 1968: 41; Kashikar 1976, Houben 1991: 21 sqq.

88 See Oldenberg 1915.

89 KaṭhB corresponding to TĀ 2.9-12, see v. Schroeder 1898: 53sqq

90 [See the photo in J. F. Staal 1983: 373; cf. Ikari 1983: 171].

91 This is only supplied in the late Vedic Śrautasūtras. In the *brāhmaṇa* style texts, however, other principles obtain.

92 While the *brāhmaṇa* style texts generally follow the order of the ritual procedures, they do not adhere to this order persistently. Various 'digressions' arising from the stream of consciousness of the Brāhmaṇa author are interspersed, such as mythological references and tales, discussion of *ad hoc* ideas, popular sayings, objections of rivaling persons and schools, etc. In addition, there are many ritual items and discussions added in smaller or larger sections, sometimes in an appendix to the ritual in question, sometimes much later in the text.

order,[93] but an explanation, *why* they have to do it, and why in a particular way.

Such *brāhmaṇa* explanations will not be understood easily by the modern reader, whether Hindu or not, as they are based on a ancient system of thought, the main assumptions of which are widely different[94] from our contemporary thought.

§3.1. Identification technique

One of the main features of Vedic thought is the use of an 'identification'[95] technique that establishes links, equivalents, nexus [or correlations] between, or identity of two entities, things, beings, thoughts, states of mind, etc. Both entities are unrelated, according to our way of thinking. When the text says, e.g., 'the *muñja* grass is strength' and 'the *udumbara* tree is strength', or 'Prajāpati is thought' and 'Prajāpati is the sacrifice', it will not be clear why some kind of grass (a living being, or dead material) could be the *same*[96] as 'strength' (an abstract idea, or a force experienced); or in the second case, why and how the god Prajāpati, 'the lord of creation,' could be the same as 'thought/thinking', and, at the same time, the act or idea of ritual ('sacrifice', *yajña*).

Such sentences constitute the notorious 'identifications' of the Brāhmaṇas, which, since long, had been the laughing stock of occidental scholarship. In the eyes of Max Müller and L. v. Schroeder, they are worthy of study only as the 'literary production' of weakly-minded people living in an asylum.[97] Even Keith still

---

[93] The order of all Śrauta rituals and the discussion of individual rituals generally follow that of the ritual procedures (cf. Kashikar 1968). For the ancient arrangement of Śrauta topics, followed from the oldest Yajurveda Saṃhitās (MS, KS) onwards, see the detailed discussion in my forthcoming book *The Veda in Kashmir,* chapter IX. These texts typically begin with the mantras of the Darśapūrṇamāsa and Soma rituals (reflecting the blueprints of the Iṣṭi and Soma rituals), and the peculiarities of the *yajamāna*'s participation and then discuss the Agnihotra, Cāturmāsya, Soma, Vājapeya, Rājasūya, Sautrāmaṇī, Agnicayana, Aśvamedha and Sattra rituals.

[94] Cf., however, below, on the similarities of the underlying systems of thought as such.

[95] [Often better: 'correlation' instead of 'resemblance, identification,' etc., for which see now: S. Farmer, J.B. Henderson, M. Witzel, Neurobiology, Layered Texts, and Correlative Cosmologies: A Cross-Cultural Framework for Premodern History. *Bulletin of the Museum of Far Eastern Antiquities (BMFEA)* 72, 2002, 48-90. http://www.people.fas.harvard.edu/~witzel/BMFEAfinal.pdf].

[96] At least, *prima facie*, as the majority of the sentences establishing identifications are simple nominal clauses of the type 'x [is] z' or 'x *vai* z;' they are frequently summed by a statement 'x *eva* z.' Usually, they do not express such links as '*x is like z*' or '*x is connected with z*.' The latter case is seen, however, in a number of cases that employ *vṛddhi* formulations, such as *prājāpatya* 'coming from/connected with Prajāpati' II 23,24, 143; *ānuṣṭubha* III 233, etc. [In some other cases, they function as metaphors, see now Witzel 1979a, (cf. Arieti 1967: 373), and cf. Wezler 1996].

[97] [Cf. now Arieti 1967: 280sqq. for some features in the psychotic transformation that underlies the use of words as 'an icon of the thing it represents' and the Brāhmaṇa-like results: '... associate words not according to their meaning but according to their phonetic quality... because of their assonance...' such as 'pen ~ penitentiary,' 'frame ~ name, ~ same.' This comes close to the traditional Brāhmaṇa and Yāska-like etymologies.]

maintains,[98] in his book on the *Religion and Philosophy of the Veda and Upaniṣads* (1916/1925), 'of the puerilities the Brāhmaṇas are never tired, and this attitude must be accepted as a fundamental fact of their mental outlook' (*op cit.*, p. 312),[99] or he refers to them as 'a world of fancy', where , sometimes, a text can have 'a moment of sanity' (*op. cit.* p. 483).

This, however, was the view of 19th century Indologists. In the early 20th century, some advances have been made in the understanding of these *seemingly* nonsensical texts, e.g., by L. Lévy-Bruhl,[100] who investigated early patterns of thought and by S. Lévi[101] who described the nature of 'sacrifice' in the *brāhmaṇa* style texts and shared this with his colleagues in various fields of the humanities working in Paris. Further progress was made especially by H. Oldenberg and S. Schayer who studied the nature of Brāhmaṇa equations.[102] However, interest in the subject waned after a comparatively short period of impact on the field, along with the then increasing decline of Vedic studies. It has been picking up again only since K. Hoffmann's seminal note,[103] and notably, among his students,[104] due to his intensive teaching of *brāhmaṇa* type texts. [The matter has taken a new turn recently[105] by the resumption of collaboration between Sinologists, Indologists, and scholars in other fields which had been lacking since c. 1920 (see Henderson *et al.* 2002)].

98 In spite of Oldenberg's book on the concept of the world in Brāhmaṇa texts, published in 1919, which is actually quoted by Keith.

99 I mostly quote from Keith's book as it is readily available in the Indian subcontinent in an inexpensive reprint and is in English; secondarily, and for the same reasons, I quote from the collection of anthropological articles on magic, as it is easily available in a Penguin edition: *Witchcraft and Sorcery*, ed. by Max Marwick, 1970; see also A.B. Keith 1925.

100 Lévy-Bruhl 1910. [He has frequently been misunderstood; however, he restricts the designation of a 'primitive' (paleological) mind set to its collective manifestations in the various societies concerned, not to individuals, see Arieti 1967: 123. Arieti points out survivals of such paleological thought, e.g., in modern western societies; cf. Witzel 1979a].

101 S. Lévi, 1898. For the concept of archaic ('paleological') mentality, note S. Arieti 1967: 108 sqq., 121sqq., cf. also p. 348 sqq.

102 Oldenberg 1919, Schayer 1925, *Rocznik Orientalistyczny* 2, 26-32; *RO* 3, 57-69; K. Hoffmann 1960; Renou 1946; Gonda 1965a [See now: Witzel 1979a, B.K. Smith 1989; A. Wezler 1996; summary by P. Olivelle, in the introduction to his translation of the *Upaniṣads* (1996); S. Farmer, J.B. Henderson, M. Witzel 2002, (see n. 19)].

103 K. Hoffmann 1960: 232 [= *Aufsätze*, 1992, p. 709].

104 See Benke, A. 1976 [and Witzel 1979a; B.K. Smith 1989, Wezler 1996].

105 See Benke 1976, [and Witzel 1979a; B.K. Smith 1989, Wezler 1996, see n. 102].

§3.2. Identifications, Equations, Equivalences, Correlations, *bandhu/nidāna.*

Brāhmaṇa style texts are found in the prose sections of the Kṛṣṇa Yajurveda Saṃhitās,[106] all Brāhmaṇas proper, the Āraṇyakas, and many earlier Upaniṣads. All abound in 'equations', frequently simply stated as such, and not explained any further by the texts. A thorough look into this vast mass of literature occasionally reveals[107] some reasons as to *why* a particular link or identification was made.[108] On closer analysis, it will be found that such reasoning is based on a [paleological[109] and] *magical* interpretation of the world (*magische Weltanschauung*), according to which, in a

[106] Thus, in the Maitrāyaṇi, Kaṭha, Kapiṣṭhala, and Taittirīya Saṃhitās.

[107] This is due to the belief that the whole cosmos is an *organized* unity in which everything has its relationship with and bearing on another thing, cf. Keith, *Rel.* p. 487.

[108] Scattered over various parts of the TS, for example, is the explanation about why the horse (*aśva*) is like/connected with Prajāpati (Prajāpati cried; from his tear, the horse developed). [On this myth, see now Witzel 1979a].

[109] [See S. Arieti (1967) who uses this concept, relying on the *von Domarus principle,* (von Domarus 1944) which states: "Whereas in nature (or secondary process) thinking identity is accepted only upon the basis of identical subjects, in paleological (or primary process) thinking identity is accepted on the basis of identical predicates," which is a good description of the Brāḥmaṇa procedure of linking and identifying items if they share just one common predicate (see immediately below). Arieti (1967: 120; cf. also Doty 2000: 88 sqq) quotes von Domarus and adds: "The predicate which leads to the identification is called the identifying link or identifying predicate. At this level identity cannot be based upon identical subjects, because 'logical' subjects are in reality only concepts, and clear concepts have not been formed. Clear concepts must include all essential predicates." (cf. also p. 275, 359, 373.) In other words, Brāhmaṇa correlations and identifications are based on (partial) *bandhus* that do not cover all aspects of the linked items, though they are clearly stated as thus in the texts. I therefore think that my friend A. Wezler (1996) goes too far when he argues philosophically about such correlations 'before the fact,' that is *before philosophy* and before the authors of the texts and the users of the correlation scheme had analytically thought about it as a philosophical system or as *weltanschauung.* The quotes from psychologists and anthropologists working on similar systems of thought, magic and sorcery (Arieti 1967; Gluckmann and Horton (in Marwick 1970; see §3.4), Tambiah 1990) clearly indicate that adherents of such systems typically cannot perceive their system 'from the outside,' that they are bound by it and remain 'inside the box.' Notably, even one of the first philosophical systems, that of Mīmāṃsā (note *iti mīmāṃsante* in the Br. texts), still works along the culture-specific pathway dependencies first established by the Brāhmaṇa authors (see Farmer *et al.* 2002). Its thinkers remain inside the Vedic 'box.' They take it for granted that ritual leads to heaven and they merely discuss, in much refined, quasi-philological fashion, the *interpretation* of the very same Brāhmaṇa texts. They do *not* question (as Horton underlines for an African context) the very foundation of the correlation system, instead, they take its outcome for granted. They do not develop an analysis of the (system of) correlations themselves, which, in fact, has so far not been done by Indologists either. In order to come closer to an understanding of the intricacies of the Vedic system of thought, a detailed study is needed of the *vai* and *eva* sentences as well as the Vṛddhi derivatives used in establishing correlations. I have collected many such correlations since 1970, on and off, and am now working on a computer program depicting them; easy access to a large section of such *bandhus* is possible, for the time being, via the almost unknown and unused *Brāhmaṇoddhārakośa* of Vishva Bandhu (1966).]

fashion somewhat similar to modern natural science,[110] everything in the world is closely interrelated and interdependent with its particular cause. The existence of a nexus (*bandhu, nidāna*) of cause and effect is a given; the link is inevitable and compulsory. It is the aim of the Vedic priest and 'theologian' (*brahmavādin*) to discover such relationships of cause and effect, to establish their *bandhu*.[111] His joy of discovery is visible in discussions sometimes reported as having taken place between protagonists of various ritualistic opinions.[112]

The *bandhu* usually is threefold: something in nature (macrocosm) has its *equivalent* in the human sphere (microcosm)[113] and in the sacrifice/ritual (*yajña*). This is the famous *adhidevata, adhyātma, adhiyajña* interpretation of the world found in the later Brāhmaṇas and in the Upaniṣads. (The earlier texts use the same system, though their terminology is not yet developed to that extent.)[114]

Such traditional reasoning (whether in India, Africa or elsewhere) makes use of many ways of linking cause or effect, i.e., the concept of "converging causal effects (the possibility that a result, E, is attributable to any of a set of causes A, B, C, D, etc." (Horten 1970: 361) while scientific thought assigns distinctive effects to differing causes. The traditional system almost never allows "a confession of ignorance about the answer to some question which the people themselves consider important." It cannot tolerate "the development of concepts which formally recognize the existence of various kinds of limitations upon the possible completeness of exploration and prediction," i.e. coincidence, chance, probability.[115]

Such identifications are the hallmark of sorcery, as is easily seen in the manipulation of Voodoo dolls representing an enemy. If the doll and the enemy are somehow linked or *correlated* (by using hairs, nail clippings etc. of the enemy), can he be affected. The *bandhu* in this case is the *similarity* of shape, *identity* of substance (hair, nails, etc.), and *identity* of name (given to the effigy, *kṛtyā*). The link is established in ritual (sorcery, action, words) -- though African or Carribean sorcery usually does not pay as much attention to the formulation of mantras as seen in

---

110 The thought of these Vedic texts has, in fact, been labeled by Oldenberg (1919) as 'Vorwissenschaftliche Wissenschaft' (science preceding science); Schayer more precisely defined it as a speculative achievement, the source of the spiritual culture of Old India, the source of many of the later technical sciences and philosophy (1925: 283sq, 291); cf. also Keith, *Rel.* p. 381 n. 8; cf., however, below on the view of ethnology (cf. Frazer 1922: p.48).

111 It is important to note that it is enough to know this *bandhu* as to master it. This is the origin of the importance given to (secret/esoteric) knowledge, so typical for Hindu and Buddhist thought ever since.

112 Occasionally, already in the early YV prose texts (MS, KS, TS), but especially so in ŚB; note KaṭhĀ II 143. [See now Witzel 1987a; on Yājñavalkya's discussion with the Carakādhvaryu, see Witzel 1982].

113 From the Puruṣa *sūkta* (RV 10.90) onwards, microcosm and macrocosm have been distinguished and compared, see Keith, *Rel.* p. 486.

114 Note the Ṛgvedic (and later) concept of eye ~ sun (RV 6.51.1; 7.61.1, 7.76.1; 1.155.5; 5.26.2; 7.32.22, 10.90.13, 10.16.3 etc.), fire ~ sun (cf. 1.115.1, see n.173), ritual fire ~ heaven, etc. (see also n. 232, 244, 249-255, KaṭhĀ II 107-8, see n. 199, 209, 254-55).

115 Horton 1970: 362. The same is stressed by Keith (*Rel.*, p. 483): "The theologians of the Brāhmaṇas are not prepared to admit to ignorance of any sort."

Indian ritual. (For a detailed discussion, see below §3.4, §4).

§3.3. Vedic Magic

This presupposes that one of the major underlying features of Vedic ritual is that of magic.[116] This has been denied sometimes,[117] but will become clear enough from the following paragraphs that, at least for the ritual in question, (the Pravargya in an Āraṇyaka text), *yajña* is *not* the giving of gifts to all-powerful gods, not just an act of *dō ut dēs*, but an instance of a rather developed and systematized form of magic, permeating all words and acts of the ritual, as well as the reasoning given for the use of certain implements,mantras, and so forth.

Keith (*Rel.*, p. 260) sums up the question as follows. "In the theosophy of the Brāhmaṇas it is an accepted fact that the ritual has a power of its own... and the question arises whether the Ṛgveda shows any real trace of the belief in the magic efficacy of the sacrifice." (This, he denies). "The later literature ... openly says so, and provides the believer with magic devices in order to bind hard the Ādityas until they yield what is desired ... and ... tie[s] up Indra in disgraceful fashion."[118]

---

116 Similarly in a negative vein, though, as usual, more balanced, Keith, *Rel.* p. 258: "... the nature of the ritual can be solved at once by the application of the concept of sympathetic magic, and this is one of the most obvious and undeniable facts in the whole of the Vedic sacrifice: it is from beginning to end full of magic elements, which can as a rule be perfectly easily disentangled from the rest of the rite... The nature of the ordinary offering to the gods is expressively stated to be an offering made to the god to attract his attention and goodwill ... this theory of the sacrifice and its result as an exchange of gift ... is the fundamental fact of the whole of Vedic religion." [For the concept of exchange, see Sahlins 1972].

117 E.g., by Heesterman 1985, due to his idiosyncratic view of the purpose of Vedic ritual (cf. Lévi 1898, Falk 1997, Witzel 1998), in spite of such clear passages as those found in KaṭhĀ II 30-36, and in spite of the existence of the special *kāmya* forms of certain Śrauta rituals (*kāmya iṣṭi, kāmya paśu*) intended to magically bring about particular, well-defined benefits for the sponsor (*yajamāna*) of the ritual in question, see Caland 1908. Incidentally, this trends continues even in (later) Buddhism, see for example the last chapters of the Mañjuśrīmūlakalpa. Cf. also Aguilar (1976) who, however, denies the obvious *dō ut dēs* character seen in much of Vedic ritual and instead interprets it in a rather theological fashion.

118 However, Keith continues: "It would be a complete error to assume that the magic side of the sacrifice is the primitive one, and that the whole sacrifice is really a magic performance..." I cannot agree. The basis of the Śrauta rituals is the identification of the offering ground and the fires with the universe and its entities, and that of the priests with the gods. Whatever they do in ritual has unavoidable repercussions in macrocosm and microcosm (see below §4.1). - - Keith expands on other concepts of the *yajña*, *Rel.*, p. 262 sqq. (cf. below, n. 161): sacrifice as a piece of magic to secure a periodical renewal of the growth of life; as a means to remove sin [which is not a Vedic concept, rather: evil] 'by *yajña* and magic,' p. 264 sqq.; as a sort of communion and sacrament with the gods, p. 268 sqq., as union with the deity, p. 274, as divine ecstasy, p. 275. All of these certainly are aspects of *yajña*, but they do not adequately describe it in its character and entirety. Keith, however, sums up (p. 277): ... "the view that the sacrifice is primarily an offering to please the god seems to be borne out by every possibility, ... [those who think differently] have always allowed themselves to be influenced unduly by the theories of the Brāhmaṇas as to the nature of sacrifice, and have underestimated the purely speculative and learned character of these suggestions." This seems to echo the view of the 19th

While Keith believed (*Rel.* p. 379) that the RV is a book in which magic is not dealt with, except for a very few cases in a few late hymns, that the AV is a book of magic (popular magic, changed much by the priests), and that the Brāhmaṇas show that the whole sacrifice was penetrated by conceptions of magic, he says, however, that "we cannot believe that there was ever a time when Vedic sacrifice was not filled with magic elements, ... and that the desire to see magic in everything was growing in the period of the Brāhmaṇas, which degrade the sacrifice from the position of an appeal to the bounty of heaven to the greatest power on earth, which controls the gods and produces whatever is desired by the priest."

This attitude towards the gods was never to leave the Hindu religion, in spite of all later developments of Advaita, Bhakti, etc. For example, Tantric priests, both Buddhist and Hindu, can still command the gods as they please. Thus, the mighty Indra was captured and put in a cage by the legendary Yogi Macchendranāth in Nepal as to stop excessive rains, and this is still repeated every year during the Indrajātrā at Kathmandu, held towards the end of the rainy season. A figure of Indra is put into a cage at the bottom of Indra's pillar (*indradhvaja*)and exhibited publicly near the former royal palace, Hanuman Dhoka.

§3.4. Magic in anthropology and in the Veda

As for magic in general,[119] it is perhaps useful to compare some findings of modern anthropology on this subject, many of which are collected in the handy volume *Witchcraft and Sorcery* edited by Max Marwick;[120] note, e.g., the definition: "Magic ... is a morally neutral term in the sense that magic may be used with or without social approval. It refers to the activities or craft of the magician, a person who, suitably prepared, performs rituals aimed at controlling impersonal supernatural forces held responsible for the succession of event. In these rituals, material substances, often with characteristics or origins symbolically related to the objectives desired, are used to the accompaniment of verbal formulae" (Marwick, *op cit.* p. 12).[121] This definition holds

---

century, repeated until late into the 20th, that the Brāhmaṇas in reality are nothing but the 'twaddling of idiots' or 'primitive thought' with a rare 'moment of sanity.' While this approach unneccessarily neglects the important contemporary 'native commentary' present in the *brāhmaṇa* style texts, the nature of RV ritual should be explained first before proceeding with the Mantra and YV Saṃhitā/Brāhmaṇa level. [For some recent, mostly preliminary approaches see now Falk 1997; Witzel 1989b, 1995; Proferes 1999, Oberlies 1998-1999, Witzel 2004].

119 On the nature of Vedic magic, see Keith, *Rel.* p. 380 sqq.; for magic in ritual, see Keith, *Rel.* p. 396 sqq., where he repeats his low opinion of post-RV religion: "the sacrifice is degraded to mere magic." For Frazer's definition of magic, which had some influence on Vedic scholars at the beginning of the 20th century, see Frazer 1922: 48 sqq., p. 11 sqq.: [the two major rules operating in magic are those of 'like produces like' (effect resembles its cause, such as in imitation of rain as to produce it, note the steam of the Pravargya ~ rain in KaṭhĀ II 123), and items that were in contact continue to do so long after they have been separated (such as in the Voodoo doll case), cf. Arieti 1967 : 433].

120 Marwick 1970/1975. [To be added: Tambiah 1990, Moreau 2000].

121 Among the contributions to this volume, the following ones may be relevant here: Firth (1970: 38) "Magic... comprises a rite and verbal formulae projecting man's desires to the external world on a

for a description of Vedic ritual as well, though the aspects of sorcery are more subdued and directly apparent only in AV rituals.[122]

It is important to study closely the *world view* that produced such magic-based rituals. R. Horton (1967, *op. cit.*, p. 342) traces the following similarities between traditional African thought and 'Western' science. Both systems aim at an explanation of the world establishing "unity underlying apparent diversity... The gods of a given culture therefore do form a scheme which interprets the vast diversity of everyday experience in term of the action of a relatively few *kinds* of forces." Such[123] "theory places things in a causal context wider than that provided by common sense ... In evolving a theoretical scheme, the human mind seems constrained to draw inspiration from analogy between the puzzling observations to be explained and certain already familiar phenomena..."

This is exactly the way the notorious Brāhmaṇa identifications [or, correlations] are made (see below): "only a limited aspect of such phenomena... is incorporated into the resulting model... Other aspects are ignored; from the point of view of explanatory function, they are irrelevant. ... A theoretical world, once built, is developed in ways which sometimes obscure the analogy on which it was founded." A typical case would be the identity of *ātman* and *brahman*, which developed from earlier identifications of single entities, such as wind = breath (RV 10.90.13);[124] this was followed by a *series* of such apparent 'identities' in macrocosm and microcosm. Although there are many similarities between both the African and Indian systems, the differences, however, are equally diverse. "In traditional cultures, there is no developed awareness of alternation to the established body of theoretical tenets ... traditional cultures are 'closed'... even [if someone] were a skeptic, he would express his doubts only in terms of the beliefs held by all around him (Evans-Pritchard)." We may compare the gradual development of new concepts regarding *ātman* and *brahman* in the Āraṇyakas and even in the older Upaniṣads, all of which still use the traditional sacrificial terminology, along with old legends and examples.

---

theory of human control, to some practical end, but as far as we can see based on false premises. ... A broad classification: A. productive [magic], B. protective, C. destructive..." -- B. Malinowski (1970: 210 sqq.) emphasizes the role of the origin of certain magical rites, stressing the situations where control over a happening is longed for, resulting in spontaneous ritual, which, once fixed, becomes traditional magical ritual, 'revealed' to outstanding personalities. Thus "magic is the bridge between the golden age of primeval craft and the wonder-working powers of today. Hence, the formulas are full of mythical allusions, which, when uttered, unchain the powers of the past and cast them into the present. ... Myth ... is the historical statement of one of those events which once for all vouch for the truth of a certain form of magic."

[122] The distinction between 'black' and 'white' magic (magic in general and sorcery for an evil purpose) which plays a great role in ethnology, is not of peculiar importance in the Veda. Both are too close to each other in actual practice for the Vedic priest. They are not kept apart even in the *brāhmaṇa* type texts (see below II 30 vs. II 31, etc.). The RV, however, distinguishes between *yātudhāna* and other sorcerers, see RV 7.104.

[123] All quotes in the followings paragraphs are from Horton's paper, unless indicated otherwise.

[124] Wind ~ breath also KaṭhĀ III 218.

Coming to the underlying tenets of traditional systems, one can observe that there is a magical attitude towards *words*. "To know the name of a being or thing is to have some degree of control over it ... this is one reason why the true or 'deep' names of gods are often withheld..." The Atharvaveda, and especially the *brāhmaṇa* style texts, indeed put great stress on the secret names of entities (see below) which they, nevertheless, can reveal, as the Brāhmaṇas are texts composed by Brahmins for Brahmins: these are professional compendia used for teaching the young students.[125]

Secondly, "thought does not appear as something distinct from and opposable to the realities." The traditional thinker cannot 'get outside of his system' and "cannot see it as a *system*. He has to get on with the work of explanation [of the world] without pausing for reflection upon the nature of rules of his work." Therefore, we do not find reflections in the *brāhmaṇa* style texts about their own system of thought. It had been in place since the early post-Ṛgvedic period. There was no need to reflect on the system as such; instead, all *brāhmaṇa* style texts are full of 'getting on with a Brahmin's work' of finding further links, equivalences and identifications. He "cannot start to formulate generalized norms of reasoning and knowing." Even though the Upaniṣads explain the world, i.e., the true nature of *ātman* and *brahman*, they are not *real* philosophy, as they do not ask about the nature of the reasoning that they use to establish these insights. Further, the traditional system is constantly kept valid by *ad hoc* excursuses, known in ethnology as 'secondary elaboration,' e.g., in a case of wrong divination, which may be blamed on the operator's dishonesty or incompetence.

Keith (*Rel.* p. 482 sqq.) also denies that Vedic literature shows any signs of a "development of logical theory." Only TĀ 1, a rather late Vedic text,[126] gives what he terms as 'a late popular view' with epic parallels (*smṛti* 'tradition,' *pratyakṣa* 'perception,' *aitihya* 'communication by one who is expert,' *anumāna* 'reasoning'). The real distinction of the Brāhmaṇa texts, he holds, "is between what is normally perceived (*pratyakṣa*) and what is beyond mere perception (*parokṣa*) ... What is *parokṣa* for men is *pratyakṣa* for the gods." Special insight --and power-- is gained by *tapas*,[127] the power of asceticism necessary to achieve an understanding of *parokṣa* things and situations.

The Veda only knows of "the deep consideration of topics, styled Mīmāṃsā which always relates to questions of ritual" (see KaṭhĀ III 143). "*Vicikitsā* ... denotes the doubt which prompts inquiry, while the final result is denoted by *sthiti*, the station attained." As for the results of such deliberations, Keith (*Rel.*, p. 483) still is quite derogatory: "The conception of causality remains wholly obscure; ... the most fantastic conception of cause and result ... we have endless identifications ... which may

---

[125] [Carried out on the offering ground next to the three sacred fires, as per J. Narten, personal comm., c. 1970].

[126] A section taken over from the late Kaṭha Brāhmaṇa, cf. Witzel 1977, cf. the late-, post-Vedic and Purāṇic data in Witzel 1972: 180, n. 12.

[127] Note the late Vedic story about a Ṛṣi, accumulating *tapas* behind the *gārhapatya* fire, in VādhB (Caland AO VI 190sqq [= 1990: 490sqq]) which gave Indra a headache, so that he must act, which reminds of many similar tales in the Epic.

suit the moment ... Reasoning, indeed we find, but of a peculiar character: ... the general principle [is] asserted as the cause of reasoning ... the identification ... renders the general principle apposite... There is no effort at induction, which is found only in the Upaniṣads, and even then only in the form of arguments which exhaust a series of possibilities, assumed not proved..." This clearly is the state of affairs described by Horton (see above).

M. Polanyi (1958), *op. cit.* p. 332 sqq., also stresses the *stability* of a given system of belief which endures, as the followers of a particular world view "reason excellently in the idiom of their beliefs, but they cannot reason outside or against their beliefs because they have no other idiom in which to express their thoughts." Such a system is circular; stability is ensured by an "automatic expansion of this circle ... [to] cover almost any conceivable eventuality," and the system "denies to any rival conception the ground in which it might take root: ... such evidence [against it] cannot accumulate in the minds of people... each of them is disregarded ... for lack of the concept which would lend significance to it."

These observations of ethnologists dealing with African or Oceanic magic have their bearing on Vedic magic and ritual as well. The Vedic evidence, however, was studied much earlier than the articles above were written. Ethnologists could have learned (and still can learn) quite a lot from the large corpus of magical texts contained in post-RV literature, but, except for the anthropologists J.G. Frazer, Hubert & Mauss, the Indologist S. Lévi and the Sinologist M. Granet,[128] these fields have hardly interacted, certainly because of the Vedic scholars' own conception of these texts as the 'mutterings of mad men.'

The Vedic texts constitute, in fact, ideal ethnological materials rarely found in anthropology in this abundance: they provide perfectly 'transcribed' ritual formulas (in the *Saṃhitās*), a detailed ritual handbook (in the *Sūtras*), *and* the opinions and interpretations of the 'indigenous informant' in the form of interpretations contained in *brāhmaṇa* style texts. In addition, the texts provide an unusual breadth of historical perspective (some 1000 years), further expanded by the persistence of these rituals into present times: medieval texts and even *living* performers may provide contemporary explanations. This ideal situation is hardly ever seen in the materials found, used and interpreted in anthropological accounts, be it village studies or investigations of a whole civilization.

---

128 Frazer 1922, Hubert & Mauss 1902-3, Hubert & Mauss 1987-1898; note the seminal work of S. Lévi, *La doctrine du sacrifice* (1898) that influenced his contemporaries Hubert and Mauss as well as the Sinologist Marcel Granet (1934). [Henceforth, Sinologists have spoken of 'correlations.'] Note also the reflections in Oldenberg (1919), J. Gonda 1960. [However, see now Henderson *et al.* 2002]. -- In light of the preceding section, Evans-Pritchard (1970: 21, originally published in 1926) was not correct but simply uninformed in calling 'the native viewpoint [on black or white magic] ... little studied.' [Also discussed by S. Arieti 1965, see above, n.100].

§4. Identifications, equivalances, correlations

§4.1. The nature of identifications

The links between the realms of macrocosm, microcosm, and ritual [or mesocosm][129] can be established in various ways. All of them, however, make use of the 'identification' or equivalence [or 'correlation'][130] technique mentioned earlier.[131] This technique is never explicitly explained in the texts,[132] as could be expected as per Horton (*op. cit.*, 1967). However, it can be closely observed in its intricate steps many times, on every page of a particular post-RV prose text. The technique rests on the assumption that two entities, beings, things'[133] or substances[134] are closely linked [or correlated], and that they are even *identical* with each other if just *one* of their attributes is common.[135]

(a) Such identical attributes will sometimes be readily understood even today,

---

[129] [It is curious that the term has not been used in this context before. I borrow it from R. I. Levy (1990). Levy uses the term to describe the realm of rites and festivals mediating between gods and humans in the traditional town of Bhaktapur, Kathmandu Valley. Note that Arieti (1967: 138), similarly, uses 'mesocosm' for the world we understand according to our traditional Euclidian-Newtonian-Kantian framework of thought].

[130] [The term has recently been used by J. Brereton, in his insightful introduction to selections from the Upaniṣads (1990: 119).]

[131] In the sequel, I mainly draw on the work of Oldenberg (1919) and Schayer (1924, 1925); cf. also Keith *Rel.*, p. 487: "form naturally serves as the basis of identifications, for almost everything can be said to be the form of another, either on solid or fanciful grounds." [See now Witzel 1979a, Wezler 1996, etc.; and above, n.96].

[132] The reason is explained (for Africa) by Horton 1970: 342 (see above §3.4.). The identification [or correlation] technique was already taken for granted by the earliest prose texts of the Black YV. It had been introduced much earlier: the preceding period of literary activity, the so-called Mantra period, has examples of it. This is evident from fragments of such thought found in the Black YV Saṃhitās (see K. Hoffmann, Der Mantra *yán navám áit*, 1975-6: 509). Apparently, some identifications were already made in the time between the RV and the beginning of YV prose. For example, equations such as *agnir vai retas* are never explained. Some rudimentary equations are seen even in the RV (eye = sun RV 10.90.13, 10.16.3, see n. 113, 151, 255.) -- The reason for *not* discussing the [correlation] technique in any of the Vedic texts is obvious if one follows the explanation by given Horton, above §3.4.

[133] A special case is the one mentioned above, i.e., a substance that is attached to something 'naturally' or by accident. This could be submitted under section (a) as well.

[134] In the widest sense, things in nature, but even ideas such as mathematical numbers, states of mind like 'fear,' menacing 'powers,' or conditions of the body like 'fever', were thought of as material entities or living beings. Such 'substances' are often attached to things/beings (like 'strength' to the tiger, the bull); or they are accidentally connected with things (they can leave the object they normally are attached to, as to settle here or there). They also can be influenced by knowing their equivalents (see below).

[135] [See Schayer 1925; Witzel 1979a, see n. 100.]

for instance when it is said that 'breath is the wind.'[136] The movement of air suffices to identify the meteorological phenomenon with the biological one. Other identifications will not so readily be understood.

(b) The linking [or correlation] goes so far that even identity of number is enough to establish the identity of two things: The word *saṃ-vat-sa-ra* ('the year') has four syllables. The word *ya-ja-mā-na* (the one who makes an offering , the one who institutes and pays for a ritual) also has four syllables. Therefore, they both are 'identical'[137] [or at least, closely correlated]; ŚB 12.3.2.1.

(c) Etymology -- whether an acceptable one which linguistically relates two words back to a common root, whether a 'popular etymology' that is merely playing on the similarity of sounds, or whether an invented one set up *ad hoc* to establish a relationship for a particular cause:

> "The sun, moving upwards, leads all beings forward (*praṇayati*)[138]; therefore he (the sun) is called 'breath' (*prāṇa*)"... (AB 5.31.3 *udyann u khalu vā ādityaḥ sarvāṇi bhūtāni praṇayati, tasmād enam prāṇa iti*).

Here the similarity in sounds is used to explain a name of the sun. The idea underlying this is: knowledge about the name (*nāman*) of something will include knowledge about its real/secret nature (*rūpa*, form).

(d) mythological or pseudo-mythological tales (often invented or modified *ad hoc*) which frequently include etymologies or other identifications not always stated explicitly.

> "Prajāpati did not know to whom to give the offering fee (*dakṣinā*). He put it in his right hand (*dakṣiṇa*). He took it (pronouncing the mantra) 'For fitness (*dakṣa*) I take you, the offering fee (*dakṣiṇā*).' Therefore, he became fit (*adakṣata*). The one knowing this who receives the offering fee (*dakṣiṇā*) becomes fit (*dakṣate*)." (TB 3.11.8.7-8).[139]

---

[136] Note already the equation made in RV 10. 16.3.

[137] *caturakṣaro vai saṃvatsaraś caturakṣaro 'yaṃ yajamāno, 'tra tat samaṃ*; cf. VādhB, *AO* VI: 152: the Upasads (which follow the Avāntaradīkṣā of the Soma ritual) end with the monsoon, in the month of Āṣāḍha.

[138] *pra-ṇayati* 'he leads forward' has no linguistic connection with *prāṇa* 'breath' as *prāṇa* is composed of *pra* 'forwards'+ **āṇa* 'breath,' while *pra-ṇayati* is derived from *pra+ nī* 'to lead forward.' Only for the sake of 'etymology,' did the Brāhmaṇa authors want to create a denominative verb *praṇa-ya-ti* belonging to a hypothetical **prāṇ* 'to breath,' or something similar. Many of such 'etymologies' are taken seriously even nowadays by followers of Yāska and even by trained Indologists, see for example Fatah Singh (1970). In this way, everything can be explained by everything, quite after the fashion of the Brāhmaṇas, classical Greek (Plato's *Kratylos*) or Latin authors (*'lux a non lucendo'*). But all of this cannot be called linguistic science. [A more careful approach to 'etymologies' in Vedic texts is seen in Nargis Verma 1992; cf. also E. Kahrs 1998. -- For etymological correlations made on a superficial similarity of sound, see Arieti 1967, above n. 100]

[139] It makes use of the following devices.

- The offering fee is called so because it is taken with the right hand (not explained here, a sign of politeness; also used in affirming agreements).
- Prajāpati uses a mantra, wishing for fitness. This produces fitness for him; at the same time, as a

This pseudo-mythological tale shows the practical application of esoteric knowledge, of the one 'who knows thus.' He can put such identifications to use for his own or others' benefit, both material and spiritual. In ritual, it is not enough just to receive the *dakṣiṇā* to become 'fit' (or rich), one also has to *know* the secret meaning of the word *dakṣiṇā* (and how it came about) in order to attain the desired aim.

This train of thought[140] permeates the reasoning of all post-RV texts. It still is a very important factor in Upaniṣadic and early Buddhist philosophy: only the one who knows the identity, the secret nature of being, or the Buddhist who *knows* the four noble truths, or the Hindu who *knows* the truth of the identity of *ātman* and *brahman* can reach deliverance and salvation.

As Schayer seems to have given the best description of the magical interpretation of the world (*magische Weltanschauung*) and of the method of identifying microcosm, *yajña* and macrocosm that is used in the YV Saṃhitās and in the subsequent Brāhmaṇas, Āraṇyakas, and Upaniṣads, I add his summary (*op. cit.* p. 292, in my translation).

> "Ritual technology is a kind of hieratic, expressively official and priestly magic, based on the principle of equivalence between [certain] substances. Its aim is to secure the well-being of mankind, to gain mastery and power over substances

---

primordial being, he solves the theological problem of how to dispose of the sacrificial fee that is necessary at the conclusion of a ritual: he gives it to himself! The giving of *dakṣiṇā* produces fitness for him. Underlying this is the identification of the word *dakṣiṇā* 'fee' with *dakṣ* 'to become fit.' This identification is not quite so unscientific as *dakṣiṇā* 'fee' is indeed derived from *dakṣinā* 'right, dexterous' (the right hand is the 'fit, dexterous' one; see above).

140 It would be an interesting task to study the development of the method of magical [correlations and] identifications (cf. n. 281). It is commonly believed by scholars that the Ṛgveda is a collection of hymns that praise the Vedic gods who still are mighty personalities that have to be asked with mantras and by offerings to confer goods on their supplicants (see Keith, *Rel.* 379sqq; cf. 311sq). The AV, however, is regarded as traditional primitive magic that has 'fallen into the hands of the priestly class' and has been properly ṛṣified and brahmanized. Third, the YV texts are said to represent something altogether new: the mighty gods of the RV (and to some extent those of the AV) have fallen into eclipse: everything can be effected through the magic of *yajña*. The gods frequently are no longer *devas* but just *devatās* (deities, such as the cardinal directions, the meters, etc.). As such, they can be forced to do something according to the wishes of the priest. -- I cannot fully subscribe to this interpretation. First of all, the mantras of the YV (which are older than the prose sections in the YV) already clearly contain such identifications (see above n. 132), and as mentioned, there are even some fragments in pre-YV prose (K. Hoffmann 1975-6: 509). A part of AV 15 (the Vrātya chapter) is a typical piece of Brāhmaṇa prose. Finally, there are some identifications in the RV itself which indicate the existence of the magical view of the world. Secondly, the difference between RV and (pre-)YV prose and mantras seems to be one of style and ritual application. The Ṛsis of the RV *sūktas* were less interested in (ritual) magic but in artful praise of the gods (in ancient, Indo-Iranian and Indo-European manner). Yet, here and there, not just 'primitive' magic (e.g., *satyakriyā*) show up, but also the ritual magic of later times (e.g., in the Ṛgvedic fire and Soma rituals and the horse sacrifice). This was codified in YV prose, see below §6. All of this has to be properly investigated before taking any definite stand that goes beyond the impressions mentioned here. -- As for some specific developments in the Atharvaveda, note Prajāpati, Skambha, Kāla, *Puruṣa* as highest reality; or the importance given to 'insignificant' items such as the *brahmaudana, ucchiṣṭa, gauḥ*, etc., cf. Keith, *Rel.* p. 444, sq.

bringing good luck and as to ward off hostile attacks and dangers. In addition, one strives to establish magical relationships according to an eternal absolutely valid order and to implement the magical law. Man, i.e. microcosm, flourishes only if the 'big world' does so too, that is, if every substance is based on its proper *pratiṣṭhā*, secured and well supported, and bound to its *āyatana* by the ties of *nidāna* and *bandhu*. The highest goal that one seeks to gain with the help of sacrifice --immortality after death-- is the state of final, secure order, the implementation of the magical 'norm.' Then, the liberated person looks down from the heavenly heights, down on the rotation of day and night, 'as if he, standing on a chariot, would look at the revolving wheels,' ŚB II 3.3.7" [cf. JUB 3.28, KU 1.4].

§4.2. Technical terms

The technical terms used in the identifications include (mostly following Schayer, cf. his statement, §4.1):[141]

1. • *tanū* '(magical) substance,' (such as wealth, offspring, fever, panic, fame, splendor, guilt, etc.) belonging to nature, ritual or the human body;[142]

• *rūpa* 'form, magically essential substance of something.'

2. • *pratimā* ' (magical) equivalence; likeness, image' of something;[143] *abhirūpa* magically conform,' *rupasamṛddha* 'perfect in its magical equivalence;'[144]

• *sammita* 'having the same measure, congruent,' used to indicate equivalences based on identity of numbers;

• *sampad* 'falling together, congruence.'

3. • *nidāna* 'symbolical connection, binding;' *nidānavant* 'controlling magical substances by *nidāna*'; *nidānena* 'because of symbolical connection;'[145]

• *bandhu* 'relationship, magical connection;'

• *brāhmaṇa* 'liturgical-cosmological equivalence' derived from *bráhman* '(magically powerful) formulation (of a truth)' (Thieme); here, the truth of the (secret) equivalence of macrocosm, *yajña* [or mesocosm], and microcosm;

• *upaniṣad* 'formula of magical equivalence.'[146]

---

141 In this section, I follow Schayer's article closely (*op.cit.*, p. 292-299), though with some additions of mine. Cf. also Keith, *Rel.* p. 380 sqq., especially p. 382-401; see §3 and n. 131.

142 Cf. also Keith, *Rel.* p. 380, with n. 4., p. 486 sq.: "...derives its origin from the corporal aspect of a thing."

143 Cf. Gonda 1969: 64.

144 Cf. Keith, *Rel.*, p. 486 sq. "comes from the idea of appearance."

145 Cf. Gonda 1969: 63.

146 [See now also H. Falk 1986a].

4. • *āyatana* 'area, place, abode (of a substance)'; equivalent substances have the same abode;[147] *āyatanavant* 'magically safe, immune,' cf. *nidānavant, bandhuvant*;
• *dhāman* 'abode;'[148]
• *pratiṣṭhā* 'firm support,' the magical basis of each substance. Having 'support' in a magical substance is having power over it (similarly, *śānti, kḷpti*); *apratiṣṭhita, aśānta* 'not having firm support, insecure.'

§5. Setting speculation to use: practical application of Vedic speculation

The pre-Upaniṣadic Vedic texts are thus constantly concerned with establishing various kinds of links, correlations and identifications, such as mentioned above, putting them to use for a particular purpose in ritual, in everyday life, or to 'attain heaven.' This can be done most effectively in a ritual (*yajña*), which has equivalents both in nature (macrocosm) as well as in man (microcosm).[149] In a *yajña*, magically powerful words (*mantras*) are combined with meaningful actions (preparation and use of utensils, various offerings, circumambulations, special dress, etc.). Only if the secret meaning of both words[150] and actions is known[151] does a *yajña* have the desired effect; if not, or if the ritual is executed with even minor faults, it can have disastrous consequences.[152]

---

[147] See also Gonda 1969.

[148] Cf. Keith, *Rel.*, p. 487, Hillebrandt, 1987: 281-292 (meaning 'Stätte,' i.e. place, locale, site, spot, resort) ; Gonda 1967 ("may be complemented by *yoni*, 'the womb'," see further, Gonda, *āyatana* p. 31).

[149] See especially Lévi (1898) *La doctrine du sacrifice dans les Brāhmaṇas,* which also includes many passages from the early YV Saṃhitās available at the time, i.e. with the exception of KS, KpS; [note also the excellent discussion of Brāhmaṇa time thought by Paul Mus (1935: 79-121)]. Keith, *Rel.*, p. 454 characterizes the ritual as magic: "the sacrifice in the Brāhmaṇas is a piece of magic pure and simple. This is assuredly not the attitude of the average seer of the hymns of the Ṛgveda." (cf. above, n. 114, and §3.3.) "The basis of the whole system is the identification of the sacrifice with Prajāpati," the creator of the universe, who "as the first sacrifice,. ... also is the first victim to be offered, ... he is the first to wish the reward of the sacrifice and to ascend to the sun." (Keith, *Rel.* p. 455). Note the similar situation of Odin, hanging on a tree, as an offering to himself.

[150] Cf. KaṭhĀ III 233; Keith, *Rel.*, p. 455 sq. on 'speech.'

[151] Another prerequisite for the success of a ritual is *śraddhā*, 'the belief [in the magically powerful nature of the *yajña* and its effects in this world and after death] by the *yajamāna*.' See Koehler 1973, Hacker 1963; Hara 1964, cf. also Rao 1971 and already Caland, *AO* VI: 208. -- Without *śraddhā* the ritual has no effect, cf. Keith, *Rel.*, p. 462, with further details.

[152] See Keith, *Rel.*, p. 463, n.1; note the case of mispronouncing *indraśatru*, below n. 215.

§5.1. Application in ritual

The main preoccupation of Vedic priests and their *yajamānas*, however, was to attain results in *this* world.[153] Aims included obtaining long life, offspring and wealth (cattle), gaining a 'secure stand' (*pratiṣṭhā*) in Vedic society which was ever threatened by petty wars and hunger,[154] producing rain,[155] sons, spoiling a rival, regaining lost kingship, etc. To such individual ends, specially modified forms of the great rituals were performed, especially the Soma *yajña* and the New and Full Moon offerings. They always included a particular offering, and a *dakṣiṇā*, etc. magically suited for the intended purpose.[156] After having magically established equivalents for all utensils, actions, mantras, etc. both in macrocosm and microcosm,[157] a priest could influence, through these *yajñas*, both nature and man in the desired way, by using proper words and actions, accompanied by knowledge of their inherent secret impact.

All of this is not just 'primitive' magic or malicious sorcery.[158] By *kḷpti, śānti, pratiṣṭhā*,[159] etc., the priest, in fact, wants to restore the world[160] to its true and salutary order.[161] For, *yajña* is not only a force ordering both cosmos and man, but it also supplies their *original* pattern.[162] Since acts in the ritual take place in a particular way, they *therefore* also do so in nature and in man. Examples of this kind of reversal of natural causality are legion: the sun rises *because* the fire is kindled during the

---

153 Note the frequent prescription in the texts to bring back the *yajamāna* from 'heaven' (Āhavanīya fire), e.g. KaṭhĀ II 109, III 177; cf. II 37, III 199, 232, 233; note the opposite, climbing up to the other world at KaṭhĀ II 23, 110, III 199, 231, 240.

154 See W. Rau 1957: 22.

155 See KaṭhĀ II 123.

156 See Keith, *Rel.* p. 461.

157 Sacrifice (= gods) = Prajāpati (cf. KaṭhĀ II 24, 143, cf. II 1), see Keith, *Rel.*, p. 459.

158 Cf. the distinction between white and black magic or magic / sorcery / witchcraft in Marwick, *op. cit., passim.*

159 See Schayer, *op. cit.* p. 282 sq.

160 Such as by the (common) regeneration of Prajāpati each year, or for example by referring to the primordial state in charter myth such as in KaṭhĀ II 10 on *iyaty agre sthaḥ*, cf. III 199 on the boar, etc.

161 This is quite similar to the Ṛgvedic idea of *ṛta* 'truth,' with its *inherent implementation* in cosmos and among men ('active truth'). Schayer (*op. cit.* p. 283), however, thinks that *ṛta* in the RV is a force *outside* of man, that is, actively influencing the cosmos and the behavior of men (morals, etc.), while in YV prose it is man who is *gopā ṛtasya* 'the protector of *ṛta*,' and a god who governs the world is thus superfluous. (This is similar to the position of *pūrvamīmāṃsā*).

162 This is exemplified by the many legends (charter myths) about the first sacrifice of the gods (or of Prajāpati) when the giant Puruṣa (or Prajāpati himself) were sacrificed. Such charter myths frequently occur in the KaṭhĀ, for example, in the main and smaller myth fragments detailed in §5.2 (or snippets such as in II 10/III 239a, end, about the size of primordial earth). Keith thinks (*Rel.* p. 261, see n. 149) that this is "in the strain of shallow mysticism" which he sees as characteristic of Vedic conceptions, while it is a natural consequence of the concept of *yajña* as the *pratimā* of cosmos and man.

morning *agnihotra*, etc.[163] In addition, *yajña* is also regarded as "a perpetual series of deaths, and of coming again to life again... [it] is the eater, for it lives on all creatures, but at the same time is the universal principle of life."[164] This has been stressed since Lévi's seminal book in which he underlined the (self-)sacrifice of Prajāpati, whose life force wanes during the course of the year and needs to be restored by ritual. [This is based on an agricultural point of view, superimposed on the ancient, paleolithic and later, sacrifice and dismemberment of a sacrificial victim (universal *puruṣa*, bear, dog); later a ram, bull, horse, etc. by hunter-gatherers and then, food producing tribes.]

§5.2. Applications of magic

The ways in which this particular kind of magic is actually carried out in various *yajñas* falls under the following heads.[165]

(1) direct magic, such as

(a) By rubbing off, shaking off, or washing off dangerous, damaging substances. Note, for example, the use of the *apāmārga* 'wipe-off' plant in the Atharvaveda (4.18.7 *apāmārgo 'pa mārṣṭu*), etc.

(b) By removing those things, parts of the body, etc. which have been in contact with or which came from dangerous things or beings. At KaṭhĀ II 10, *varāhavihata* clay is used. The mythological reason is that the earth had been brought up from the bottom of the ocean by a boar.[166] It seems that the boar has particular power, note for example the atonement at III 199, prescribed after viewing a boar eating a lotus shoot. This reminds one of the creation of the earth, brought up by the 'earth diver' boar, and floating on the ocean, 'just that large' (KaṭhĀ II 10).[167]

(c) By touching those items that have gained magical potency through contact with an (in)auspicious thing/being, or by transferring a (damaging) influence to other things/beings while touching them.

(d) By using powerful mantras that contain their own force (mostly, through inherent truth).[168] These categories are also used in black magic (*abhicāra*),

---

163 See below n. 228.

164 Keith, *Rel.* 460; See Lévi 1898; cf. Keith, *Rel.* p. 455.

165 As indicated above, I follow Schayer's article closely (*op.cit.*, p. 292-299), though with some additions, as I believe that he has best understood the system; cf. Keith, *Rel.*, p. 380 sqq. and especially p. 382-401 (see n. 118): §3: removal of hostile influences, §4 attraction of beneficial substances and powers, §5 mimetic magic, §6 divination and ordeal, §7 magic spell, §8 Magic sacrifice. -- For a similar but less detailed analysis of magic, see Marwick, 1970: 38 sqq.

166 PS 6.7, KS 8.2, cf. TS 7.1.5.1, TĀ 1.10.8, ŚB 14.1.2.11; at KaṭhĀ II 9 identified with Prajāpati, later with the boar incarnation of Viṣṇu.

167 [This mytheme is the Indian version of the well-known earth diver myths found in Siberia and North America, where the diver usually is a bird or a musk rat. Cf. Witzel 2004.]

168 Cf. on *satyakriyā* (see below, at the end of §5.2 and n.140). These mantras certainly are *not* "chosen without any appropriateness from the vast body of existing sacred literature." First of all, virtually any mantra that contains *some* kind of magical power -- inherent in any artfully formulated hymn (*bráhma*) -- could be chosen to serve as the 'accumulator' of magical power needed for effecting a spell

where an enemy is sought to be damaged or destroyed.
(2) Symbolic magic, involving the establishment of equivalents (*bandhu, nidāna* etc.), such as

(a) By using an artificial model (*kṛtyā*) of the object that is to be influenced;

(b) By divination: the future event will be known by observing the actions that an equivalent object is subjected to (such as the way smoke rises from the offering fire or one's reflection in a vessel filled with ghee);

(c) By using the *names*, especially the *secret* names (*guhya nāman*) of things/beings to be influenced (the name of something is its true essence); see RV 7.87.4 the three times seven names of the 'cow'; KaṭhĀ II 117 *vedānāṃ guhyāni nāmāni;* III 233 (*a*)*nirukta nāmadheya;* further, etymologies of Rudra, Śarva, Bhava, Mṛḍa, II 100 (cf. ŚB 1.7.3 on Śarva); note the frequent maxim: 'the gods love the recondite' (*parokṣapriya, °kāma*);[169]

(d) Even knowledge of the *origin* of the relationship (*bandhu*) in question suffices to influence it. This accounts for the many etymologies and also for the (pseudo-)mythological stories in Brāhmaṇa style texts. In KaṭhĀ, mythological stories about the Pravargya, mostly stereotypical stories about the contests of the gods and the Asura,[170] include

II 100 Rudra ascends to Heaven and frightens the gods;
II 115 The Aśvins restore the head of the sacrifice;
II 207 Rudra's head is cut off by his bow.

Further, many small fragments and variants of well-known myths:

II 8 Heaven and earth fear the Pravargya
II 9 Prajāpati's creation; Prajāpati as boar
II 11 Indra kills Vṛtra
II 76 sq. The worlds fearing the Pravargya are protected by Prajāpati
II 79 The directions of the sky, *ditto*
II 117 The gods milk speech
II 130 The worlds and directions want a part of the Pravargya drink
II 137 The gods and Asuras compete at the Pravargya
III 207 The Jyotiṣṭoma as sacrifice
III 225 The gods exclude Rudra, he turns on them with his bow
III 226 The gods and the Asura compete at the sacrifice
III 229 The gods fear the glowing Parvargya and ask Prajāpati for help

---

(Lüders 1944; Thieme 1964: 10-11). The spell may be added as an additional stanza (Thieme 1964: 36, 39). It is better if both the 'accumulator' (the hymn) and the actual mantra (the actual spell) releasing such power thus accumulated have something in common. For example, the crossing of streams by king Sudās (RV 3.33, Thieme 1964: 34sqq.) is used as a spell helping a pair of bullocks to ford a stream (Thieme 1964: 36), or the KaṭhĀ Mantras I 98sqq., which, however, are used in the AV (AVŚ 2.2.1, PS 1.7.1, Kauś.S. 8.24; 94.15; 95.4; 96.4; 101.3; 114.3; cf. Vāit. 36.28) as a spell against loss in playing dice. When a mantra is selected, this is usually done on the basis of at least *one* word that seems to be effective in the context, cf. KaṭhĀ II 115 *sapema* : progeny :: penis , see below n.190-91 on KaṭhĀ II 115).

[169] See Keith, *Rel.*, p. 456 n. 8.

[170] Cf. Keith, *Rel.*, p. 456 sq.; [cf. now Houben,1991: 26 sqq.]

III 233 The Aṅgiras go to Heaven

(e) By *satyakriyā, 'sorcery by truth' (*Wahrheitszauber*).

This is carried out by a magical equation (*upamā*) that establishes the identity of two actions or facts; one of them is a well known fact that exists or has happened; the other one is something that one wishes for: "just as the sun rises every day, so shall this or that happen." This method uses well-known facts, common occurrences or (well) known, (and implicitly true) mythological tales.

The act of **satyakriyā* is very common in Pāli texts (*saccakiriyā*) and in the Epics; it has been discussed by Lüders[171] in a detailed study of this phenomenon. The RV contains several examples, e.g., the added 13th verse of RV 3.33.[172] Even if the equation is not explicitly mentioned, (pseudo-)mythological tales (modeled on existing myths) are used to account for the magical potency of a particular substance (cf. 2.d.)

Examination of the practical applications of Vedic speculation leads to a more detailed investigation of the nature of solemn Vedic ritual (*yajña*).

§5.3. The nature of Vedic Yajña

The constant use of such individual magical procedures in Vedic rituals and the very structure underlying solemn *yajñas* such as the Agnihotra[173] does not allow, in my opinion, for any simple procedure to determine the (original) 'meaning' of most *śrauta* rituals. These rituals are laid down in the Sūtras and earlier on, since the Kṛṣṇa Yajurveda Saṃhitās, composed in 'ritualistic prose.' They thus have a history of continuous development even in the late Brāhmaṇa prose and in Sūtra texts, due to activities of the ever cogitive and disputing Vedic priests.[174]

This situation does not allow one, in most cases, to trace the exact Ṛgvedic form of a given ritual. Rather, one has to take into account the time between the (late) RV and the ritualistic prose of the earliest Brāhmaṇa type texts, found in the Kṛṣṇa Yajurveda Saṃhitās. From a linguistic point of view, the so-called Mantra period (AV, mantras of the YV, SV, RV Khila) intervenes between them, and its actual length cannot be estimated at present.[175] It is, however, significant that even during this intervening period, *brāhmaṇa* style 'theological' discussions occurred regarding the

---

171 Lüders 1951,1959. See already Schayer 1925: 299.

172 Thieme 1964: 36.

173 With its identification of the fire and the sun (already an Indo-Iranian feature; see below n. 255).

174 [E.g. cf. ŚB 3.8.2.24 on *Carakādhvaryu*, see Witzel 1982: 172 sqq; cf. Falk 1988: 246.]

175 [See now, however, Proferes (1999); he establishes just four generations between the poet/priest Kavaṣa of RV 7.18 and his great-grandson Kāvaṣeya in connection with the Agnicayana (ŚB 9.5.2.15 where Śāṇḍilya tells of Tura Kāvaṣeya's Agnicayana on the Kārotī; cf. further AB 3.26: *purohita* of Janamejaya Pārikṣita; KĀ 8.11, ŚB 10.6.5.9 in a *vaṃśa*, BĀUK 6.5.4). [According to Kuiper (1991) Kavaṣa was a non-Indo-Aryan, local name; cf. Mayrhofer, *EWA* I 327; for such non-IA names in Vedic Kurukṣetra, see Witzel 1999. -- Incidentally, this is the same kind of genealogy seen in the YV Saṃhitās and the Upaniṣads with Aruṇa-Āruṇa-Āruṇi-Āruṇeya.]

ritual.[176] The rituals, as reconstructed from the scanty testimony of the RV (outside the Soma ritual), must have undergone multifarious developments during the Mantra period that obscured the 'original' meaning of the ritual in question. In addition, even the Ṛgvedic stage is just a snapshot of the long, prehistoric development of Indo-Iranian rituals.[177]

Secondly, various statements of YV ritual prose about the *yajña* cannot be taken as other than *cum grano salis*. Few criteria allow distinction of a 'secondary' trait from an original one,[178] even when one compares several versions of closely related and unrelated Vedic schools (*śākhā*).

Perhaps it will be useful to introduce, at this stage, terminology parallel to that used by K. Hoffmann[179] to distinguish several layers of development in the oral tradition of a given mantra, i.e. the *authentic* and the *original* traits.

An *authentic* trait of a particular ritual is the earliest one that is actually traceable for a particular Vedic school (*śākhā*). An original trait and, thus, the original meaning(s), however, precede attestation in various Vedic schools, and can be of the Mantra period. Therefore, it is materially different from an authentic one. Ideally, it should represent the form and meaning of the ritual in question that can be reconstructed for the Ṛgvedic period, or preferably, for an even earlier time.

The problem, however, is how to go about such investigations and reconstructions. Merely transporting a ritual, as recorded in the Sūtras or in ritualistic YV prose, back to the RV period would be over-hasty. The RV usually does not supply us with copious details about the actual ritual.[180]

One could certainly begin the study with YV mantras that form the skeleton of any *śrauta* ritual, as every action has to be accompanied by an appropriate mantra. Yet, even here there is need for caution. Firstly, it is well known that some of the mantras were taken, at least in part, rather 'haphazardly' from the RV as to fit a particular action.[181] Secondly, there has been a lot of ritual development in post-RV, pre-Mantra time, as can be observed in a comparison of materials from the Ṛgveda, Mantra, and YV Saṃhitā prose. Thirdly, there is the curious fact of frequent interrelation of and mutual influence by the same or similar acts in separate, individual rituals (extending to their accompanying mantras). This has not yet been

---

176 See K. Hoffmann 1975-6: 509.

177 Note the horse sacrifice, fire ritual, animal sacrifice, Soma, and seasonal rituals (also, in part, in the Avesta), or the Pravargya [for details see now Witzel 2004; cf. the data for the Indo-European fire rituals and the horse sacrifice, see Puhvel 1987].

178 Note that the various interpretations of the Pravargya ritual proposed so far are mutually exclusive; for references see n. 227.

179 See his *Aufsätze* 1975-6, Index, s. v. *Vedisch* and *Methodisches*, p. 688sqq and cf. J. Narten 1964: 307sqq., s.v. *Mantravarianten, Mantrarekonstruktion, Modernisierungen, Textfehler, Überlieferungs-varianten*; [see now also Witzel 1980: 22 sq.]

180 Cf. also Aguilar 1976 (though stressing the theological aspects of sacrifice) [and now, Proferes 1999].

181 [See however J. Gonda 1980].

studied at length.[182]

Under these circumstances, it will be prudent to combine the following procedures.[183]

- Reconstruction of a particular Ur-YV ritual on the basis of a comparison of relevant mantras of all available *śākhās* (while cautiously adducing *vidhi* elements from ritualistic YV prose, cf. Tsuji 1934), and contrasting this with materials from RV, SV, AV texts;
- Controlling the reconstructed ritual facts or by statements made in the RV, if any;
- Comparison of the reconstruction with non-Vedic material (especially from the Avesta), if any.

In a best case scenario, one could arrive at a particular Indo-Iranian ritual. This seems possible with some forms of the fire ritual and the Soma ritual. In very rare instances one might obtain a glimpse of Indo-European antiquity (horse sacrifice, libations, fire rituals, and ancestor worship).[184] The normal result, however, will be a reconstructed *Ur*-YV ritual, usually without input or proof from Ṛgvedic sources.

Practically speaking, it will be useful to restrict oneself to the YV mantra material, proceeding further only after a reconstruction of the *Ur*-YV ritual to compare it with pre-YV materials (in the RV). This will provide a healthy countercheck for the reconstruction. In doing so, one will then be able to distinguish the following levels (with very rough dates[185] supplied).

---

182 [See now, however, Ikari 1983].

183 [For the procedure proposed here, see now Witzel 1981/2].

184 [For the horse sacrifice, see now J. Puhvel 1987: 69-276; for fire see Puhvel, *op. cit.* p. 65; for ancestors and all the above, see now J.P. Mallory and D.Q. Adams 1997].

185 Such dating will remain in flux as long as we do not have a generally agreed date for the introduction of iron in the Indian subcontinent; iron is missing in the RV and is first found in Mantra time texts as 'black metal.' Recently [in the Seventies], dates around 1200 BCE have replaced later dates. The lower end of the scale depends on the date of the older Upaniṣads and the Buddha [now believed to be around 400 BCE. -- However, since the end of the Nineties, the early archaeological dates for iron have again been reversed; they have been lowered for the Panjab (and thus for the RV) to c. 1000 BCE, while Kashmir and eastern Uttar Pradesh are said to have dates that are up to some 1000 years earlier.]

	*Pre-Vedic	*Proto-rite
c. 1500/ 1200 BCE	Ṛgveda	ORIGINAL Vedic rite
	late RV (10, 1)	
		Ur-YV ritual * and of other Vedas
1200/ 1000	[Kṛṣṇa YV Saṃhitās:] YV Mantras (and early, lost Brāhmaṇas)	
		AUTHENTIC rite as per *śākhā*
1000/ 800	*vidhi* portions of brāhmaṇa type prose[186]	
	[Brāhmaṇas, Āraṇyakas] [early Sūtras, BŚS, Vādh.S.]	
500- BCE	Sūtra descriptions of rituals later syncretism[187]	

Only when various layers of the continuous development of a ritual have been put into this perspective and traced back as indicated, can the 'meaning' of Vedic ritual or of an individual ritual (and implicitly, the original ritual or even the proto-rite) be traced.[188] Otherwise, one can merely establish the 'meaning' of a ritual for the Āraṇyaka period, for the Brāhmaṇa period, etc.[189]

This is what van Buitenen did not take into account when studying the Pravargya. His interpretation of the Pravargya as an iconic fertility rite (with the vessels seen as

[186] The extant prose portion of the Black YV, the Brāhmaṇas and the Āraṇyakas occasionally contain mantras not recorded in the RV, AV, and YV Saṃhitās. This situation even holds true for the Sūtras. However, the important point here is that of Brāhmaṇa type prose *vs.* earlier Mantra prose (or verse) *vs.* still earlier RV verse.

[187] Note the constant (even late/post-Vedic) addition of certain rituals to the Vedic corpus, see H. Falk 1988, cf. n. 174.

[188] Note Kashikar's and Keith's cautioning with regard to the interpretation of a ritual: they hold that "the explanations of the Brāhmaṇas are always to be taken with the utmost care," as Keith, *Rel.*, p. 7, has it; cf. Kashikar 1972.

[189] [I leave aside J.F. Staal, The meaninglessness of ritual, 1979; cf. also Houben 1991: 8, n. 11, Witzel 1992].

representing a human shape and *liṅga*) is merely based on AB[190] (and cf. KaṭhĀ II 115, which he did not know of). It covers just *one* aspect of the manifold explanations that the Brāhmaṇa and Āraṇyaka authors provided for the ritual, and a comparatively late one.[191] The RV ritual, however points to a simple milk offering to the heavenly Twins, whatever its original intent (see Keith, *Rel.* 332sq.)[192]

Taking into account the well-known complexity of each individual Śrauta ritual, a detailed investigation of the Pravargya is not given here. However, it may briefly be pointed out that -- as is well known --the Pravargya has its origins in the Ṛgvedic milk offering to the Aśvins.[193] Secondarily, this rite has been introduced into the ancient, elaborate Soma ritual. The mythological reasoning is given in tales relating how the secret (the head of the sacrifice) was obtained by the Aśvins from the mouth of Dadhyañc Atharvan.[194] The fusion of the Pravargya and the Soma rituals is still very obvious in the texts that discuss the facultative nature of this ritual (see §2, §6.6);[195] it also is visible in the combination of two types of mythological tales that justify, as charter myths, the nature of the new, extended Soma ritual that incorporates the Pravargya.[196] Due to the complex nature of the enlarged ritual, the 'original' meaning of the (Ṛgvedic) Pravargya milk offering has been obscured, and various secondary interpretations[197] have been introduced (see below §6).

---

190 Cf. Kashikar 1972: 7, and already Keith, *Rel.* p. 333.

191 However, the Mantra at KaṭhĀ II 115 does *not* invite a sexual interpretation, while the Brāhmaṇa section merely has the usual reference to fertility; cf. n. 168, n. 220, and Caland *ad* ĀpŚS 10.23.8.

192 [See now Witzel 1981/2, Houben 1991: 28 sqq; he wants to add RV 1.164.43 to the references on the Pravargya in the RV].

193 [RV 1.119.2; 3.53.14; 5.30.15; 7.70.2; 8.9.4; 8.87.2; note especially 7.103; cf. also 1.164.28; 1.180.4; 5.19.4; 5.73.8; 8.9.7; 8.88.7].

194 [For this *charter myth* justifying violence used in the Śrauta ritual, carried out for the Adhvaryus by other para-priests, see now Witzel 1987a: 412, n.103; cf. below n.229.]

195 [For the technique and background on the development of the Śrautra ritual and the insertion of the Pravargya into the Soma ritual, see now Witzel 1995/97].

196 Note KaṭhĀ II 21, II 137, III 239a, and the fragment fol. 357b. [For the combination of Pravargya and Soma ritual, see now Witzel 1987b; an earlier version of this paper was intended for the 1972 *Orientalistentag*, but not delivered as I moved to Kathmandu in Sept. 1972].

197 Including the most standard ones, met in all Śrauta rituals, such as the wish for health, long life (*āyus*), rain, cattle, sons and attaining heaven after death. In general, see Keith, *Rel.*, p. 332-333, Houben 1991: 7 sqq.

The probability of the descriptions and conclusions made in the preceding paragraphs is borne out by a comparison of multifarious details found in discussions of the Pravargya ritual, as described in the KaṭhĀ.[198] Data from such discussions are given in the following sections.

§6. The various levels of interpretation in the KaṭhĀ

Brahmanical speculation can be observed throughout the Kaṭha Āraṇyaka. It appears in various forms, done for various aims, and executed on various levels of esoteric interpretation. It involves the three spheres (macrocosm, *yajña* [mesocosm], and microcosm). But, as is only natural in a ritual text, KaṭhĀ is centered on the ritual itself and starts most explanations from that point.

§6.1. The ritual itself.

The sponsor of the ritual (*yajamāna*) has to undertake the Pravargya ritual with thought, speech, and action.[199] This begins with the intention (*saṃkalpa*) to actually undertake it (and with *śraddhā*)[200] by inviting the priest, and proceeds by uttering certain mantras[201] and performing certain actions reserved for him[202] and his wife,[203] while nearly all other actions during the artifice are performed by the priests, mainly the Adhvaryu.[204]

§6.2. Priests

The priest performing the ritual gains special powers in doing so, and he is actually

[198] Detailed comparisons with the other *brāhmaṇa* style Pravargya texts (TĀ 4-5, ŚB 14.1-3) are not included here, as that would lead too far astray in the present context; [see now Houben (1991) for TĀ, and for some comparisons with ŚB and KaṭhĀ].

[199] After the example of Prajāpati; KaṭhĀ II 1, cf. II 5; for 'speech,' see also III 215 (beginning and end of the observance) and III 233. -- The *yajamāna* is identified with Prajāpati, the first 'sacrificer' (implied in KaṭhĀ II 79; cf. II 1); the most elaborate identification of both seems to occur in the Agnicayana ritual, see Keith, *Rel.*, p. 466 (sun = *agni* = *yajamāna*). [On the triad of thought, speech and action also seen in Zoroastrianism and, through this, in Christian formulas, see Witzel 1996; cf. below n. 224 and cf. S. Zimmer 2003: 17 (with examples from Indo-Iran. and Celtic)].

[200] See n. 151, 214, 224sqq.

[201] The *yajamāna* appeases the Aśvins with a mantra, II 133a.

[202] He partakes of the *havis* offering, II 143.

[203] She is brought in and shielded from the Mahāvīra vessel, III 177.

[204] The priest places various entities into the *yajamāna:* cattle II 19, breaths 96, 97; he joins him with the Apsaras (in heaven, after death?) II 101, makes him go to heaven II 109; Soma (drink) is invoked for him II 137; his progeny is protected II 207 (end); the *yajamāna* obtains long life III 235b, 236, 237, and success, long life and virility III 234, cf. also II 70.

identified with some gods during the *yajña*.[205]
• The *yajña* is in the *brahmán* priest, who is identified with *bráhman*, the artfully formulated *mantra*, the (later) 'absolute' behind all manifestations of the universe, see (KaṭhĀ II 48). The *brahmán* priest must have knowledge of the whole ritual and 'cure' any lapses by performing certain *prāyaścittas*,[206] often taken from the Atharvaveda.
• The *bráhman* priest is expressively identified with the god Brahmaṇaspati or Bṛhaspati, 'the lord of magical formulation,' KaṭhĀ II 3, II 5.[207]
• Another priest, the *Hotṛ*, is identified with the recitation. It is his duty to recite from the Ṛgveda (II 93, 97) while the *Udgātṛ* (II 233: 98.6) sings from the Sāmaveda. The rest of the references refers to the *Adhvaryu* priest, who mumbles *yajuṣ* and mantras from the Yajurveda while actually performing the multiple acts of the ritual.
• He is instigated to perform the ritual by Savitṛ, the god 'Instigator,' II 2, cf. II 27, 107-8, 120.
• He acts with his arms, having become those of the Aśvins, and his hands, those of God Pūṣan,[208] I 2
He looks on the Pravargya vessel 'with the eye of the sun,' cf. II 86, cf. II 26, III 169-170, I 218e.[209] Thus, he represents [and embodies] certain gods,[210] yet he also moves about the universe when he walks on the offering ground.
• He 'climbs the three worlds' II 22, as the *gārhapatya* fire is this world (the earth) and the *āhavanīya* fire is the sun/heaven (III 231, 232). The *uttaravedi*, too, is identified with heaven. The priest, when moving back towards the *gārhapatya*, 'comes down to this world,' to the earth, II 36. On the other hand, when the Pravargya vessel is held up with the two pincers (*śaphau*), it is 'held by heaven and earth' (II 126) and thus, is situated in the intermediate space (*antarikṣa*), II 127.

§6.3. Implements

Just as the priest gains special powers during the *yajña* and the offering ground turns into a replica of the universe, the implements that are used have to be of a special type in order to become powerful and effective.

Thus the 'chair' for the Pravargya vessel is made of *udumbara* wood, as this tree is identified with strength (III 239a); the same is said of the strings of *muñja* grass woven to form the actual seat. The antelope skin that covers the seat is identified with *bráhman*, whose magical potency thus carries the Pravargya. The legs of the chair are

---

205 [See now Minkowski 1992; Falk 1986b].

206 See KaṭhĀ III 234-239a.

207 For Brahman = Bṛhaspati, cf. Keith, *Rel.* p. 449, H.-P. Schmidt 1968.

208 Already an identification that was made during the Mantra period, preceding the formulation of the Kṛṣṇa YV Saṃhitā and the Brāhmaṇa texts. It appears in the most common mantras, is used in almost all *yajñas*, and shows that the concept of the identification technique had developed early.

209 Cf. also 'eyesight' in III 147a; and cf. II 89-91 for the protection from sun/Rudra.

210 [See now Falk 1986b; Minkowski 1992; Oberlies, 1998-9].

to be one cubit long, as this is the original size of 'the two worlds' (III 239a) before they were expanded by Indra.

Similarly, the Pravargya vessel, the central implement of this ritual, has to be made according to very detailed instructions,[211] most of which are 'theologically' motivated by making use of the identification [or, correlation] technique.[212]

§6.4. Actions

One of the two most important aspects of any ritual are the many simple or more elaborate actions performed during the *yajña*. When the priest calls the cow for milking (II 115-117), he does not just call her, he calls her 'from heaven, from the atmosphere, from the earth.' When milking her, he has to first let the calf suckle; the calf is identified with *bráhman*, and the cow's teats are the *four* Vedas (II 117). Thus, milking the cow means to collect the essence of the four Vedas, and this is achieved by the agency of *bráhman*. Again, the milk of the cow and goat are said to be 'strength' (II 120), and in putting them into the Pravargya vessel, the priest 'strengthens the *vīra*,' that is the *gharma*/Pravargya vessel.

In this way, almost all acts of the priests and *yajamāna* during the ritual have esoteric meanings. This becomes very evident when the Āraṇyaka author discusses, in early Mīmāṃsā fashion, such questions as: 'should one eat of the remnants of the offering or not?' (II 147). The Talmudic solution is: one should just sniff at them: in this way, one neither eats nor does one not eat, and thus, one avoids the dire consequences believed to inherent in both alternatives. Similarly, in one case (II 128a), one should only say some mantras and leave out the offering as to protect the cattle from Rudra.

The *sāmans* used during the performance of a Pravargya are treated in detail at III 233 (end), for the first time in Vedic literature. They are especially effective according to the concepts magically connected with them:

---

211 See I 1-21 and cf. III 239 (end) for making the Pravargya vessel; for making the throne of the Pravargya, see III 239a-240.

212 It is important to note that the preparation of the *ukhā* vessel used in the Agnicayana ritual is quite similar to that of the Pravargya vessel; in addition, the mantras used are similar or identical. The Agnicayana belongs only to the third layer of (mantras used in) rituals in the YV (Oldenberg 1888). Therefore, the question arises: which of the two subrites (preparation of *ukhā* or *mahāvīra* vessel) was earlier and influenced the other? [Y. Ikari (1983) has now determined that the preparation of the Ukhā was modeled on that of the Pravargya vessel. This will allow for the following history: metal Pravargya vessel (RV) > clay Pravargya vessel (early YV) > clay Ukhā vessel (YV Mantras, stage III, see Oldenberg 1888). As we know that the Ṛgvedic Pravargya rite was carried out with a metal vessel, the preparation of the earthen Mahāvīra vessel is an *innovation* [though it looks more archaic: such archaization is a feature of the Kuru reform of Ṛgvedic rituals, see Witzel 1995/7; differently, Houben 1991: 28 sqq. It seems that both rites were developed during the Mantra period in close interdependence by priests who systematized the ritual. We may now date the development of the Agnicayana to a period of four generations after RV 7.18 (Proferes 1999). The case can serve as a test case for the study of the mutual influence of mantras and ritual actions across the board, see n. 182; for details on the Pravargya/Ukhā see Ikari 1983].

- the Śārga Sāman is heat: one gains heat (*tejas*) by singing it;
- the Śukra and Candra Sāmans are sun[213] and earth; one gains both with them;
- the Gharmasya Tanvau Sāmans let one gain one's own form;
- the Vrata and Pakṣa Sāmans are a *vajra* against the *rakṣas* ('damages');
- the Aśvinavrata Sāmans spice the Pravargya;
- the Rajana and Rauhiṇa Sāman are Sun and Moon, and are identified with the
- eyes of the Pravargya; one gains eyesight;
- The Āṅgirasa Sāman is the heavenly world; one obtains it.

§6.5. Speech

All acts during the ritual will be without effect unless accompanied by fitting words, i.e. by magical formulas in prose or verse, the mantras. These are taken mostly from the Yajurveda Saṃhitās, Ṛgveda and Atharvaveda, with the addition of a few that are first encountered in the present text. The combination of magically powerful acts and words produces the desired effect.[214] This explains the special position given to 'speech' (*vāc*) in all Brāhmaṇa and Āraṇyaka texts. After the *yajamāna* has conceived of and decided (*saṃkalpa*) to undertake the *yajña*, it is performed by speech, thought, and action (II 1). It is by speech that the clay used in making the Pravargya vessel is collected (II 6). There is a long praise of speech in III 208-212.

Just like performing or omitting certain actions (see above §4), the application or alternation of certain mantras has peculiar effects. At II 128a-129, it is said that one should not offer to Rudra with certain mantras (intended for some other gods) as "some deities have a share in the offering formulas, others in the poured out offering."

The way that the mantras are recited has unavoidable consequences[215] of their own. At II 133, it is related how the gods succeeded with the Pravargya ritual as they performed it by receiving certain ritual formulas aloud; their rivals, the Asuras, did not, and just mumbled (*upaṃśu*) them.

Special importance is given to the recitation (by the *yajamāna*?) of the *avakāśa* mantras, used when looking down on the glowing Pravargya vessel (II 227-9). The text again relates how the gods prospered and the Asuras lost, because of the application viz. non-application of these formulas (II 226).

In spite of the stress seen in *brāhmaṇa*[216] type texts on the correct application

---

213 See II 233.

214 As pointed out above, n. 151, this has also to be accompanied by the the *yajamāna*'s belief in the efficacy of the ritual: *śraddhā* is trustful belief in the effects of the *yajña*. Manu, as the first offerer, is the prototype of a trustful *yajamāna*, see MS 4.1.6, cf. also TB 3.11.8/KaṭhUp 1.1.2 *śraddhāviveśa*.

215 The most famous legend about the power of a mantra is related in ŚB I.6.3.10, where the mispronunciation of one word, i.e. that of *indraśátru* 'enemy of Indra' as *índraśatru* 'having Indra for an enemy,' produces disastrous results: Indra comes rushing and cuts off the head of Viśvarūpa who had mispronounced it; cf. Patañjali, Mahābhāṣya, introd., and Keith, *Rel.* p.464, n. 1.

216 The 'theological' prose portions of the YV Saṃhitās, the various Brāhmaṇas and Āraṇyakas of all four Vedas.

of mantras by Vedic priests, there sometimes is a considerable divergence for a certain act.[217] The causes for this are manifold.[218] At II 129, for example, the mantra "to you, o Agni, who possesses riches, *svāhā*" is thought, in the Brāhmaṇa passage discussing it, to let a whole group of divinities partake in the offering. One may argue that it is only *through* Agni that the offering is conveyed to the gods, to heaven. However, in the present case, the apparently wrong use of a mantra (Agni : deities) is explainable within the framework of the whole section surrounding it. It is part of the discussion of *which* gods are partaking in a ritual, and in what way (see above §4).

Sometimes, however, a mantra is indeed misunderstood, whether accidentally in the course of tradition[219] or intentionally so. A point in case is II 115 'having / possessing Tvaṣṭṛ, we wish to dedicate (*sapema*) ourselves to you' which the Brāhmaṇa understands as 'from here (from the penis) progeny is produced: this serves to produce progeny.' The word *sapema* (from *sap* 'to follow, serve') is connected by intentional, but linguistically wrong, etymology, to *sapa* 'penis.'[220]

Normally, each mantra is closely attached to the ritual action performed together with its recitation, as is seen in the following KaṭhĀ passages.

II 133 The gods, to whom the offering of hot milk is made, are actually called upon in the accompanying mantra: 'to the gods drinking the hot (milk, I offer) you, *svāhā*,'

II 136 All classes of people are benefited by offering with the mantra: 'Swell for this Brahman, for this Kṣatriya, for this tribe,' while

II 137 the *yajamāna* alone is named in the mantra: 'for this (Soma) pressing *yajamāna*.'

This type is most common and too numerous to be quoted in detail; however a few instances include: at III 188, water is poured out while reciting 'the waters shall be friendly towards us.' At II 22, the Pravargya vessel is put down in the sunlight to dry with the mantra, 'be baked by the heat of the sun;' it is fumigated with horse dung while saying 'the wives of the gods shall fumigate you with the dung of the stallion!'

Sometimes a mantra may not seem to fit an action, but will do so when scrutinizing the text more thoroughly. Thus, at II 141, offerings are made to the directions of the sky by saying 'to energy, you; to brilliance you; to prosperity, you; to bodily strength, you!' These words do not seem to have any relation with the cardinal directions (see above §4.2, no.2). Apparently, it is just the number 'four' which has led to the identification of the four cardinal points with this set of four mantras.

§6.6. The *yajña* itself

---

[217] According to the Vedic texts, a mantra should always accompany a ritual action, see the Paribhāṣā section of ĀpŚS, transl. by M. Müller, SBE 30, 315-364.

[218] Hillebrandt (1897) thought that mantras were quite haphazardly taken from the RV and other texts, and thought to fit a particular action if just one or two words pertained to the action undertaken. [See now Gonda 1980, see above n. 181].

[219] See K. Hoffmann 1976-6: 509.

[220] See Caland on ĀpŚS 10.23.8; the same 'etymological' connection is seen at KS 24.4:93.20, MS 3.7.7: 84.9; cf. above n. 168, 191.

In the preceding paragraphs it has been apparent that all persons taking part, and all implements used in a *yajña,* have special significance attributed to them by the 'theological' Brāhmaṇa texts. A whole particular *yajña* is also interpreted in various ways and on various levels.

One is the re-creation of the universe --on a small scale-- on the offering ground, as has already been mentioned (§2). The three ritual fires *are* the earth, moon and heaven/sun; the priest moving about on the offering ground is expressively said to go to that world (heaven) or this world (the earth).

As the *yajña* is identified with the universe, it also can be identified with Prajāpati, the god of creation who caused it to 'flow from him' (*pra-sṛ*, II 9). Prajāpati is not merely identified with the *yajña*, he frequently is the actual victim that is slaughtered and dismembered.[221]

The sacrificial actions (or their outcome) that take place on the offering ground, i.e. the *yajña* itself, are said to 'go to heaven' (II 110, 111; cf. 130-131) or to the gods in heaven (II 132, 133). Or, in the case of the Pravargya milk offering, to go just to the Aśvins (II 139a).

This reflects the old (pre-)Vedic concept of ritual as guest worship:[222] the gods are invited to sit on the offering ground and are fed. In other instances, the offerings are transferred to heaven by the ritual fire. How this is achieved is explained at II 49-54, where the ritual is likened to a chariot that carries offerings to the gods.

The chariot must, first of all, be put together (just as its mundane counterpart is before any use).[223] This is done by the *yajamāna*[224] (II 51) through his 'thinking.'[225] Then, the chariot is yoked by *yajuṣ* formulas; this is done by the Adhvaryu priest who also knows the path (*adhvan*) of the *adhvara* (ritual), and is therefore 'the leader of all priests' (II 49, III 168). The nave of the chariot wheel is oiled by the melodies (*sāman*, II 50), and the chariot is drawn by recitations from the Ṛgveda (*ṛc*, II 54). In this way, the Vedas are instrumental in performing the ritual, and it therefore can even be said that the *yajña* is carried out with the 'truth of speech' (II 55)[226] as Vedic mantras are inherently truthful.

The *yajña,* as such, is established and explained by adducing (pseudo)-

---

221 Reminding of the primordial Puruṣa (RV 10.90); for details see Keith, *Rel.*, p. 81, 455sq.

222 As stressed by Thieme 1964: 9 sq. [For an update on the Proto-Indo-European idea of guest worship see S. Zimmer 2003: 16.]

223 Chariots were usually stored in a dismantled fashion and put together only for actual use; in this way, deformation of the wheels was avoided; note, e.g., the Egyptian chariots found in the grave of Tut Ankh Amun); [cf. now M. Sparreboom 1985].

224 That is, at the very beginning of the ritual; it begins with the intention of the *yajamāna* to carry it out (*saṃkalpa*) and his accompanying *śraddhā* belief in its effectiveness; it is then carried out by thought, speech, and action (cf. above n. 181), cf. the next note.

225 This correlates with KaṭhĀ II 1: the ritual is conceived by thought (apparently equaling, at least in part, *śraddhā*); it is also concluded in this fashion: III 143 *manasā ... yajñaṁ saṃtanoti* (cf. above. n. 199).

226 In the present case, *bhūr bhuvas svaḥ*, the so-called *vyāhṛtis*, often identified with the three Vedas.

mythological reasons. Many customs, rites, etc. are given the aura of having been instituted in the remote past by the *ṛsis* or the gods themselves (Malinowski's *charter myth*). In the present text, recourse is taken to the well-known myth relating how the head of the sacrifice was cut off and, later on, rejoined with the help of the heavenly physicians, the Aśvins (II 115, III 207), to make the headless sacrifice effective. There are many versions of this myth, always changed slightly as to suit various *yajñas*, and they have found many interpretations.[227]

A comparison of such mythological stories indicates that they are used to explain a particular ritual and the incidental differences peculiar to various other rituals. That means, just like any assertion or identification in the *brāhmaṇa* style texts, a particular legend or myth cannot be regarded in isolation. The very existence of variant tales points to the fact that they have been changed as to fit a particular local or ritual purpose.[228]

Thus, in the case of the Pravargya ritual, there are two main versions of the etiological legend relating the origin of the rite: the one mentioned above (§5.2, §6.5: II 115/III 207), and another narrating how Rudra was excluded (II 100sqq). When the gods had succeeded in 'going to heaven,' they could not recognize him, as he eventually ascended and approached them, sun-colored and boasting of his power. This version is unique and has gone so far unnoticed. It is one of the earliest stories that explain some of Rudra's many names (Bhava, Śarva, Śiva, Mṛḍa). The way the gods (or the *yajamāna*) obtain heaven was by performing a ritual, the Pravargya. From this, they excluded Rudra, told in another slightly shortened version (II 115, III 207). This merely relates the threat by Rudra, with bow and arrow in hand, and the compliance of the gods by including him into the Pravargya ritual. This tale closely parallels how the Aśvins were included in the gods' Soma ritual.[229]

The various Kaṭha versions of the present legend speak of Rudra as excluded from ritual and not going to heaven or of his head cut of by his own bow string (III 207). However, other Brāhmaṇa texts dealing with the Pravargya (ŚB 14.1.1.6 and TĀ 5.1.2) instead have (Makha-)Viṣṇu viz. Makha Vaiṣṇava as the one who was killed. KaṭhĀ specifies that it was Indra in the form of an ant who cut the bow string (III

---

227 Garbe 1880, Hillebrandt 1897: 134sqq, Oldenberg 1917/1923 : 446 , Keith, *Rel.*, 332 sqq; Rönnow 1929, Lüders 1951, 1959 : 359-368, van Buitenen 1968, Rolland 1973, Kashikar 1972, 1976, [1982, Gonda 1979, Heesterman, J.C. 1985, Houben 1991, especially p. 3 n. 3, p. 7 with n. 9 sqq.]; note, also, the mistaken approach of Kramrisch 1975, criticized by Kuiper 1984, cf. above n. 188.]

228 Just as the Brāhmaṇa texts frequently argue in reverse logical order as well, *e.g.* TS 5.1.7.3: "(the Adhvaryu speaks towards the fire pan, just made of fresh clay:) 'may they cook' he says twice: therefore twice in the year the corn does ripen." It is a fact that corn (barley/wheat and rice) does in fact ripen twice in the Gangetic plain due to its favorable climate. Speaking the mantras twice is connected with this natural phenomenon (*pac* means 'to cook' and 'to ripen') rather fancifully, by an identification based on the meaning of *pac* and on the number 'twice.' At TS 5.1.2, when an ass is led behind a horse (that is considered better than the ass): 'therefore the worse always follows the better' (cf. also W. Rau 1957: 61 sq. on *pāpa* status).

229 [For the integration of (nearly all) such Aśvin tales into one frame story, see now Witzel 1987b; for the (unnoticed) charter myth-like inclusion of the Aśvin/Adhvaryu, see Witzel 1987b and 1987a: 412, n. 103].

207), while the other texts just mention the ants.

The apparently late inclusion of the Pravargya ritual into the Soma ritual is provided for in the latter portion of the Brāhmaṇa text of KaṭhĀ. At III 207, it speaks of the gods putting the Pravargya ritual *before* the actual (Soma) *yajña*, to which it serves as its (lost) 'head.' Their *yajña* was a *jyotiṣṭoma* ritual, the blueprint (*prakṛti*) of all other complicated Soma rituals. There are a few more hints on the inclusion of the Pravargya into the Soma ritual. At II 137, a mantra is supplied (*asmái sunvaté yájamānāya pinvasva*) which would allow for this inclusion already at the time of composition of prose mantras, i.e. during the so-called Mantra period. Otherwise, KaṭhĀ II seems to be devoid of references to the Soma ritual.[230] However, in the presumably later section, KaṭhĀ III 173-176, implements or buildings are mentioned, typical for a Soma ritual; or at III 232-3, regulations and explanations are given for the Pravargya performed at the midday pressing of the Soma ritual.

Peculiar to KaṭhĀ is the inclusion of the Pravargya ritual into the three Cāturmāsya and the Śunāsīrīya ritual (III 233), which reminds of another Kaṭha peculiarity, the Kaṭha Agnicayanas preserved in TB 3.10-12 and TĀ 1 as part of the so-called *aṣṭau kāṭhakāni*; their respective fragments are found in KaṭhB[231].

§6.7. The effects of *yajña*

The preceding paragraphs have indicated how a *yajña* was thought to take place -- with all participants and implements used as well as which exceptional, supernatural conditions and results it created. Like other rituals, the Pravargya was said to bring about multifarious results in nature, society, and for the sponsor of the ritual (*yajamāna*).

§6.7.1. Nature

One of the foremost features of the Pravargya ritual is its dangerous appearance as a glowing vessel identified with the sun[232] and with Rudra Mahāvīra (II 89, II 100, III 207 (end), 233, 238). The red-hot vessel threatens all beings and even Heaven and Earth. Special protection is necessary for the priest (II 80 sqq., II 180, 182-183), for the *yajamāna* (III 150, 173-76, etc.), for his wife (III 207, 177), even for the future offspring of the *yajamāna* (II 38, III 207), which otherwise would be born blind.

Protection for Heaven and Earth is effected by putting a golden or silver plate on top viz. under the Pravargya vessel (II 76, 91); protection of the intermediate space (*antarikṣa*) is created by putting 'trees', i.e. fire wood, on top of 12 other kindling sticks representing the rays of the sun (II 90, cf. also III 178-183). Even the cardinal

---

230 Perhaps with the exception of the *brāhmaṇa* conclusion in II 21 that the sponsor becomes a *somapīthá*.

231 L. v. Schroeder (1898) lists and prints some examples corresponding to TB 3.10-12, TĀ I, II.

232 The vessel is connected with Rudra, as it is baked by the sun II 22, cf. II 89, and the *udvāsana* of the utensils takes place in the shape of the sun(?) II 151-54; further, the heated vessel is round like the sun and glows like it. [Cf. now the discussion by Houben 1991 : 10 sqq.]

directions have to be protected, carried out by the *yajamāna* (who is likened to Prajāpati, II 79) who 'measures' a span (from the thumb to the tip of the index finger). The directions, in turn, provide protection for the *yajamāna* and/or the priest,[233] as well as for other 'minor *devatās*,' such as the gods linked to the directions of the sky (Agni, etc.), the meters (Gāyatrī, etc.), the seasons (spring, etc., II 58-63), the waters (II 72), in sum, 'the year and all *devatās*' (II 73). One of the more remarkable effects of this ritual is the production of rain: the steam[234] rising from the milk boiling in the Pravargya vessel is believed to form clouds and to return as rain (II 123). This is a clear instance of analogical magic and may be one of the earliest interpretations, or even one of the original intentions, of this ritual in the Yajurveda.[235]

§6.7.2. The effect on the *yajamāna*

This aspect is mentioned in much more detail and variation. In the first place, he gains all usual benefits caused by the performance of Śrauta rituals:

(a) strength (II 32-34, III 154),
power of eyesight (III 147a, 153 a(?), 158, 233),
power of hearing (II 97, III 148),

---

233 Frequently, the text is not clear enough: it is not said who (*yajamāna* or *adhvaryu*) will be protected; the subject of such *brāhmaṇa* sentences is mostly unexpressed; though the *yajamāna* is likely to be the intended goal of these mantras, this remains uncertain.

234 [See now the impressive video film of a Pravargya performance by J.E.M. Houben (1996); cf. J.F. Staal's Agnicayana film (1976), and notably, the Pravargya ceremony in some of the 30 related black/white Betamax videotapes (preserved at Instituut Kern, Leiden University), as well as his book *Agni*, 1983: 373.]

235 Perhaps already alluded to in the RV 7.103 in linking the Pravargya, frogs, and rainy season, cf. Keith, *Rel.*, p. 332-3(cf. VādhB, Caland AO VI: 152). The Pravargya apparently existed already in (late) Ṛgvedic times in a form somewhat similar to the one appearing in the *brāhmaṇa* style texts. This much is apparent in the allusion to the *gharma* vessel and the arrival of the great rains in the (late) frog hymn (RV 7.103.9). However, due to the composition of most RV hymns in the (nearly) monsoon-less territories of Afghanistan, Gandhara, and the Panjab, reference to the monsoon rains following the hot season (*gharma*) is less likely than this interpretation found in the late RV and in the YV. [See now: Vajracharya 1997]. What then could be the reason for, and what could be the age of, an offering of a hot milk drink to the Aśvins, as compared to that of (unheated) Soma to the gods? In the interpretation of Brāhmaṇa passages (MS, KS, TS, Br., Ār.), just as in that of the mantras, one has to be very careful in separating original intent from Brahmanical speculation and the schematic application of the more common categories of magical identifications. Otherwise, one is likely to become a Brāhmaṇa author oneself, or indeed the writer of a new (personal) mythology. Note, for example, Kramrisch (1975) on Soma and the *pūtika* mushroom, severely criticized by Kuiper (1984) (see above, n. 227). [Note also other contemporary authors' *brāhmaṇa*-like speculations on Vedic texts that proceed in free association well beyond likely suggestions permissible boundaries of Brāhmaṇa philology. Notably, Vishva Bandhu's *Brahmaṇoddhārakośa,* which could provide some Brāhmaṇa-*inherent* associations (and indicate their limits), is not used in such free style associations (cf. above n. 97).]

breathing (in, out, asunder, II 96[236]),
virility (II 18, 32-34),
long life (II 74, III 149, 150, 151, 173-76, 174),
(b) reputation (*varcas*) (III 205), but not *yaśas* [237]
Brahmanical fame (II 30, 139, 143, III 167-8, 232, 233)
brilliance (*tejas*, II 17), *prakāśa* (III 170, 197, 232),
bráhman (II 17),
(c) offspring (II 115, cf. III 239)
cattle (II 19, 32-34),
wealth (II 138, 147),
food (III 146, 198),
good luck (III 187),
success (III 234),
prosperity (III 193, 'becomes fat'[238])
a firm support (on this earth, II 144, IIII 177),
power (II 18, 32-34),
pre-eminence in society III 207
supreme power II 100 (end, like Rudra).

On the other hand, a different, major effect of the Pravargya ritual seems to be its production of sacred knowledge (see point *c.*, above). There is a special injunction in III 167-168 forbidding the Pravargya for someone who does not study the Veda:[239] by a Pravargya, he would become 'learned' (without previous Veda study).

If this fact is combined with the frequent injunction[240] not to perform the Pravargya at the first Soma ritual undertaken in one's sacrificial career,[241] it seems that the performance of the Pravargya adds special power to the *yajamāna* as well as to the Soma *yajña*: it supplies 'the head.' This also explains[242] why the special *dīkṣā* for a Pravargya ritual is called *avāntaradīkṣā*, 'intermediate consecration.' The normal *dīkṣā*

---

236 This seems to allude to the set of 3 or 5 *prāṇas* (see Benke 1976) mentioned in the late Brāhmaṇas and Upaniṣads. The *prāṇas* are not simply, as frequently translated, the various 'breaths' of man (as in the present quotation). They indicate the major bodily, and indeed, vital functions of man, i.e. eyesight, hearing, mind, etc.; *prāṇāḥ*, in this sense, is just an instance of the well-known grammatical feature of the elliptic plural ('the breath and the other functions,' cf. *mātarau* 'parents,' etc.). Note the occasional translations by some authors who came quite close to this concept, i.e. Schayer. [See now Bodewitz 1986b].

237 The text focuses, next to material success, on the spiritual qualities of the *yajamāna*, such as *bramavarcas*.

238 A sign of wealth.

239 Cf. TĀ 5.8.13, 5.2.2 [See now Houben 1991: 23].

240 Cf. III 207: 80.9; ĀpŚS 15.1.2, with Caland's note on TĀ 5.2.2, ĀpŚS 15.12.10; see Keith *Rel.*, p. 332, KaṭhĀ III 168, and contrast III 207. [See now Houben 1991: 107 n.11].

241 Starting with the *ādhāna*, *agnihotra*, etc., and progressing with the various Soma sacrifices and beyond, [see Witzel, 1995/7].

242 Caland, transl. of ĀpŚS 15.20.1: "weshalb diese Dīkṣā 'die Avāntaradīkṣā' heisst, weiss ich nicht zu sagen."

for a Soma ritual has to be undertaken first; just before the Pravargya begins, the *avāntaradīkṣā* is inserted. It includes many more severe observances and is concluded just before the selection of the priests and the animal sacrifice at the *dīkṣā* takes place. The *dīkṣā* of the Soma *yajña*, however, ends only with the end of the ritual itself. The problem is more complex as the *avāntaradīkṣā* is also applied to the study of the Pravargya texts (III 198). An explanation would lead too far astray here and will be attempted separately.[243]

In addition to the various entities mentioned above, the *yajamāna* also has to be protected from the glowing Pravargya vessel (III 150, 173-6, 194; II 58-70) viz. from Rudra who frequently is identified with the glowing vessel: III 154; cf. III 159-162 (from Rudra's rain), 163-165 (from his wind), and from his poisonous(?) food (III 166-166b) -- all of which are Rudra's weapons. Further, from Rudra identified with Pūṣan (III 173), from Rudra's glow/heat that is present in heaven (as sun), in the intermediate space (*antarikṣa*) and on earth, as well as in certain meters, *stomas*, and parts of the offering ground (cf. III 177-183a). Rudra himself is appeased by an offering of fire wood (III 195), because he --as the Parvargya vessel-- is the head of the sacrifice rejoined (III 207), or he is called to sacrifice with 'his dear name' (III 220).

There also is a whole section on expiation (*prāyaścitti*), aiming at the protection of the *yajamāna* from Rudra (III 235 sqq.). The *yajamāna* retains long life when atoning for an accidental boiling over of the *gharma* vessel, or when atoning for thunder (= sorrow), rain falling during the Pravargya ritual (= hitting by a *vajra*), or setting of the sun (= bad luck) while the Pravargya still is underway. He gains cattle and long life by atoning for the sitting down of the *gharma* cow (III 238, 239); he provides for offspring by expiating for an approach of birds (= offspring, III 186) or ferocious wild animals to the Pravargya vessel (= Rudra = Yama = death, III 239-239a).

It is, however, not only Rudra who can deprive the *yajamāna* from certain benefits of the ritual, it can also be done by other gods. Frequently, it is accidental mistakes in the performance of the ritual or intentional sorcery (*abhicāra*) by malevolent priests (or directed against him by his enemies). Thus, the *rakṣas* ('damage') are 'beaten away' by singing the *vrata* and *pakṣa sāmans* (III 233). Malignant gods who would not get a share in the offering have to be appeased in order not to hurt him (II 129, III 170); Agni, etc., protects his senses and other biological functions (II 80-89a).

A priest who wants to spoil his own *yajamāna* for one reason or another just has to alter one syllable (*sam-ardh•* > *vy-ardh•*, II 31,33, 35). An intentional act of sorcery (*abhicāra*) against enemies is seen at III 189, where the waters are meant to hurt. Even the smallest mistake in ritual might lead to disaster: if certain mantras would be said loudly, Rudra would kill the *yajamāna*'s cattle (II 128a, cf. III 229).

---

243 Discussed in my forthcoming book *The Veda in Kashmir*, ch. VI; this feature has some bearing on the original constitution of the text corpus of the Kaṭha *śākhā* as well, see Witzel 1977 [and cf. now also Witzel 1980, 1981, Houben 1991: 21sqq.]

§6.7.3. Social position of the *yajamāna*

The *yajamāna*'s position in society is also enhanced by the effects of the Pravargya ritual, as has been briefly indicated above. Like Rudra, who was at first excluded from the companionship of the gods in heaven and who finally succeeded in going there by himself, approaching the gods as a powerful deity, the *yajamāna* not only reaches heaven (cf. below), but also achieves supreme power (II 100) like Rudra; he becomes one 'at the top' (*mukhya*, II 207) and is 'exalted' (*mahiman*, III 220).

He attains special status as a learned person because he has 'come together with the Vedas' (II 101); he is provided with splendor and Brahmanical fame among men (III 207, 233). He will know the secret names of the four Vedas when he has studied the text (II 117), and, through this, he will gain long life, Brahmanical fame, and food. By some special mantras (I 136, 137), he is made to partake of the offering, otherwise intended for the gods.

§6.7.4. Supernatural effects

Finally, the ritual also produces supernatural effects for its sponsor, the *yajamāna*. By performing this or another one of the many Śrauta *yajñas*,[244] the sponsor carrying out the Pravargya will go to 'heaven.'[245] This is clearly expressed in many passages of KaṭhĀ (II 109, 110, 231, 233, cf. II 98), for example, by offering into the *uttaravedi* fire (identical with heaven, III 233: 91.1-2, *svargó vái loká auttaravedikás*), or by singing the *ārūḍhavat* sāman ('the Sāman having ascension' III 233, end). By this melody the Aṅgirasa went to heaven; it is said to be identical with heaven, and thus, the sponsor will 'go to heaven' himself.

The *utsādana* that takes place at the end of the ritual entails the 'taking out' of the Pravargya implements and their arrangement on the ground in various patterns. Carrying the implements, the participants in the ritual go towards the east, identified with the world of the gods (III 177).[246] The *yajamāna*'s wife accompanies him so that he may 'not be single' in going to the other world. To be married is a requirement for all those who offer Vedic rituals.[247]

---

[244] However, he does not want to stay there until he has lived out his full life (*āyuṣ*); therefore, he reverses the process and returns to 'earth' again (cf. Keith, *Rel.* p. 461, 463 and KaṭhĀ III 231 (end), III 232; cf. II 143). If the *yajamāna* and the priests would loose their 'firm stand' in this world, on earth, and remain at the Āhavanīya fire or on the *Uttarā Vedi*, that is in 'heaven,' they could not live out their life span (*āyus*); cf. also Keith, *Rel.* p. 463; for the full life of 100 years as a desideratum to be gained in ritual, see Keith, *Rel.*, p. 467 (effected by the Agnicayana, as explained by ŚB 10).

[245] For examples, see above, n.153, 197, 204 and below n. 277.

[246] The offering ground is in fact prescribed to be on a ground slightly sloping towards the east and northeast (VādhB, see Caland AO VI: 208; cf. ĀpŚS 10.2.9). It is well known that the gods live in the eastern or northeastern directions of the sky.

[247] [Here, however, it seems that the idea of *sahānugamana* is alluded to. However, actual *satī* is otherwise unattested in the Vedas; Greek sources attest to it during Alexander's time in the area of the Kaṭhas, Gr. *Kathaioi*.]

The various items discussed so far follow a common method, known from other *yajñas* as well. The heavenly world was believed to in the sun or to be reached through the sun.[248] As is well known, in Vedic ritual the eastern (*āhavanīya*) fire is regarded as heaven while the opposite, western (*gārhapatya*) fire is identical with the earth, and the southern (*dakṣiṇāgni*) fire is the moon. It was already a pre-Vedic (Indo-Iranian) belief that fire on earth, when used on the offering ground, was identified with fire in the sun. This is the ultimate reason for Avestan fire worship[249] and it is apparent in Vedic literature from RV passages[250] onwards. The present text, too, contains a mantra explicitly identifying both, III 222:

> "The one is speech in the fire, the other one the eyesight in the sun;[251] -- one is in the fire, the other in the sun; one is in the fire, the other one is in the fire." (cf. below, §7)

This is a prose mantra that could have been composed during the Mantra period, intervening between the late RV and the old expository prose found in the Black Yajurveda Saṃhitās.[252] Clearly, we deal here with mantras and not *brāhmaṇa* sentences. The passage thus does not follow the well-known expository *brāhmaṇa* style, yet its contents would fit into a typical *brāhmaṇa* passage without problem. In fact, such a *Brāhmaṇa* could easily be reconstructed for the Mantra period [253] perhaps as follows:

> *Fire is speech.[254] (Fire produces peculiar sounds when offerings of ghee are poured into it). The Sun is the eye (of Mitra and Varuṇa).[255] (Both are linked by their relationship as vital functions (*prāṇa*).) The sun is this fire.*

Or, if the apparent intention of the author of KaṭhĀ III 222 is followed more strictly:

---

248 A concept especially prominent in the Upaniṣads, e.g., Chāndogya Upaniṣad 8.6.5.

249 Both are identical with (an aspect of) Ahura Mazdā, see J. Narten 1971/1992; Witzel, 1992 see p. 811, n. 13.

250 See n. 114 (see also n. 232, 246, 249sqq, KaṭhĀ II 107-8, with n. 199, 209, 254-55). [For post-Ṛgvedic occurrences (KS 6.3: 51.9, etc., cf. Witzel 1992: 810sq., n. 8, 13]; it also underlies the original concept of the Agnihotra (*agnir jyotir...jyotir agniḥ/ jyotiḥ sūryaḥ*), offered before the sun sets; the fire of the sun is protected in the sacrificer's fire on earth and rekindled the next morning so that the sun must rise again (analogical magic); [see now Witzel 1992: 810, n. 8 (TB 2.1.29, ŚB 2.3.1.3, JB 1.8, etc., and in Old Iranian: Yasna Haptaŋhāiti 36.3.6].

251 The sun is the eye of Mitra and Varuṇa, watching all humans, RV cf. 10.90; see above n. 33. This concept is perhaps even Indo-European, note Iliad Γ 277, see Witzel 1972:188 n. 37, and Witzel 1984a: 222, 230, n. 44.]

252 See K. Hoffmann 1975-6: 509.

253 'Theological' texts in *brāhmaṇa* style existed already at that time, see K. Hoffmann, 1975-6: 509 (see above n. 140).

254 Fire = speech, see already RV 1.1.1 where Agni is identified as the Hotṛ priest who has to recite mantras, see Thieme 1964: 16; KaṭhĀ III 236.

255 Sun = eye, found in the Puruṣa hymn RV 10.90.13; in the death hymn RV 10.16.3; as Mitra's and Varuṇa's eye (see n. 114); sun = eye = Mitra in KaṭhĀ III 169, cf. I, III 218; KaṭhĀ II 231 *svar = jyotiṣ* in a mantra, where it is apparently identified with the sun in a Brāhmaṇa portion; cf. also, for the Agnicayana: sun = fire = *yajamāna*, see Keith, *Rel.*, p. 466.

> *Fire is speech, the sun is the eye. (Both are *prāṇas*, therefore) the sun is this fire (on earth) and that fire (in the sun).*

KaṭhĀ III 222 then states: "The two eyes (of Rudra) he praises thus. Good luck (*Bhaga*, another Āditya, like Mitra and Varuṇa) is blind.[256] His (the *yajamāna*'s) offspring are not born blind (because the eyes of Rudra have been praised)."

This implies a further identification of the 'heavenly' eye (the sun) and the mundane one (the fire) with the eyes of Rudra.[257] The identifications [or correlations], underlying the *brāhmaṇa* statement and the mantra portion of III 222 are born out frequently in KaṭhĀ:

- *agni* = Rudra (Mahāvīra) II 226,
- *agnir vai rudraḥ* III 239,
- *agni* = Rudra Mahāvīra = sun, III 233, 238, (mantra: = *jātavedas*; prose: *asau vā ādityo rudro mahāvīras*).

The simple assertion that the *yajamāna* would go to heaven and gain a heavenly abode is, however, not enough. There must be one symbolic act effecting change during the ritual. This is not only done by merely walking on the offering ground towards the east (heaven) as in some of the common rituals. The Pravargya offers a spectacular event that makes the *yajamāna* go to heaven with a *substitute* body.[258] It is reflected by the myth of Rudra, of 'sun-colored' skin, ascending heaven (II 100). The gods had excluded him from their ascent, and yet he managed to follow them and threatened them into submission.

As seen above, the *yajamāna* is implicitly identified with Rudra during the Pravargya (II 100-101). Like Rudra, he gains a new bodily form, *svargākṛti*[259] (II 143, cf. III 225), a 'heavenly body.' This can be done in several ways. After taking the Pravargya vessel and the other utensils eastwards (III 177), all are laid out in the from of a man (for details, see immediately below). This action creates a new body for the *yajamāna*,[260] with the Pravargya vessel that glowed during the ritual as his head. In sum, the sponsor of the ritual also becomes *ādityavarṇa* 'sun-skinned,' and goes to heaven like Rudra (III 183).

Apparently unique to the KaṭhĀ I is the further laying out of the Pravargya vessel and the utensils in the form of a head (III 219). The two forms of laying out the utensils, as body and as head, are expressively explained in the preserved sections of the text. They are compared in the following table.

Laying out of the Pravargya utensils

---

[256] This is apparently a proverb; another proverb is found at III 151 (*āyur vai madhu*).

[257] Cf. III 219: *jyotīṁṣi* (eyes?) = *sāmans*.

[258] For earlier ideas, see RV 10.14-18, on death; AV 18.2.26, 18.4.64 on restoring limbs in the other world.

[259] *agnihotravidhíṃ juhoti. sáṃsthitir eváiṣā́ svargā́kṛtir.* "He offers according to the procedure of the Agnihotra. That heavenly form is the conclusion." However, see above, *Introduction*, n. 33.

[260] See AB 1.22, KB 8.3-7; Keith, *Rel.*, p. 333, Pischel, R. and K.F. Geldner 1889-1901: II, 135.

as man III 183a	utensils used	as head III 219
hair	grass brush	hair
skull bones	pot sherds	skull bones
eyes	metal plates (silver plate (golden plate	eyes northern[261] eye) southern eye)
-	2 fan sticks	2 nostrils
	caru vessel	mouth
mouth	2 milk vessels	-
-	2 spare *mahāvīra* vessels	neck bones/ spine
throat/neck	*sruva* ladle	-
arms	2 *śapha* pincers	chin bones
-	not hollowed spoons, round ladles	canine teeth
breast bones	two fans	ears
belly	saucer and bamboo shavings	tongue
navel	third fan	-
-	puroḍāśa cake[262]	brain
loins/womb	two elephant-lipped vessels	-
shanks	poles	teeth

[261] This would indicate the position of the head, its skull pointing eastwards; similarly, III 183a several times explains that the next implement has to be put *paścāt* 'west' of the preceding one. The head, therefore, is in the east; the eyes of the Pravargya = sun and moon, III 158, III 233 (end); = sun (Mitra, not Varuṇa) III 189; = sun (in goose form III 183a, cf. RV 4.40.5 and also RV 1.65.9, 10.124.9).

[262] Note the similar identification of the underground termite nest (*valmīkavapā*) with the brain (see Smith and Carri 1994).

feet	2 fire rakes	-
-	coals	flesh
-	ghee	marrow
-	cow and goat milk	fat
breast	pravargya throne, put on top	-
skin(?)	*ditto*, covered by antelope skin (form of *bráhman*)	-
body hair	*ditto*, covered by muñja grass (= strength), sour milk and honey (sprinkled all over = heat)	-
		form of the body = *ṛc*;[263] *prāṇas* = yajuṣ; *jyotīṁṣi* (eyes?) = sāman;[264] hearing = cardinal directions
		sacrifice has a head; *yajamāna* is provided with a head, with a top position

Immediately following the laying out in the form of a man, however, KaṭhĀ provides for another, equally unique model. The passage is unfortunately very much destroyed in the manuscript, yet the main train of thought can be inferred (III 183, at the end):

> "He makes (a figure) in the form of a goose (*haṁsa*). The sun is a goose(?)[265] .. (3 lines broken off) ... pouring ... pouring water he goes around the (Pravargya vessel, with the mantra:) 'you are agreeable, a giver of strength.' Thus, he lets him (the *yajamāna*) gain strength. 'You are a small child (*śiśu*) that feeds people.' He declares its (the vessel's) form to be greatness.
>
> If birds should sit down (next to the vessel), he should know: 'this offspring wants to sit next to the *gharma* vessel.' Therefore, he protects himself from the birds (with the mantra:) 'as one with bloody mouth...' and 'like someone going through the cows(?)...' and by offering two (spoonfuls of ghee). Yama is death,

[263] Cf. *ṛc, sāman, yajuṣ* = *gharma* III 234.

[264] Cf. *śukriya sāman* = sun, *candra* = earth III 233.

[265] KaṭhĀ III 183; for RV passages, see above, n. 261and cf. next note.

he appeased him with his own share."

The reason for the identification of the birds, especially the goose,[266] with death is the belief that the dead sometimes reappear as talking golden geese. In the story[267] of Keśin Dālbhya, for example, the deceased king Sutvan Yājñasena comes to Keśin in the form of a golden goose (*hiraṇmayo haṃso bhūtvā*) and asks him for a method not to loose his sacrificial benefits in the other word (*iṣṭāpūrtasyākṣiti*).

In the Pravargya, the *yajamāna* apparently is provided with a body that he would otherwise only gain after death,[268] i.e., that of a golden[269] goose. The sun is often identified with a bird, a goose, and the identification of the Pravargya vessel with the sun and Rudra was seen above. Now, if other (apparently, predatory) birds sit next to the Pravargya vessel, they are thought to be his offspring (i.e., the deceased to be reborn as his future children).[270] The link between the deceased/children, death (Yama) and the Pravargya vessel is made by calling it, in the mantra applied here, a 'baby' (*śiśu*). The birds (his deceased relatives, his future children) try to disturb him, take away his food, or even kill him. Therefore, he must protect himself from death, from Yama.[271]

This leads to another important motive for performing a Pravargya ritual, the belief in the gradual reduction and final disappearance of supernatural benefits (*iṣṭāpūrta*)[272] gained by ritual. This resulted, in the late Brāhmaṇas and the Āraṇyakas, in the wish to avoid a second death (*punarmṛtyu*) after death.[273] Like other *yajñas*, the Pravargya is said to 'beat off recurring death' (*punarmṛtyum apahanti*, III 219). The discussion of recurring death represents the intermediate stage in the development of Upaniṣadic thought, emerging as the theory of rebirth with *karma* in the

---

[266] This may be understood as the sun identified with a goose, see ŚB 6.7.3.11: *asau āditya haṁsaḥ śucuṣat*, AB 4.20 *eṣa vai haṁsaḥ śuciṣad.*

[267] VādhB, ed. Caland, *Acta Orientalia* VI: 147 sqq. [= *Kleine Schriften:* 447]; also JB 2.53 (§124) and KB 7. 4.

[268] Here, the identification of the 'man in the sun' with the 'man in the eye' (i.e. in the human pupil) and with death should be taken into account. ŚB 10.5.2.13 *sa eṣa eva mṛtyuḥ | ya eṣa etasmin maṇḍale* (= sun) *puruṣo yaścāyaṃ dakṣiṇe 'kṣan puruṣaḥ* (cf. ŚB 10.5.2.7 sqq.); cf. also TĀ 1.8.4 (a Kāṭhaka chapter from the lost KaṭhB): *amum* (the sun) *āhuḥ param mṛtyum*; JB 1.27 *eṣa vai mṛtyur yad āditya mrocann eva nāma.*

[269] The heated Pravargya vessel will be *ādityavarṇa*, too.

[270] [Cf. Witzel 1984b].

[271] Another interpretation might be according to the fragment in KaṭhĀ III 187a: "he makes (the laying out of the Pravargya utensils) in the form of a goose. The sun is a goose..." (see n. 261). This may point to laying out the utensils in the form of the sun, cf. ĀpŚS 15.14.9, etc. The mantras used and the action performed, however, correspond to those of KaṭhĀ I 151-153a; cf. *Introduction*, notes 40, 41. Note, however, that the sun = death, too; cf. Keith, *Rel.* p. 464.

[272] [See now J. Sakamoto-Gotō 2000].

[273] For the difference between a life after death subjected to *punarmṛtyu* and immortality after death (with the gods) effected through ritual, see Keith, *Rel.*, p. 464 sq. [See now also Witzel 1984a, n. 6, 105; 1989: §8.2 with map (p. 202); H.-P. Schmidt 1967, 1997, Bodewitz 1986a].

Upaniṣads.[274]

It is interesting to note that this passage occurs in the treatment of the *avāntaradīkṣā* and, therefore, during the study of the Pravargya texts. How 'second death' is to be affected seems to be dependent on the effect of this additional and more severe *dīkṣā*. It is significant that the undertaking of this special observance results -- just like that of a normal *dīkṣā* -- in a kind of rebirth of the *yajamāna*. [275] In the present case, he not only becomes another consecrated person with a new name, a *dīkṣita*, but in addition, he also separates himself from death by undergoing the *avāntaradīkṣā* in the wilderness: 'the village is the cow pen of death; now, the wilderness is (the cow pen) of the gods, he who knows this, conquers second death. ... He becomes three times lustrous, who knows thus' (III 219).

§7. On the Position of KaṭhĀ in Vedic Thought

The KaṭhĀ clearly stands at the crossroads of traditional *brāhmaṇa* ideas and the beginnings of Upaniṣadic thought. As indicated above, the idea of *punarmṛtyu* (KaṭhĀ III 219 *ápa punarmṛtyúm jayati, yá evám̐ véda*) is one of the steps leading to the Upaniṣadic concept of karmic rebirth. In fact, there were several strands of beliefs that, for the first time in Vedic thought, resulted in the idea of constant rebirth, seen gradually developing in the older Upaniṣads.[276] Their development was mainly due to the combination of a belief in the gradual waning of the beneficial effects of ritual (*iṣṭāpūrta*) and the belief in a second death after death (*punarmṛtyu*), that is after a period in heaven (MS 1.8.6: 123.19-124.3).[277] This concept was joined or influenced by the popular(?) belief of a reverse world, where the roles of slayer and victim are reversed; this concept does not agree with the more optimistic view of an automatic stay in heaven based on *iṣṭāpūrta*.[278]

At the same time, the late Brāhmaṇas and Āraṇyakas gradually evolved a means to avoid rebirth: proper insight into the true nature of the self (*ātman*), which finally lead to the famous Upaniṣadic identification of *ātman* and *brahman*. An indication of these developments in KaṭhĀ is the appearance of the word *upaniṣad* itself,

---

[274] H.-P. Schmidt 1967, [cf. Witzel 1987a: 390 sq., 412 sq.; cf. 1987b; Schmidt 1997; J. Sakamoto-Gotō 2000]; note ŚB 11.6.1 and JB 1.42-44 on retribution after death.

[275] On the rebirth of the *yajamāna* through *dīkṣā*, see Gonda 1965b: 315sqq.

[276] See Keith, *Rel.*, p. 464 sq. For theological and spiritual developments from the Brāhmaṇas to the Upaniṣads, e.g., in ŚB 10.6.4, see Keith, *Rel.*, p. 467, [see now Ikari 1989, Witzel 1984b, Bodewitz 1996].

[277] The importance of this early attestation (in an untranslated text) of a limited stay in heaven and a return to earth (as shooting stars) has escaped attention. [Cf. now also Bodewitz 1998]. Note VādhB on *punar jan* Caland AO VI: 198.

[278] See Keith, *Rel.* p. 409, 478, n. 5, 573, n. 11; H.-P. Schmidt 1967 [and now Schmidt 1997, Sakamoto-Gotō 2000]; note the ŚB, KB, and JB passages on retribution, see n. 274.

unfortunately in a slightly mutilated passage, as *pravargyopaniṣád* (III 229).

In the present text, one can notice the beginnings of multiple identifications, that is equating parts of macrocosm and microcosm in sentences such as[279] *vāg vā anyat...* (see above, §6.7.4):

> "The one is speech in the fire, the other one is the eyesight in the sun;[280] one is in the fire, the other in the sun; one is in the fire, the other one is in the fire."

This establishes a simple localization of speech and of eyesight in the fire *viz.* in the sun. The text does not *explicitly* identify fire with speech nor the sun with eyesight. However, this is something already presupposed *behind* the formulation of this mantra. It has precedents in the Ṛgvedic identification apparent in the (poetical) description of god Fire (Agni) and speech because of the sounds fire produces when burning ghee or wood. As pointed out above, the sun, too, is described in the RV as the eye of the god Mitra, seeing everything on earth.[281]

One has to take into account that the passage in question is a mantra, and thus considerably older than the prose text of the present Āraṇyaka that makes use of it. However, the *brāhmaṇa* passage preceding and following the mantras of III 222 is based on the identification of Rudra and his vital functions (eyesight, etc.) with those of the *yajamāna* (*viz.* those of the Veda student who learns the Pravargya text by heart). Taking together the links made between fire and speech (RV+), the sun and the eye (RV+), Rudra and eyesight (KaṭhĀ), Rudra and the sun/fire (KaṭhĀ), diverse connections and identifications are made in the present text. This procedure thus establishes *multiple* links between macrocosm, microcosm and ritual.

In the present text, a few such developments can be found. Macrocosm, ritual and microcosm are linked when various ritual implements are at first identified with parts of the human body, and then identified with the sun (and Rudra-Mahāvīra). In this way, the *yajamāna* apparently gains a new heavenly body.

This kind of threefold, multiple linkage and identification (e.g., III 219) is the most developed one found in a YV Āraṇyaka. The procedure was later formalized in the Upaniṣads with their three- and five-fold identifications (Benke 1976).

In sum, even this neglected, fragmentary text can provide important indications of the developments in Vedic thought.

---

[279] Cf. II 107 Mantra and Brāhmaṇa: *sám agnír agnínāgata, sáṃ devéna savitrā́, sáṁ sū́ryeṇa rocate svā́héty. átra vā́ eṣá etárhy agnír agnínā sáṅgaśchate.*

[280] The sun is the eye of Mitra and Varuṇa, watching all humans, (see above, n. 114) RV 6.51.1; 7.61.1; 6.67.5; 7.61.3, cf. Geldner *ad* 1.72.10; 10.127.1; see n. 114; for a Greek reference (Iliad Γ 277, see above n. 251).

[281] This opens up the interesting question of (cf. above, n. 140) whether there was a development between the Ṛgvedic concepts of simile and metaphor on the one hand and Yajurvedic linking and identification on the other; or whether these are just two ways to look at the same thing, one in poetic and the other in expository fashion.

ABBREVIATIONS

AB	Aitareya Brāhmaṇa
AO	Acta Orientalia
ĀpŚS	Āpastamba Śrauta Sūtra
Ār.	Āraṇyaka
BORI	Bhandarkar Oriental Research Institute
BŚS	Baudhāyana Śrauta Sūtra
IIJ	Indo-Iranian Journal
JB	Jaiminīya Brāhmaṇa
JNRC	Journal of the Nepal Research Centre
KaṭhĀ	Kaṭha Āraṇyaka
KaṭhB	Kaṭha Brāhmaṇa
KaṭhŚS	Kaṭha Śrauta Sūtra
KB	Kauṣītaki Brāhmaṇa
KGS	Kāṭhaka Gṛhya Sūtra
KS	Kaṭha Saṃhitā
LŚS	Lāṭyāyana Śrauta Sūtra
MS	Maitrāyaṇī Saṃhitā
MSS	Münchener Studien zur Sprachwissenschaft
PB	Pañcaviṃśa Brāhmaṇa
RO	Rocznik Orientalistyczny
RV	Ṛgveda Saṃhitā
ŚB	Śatapatha Brāhmaṇa
SBE	Sacred Books of the East
ŚBK	Śatapatha Brāhmaṇa, Kāṇva recension
ŚŚS	Śāṅkhāyana Śrauta Sūtra
StII	Studien zur Indologie und Iranistik
TĀ	Taittirīya Āraṇyaka
TB	Taittirīya Brāhmaṇa
VādhS	Vādhūla Sūtra (and Anvākhyāna)
VaikhŚS	Vaikhānasa Śrauta Sūtra
WKZM	Wiener Zeitschrift zur Kunde des Morgenlandes
WZKS	Wiener Zeitschrift zur Kunde Südasiens
WZKSO	Wiener Zeitschrift zur Kunde Süd- und Ostasiens
YV	Yajurveda
ZDMG	Zeitschrift der Deutschen Morgenländischen Gesellschaft

BIBLIOGRAPHY

Aguilar, H. *The Sacrifice in the Ṛgveda.* Delhi: Bharatiya Vidya Prakashan 1976

Arieti, *The intrapsychic self; feeling, cognition, and creativity in health and mental illness.* New York: Basic Books 1967

Aufrecht, Th. *Catalogus catalogorum. An alphabetical register of Sanskrit works and authors.* Leipzig: F. A. Brockhaus 1891-1903

Baroda Alphabetical List, see R. N. Siromani

Benke, A. *Die Magie in der Brāhmaṇa-Zeit.* [MA Thesis] Erlangen 1976

Bhagavad Datta, *Vaidik vāṅmay kā itihās. History of Vedic Literature.* Lahore 1927

Bloomfield, M. *A Vedic Concordance.* Cambridge: Harvard Oriental Series 1906

---, F. Edgerton, and M. B. Emeneau. *Vedic variants: A study of the variant readings in the repeated mantras of the Veda.* Philadelphia 1930-34

Bodewitz, H. W. Redeath and its relation to rebirth and release, *StII* 20, 1986a, 27-46

---, Prāṇa, apāna and other prāṇas in Vedic literature. *Adyar Library Bulletin* (Golden Jubilee Volume) 50, 1986b : 326-348

---, The Hindu doctrine of transmigration: its origin and background. *Indologica Taurinensia* (Professor Gregory M. Bongard-Levin Felicitation Volume) 23-24, 1998, 583-605

Brereton, J. The Upanishads. In: *Eastern Canons: Approaches to the Asian Classics,* ed. by Wm.Th. de Bary and I. Bloom, New York: Columbia University Press 1990: 115-135

Bühler, G. Eine Notiz über einige Sanskrit MSS. aus Kaçmîr in der K. K. Hof-Bibliothek zu Wien. *Monatsberichte der Preußischen Akademie der Wissenschaften zu Berlin aus dem Jahre 1879.* Berlin 1879: 200-202

Caland, W. *Altindische Zauberei, Darstellung der altindischen "Wunschopfer".* Amsterdam : J. Muller 1908.

---, *Indischer Ahnencult. Das Śrāddha nach den verschiedenen Schulen mit Benutzung handschriftlicher Quellen dargestellt.* Leiden 1893

---, *The Baudhāyana Śrauta Sūtra belonging to the Taittirīya Saṃhitā.* Calcutta: Asiatic Society, 1904-1924.

---, Brāhmaṇa en Sūtra aanwinsten. *Verslagen en mededeelingen der Koningklijke Akademie van Wetenschappen, Afdeeling Letterkunde,* vijfde reeks, vierde deel, derde stuk. Amsterdam 1920, 478-498

---, *Das Śrautasūtra des Āpastamba* (3 vols.) Göttingen 1921, Amsterdam 1924,1928.

---, *The Kāṭhakagṛhyasūtra with extracts from the three commentaries, an appendix and indices edited for the first time.* Lahore 1925

---, Über das Vādhūlasūtra; Eine zweite / dritte / vierte Mitteilung über das Vādhūlasūtra. *AO* 1, 3-11; *AO* II, 142-167; *AO* IV, 1-41, 161-213; *AO* VI, 97-241.1922. 1924.1926.1928. [= 1990, pp. 268-541]

---, A Vaidic wedding song. *AO* VII, 1929, 305-311

---, *Kleine Schriften,* M. Witzel (ed.) Wiesbaden 1990

Devi Prasad. *Catalogue of Sanskrit Manuscripts in Oudh for the year 1882-90.* Allahabad 1883-93

Dreyer, C. *Das Kāṭhaka-Gṛhya-Sūtra, mit Vivaraṇa des Ādityadarṣana, Bhāṣya des Devapāla, Gṛhyapañcikā des Brāhmaṇabala; kritische Edition mit Anmerkungen.* Stuttgart: F. Steiner 1986

Deambi, Bh. K. see: Kaul Deambi

Doty, W. G. *Mythography. The study of Myths and Rituals.* Tuscaloosa/London : The University of Alabama Press 2000

Evans-Pritchard, E.E. Sorcery and Native Opinion. In: Marwick 1970: 21-26

Falk, H. Upaniṣád. *ZDMG* 136, 1986a, 80-97

---, *Bruderschaft und Würfelspiel.* Freiburg 1986b

---, Vedische Opfer im Pali-Kanon, *Bulletin des Etudes indiennes* 6, 1988, 225-254

---, The purpose of Ṛgvedic ritual. In: Witzel 1997a: 67-88

Farmer, S., J.B. Henderson, M. Witzel. Neurobiology, Layered Texts, and Correlative Cosmologies. A Cross-Cultural Framework for Premodern History. *Bulletin of the Museum of Far Eastern Antiquities (BMFEA)* 72, 2002, 48-90

Firth, R. Reason and Unreason in Human Belief . In: Marwick 1970: 38-44

Frazer, J.G. *The Golden Bough. A Study in magic and religion.* Abridged ed. 1922, London 2nd ed. 1923

Fujii, M. On the Formation and Transmission of the Jaminīya-Upaniṣad-Brāhmaṇa. In: Witzel 1997a: 89-102

Garbe, R. Die Pravargja Ceremonie nach dem ĀpŚS. *ZDMG* 34, 1880, 319-370

---, *Āpastambaśrautasūtra, Taittirīyasaṃhitāsambandhitā Āpastambapraṇītam Rudradattaviracita-bhāṣyasahitam.* Calcutta: Baptist Mission Press 1882

Gonda, J. *Die Religionen Indiens, I. Veda und älterer Hinduismus*, Stuttgart 1960

---, Bandhus in the Brāhmaṇas. *Adyar Library Bulletin* 29, 1965a, 1-29

---, *Change and continuity in Indian religion.* The Hague: Mouton 1965

---, The meaning of the Sanskrit term *āyatana*, *Adyar Library Pamphlet Series*, no. 38 [= repr. of *Adyar Library Bulletin* 33] Madras 1969

---, *The meaning of the Sanskrit term dhāman. Afhandelingen der Nederlandse Akademie van Wetenschappen.* Amsterdam 1967

---, A propos of the Mantras in the Pravargya section of the Ṛgvedic Brāhmaṇas. *IIJ* 21, 1979, 235-271

---, *The Mantras of the Agnyupasthāna and the Sautrāmaṇī.* Amsterdam 1980

Granet, M. *La pensée chinoise.* Paris 1934 [repr. Paris 1988]

Hacker, P. *śraddhā. WZKSO* 3, 1963, 151-189

Hara, M. Note on two Sanskrit religious terms: *bhakti* and *śraddhā. IIJ* 7, 1964, 124-145

Heesterman, J.C. The case of the severed head. In: *Essays in Indian Ritual, Kingship and Society.* Chicago 1985, 45-58

Hillebrandt, A. *Rituallitteratur.* Strassburg 1897

---, *Kleine Schriften* (ed. R.P. Das). Stuttgart: F. Steiner 1987

Hoffmann, K. Die magische Weltanschauung im Veda. *Indologentagung 1959. Verhandlungen der Indologischen Arbeitstagung in Essen-Bredeney, 13.-15. Juli 1959*, ed. E. Waldschmidt, Göttingen 1960, p. 232 [= *Aufsätze*, 1992, p. 709]

---, Remarks on the New Edition of the *Paippalāda Saṃhitā. IIJ* 11, 1-10 = 1975-6: 228-237

---, *Aufsätze zur Indoiranistik* (ed. J. Narten). [2 vols.] Wiesbaden 1975, 1976

Horton, R. African Traditional Thought and Western Science. In: Marwick, 1970: 342-368

Houben, J. E. M. *The Pravargya Brāhmaṇa of the Taittirīya Āraṇyaka. An ancient commentary on the Pravargya ritual.* Delhi: Motilal Banarssidas 1991

---, *The Vedic Pravargya Ritual. Performances in Delhi, December 11-12, 1996. A film by Jan E.M. Houben and Nandini Bedi.* Stichting Namarupa, p/a Marnixstraat 5, 2316 EJ Leiden. The Netherlands

Hubert, H. & M. Mauss. Esquisse d'une théorie générale de la magie, *L'année sociologique*, vol. 7, Paris 1902-3

---, Essai sur la nature et la fonction du sacrifice. *L 'Année sociologique* 1987-1898. [Transl. by W. D. Hall: *Sacrifice: its nature and function.* Chicago 1964]

Ikari, Y. Ritual Preparation of the Mahāvīra and Ukhā pots. J.F.Staal, *Agni*, vol. II. Berkeley 1983: 168-177

---, Veda saishiki-bunken ni mirareru saisei-kannen no shosō. [Aspects of the ideas about rebirth observed in Vedic ritual literature]. *Zinbun-gaku-hō* 63, 1989, 69--78

---, Vādhūla Śrautasūtra 1.1-1.4 [Agnyādheya, Punarādheya] - A New Critical Edition of the Vādhūla Śrautasūtra, I. *Zinbun: Annals of the Institute for Research in Humanities - Kyoto University*, 30, 1995, 1-127

---, and H.F. Arnold. *Baudhāyana Śrautasūtra X*, in: J.F.Staal, *Agni*, vol. II. Berkeley 1983: 478-675

Jolly, J.*Viṣṇu-Smṛti.* Calcutta: Bibliotheca Indica 1881

Kahrs, E. *Indian semantic analysis: the nirvacana tradition.* Cambridge/New York: Cambridge University

Press 1998
Kashikar, C.G. *A Survey of the Śrautasūtras*. Bombay 1968
---, Apropos of the Pravargya. *CASS Studies*. Centre of Advanced Studies in Sanskrit, Poona, 1, 1972, 1-10
---, The Avāntaradīkṣā of Pravargya, *Bulletin of the Deccan College Research Institute* 35, Poona 1976: 66-72
---, The Concept of Mahāvīra in the Pravargya. *Golden Jubilee Volume*. Poona: Vaidika Saṃśodhana Maṇḍala 1982: 136-139
Kaul, M.S. *Laugākṣi-Gṛhyaṣūtra*. Bombay 1928-34
Kaul Deambi, B. K. *Corpus of Śāradā inscriptions of Kashmir: with special reference to origin and development of Śāradā script*. New Delhi: Ariana Pub. House 1985
Keith, A.B. *The Religion and Philosophy of the Veda and Upanishads*. Cambridge: Harvard Oriental Series 1925 [Repr. Delhi 1970]
---, The Veda of the Black Yajus School entitled Taittirīya Sanhita. Cambridge: Harvard Oriental Series 1914
Koehler, H.-W. *Śrad-dhā- in der vedischen und altbuddhistischen Literatur* (K. L. Janert, ed.). [Diss. 1948]. Wiesbaden 1973.
Kramrisch, S. The Mahāvīravessel and the plant Pūtika, *Journal of the American Oriental Society* 95, 1975, 222-235
Kuiper, F.B.J. *Aryans in the Rigveda*, Amsterdam-Atlanta: Rodopi 1991
---, Was the putīka a mushroom? In: *Amṛtadhārā. Prof. R.N. Dandekar Felicitation Volume*. Delhi 1984: 219-227
Lévi, S. *La doctrine du sacrifice dans les Brāhmaṇas*. Paris 1898. [Repr. Paris 1966]
Levy, R. I. with the collaboration of Kedar Raj Rajopadhyaya. *Mesocosm: Hinduism and the organization of a traditional Newar city in Nepal*. Berkeley: University of California Press, 1990.
Lévy-Bruhl, L. *Les fonctions mentales dans les sociétes inferieures*. Paris: Alcan 1910
Lokesh Chandra, *Sanskrit Texts from Kashmir*. Śatapiṭaka Series 298sqq. New Delhi 1982-
Lüders, H. Die magische Kraft der Wahrheit im alten Indien, *ZDMG* 98, 1944, 1-14
---, *Varuṇa*. (L. Alsdorf, ed.). Göttingen 1951, 1959
Malinowsk, B. Magic, Science and Religion. In: Marwick 1970: 210-216
Mallory, J.P. and D.Q. Adams, *The Encyclopedia of Indo-European Culture*. London/Chicago: Fitzroy Dearborn 1997
Marwick, M. (ed.) *Witchcraft and Sorcery*. Hammondsworth: Penguin Education 1970, 3rd ed. 1975
Mayrhofer, M. *Etymologisches Wörterbuch des Altindoarischen*. Heidelberg: Carl Winter 1986-2001
Minkowski, C. *Priesthood in ancient India : a study of the Maitrāvaruṇa priest*. Vienna: Sammlung de Nobili, Institut für Indologie der Universität Wien 1992
Moreau, A. & J.-C. Turpin. *La magie: actes du colloque international de Montpellier, 25-27 mars 1999*. Séminaire d'Etudes des mentalités antiques. Montpellier: Université Paul Valéry 2000
Müller, M. Āpastamba's Yajña-Paribhāṣā-Sūtras. In: M. Müller (ed.) *Sacred Books of the East*, Vol. 30, Oxford 1892: 315-364
Mus, P. *Barubuḍur. Esquisse d'une histoire du bouddhisme fondée sur la critique archéologique des textes*, Hanoi 1935
Narten, J. *Die Sigmatischen Aoriste im Veda*. Wiesbaden 1964
---, *Der Yasna Haptaŋhāiti*. [Habilitationsschrift 1971] Wiesbaden 1986
Oberlies, Th. *Die Religion des Ṛgveda. 1. Teil. Das religiöse System des Ṛgveda*. Wien: Institut für Indologie der Universität Wien 1998; *2. Teil. Kompositionsanalyse der Soma-Hymnen des Ṛgveda*. Wien: Institut für Indologie der Universität Wien 1999
Oldenberg, H. *Die Hymnen des Rigveda, Band I. Metrische und textgeschichtliche Prolegomena*. Berlin : Wilhelm Hertz 1888.
---, Die *Religion des Veda*, 2nd. ed. Stuttgart 1917, 1923, [repr. Darmstadt 1970, Engl. transl.: *The Religion of the Veda*, 1896]

---, *araṇya* (1915) = Kleine Schriften, Wiesbaden 1967: 419-438
---, H.Oldenberg, *Vorwissenschaftliche Wissenschaft. Die Weltanschauung der Brāhmaṇa-Texte*. Göttingen 1919
Olivelle, P. *Upaniṣads* Oxford: OUP 1996
Parpola, A. *The Śrautasūtras of Lāṭyāyana and Drāhyāyaṇa and their commentaries. An English translation and study.* [vols. I:1, I:2.] Helsinki 1968, 1969.
Paulys Realencyclopädie der classischen Altertumswissenschaft, neue Bearbeitung unter Mitwirkung zahlreicher Fachgenossen, hrsg. von Georg Wissowa [*et al.*]. Stuttgart: Metzler 1894-1980.
Pischel, R. & K.F. Geldner. *Vedische Studien.* Stuttgart: Kohlhammer 1889-1901
Proferes, Th. *The Formation of Vedic liturgies.* Ph.D. Thesis. Harvard 1999
Puhvel, J. *Comparative Mythology.* Baltimore & London: The Johns Hopkins Press 1987
Raghavan V. & Raja, K. *New catalogus catalogorum; an alphabetical register of Sanskrit and allied works and authors.* Madras: University of Madras 1949-
Raghu Vira, Fragments of the Kāṭhaka Śrautasūtra. *Oriental College Patrika.* Lahore 1928: 9-23
---, *Kapiṣṭhala Saṃhitā.* Lahore 1932. [Reprint: Delhi 1968]
---, Kāṭhaka-Śrautasūtra Fragments. *Journal of Vedic Studies* 2, 1935, 104-107
---, Śākhās of the Yajurveda, the discovery of a unique chart of Yājuṣa recensions. *Journal of Vedic Studies* 2, 1935, 61-77
Rao, K.L.S. *The Concept of śraddhā (in the Brāhmaṇas, Upaniṣads and the Gītā).* Patiala 1971
Rau, W. *Staat und Gesellschaft im alten Indien nach den Brāhmaṇa-Texten dargestellt.* Wiesbaden 1957
---, Notiz zum cerebralen ḷ in südindischen Sanskrit-Handschriften. *MSS* 42, 1983, 187-189
Realenzyklopädie des klassischen Altertums, see Pauly
Renou, L. Connexion en védique, cause en bouddhisque. *Dr. Kunhan Raja Presentation Volume*, Madras: Adyar Library 1946: 55-60
---, *Les écoles védiques et la formation du Veda.* Cahiers Societé Asiatique IX. Paris 1947
---, The Vedic Schools and the Epigraphy. In: *Dr. Siddheshwar Varma felicitation volume: being a collection of papers presented to him on his 90th birthday edited by K. V. Sarma.* Hoshiarpur: Vishveshvaranand Vishva Bandhu Institute of Sanskrit and Indological Studies, Panjab University 1978 : 1-8
Rieu [Note in Weber, *Indische Studien* 1, 1850, 70]
Rönnow, K. Zur Erklärung des Pravargya, des Agnicayana und der Sautrāmaṇī. *Monde Oriental* 23, 1929, 113-178
Rolland, P. *Le Mahāvrata. Contribution à l'étude un rituel solonnel védique.* Nachrichten der Akadademie der Wissenschaften in Göttingen. Phil.-Hist. Klasse, Jg. 1973: 53-79
Rosenfield, S. Kaṭha Brāhmaṇa Fragments. A Critical Edition, Translation, Study. Harvard PhD thesis 2004
Sahlins, M.D. *Stone Age Economics.* Chicago 1972
Sakamoto-Gotō, J. Das Jenseits und *iṣṭā-pūrtá* "die Wirkung des Geopferten-und-Geschenkten" in der vedischen Religion. In: Forssman, B. & R. Plath, *Indoarisch, Iranisch und die Indogermanistik. Arbeitstagung der Indogermanischen Gesellschaft vom 2. bis 5. Oktober 1997 in Erlangen.* Wiesbaden: Reichert 2000: 475-490
Saletore, G.N. *An Alphabetical Index of Sanskrit Manuscripts in the State Archives of Uttar Pradesh.* Allahabad: State Arhives of U.P. 1970
Satvalekar, D. Maitrāyaṇīyam Āraṇyakam athavā Maitrāyaṇīya Upaniṣad, In: *Maitrāyaṇī-Saṃhitā*, Aundh 1942: 543-564
---, *Kāṭhaka-Saṃhitā.* Aundh 1943
Schayer, S. Die Weltanschauung der Brāhmaṇatexte, *Rocznik Orientalistyczny* 2, 1924, 26-32
---, Über die Bedeutung des Wortes *upaniṣad, Rocznik Orientalistyczny* 3, 1925, 57-67
---, Die Struktur der magischen Weltanschauung nach dem Atharvaveda und den Brāhmaṇatexten, *Zeitschrift für Buddhismus* 6, 1925, 259-299
Scheftelowitz, I. Zur Textkritik und Lautlehre des Ṛgveda. *Wiener Zeitschrift zur Kunde des Morgenlandes*

21, 1907, 85-142

Schmidt, H.-P. The origin of *ahiṃsā. Mélanges d'indianisme à la mémoire de Louis Renou.* Paris 1968: 625-655

---, Ahiṃsā and Rebirth. In: Witzel 1997: 207-234

v. Schroeder, L. Zwei neuerworbene Handschriften der k. k. Hofbibliothek in Wien mit Fragmenten des Kāṭhaka. *Sitzungsberichte der kaiserlichen Akademie der Wissenschaften, Philosophisch-historische Classe, Bd. 133.* Wien 1896: 1-38

---, Die Accentuation der Wiener Kāṭhaka-Handschrift. *ZDMG* 45, 1891, 432-438

---, Das Kāṭhaka, seine Handschriften, seine Accentuation und seine Beziehung zu den indischen Lexicographen und Grammatikern: *ZDMG* 49, 1895, 145-171

---, Die Tübinger Kaṭha-Handschriften und ihre Beziehung zum Taittirīya-Āraṇyaka. *Sitzungsberichte der kaiserlichen Akademie der Wissenschaften, Philosophisch-historische Classe* 137.4. Wien 1898:1-126

---, *Maitrayaṇī-Saṃhitā. Die Saṃhitā der Maitrāyaṇīya-Śākhā.* Leipzig. 1881-86. [Repr. Wiesbaden 1970-72]

---, *Kāṭhakam. Die Saṃhitā der Kaṭha-Śākhā.* Leipzig. 1900-1910 [Repr. Wiesbaden 1970-72]

Singh, F. *The Vedic Etymology. A Critical evaluation of the Science of Etymology as found in Vedic Literature.* Delhi: National Publishing House 1970

Siromani, R.N. *An Alphabetical List of Manuscripts in the Oriental Institute Baroda. Vol. I. Vedic.* Baroda: Oriental Institute 1942

Slaje, W. Katalog der Sanskrit-Handschriften der Österreichischen Nationalbibliothek (Sammlungen Marcus Aurel Stein and Carl Alexander von Hügel). Wien: Verlag der Österreichischen Akademie der Wissenschaften 1990

Sparreboom, M. *Chariots in the Veda.* Leiden: Brill 1985

Smith, B.K. *Reflections on resemblance, ritual, and religion.* New York/Oxford 1989

Staal, J.F. *Nambudiri Veda Recitation.* 's Gravenhage 1961

---, The meaninglessness of ritual. *Numen* 26, 1979, 2-22

---, and R. Gardener. *Altar of Fire. Produced by Robert Gardener and Frits Staal.* The Film Study Center. Cambridge: Harvard University 1976

---, *Agni: The Vedic ritual of the fire altar.* Berkeley 1983

Surya Kanta, *Kāṭhaka-Saṃkalana, Extracts from the lost Kāṭhaka-Brāhmaṇa, Kāthaka-Śrautasūtra and Kāṭhaka-Gṛhyasūtras.* Lahore 1943

Tambiah, S. *Magic, science, religion, and the scope of rationality.* Cambridge/New York: Cambridge University Press 1990

Thieme, P. *Gedichte aus dem Rig-Veda.* Stuttgart: Reclam 1964

Tsuji, N. (*a.k.a.* N. Fukushima). A collection of the Sūtra-elements from the Kāṭhakam (Prolegomena) in *Commemoration Volume of the Science of Religion.* Tokyo: Imperial University 1934: 243-272

---, *On the relation between Brāhmaṇas and Śrautasūtras, [Burāhumana to shurauta sūtora to no kanken].* Tokyo 1952. Repr. 1982, 1-247 [Engl. summary, pp. 181-247].

---, *Genzon Yajurveda Bunken* (*Existent Yajurveda Literature*), Toyo Bunko Ronso, Ser. A, Vol. LII, Tokyo 1970

Vajracharya, The Adaptation of Monsoonal Culture by Ṛgvedic Aryans: A Further Study of the Frog Hymn. *EJVS* 3-2, 1997
http://users.primushost.com/~india/ejvs/issues.html].

van Buitenen, J.A.B. *The Pravargya: An ancient Indian iconic ritual described and annotated.* Poona 1968

Verma, N. *The Etymologies in the Śatapatha Brāhmaṇa.* Delhi: Nag Publishers 1992

Vishva Bandhu. *Cārāyaṇīya-Mantrārṣādhyāya.* Lahore 1935

---, *Brāhmaṇic Citations (Brāhmaṇoddhārakośa).* Hoshiarpur 1966

Vaidikamantrakalpalatā, ed. Pt. Viśvanāth. Srinagar 1913

von Domarus, E. The specific laws of logic in schizophrenia. In: Kasanin, J.S. (ed.) *Language and Thought in Schizophrenia: Collected Papers.* Berkeley: University of California Press 1944

Wackernagel, J. *Altindische Grammatik.* Bd. I. Göttingen: Vandenhoeck & Ruprecht 1896/1957

Weber, A. Ueber den Taittirîya-Veda, astronomische Data aus den beiden Yajus, und eine Stelle des Taitt. Brâhmana über die naxatra. Indische Studien 1: 68-100

---, [note in: G. Bühler 1879: 201, n. 1]

Wezler, A. Zu den sogenannten Identifikationen in den Brāhmaṇas. *Veda-Vyākaraṇa-Vyākhyāna. Festschrift Paul Thieme zum 90. Geburtstag am 18. März 1995 dargebracht von Schülern, Freunden und Kollegen*, ed. by Hanns-Peter Schmidt and Albrecht Wezler = *Studien zur Indologie und Iranistik* 20, 1996, 485-522

Witzel, M. Āraṇyakas. In*: Kindlers Neues Literatur Lexikon* 1972, 1992, Bd. 18: 133-4

---, Jungavestisch *apāxəδra-* im System der avestischen Himmelsrichtungs-bezeichnungen. *MSS* 30, 1972, 163-191

---, An unknown Upaniṣad of the Kṛṣṇa Yajurveda: The Kaṭha-Śikṣā-Upaniṣad. *JNRC* 1, 1977, 139-155

---, *On Magical thought in the Veda.* Leiden: Universitaire Pers 1979a

---, Die Kaṭha-Śikṣā-Upaniṣad und ihr Verhältnis zur Śikṣāvallī der Taittirīya-Upaniṣad. *WZKS* 23 (1979b) 5-28, 24 (1980) 21-82

---, Review of J. Gonda, *The Mantras of the Agnyupasthāna and the Sautrāmaṇī.* (Amsterdam 1980). *Kratylos* 26, 1981/2, 80-85

---, Materialien zu den vedischen Schulen: I. Über die Caraka-Schule. *StII* 8/9, 1982, 171-240

---, Sur le chemin du ciel, *Bulletin des Etudes indiennes* 2, 1984a, 213-279

---, The earliest form of the concept of rebirth in India, (Summary). 31st CISHAAN (Tokyo-Kyoto), *Proceedings*, ed. by T. Yamamoto, Tokyo 1984b: 145-146

---, The case of the shattered head. *Festschrift für W. Rau, StII* 13/14, 1987a, 363-415

---, On the origin of the literary device of the 'Frame Story' in Old Indian literature. *Hinduismus und Buddhismus. Festschrift für U. Schneider*, H. Falk (ed.), Freiburg 1987b: 380-414

---, Tracing the Vedic dialects. In: Colette Caillat (ed.), *Dialectes dans les littératures indo-aryennes.* Paris 1989: 97-264

---, The Realm of the Kurus: Origins and Development of the First State in India, *Nihon Minami Ajia Gakkai Zenkoku Taikai, Hōkoku Yōshi*, Kyoto 1989b: 1-4

---, Meaningful ritual. Structure, development and interpretation of the Tantric Agnihotra ritual of Nepal. In: A.W. van den Hoek, D.H.A. Kolff, M.S. Oort (eds.) *Ritual, State and History in South Asia. Essays in honour of J.C. Heesterman*. Leiden 1992: 774-827

---, Kashmiri Manuscripts and Pronunciation. In: Ikari, Y. (ed.) *A study of the Nīlamata - Aspects of Hinduism in Ancient Kashmir -.* Kyoto: Institute for Research in Humanities, Kyoto University 1994: 1-53

---, Early Sanskritization. Origins and development of the Kuru State. B. Kölver (ed.), *Recht, Staat und Verwaltung im klassischen Indien. The state, the Law, and Administration in Classical India.* München : R. Oldenbourg 1997, 27-52 ~ *Electronic Journal of Vedic Studies* (*EJVS*), vol. 1-4, Dec. 1995, http://www1.shore.net/~india/ejvs

---, How to enter the Vedic mind? Strategies in Translating a Brāhmaṇa text. In: Garzilli, E. (ed.) *Translating, Translations, Translators From India to the West.* Harvard Oriental Series, Opera Minora, 1. Cambridge : *Harvard Oriental Series* 1996: 163-176 http://www.people.fas.harvard.edu/~witzel/How-to-Enter.pdf

---, (ed.) *Inside the texts, Beyond the Texts. New Approaches to the Study of the Vedas.* Cambridge: Harvard Oriental Series, Opera Minora 1997a

---, The Development of the Vedic Canon and its Schools: The Social and Political Milieu. (Materials on Vedic Śākhās 8). In: Witzel 1997a: 257-345

---, Macrocosm, Mesocosm, and Microcosm. The persistent nature of 'Hindu' beliefs and symbolical forms. in S. Mittal (ed.), *IJHS Symposium on Robert Levy's MESOCOSM, International Journal of Hindu Studies,* 1.3, 1998, 501-53

---, Aryan and non-Aryan Names in Vedic India. Data for the linguistic situation, c. 1900-500 B.C. In: Bronkhorst, J. & M. Deshpande (eds.) *Aryans and Non-Aryans. Evidence, Interpretation and*

Ideology. Cambridge: Harvard Oriental Series, Opera Minora 3, 1999, 337-404
---, The Ṛgvedic Religious System and its Central Asian and Hindukush Antecedents. A. Griffiths & J.E.M. Houben (eds.). *The Vedas: Texts, Language and Ritual.* Groningen 2004
Zimmer, S. Review of Idg. Altertumskunde II, Geistige Kultur. *Kratylos* 48, 2003, 1-25

Zur Kaṭha-Schule und ihren Texten

Das Kaṭha-Āraṇyaka, das hier zum ersten Mal in einer kritischen Edition vorgelegt wird, gehört zu den zahlreichen oft nur fragmentarisch erhaltenen und bisher nicht, unvollständig oder nur flüchtig edierten Texten der Kaṭha-Schule des Schwarzen Yajurveda. Von den üblicherweise den Kanon einer YV-Schule ausmachenden Texten sind nämlich in dieser Śākhā vollständig erhalten und bisher ediert lediglich: die Saṁhitā,[1] die berühmte, allerdings späte Upaniṣad,[2] das Gṛhyasūtra,[3] der Cārāyaṇīya-Mantrārṣādhyāya,[4] und die spät überarbeitete, sich im Kern aber wohl an die Kaṭha-Schule anschließende Viṣṇu-Smṛti.[5] In den sogenannten Ṛcaka,[6] den Ritualhandbüchern der kaschmirischen Brahmanen, finden sich aber in bunter Mischung mit RV-, RVKh- und KS-Liedern, späteren Kommentaren und Paddhatis auch Teile des wohl als Ganzen verlorenen Brāhmaṇa,[7] des Āraṇyaka,[8] der bisher unerkannt gebliebenen Śikṣā-Upaniṣad,[9] welche anscheinend den Abschluß des Vedastudiums in dieser Śākhā bildete und als die alte Upaniṣad der Kaṭhas anzusehen ist, des verloren gegangenen Śrautasūtra,[10] des Gṛhyasūtra-Mantrapāṭha,[11] und vielleicht auch von Teilen des Pitṛmedha-Sūtra,[12] des Śulba-Sūtra,[13] des Pravara-Sūtra und des Paribhāṣā-Sūtra,[14] verschiedener Pariśiṣṭas und des Dharma-Sūtra. Die vorliegende Edition des KaṭhĀ[15] macht demnach nur einen kleinen Teil einer sich in Bearbeitung befindlichen Gesamtedition[15a] der in zahlreichen Ṛcaka und z.T. auch gedruckten Ritualhandbüchern der kaschmirischen Sārasvata-Brahmanen erhaltenen Fragmente der Kaṭha-Schule aus.

Diese Śākhā repräsentiert zusammen mit der sich in ihrer Saṁhitā häufig nur durch geringfügige Abweichungen unterscheidenden Maitrāyaṇī-Schule wohl die am Frühesten fixierte YV-Tradition.[16] Der fragmentarische Zustand des Kanons beider Schulen ist deshalb umso mehr zu bedauern. Für die Kaṭhas erklärt er sich wohl aus der mangelnden Pflege dieses Veda in mittelalterlichen Verbreitungsgebiet dieser Śākhā im westlichen Nordindien und in Kaschmir, was durch die islamischen Eroberungen und das Vordringen des Weißen Yajurveda[17] mitbewirkt wurde. In der dieser Periode vorausgehenden Zeit war die Kaṭha-Schule seit dem Ende der vedischen Epoche in ganz Nordindien weitverbreitet; ihr eigentliches Ursprungsgebiet läßt sich aber aufgrund von Aussagen der Saṁhitā enger auf das östliche Panjāb eingrenzen.[18] In dieser Gegend standen die Kaṭhas, besonders auch ihre Zweigschule, die Kapiṣṭhalas, in enger, durch das Zusammenwirken beim Ritual und auch durch geographische Nachbarschaft bedingter Verbindung mit der Kauthuma-Schule des Sāmaveda.[19] Die enge Beziehung beider Schulen zeigt sich nun auch in dem bisher einzigen Zitat aus dem KaṭhĀ in einem anderen vedischen Text, dem Anupada-Sūtra,[20] - sieht man vom Sonderfall des ĀpŚS ab, das viele Bestimmungen der Kaṭhas gerade auch im Pravargya-Praśna zitiert ohne ihre Quelle zu nennen.[21]

Inhalt und Alter des KaṭhĀ

Wie in den andern Āraṇyakas des Yajurveda so macht auch im KaṭhĀ die Behandlung des Pravargya-Rituals den Kern des Textes aus. Ob sich wie in verwandten Texten, besonders aber in den Āraṇyakas des RV, den Mantras und der dazugehörigen Erläuterung des Mahāvrata bzw. Pravargya noch weitere, heterogene Textstücke anschlossen, ist eine vorläufig noch nicht mit Sicherheit zu beantwortende Frage, da das einzige erhaltene Manuskript des KaṭhĀ am Ende unvollständig ist. Vielleicht war die Śikṣā-Upanisad als der den Abschluß des Veda-Studiums bildende Text angefügt.[22] Solange keine vollständige Handschrift gefunden ist, läßt sich nur Folgendes mit einiger Sicherheit sagen: Das KaṭhĀ muß aus drei Teilen[23] bestanden haben:

KaṭhĀ I, einer Sammlung der *Mantras* des Pravargya-Rituals (nur fragmentarisch erhalten)

KaṭhĀ II, dem *Yuñjate-Brāhmaṇa*, das den eigentlichen Pravargya-Ritus 'theologisch' erläutert und

KaṭhĀ III, dem *Gharmājaṭharā-Brāhmaṇa*[24] mit ausführlichen Nachträgen und Sonderbestimmungen.

Diese Gliederung entspricht nicht ganz dem, was man aufgrund der verwandten Texte (TĀ IV-V, ŚB XIV, MS IV 9) erwarten würde. In TĀ und ŚB ist das Pravargya-Ritual nämlich in weitgehend dem Gang des Opfers folgender Weise mit Hilfe der in den YV-Saṁhitās, den Brāhmaṇas und Āraṇyakas üblichen magischen Identifizierungstechnik[25] 'theologisch' begründet und erläutert. Hier aber wird in gleicher Weise zunächst nur ein vollständiges Pravargya-Ritual vom Herstellen des Glutkessels bis zum Agnihotra, Zusammensetzen des Gharmakessels und Auslegen der zum Pravargya gehörenden Geräte behandelt, ohne nur auch mit einem Wort auf die Zugehörigkeit des Pravargya-Ritus zum Soma-Opfer einzugehen.[26] Hier liegt ein deutlicher Hinweis auf den oft angenommenen ursprünglich selbständigen Charakter dieses alten, schon im RV angedeuteten Milchopfers an die Aśvin vor, insbesondere dann, wenn dieser Teil des KaṭhĀ ein gegenüber den entsprechenden Abschnitten von TĀ und ŚB höheres Alter beanspruchen könnte. Im Falle des ŚB läßt sich diese Frage sicher positiv beantworten,[27] aber auch das Pravargya-Brāhmaṇa des TĀ trägt deutliche Züge später Abfassung, so die oft recht schematishen Identifikationen[28] und etwa auch das gedankenlose Kopieren von TS VI 4,9 in TĀ V 1,1-7.[29] Auch die Behandlung der zur magischen Begründung herangezogenen mythologischen oder ad hoc erfundenen bzw. variierten aitiologischen Legenden bekräftigt diese Hypothese: Während nämlich sowohl TĀ als auch ŚB in bereits recht systematisierender Weise die gesamte Erzählung, die von der Erlangung des Geheimnisses des Dadhyañc durch die Aśvin und dem darauf folgenden Wiederansetzen des Kopfes des Opfers durch sie berichtet, zu Beginn der Behandlung des Pravargya als Ganzes anführen, um das gesamte Pravargya-Ritual (als integrierten Bestandteil des Soma-Opfers) magisch zu begründen, so benutzt KaṭhĀ lediglich Teile der Legende[30] dort, wo es zur Erläuterung gerade angebracht ist, variiert diese selbständig nach Bedarf und ist, obwohl es sich ebenfalls bisweilen eng an die Saṁhitā anlehnt,[31] doch viel eigenständiger als TĀ. Kennzeichnend ist auch, daß komplizierte theologische Zielsetzungen in diesem Brāhmaṇa-Abschnitt (KaṭhĀ II) noch nicht auftreten: Neben den üblichen Opferwünschen ist lediglich von Regengewinnung[32] und an einer nicht recht deutlichen Stelle[33] von der 'Himmelsgestalt' die Rede, die der Opferherr offensichtlich durch die Darbringung des Pravargya gewinnen soll. Weitergehende Spekulationen über den Sinn und den Effekt des Pravargya-Rituals finden sich erst in KaṭhĀ III, dem Gharmājaṭharā-Brāhmaṇa.[34]

In KaṭhĀ II, dem Yuñjate-Brāhmaṇa, liegt demnach wohl einer der alten Teile des Kanons der Kaṭhas vor, der - weil zu den magisch gefährlichsten Riten gehörig[35] - nur auf freiem Feld, in der Wildnis (*araṇya*) gelernt werden durfte.[36] Eigentlich könnte dieser Abschnitt mit der Saṁhitā gleichaltrig sein,[36a] insbesondere da er ein altes Ritual beschreibt bzw. erläutert und auch die genaue Reihenfolge der einzelnen Bestandteile des Kanons lange Zeit nicht absolut fest war, hat aber wohl durch seine Stellung in der Erlernung der Texte - kurz vor Abschluß des Vedastudiums - und weil er schließlich nicht in die Saṁhitā aufgenommen wurde (anders als in MS: dies ist sicher der Optionalität des Ritus zuzuschreiben), längere Zeit Modernisierungen und Zusätzen offengestanden als die relativ früh fixierte Saṁhitā. Dadurch dürfte sich wohl auch die früheste[37] in einem vedischen Text belegte Nennung von vier Veden in KaṭhĀ II 117 erklären, während sonst die Dreizahl der heiligen Texte auch im KaṭhĀ mehrfach erscheint. Zeichnet sich KaṭhĀ II - vom letztgenannten Fall vielleicht abgesehen - gegenüber den verwandten Texten mehrfach durch größere Altertümlichkeit aus, so erscheint das Pravargya-Ritual in KaṭhĀ III bereits voll in die Feier des Soma-Opfers eingegliedert. Ferner bietet dieser Abschnitt viel Neues, das sonst erst aus den Sūtras bekannt ist. M. 146-149 etwa sind in fast gleichlautender Form nur im Agnihotra des ĀpŚS belegt, dort aber eine der häufigen Übernahmen aus dem Ritual der Kaṭhas.[38] Daß diese Mantras aber ihre alte Stelle im Pravargya-Ritus haben, beweist eine Bestimmung des VādhS, nach der mit einem fast gleichlautenden Spruch der Glutkessel mit der Zange umfaßt und hochgehoben werden soll.[39] Beziehen sich also die genannten Sprüche auf ein Ritualdetail, das bereits in KaṭhĀ II, M. 74ff. hätte behandelt werden sollen,[40] so enthält auch der Rest von KaṭhĀ III deutliche Nachträge:

III 150 Agnihotra (?)
151-154 Udvāsana und Auslegen der beim Pravargya benutzten Utensilien (in Sonnengestalt?)[41]
155-156 Avāntaradīkṣā, die sog. 'Zwischenweihe'
157-158 Rauhiṇa-Kuchen beim morgendlichen bzw. abendlichen Pravargya
159-168 Uttaraśānti (mit deutlichem Hinweis auf das Lehren des Textes in 167-168)
169-170 Vārṣāhara-Sāman
170 a.E. -172 Dadhigharma
173 Allsühnespenden(?)[42]
174-198 Udvāsana (mit Auslegen der Geräte in Menschengestalt, in 183a)
198 a.E. - 226 Avāntaradīkṣā, davon:

199a-207	Beginn der Uttaraśānti
207 a. E.	Erörterungen, wann der Pravargya zu vollziehen ist,
208a-214	Beginn der Pūrvakaśānti
215-219	vier Abschnitte der Uttaraśānti
219 a.A,	besondere Observanzen bei der Avāntaradīkṣā
219 Mitte:	Bestimmungen über das Lernen des Pravargya-Textes
219 a. E.	Auslegen (?) der Pravargya-Utensilien in Kopfgestalt
219m-226	ein Teil der Pūrvakaśānti
226-229	Avakāśa-Mantras
229 a.E.-231	Sāman des Adhvaryu
232-233	Sonderbestimmungen über den Pravargya am Kelterungstag und bei den Cāturmāsyas
233 a.E.-234	Solos des Prastotar[43] (*parisāmāni*)
235-239	Prāyaścittas für Störungen beim Pravargya-Ritual
239a-240	Erörterungen über das Zusammentragen der für den Pravargya-Ritus benötigen Utensilien und den Beginn des eigentlichen Rituals,

ganz am Ende des dort nur noch sehr fragmentarisch erhaltenen Textes. Zum ersten Mal in einem Brāhmaṇatext belegt oder doch ausführlich behandelt sind hier vor allem die verschiedenen Arten der Auslegung von beim Pravargya benutzten Gefäßen und Utensilien, die Zwischenweihe, das Sāman des Adhvaryu, die Parisāmāni und einige der Prāyaścittas. Die Darstellung dieser Ritualdetails scheint den letzten großen Nachtrag zur Behandlung des Pravargya gebildet zu haben, der auch schon rein äußerlich von den ersten Nachträgen (III 146-172) dadurch abgesetzt ist, daß mit III 173 der dritte (und eventuell noch folgende)[44] Anuvāka von KaṭhĀ III beginnt. Auch stilistisch unterscheidet sich KaṭhĀ III [Anuvāka] 3 (ff.) von den vorausgehenden Abschnitten durch häufig breitere, sich dem Stil der Anubrāhmaṇas der Vādhūla-Schule nähernde Darstellung.[45]

Das KaṭhĀ ist also eine bedeutende Quelle für das vedische Ritual, aber nicht allein für dieses.[46] Umso bedauerlicher ist es, daß dieser Text nur recht fragmentarisch erhalten ist und der unkritische, wegen der Arbeiten an der KS recht flüchtig hergestellte und häufig unvollständige Abdruck L. v. Schroeders zudem noch an recht versteckter Stelle publiziert worden ist,[47] so daß er weitgehend unbekannt geblieben ist.[48]

Die Handschriften; phonetische Eigentümlichkeiten des Textes

Der überwiegende Teil des KaṭhĀ liegt nur in einer[49] sehr zerstörten und am Ende unvollständigen, aber recht alten Handschrift vor. Es handelt sich um die letzten noch erhaltenen Blätter eines von Sir M. Aurel Stein 1894 in Srinagar gekauften, in Śāradāschrift auf Birkenrinde geschriebenen Ṛcaka, das er der Tübinger Universitätsbibliothek schenkte: Es trägt dort die Signatur MaI 396, Heft 10a und b. Die das KaṭhĀ enthaltenen Blätter tragen jeweils auf der Vorderseite in der linken unteren Ecke unter der Abkürzung des Titels[50] die originale einheimische Seitenzahl: fol. 337b - 357b. Davon sind nur die ersten drei Blätter leidlich erhalten; der Rest, d.h. Heft 10b, besteht nurmehr aus Fragmenten, bei denen jeweils das obere Drittel abgebrochen ist; die letzten drei Folio sind noch mehr zerstört, und am Ende fehlt mindestens ein Blatt.[51]

Das Alter der Handschrift läßt sich wegen des fehlenden Kolophon nicht ohne Weiteres feststellen. Daß der Text auf Birkenrinde geschrieben wurde, deutet jedoch bereits auf höheres Alter: nach Bühler soll Papier in Kaschmir erst um 1600 eingeführt worden sein, jedoch ist das von Baron v. Hügel schon 1836 nach Wien mitgebrachte Ṛcaka der Wiener Nationalbibliothek[52] erst 1675/76 n. Chr. datiert. - Einige Eigentümlichkeiten der Schrift des Tübinger Manuskriptes, so z.B. die Bezeichnung der Vokale,[53] zeigen aber, daß dieses Ṛcaka in der Übergangszeit zur rezenten Form der Śāradāschrift kopiert wurde. Deshalb ist - wie auch für das Manuskript des Kaschmirischen Atharvaveda der Paippalāda-Schule, das (15)19 n.Chr. datiert ist,[54] eine Niederschrift um 1500 n. Chr. anzunehmen.[55]

Außer dem Tübinger Ṛcaka (T), das vor Allem KaṭhĀ II und III enthält, standen für die Textkonstitution folgende Handschriften zur Verfügung, die allerdings jeweils nur Teile des Mantra-Abschnittes (KaṭhĀ I) enthalten: Ms. Tübingen MaI 396, fol. 274a-284b (t^1), ein Teil des o.a. Ṛcaka (T), der leider fast genau so zerstört ist, akzentuiert (aber nicht bei allen Mantras); - Paris, Nationalbibliothek, Ms. dév. 230, p. 304-317, in moderner Śāradā auf Papier geschrieben, ohne Akzente, datiert (17)80 n. Chr. (bzw. evtl. 1880); - Paris, Ms. dév. 227b, fol. 10 ff., in jüngerer Śāradā auf verschiedenfarbigem groben Countrypaper geschrieben, mit Akzentresten; - die Edition des Laugākṣi-Gṛhyasūtra durch M.S. Kaul, Vol. II p. 52-91 (leider ohne Lesarten, aber mit Devapālas Kommentar zu den Mantras).

Die Ähnlichkeit gewisser Akṣaras bzw. Ligaturen der Śāradā miteinander bringt, besonders in den jüngeren Manuskripten, viele Schreibfehler, andererseits aber auch Verlesungen mit sich. Einige der häufigeren sind die folgenden:

> *m* wechselt mit *s*, *ta* mit u, *rdh/rv/b*, *bhv/ty*, *br/vr*, *nt/tt/rt/tu*, *nv/rv*, *b/v*, *d/c*, *ru/t/ḍ*, *kt/ku*, *rth/u-*, *ṣṭh/ṣṭ/ṣy*, *yu/a-*, *tha/ṣa*, *bdh/bv*, *r*+Kons./*n*+Kons., *nn/tr;* *ṣṭh* und *ṣṭ* haben ein Zeichen gemeinsam.

Andere Fehler in den Hss. beruhen auf der lokalen Aussprache von Kaschmir. So wechseln insbesondere *e* mit *i/ī*, *o* mit *u/ū*, Konsonant + *va* mit Konsonant + *u* und umgekehrt. Vor *-r-* erscheinende Konsonanten werden häufig verdoppelt.[56] Viele der übrigen, anscheinend orthographischen Eigentümlichkeiten dieser und anderer älterer kaschmirischer Veda-handschriften repräsentieren dagegen eine gegenüber den meisten, erst aus den letzten Jahrhunderten stammenden Veda-Manuskripten und vor Allem gegenüber den danach oder nach den Schreibgewohnheiten des klassischen Sanskrit normalisierten Editionen ältere Aussprache. So ist recht häufig, wie auch im Kaschmirischen RV- und Paippalāda-Manuskript, Anunāsika (m̐) und nicht Anusvāra *(ṃ)* vor *ś*, *ṣ*, *s*, und *ḥ* geschrieben, gelegentlich auch vor *y*, *r*, und *v*, was für die Kaṭha-Schule als authentisch zu gelten hat.[57] Ob hier ursprünglich die Lautgruppe *m̐vv*, *m̐yy* vorlag, ist noch nicht mit Sicherheit zu beantworten.[58]

Altertümlich ist auch die häufig noch durchgeführte Schreibung von homorganem Nasal vor Verschlußlaut anstelle der bequemeren jüngeren mit Anusvāra, die sich im vorliegenden Manuskript aber auch schon häufig findet. Stets ist dagegen noch anstelle des in den Editionen üblicherweise durchgeführten Visarga (*ḥ*) die durch den folgenden Laut jeweils geforderte phonetische Variante geschrieben: Jihvāmūlīya ẖ [*x*] vor stimmlosen Velaren, Upadhmānīya h̭ [φ] vor stimmlosen Labialen; vor stimmlosen 'Palatalen' *ś*, vor *ś*, *ṣ*, *s* der jeweils assimilierte Zischlaut, vor stimmlosen Dentalen *s*, und vor stimmlosen 'Zerebralen' *ṣ*. Lediglich im absoluten Auslaut erscheint Visarga *ḥ*.[59]

Bisher in seiner Bedeutung nicht beachtet worden ist die konstante Schreibung *śch* für klass. Skt. *cch*, das aber in RV und MS-Handschriften als *ch* geschrieben wird,[60] und - wie die Metrik zeigt - als Konsonanten*gruppe* gesprochen wurde. Nun kann die kaschmirische Schreibung *śch* nicht auf rezenter lokaler Aussprache beruhen, da heute *c* als *[ts]* und *ch* als *[tsh]* d.h. aspiriertes *[ts]* ausgesprochen wird. Da aber andererseits die Gruppe *śch* in vielen Fällen ein idg. *sk'* repräsentiert, dürfte die übliche Erklärung als Schreibfehler (*cch*𑆖𑇀𑆗 > *śch* 𑆯𑇀𑆗) wohl auszuschließen sein.[61]

Bisher überhaupt nicht beachtet wurde das Auftreten von sogenanntem ṛgvedischen *-ḷ-* statt *-ḍ-* in Texten der Kaṭha-Schule,[62] die in der Śāradā deutlich durch ein diakritisches Zeichen voneinander geschieden sind: *ḍ* : *ḷ*. Da *-ḷ-* nun nicht allein in RV-Zitaten sondern häufig statt zwischenvokalischem *-ḍ-* auch in den Brāhmaṇapartien erscheint, hat man gegen das Zeugnis der gedruckten Ausgaben auch für die Kaṭha-Schule mit *-ḷ-* und *-ḷh-* zu rechnen.[63] Diese Laute hatten offensichtlich eine nicht nur auf den Dialekt der Diaskeuasten des RV beschränkte Verbreitung.[64] Auch in einem weiteren Punkt ist die Schreibung des Manuskriptes leider nicht konstant: Wie im RV so erscheint auch im KaṭhĀ häufig unkontrahiertes *ṛ-* nach auslautendem *-a*, oft aber auch schon die jüngere Form *-a r-*, ebenfalls ohne Unterschied in der Verteilung sowohl in Mantra- als auch in Prosapartien.[65]

Die genannten Altertümlichkeiten der Schreibung sind in der vorliegenden Ausgabe noch nicht normalisiert worden, weder nach der vedischen noch nach der klassischen Norm, sondern erscheinen in der Form, in der die Handschrift sie bietet. Als Lesehilfe wurde lediglich - neben der Interpunktion - der Avagraha durchgeführt, der im Ms. nur drei Mal erscheint.

Das Akzentuierungssystem des KaṭhĀ dagegen wurde in der Edition nicht reproduziert sondern hier wurde in der üblichen Weise normalisiert. In den Anmerkungen und Lesarten allerdings wurde, wo zum Verständnis nötig, jedes Akzentzeichen notiert. - Die Bezeichnungen der Akzente im Ms. entsprechen genau denen der akzentuierten Abschnitte der KS, die in verschiedenen Ṛcakas erhalten sind: Anudātta = ˌ senkrechter Strich unter dem betreffenden Akṣara, Udātta ˈ senkrechter Strich über dem Akṣara, abhängiger Svarita = . Punkt unter dem Akṣara, unabhängiger Svarita vor betonter Silbe = Haken unter dem Akṣara, vor unbetonter Silbe dagegen ausnahmslos Haken über dem Akṣara.[66]

Zur vorliegenden Edition

Der fragmentarische Charakter des einzigen zur Verfügung stehenden Manuskriptes, das den größeren Teil des Textes enthält, bedingte eine genaue Darstellung der zerstörten Partien und auch der Zeilen oder Akṣaras, von denen nur die obere odere untere Hälfte oder noch weniger erhalten ist. **In der Edition** sind derartige Stellen (und überhaupt unsichere Lesungen) in Schrägschrift [ursprünglich, in der Edition von 1974, mit Anführungszeichen " " unter den betreffenden Buchstaben] gekennzeichnet. Die ungefähre Zahl von abgebrochenen Akṣaras bzw. von Ligaturen ist durch **x** angedeutet, gelegentlich ein nicht erhaltenes Vokalzeichen als ə dargestellt, insbesondere wenn der zugehörige Akzent noch erkennbar war. In eckigen Klammern [ ] stehender Text ist nach Parallelstellen oder auch frei ergänzt, ergibt sich aber häufig mit großer Sicherheit durch die 'Zwangsläufigkeit' des Brāhmaṇastils.[67] Für die ersten, meist abgebrochenen Zeilen einer Seite des Manuskriptes wurde stets [...] eingesetzt, um das Ausmaß des fehlenden Textes zu veranschaulichen; dabei entspricht eine Zeile der Edition etwa einer halben des Originals.

Nur aus Gründen der Zweckmäßigkeit sind Mantras und Praiṣas - allerdings nicht mehr ganz konsequent - durchnummeriert: Da nämlich die Originaluntergliederung des Textes nur sporadisch erhalten ist,[68] dürfte Zitieren nach Mantranummer am Zweckmäßigsten sein - auch für die sich jeweils an die Mantras anschließenden Brāhmaṇa-Erläuterungen - also etwa KaṭhĀ III 207; für genaueres Zitieren empfiehlt sich aber vielleicht die Angabe von Seite und Zeile. In KaṭhĀ II und III sind die Mantras und Praiṣas durch Fettdruck [ursprünglich, in der Edition von 1974, durch Unterstreichung __] hervorgehoben; im Mantra-Abschnitt KaṭhĀ I allerdings weist Fettdruck [bzw. die ursprüngliche Unterstreichung] darauf hin, ob und wie weit der betreffende Mantra auch in den Brāhmaṇas (II und III) erhaltenist, die dann zu vergleichen sind.

Im **Lesartenapparat** wurde eine noch genauere Darstellung der beschädigten Textpartien versucht, die bei der Mehrdeutigkeit von (halb)abgebrochenen Akṣaras freilich das Faksimile nicht ersetzen kann. Schrägschrift [bzw. ursprünglich, in der Edition von 1974, Unterstreichung mit _] bezeichnet einen halb oder fast vollständig abgeblätterten Akṣara, dessen Lesung unsicher ist. Das Zeichen **x** tritt an die Stelle eines vollständig zerstörten Akṣara oder für die obere Hälfte einer Ligatur ein, während für die untere **z** erscheint. Text in runden Klammern ( ) war auf dem zur Verfügung stehenden Film des Tübinger Manuskriptes nicht lesbar: Diese Stellen sind nach Ankunft der Handschrift 1895 bereits von R. v. Roth notdürftig mit relativ undurchsichtigem Klebstreifen überklebt worden, um das Manuskript vor dem weiteren Zerfall zu schützen. In diesen Fällen wurde L. v. Schroeders Lesung (nur innerhalb der Klammern) eingesetzt, die sich bei Kontrolle der Handschrift im Sommer 1972 dann auch meist als richtig erwies.

T bezeichnet die Lesart der Haupthandschrift (Tüb. MaI 396) (KaṭhĀ II und III), **S** die Lesung L. v. Schroeders in seinem Abdruck des Textes, insoweit diese vom konstituierten Text oder von T abweicht. *S* ist deshalb - bis auf wenige Fälle, in denen das Ms. seit 1898 weiter zerstört wurde - *ohne* textkritischen Wert. Die Sigle **t1** bezeichnet die Lesarten des Mantra-Abschnittes (KaṭhĀ I) im Tübinger Ms. MaI 396, fol. 274a-284b, **P** die des Ms. Paris dév. 230, **P2** die des Ms. Paris 227b, **L** die des Laugākṣi-Gṛhyasūtra.

In der **Übersetzung**, die möglichst wörtlich die Idiomatik des Originals wiedergibt, wurden nicht im Text des Sanskrit-Originals erscheinende, aber für das Verständnis wichtige Wörter in runden Klammern ( ) hinzugefügt; dies soll selbstverständlich nicht eine Erklärung aller Eigenheiten des Textes (wie der magischen Identifikationen, aller Ritualdetails usw.) leisten, was dem hier nicht publizierten Kommentar vorbehalten ist. Eckige Klammern [ ] geben auch hier möglichst genau den Erhaltungszustand des Textes wieder.

Da vom KaṭhĀ im Wesentlichen nur eine fortlaufende Handschrift (T) vorliegt, ergaben sich für die **Textkonstitution** einige Schwierigkeiten, wenn auch die Manuskripte des Mantra-Kapitels in einigen Fällen eine willkommene Kontrolle von T boten bzw. der Text sich danach ergänzen ließ.[69] Obwohl sich T durchweg als recht zuverlässig erwiesen hat,[70] mußten in dieser Situation doch in vermehrtem Maße die verwandten Texte herangezogen werden, d.h. für die Mantras TĀ IV, MS IV 9, ŚB XIV bzw. VS XXXVII-XLIX und für die Brāhmaṇas TĀ V und ŚB XIV, auch wenn hier durch die größere Originalität insbesondere von KaṭhĀ III gewisse Grenzen gesetzt waren. Ferner waren die den Pravargya behandelnden Sūtren zu vergleichen.[71] Mit Hilfe dieser Texte, ferner mit den heute zur Verfügung stehenden Hilfsmitteln wie Bloomfields Vedic Concordance und Viśva Bandhus Vedic Word Concordance, häufig auch aufgrund der Zwangsläufigkeit des Brāhmaṇastils, konnte eine größere Anzahl von zerstörten Partien ergänzt werden.[72] Insbesondere für die Mantras konnte versucht werden, die authentische Form[73] festzustellen und sie von der originalen, soweit erschließbar, zu scheiden.

Abschließend ist es mir eine angenehme Pflicht, den Verwaltungen der Bibliothèque Nationale in Paris und der Universitätsbibliothek Tübingen für die mir zur Verfügung gestellten Mikrofilme bzw. Manuskripte zu danken. Herzlich danken möchte ich auch Herrn Dr. A. Parpola, der mir freundlicherweise ausführlich zu zwei das Ritual des Sāmaveda betreffenden Stellen[74] geschrieben und einige Verbesserungen vorgeschlagen hat, die noch im Manuskript für den vorliegenden Teildruck durchgeführt werden konnten,[75] und Herrn Dr. B.K. Deambi, der mir aufgrund seiner umfassenden Kenntnis der Paläographie der Śāradā bei einem Aufenthalt in Hoshiarpur wertvolle Hinweise geben konnte. Besonderer Dank aber gilt meinem verehrten Lehrer, Herrn Prof. Dr. K. Hoffmann, der die Arbeit an den Fragmenten der Kaṭha-Schule auch angeregt hat, für in reichem Maße gewährte Belehrung und stete Förderung, mit denen er die Arbeit an der vorliegenden Dissertation[76] begleitet hat.

Svayaṃbhūnāth
Kāṭhmāṇḍū
17. Juli 1973

Nachtrag

Der vorliegende Teildruck sollte aufgrund von lange vorliegenden festen Zusagen in Indien gedruckt werden. Nachdem aber das betreffende Institut plötzlich doch kurzfristig ablehnte, musste das Druckmanuskript in wenigen Tagen neugeschrieben werden, um die Ablieferungsfrist einzuhalten: Dies wurde weitgehend von Paljor Thondup und Vimla Lama besorgt. Es bleibt zu hoffen, daß bei der Kontrolle des Druckmanuskriptes in der Kürze der zur Verfügung stehenden Zeit keine Schreibfehler u. dgl. übersehen wurden.

Kāṭhmāṇḍū, 1.7.1974
M.W.

1) Kāṭhakam (oder Kāṭhaka-Saṁhitā), ed. L. v. SCHROEDER, Leipzig 1900-1912; ed. SĀTVALEKAR, Aundh 1943; - zur Literatur s. RENOU, *Ecoles védiques*, p.144f., 150ff. und insbesondere der vollständige Literaturnachweis bei TSUJI, *Genzon Yajurveda Bunken* (Existent Yajurveda Literature), Toyo Bunko Ronso, Ser. A, Vol. LII, Tokyo 1970, p.51, 151 Anm. 476. - Die nur in wenigen Punkten vom Wortlaut der KS abweichende Kapiṣṭhala-(Kaṭha)-Saṁhitā ist ediert von RAGHU VIRA, Lahore 1932, reprint Delhi 1968 (mit neuer Paginierung!); zur Lit. s. RENOU, *op. cit.* p.154 f., TSUJI, *op. cit.* p.54, 159 A. 519.

2) Kaṭhopaniṣad, die bekanntlich auf einen der Kaṭha-Abschnitte (cf. Anm.7) des TB III 10 zurückgeht, s. RENOU, *op.cit.* p.197 mit Lit., TSUJI *op.cit.* p.52, 154 A. 491 zu den zahlreichen Ed. und Übersetzungen.

3) Kāṭhaka-Gṛhyasūtra, ed. CALAND, Lahore 1925, derselbe Text ed. M.S. KAUL, Bombay 1928-34 als Laugākṣi-GS; s. TSUJI p. 53, 157.

4) VIŚVABANDHU ŚĀSTRĪ, Lahore 1935; wichtig zur Kontrolle des nur in einer vollst. Handschrift vorliegenden Textes der KS (cf. RENOU *op.cit.* p. 151); eine weitere umfangreiche KS-Hs. im VVRI, Hoshiarpur; - zur Lit. s. TSUJI, *op.cit.* p. 51, 153 A. 487.

5) Ed. JOLLY, Bibl. Ind. 1881, repr. Chowkhamba; übersetzt von JOLLY, SBE VII; zum Verhältnis Viṣṇu-Smṛti : Kaṭhaschule s. RENOU, *op.cit.* p.194 m. Lit., TSUJI *op.cit.* p.158 f.

6) einen Eindruck von einem Ṛcaka vermittelt die allerdings schwer zugängliche *Vaidikamantrakalpalatā*, ed. Pt. VIŚVANĀTH, Srinagar 1913, wenn auch dort die einzelnen Teile in recht willkürlicher Anordnung erscheinen. Weiteres bei SCHROEDER, insbes. SB Wien 1898: Die Tüb. Kaṭha-Handschriften...; der Charakter der Ṛcakas ist z.T. wohl mißverstanden bei RENOU, *op.cit.* p.15 f., 141, 153; s. auch TSUJI, *op.cit.* p. 154, A.488; - mir sind bisher bekannt Ṛcakas in; Berlin, Preuß. Staatsbibl. (im Krieg z.T. verloren gegangen), Univ. Bibl. Tübingen, Nat. Bibl. Wien (dort wurde keine Verfilmung erlaubt), Nat. Bibl. Paris, Oxford (Sammlung Stein: Ind. Inst. Libr.), VVRI Hoshiarpur (wo die Verwaltung mir mit dankenswerter Aufgeschlossenheit erlaubte, Mikrofilme herzustellen), Deccan College Poona (jetzt in: BORI, Poona), Akhila Bharatiya Sanskrit Parishad in Lucknow; - in der Prov. Audh gab es noch vor 90 Jahren ca. Tausend Mss. dieser Gattung: s. Cat. of Skt. Mss. for the year 1882-90, by Pt. Devi Prasad, Allahabad 1883-93; einige davon müssen in Bibliotheksbesitz in Uttar Pradesh übergegangen sein (so z.B. in Lucknow, nicht aber in Allahabad); - Ṛcakas ferner auch in Lahore, Univ. Bibl.; - für weitere Nachweise wäre

ich dankbar (cf. Anm. 13a); - zu den Ṛcakas vgl. auch TSUJI, *op.cit.* p.154 A. 488.

7) Bereits der indischen Tradition ist bekannt, daß Teile des KaṭhB (richtiger z.T. wohl: des KapB!) in das TB (III 10-12) und das TĀ (I-II) übernommen wurden: die sog. *aṣṭau kāṭhakāni*; zur Berechtigung dieser Tradition s. SCHROEDER, SB Wien 1898, vgl. auch SB Wien 1895, ZDMG 49; - vgl. RENOU, op. cit. p.146, 174 (BaudhŚS), 177 und TSUJI *op.cit.* p.52, 154 A. 488, 490. - Zu dem KaṭhB (KapB)-Fragment (= TB III 12) in der Hs. der KpS, s. ed. KpS repr. p. XIX; - Teile des KaṭhB sind abgedruckt von SCHROEDER, SB Wien 1898, SB Wien 1895; Weiteres von CALAND, Verslagen en mededeelingen der koninklijke Akademie van Wetenschappen, Amsterdam 1920; Einiges Neue auch bei SŪRYAKĀNTA, Kāṭhakasaṃkalanam, Lahore 1943 (wo allerdings meist CALAND nachgedruckt wurde).

8) ein unkritischer, oft unvollständiger und leider wegen der im Vordergrund stehenden Arbeiten an der KS recht flüchtiger Abdruck durch L. v. SCHROEDER, SB Wien 1898, p.92-120, wo das KaṭhĀ sich unter einer Menge von KaṭhB-Fragmenten findet.

9) in verschiedenen Ṛcakas erhalten, z.B. Paris, dév. 230, Tübingen MaI 396; abgedruckt aber auch schon in Laugākṣi-GS, Vol. II, p.92ff. mit Kommentar des Devapāla (auch zu den Mantras, was bei CALAND nicht gedruckt wurde). Diese Fragmente entsprechen weitgehend TU I 1.4.11.12; deshalb möchte diese Up. in Anlehnung auch an die Benennungen in einigen Mss. und an TU I als Kaṭha-Śikṣā-Up. bezeichnen; die Up. ist ohne Akzente überliefert, aber durch Devapālas Komm. abgesichert.

10) ein noch Devayajñika vorliegendes Werk von 39 Adhyāyas; Zitate aus seiner Paddhati, handschr. schon von WEBER gesammelt, ed. v. RAGHU VIRA, Oriental College Patrika, Lahore 1928; nachgedruckt und vervollständigt durch SŪRYAKĀNTA, Kaṭhakasaṃkalanam; weitere Fragmente des Sūtra ed. von RAGHU VIRA, JVS 2 p.104 ff., CALAND Ind. Ahnencult, p.212, cf. p.65 ff.; cf. ferner CALANDs zahlreiche Hinweise in seiner Ed. des KGS und die Rekonstruktionen N. TSUJIs (al. FUKUSHIMA) in Comm. Vol. of the Science of Religion, Tokyo, Imperial Univ. (Tōdai) 1934 und Brāhmaṇa to Śrautasūtra to no kankei (On the relation between Brāhmaṇas and Śrautasūtras) Tōkyō 1952 (engl. Zus. p.185 ff.); s. auch op. cit. p.156 (Ex.YV-Lit.).

11) teilweise ediert v. CALAND, Anhang zum KGS; das dort erhaltene Hochzeitslied (Sarasvatyanuvāka) wird von den Vādhūlas vorgeschrieben: AO VI 158 f., AO VII 305 f.

12) s. bereits CALAND zum Piṇḍapitṛyajña, Ai. Ahnencult, p. 212; KASHIKAR, Survey of Śrautrasūtras p.108.

13) s. TSUJI, op. cit. p.52, 157 A.500.

14) s. CALAND, KGS p.272; TSUJI, *op.cit.* p.157 A.499; - zum Paribhāṣā-S. s. CALAND, ed. KGS p.61 und cf. Baroda Alph. List, Vol. I p.158 f. No.148.

15) zur Unterscheidung vom Kauṣītaki-Ār. (KĀ) möchte ich diese etwas umständliche Abkürzung vorschlagen.

15a) zunächst ist eine Edition aller Brāhmaṇa-Fragmente vorgesehen (die über das von SŪRYAKĀNTA Gebotene hinausgeht); dann sollen die Fragmente des Śrautasūtra und der übrigen Ritualwerke, auch wichtiger Kommentare, folgen. Deshalb bin ich für Nachweise weiterer Kaṭha-Mss. (cf. Anm. 6) und auch von Zitaten in anderen Texten (insbes. auch Pūrvamīmāṁsā-Werken!) dankbar.

16) zur Gruppe MS/KS (*Caraka-Saṁhitā) cf. RENOU, *Ec. véd.* p.144, TSUJI *YV-Lit.* p.4 f., 36 f. - TS zeigt linguistisch einige jüngere Züge (anders KEITH, Introd. zur Übers. p. XCIII, s. aber XCV!; - zweifelnd RENOU, Ec. véd. p.144, positiv aber über die Mantras von MS/KS p. 152 A.1); - ferner ist TS schon bedeutend systematischer und knapper: lange Erzählungen von MS/KS sind auf wenige Sätze reduziert, - ein Verhältnis, das auch zwischen JB und PB vorliegt. MS, wohl die älteste YV-Saṁhitā, und KS zeigen schon durch einen auch nur oberflächlichen Inhaltsvergleich, daß beide Schulen eine lange Zeit gemeinsamer Entwicklung gehabt haben müssen (cf. noch Pāṇini: *kaṭhakalāpa-*), ehe sie sich schließlich in verschiedener Weise weiterentwickelten.

17) einige epigraphische Belege bei RENOU, *Ec. véd.* p.203 und ausführlicher: Festschrift S. Varma; vgl. Yajurveda-vṛkṣa, *JVS* 2; - Mādhyandinīyas bereits 641 n.Chr. in Gujarāt, dem Stammgebiet der Maitr. in den letzten beiden Jahrtausenden (*Ind. Ant.* 1886, p. 343); ihre rasche Ausbreitung ist wohl - wie in vielen ähnlich gelagerten Fällen - der Protektion der Guptas mit zuzuschreiben.

18) KS XXIII 8 : 54,12 *tasmād āpaḥ pratīcīr bhūyiṣṭhā dhāvanti* "Deshalb laufen die Wasser nach Westen am Stärksten": In Nordindien trifft dies nur auf den Oberlauf der Satlej (*Śutudrī*) und einige rechte Nebenflüsse (Bein mit Zuflüssen) und den Unterlauf der Ghaggar (Sarsuti, ved. *Sarasvatī* im Oberlauf) mit dem linken Nebenfluß Chautang (*Dṛṣadvatī*) zu, d.h. das Gebiet zwischen den Vorbergen des Himalaya im Norden, der Beās (*Vipāś*) bzw. d. parallel fließenden Black Bein im Westen, der Wüste (*maru*) im Süden und der Wasserscheide zur *Yamunā* im Osten, - auf ein Gebiet also, das auch *kurukṣetra*, das "hl. Land" der Saṁhitās, miteinschließt. Dort findet sich auch der Ort Kaiṭhal, den bereits RAGHU VIRA und SŪRYAKĀNTA auf ein **kapiṣṭhala-* zurückführen: eines der

häufigeren Zeugnisse für Ortsnamen, die auf der Bezeichnung vedischer Schulen beruhen, vgl. z.B. wohl auch: Vārāhī in Nordgujarāt (die Vāraha-Schule siedelt nach dem Yajurvedavṛkṣa in der Wüste: *marudeśe*) und Pip(pi)lī in Orissa, wo sich ja tatsächlich noch heute Paippalādins finden. - Kaṭhas und Kapiṣṭhalas (Καθαιοι, Καμβισθολοι) werden bekanntlich auch von den klass. Autoren im östlichen bzw. südlichen Panjāb lokalisiert (zum Stand der Forschung s. *Paulys Realencyclopädie d. klass. Alt.* [2512]); cf. evtl. auch Kaṭhāna, Ort ca. 30 km südl. v. Kaiṭhal und Kaṭhúā, Ort am oberen Ravī, östl. v. Jammū.

19) s. jetzt PARPOLA, LŚS-Übers. Bd.I p.91; weiter hinzuzufügen ist nun auch das *śārga*-Sāman, das im KaṭhĀ III 233 die Namensform der Kauthumas hat, während Rāṇāyanīyas und die Jaiminīyas *śārṅga* haben.

20) s. PARPOLA, loc.cit. Vol.I 2, p.106 ff., der dieses Zitat wegen der auch hier unvollständigen Ausgabe SCHROEDERs nicht verifizieren konnte: III 234 steht in einer gespaltenen Zeile und ist deshalb ausgelassen!

21) s. CALANDs häufige Verweise in seiner ĀpŚS-Übers.; direkt mit Namensnennung zitiert werden die Kaṭhas nur zweimal (s. GARBE, ed. Vol.III p.XVIII f.; zum zweiten Fall, den Kāṭhaka-Cāturmāsyas, s. CALAND ĀpŚS-Übers. XIX 15,7, Anm. 3, die CALAND in KS nicht nachweisen konnte, s. jetzt die Bestimmungen in KaṭhĀ III 233: fol.355b a.A.! - cf. auch RENOU, *Ec. véd.* p. 177.

22) CALAND, *Versl.* 1920, schreibt einige der dort von ihm veröffentlichten Brāhmaṇa-Stücke dem Āraṇyaka zu; vgl. ferner seine zahlreichen Verweise in der Ed. d. KGS, z.B. p.256. Eine weitere Ergänzung des vorliegenden Textes ist wohl bei genauer Durchsicht aller Ṛcakas zu erwarten: Zufällig fand sich z.B. ein Stück von KaṭhĀ III 199 in der Hs. Par. dév. 230 und erwies sich durch Überschneidungen mit dem erhaltenen Text von Tüb. MaI 396 als dorthin gehörig. - Vielleicht enthält auch der Kasten IV mit Fragmenten des Tübinger Ms. MaI 396 noch hierher zu Stellendes: Eine Kontrolle war mir bisher aus zeitl. oder nun aus örtl. Gründen nicht möglich.

23) vorausgesetzt wird der Mantra-Abschnitt nämlich durch die Bezeichnung des mit *yuñjate manaḥ* beginnenden Abschnittes als *prathama- anuvāka-* in Ms. Paris dév. 230. Die Kaṭhas begannen ihr Āraṇyaka (oder jedenfalls doch das Mantra-Kapitel des Pravargya) also nicht wie TĀ IV mit der Pūrvakā Śāntiḥ sondern stehen hier der Tradition der Maitrāyaṇīyas näher, welche die Śāntis erst am Ende des Mantra-Abschnittes folgen läßt. - Da das gesamte Mantrakapitel des KaṭhĀ vorläufig noch nicht vollständig zu rekonstruieren ist, werden im vorliegenden Teildruck nur die Partien gegeben, die sich in Paddhatis zum Śukriya-Vrata

fanden, vgl. Vorbemerkung zum Mantra-Abschnitt (KaṭhĀ I).

24) Diese Bezeichnung ist im Ms. nicht belegt, da kein Kolophon erhalten ist; sie wurde aufgrund der z.B. für KaṭhĀ II und zahlreiche in den Ṛcakas belegte Benennungen von Abschnitten der KS nach dem Anfangswort (bei Mantra- u. Brāhmaṇa-Abschnitten) durchgeführt, vgl. etwa KS I 1 iṣetvorjetveti-brāhmaṇa(!), X 5 pāṭhikṛtam, XXXVII 11 rāṣṭrabhṛd-brāhmaṇa usw.

25) siehe S. SCHAYER, Die Struktur der magischen Weltanschauung nach dem Atharvaveda und den Brāhmaṇatexten, *Zeitschr. f. Buddh.* 1925, u.: Die Weltanschauung der Brāhmaṇatexte, *RO* 2, 1924.

26) Selbst in den Sūtren ist - vom späten VaikhŚS abgesehen - der Pravargya noch als selbständige Einheit behandelt, auch wenn er, wie es ja in den Sūtren selbst bestimmt wird, Teil des Soma-Rituals sein soll. - In KaṭhĀ fehlt aber z.B. die ganze komplizierte Erörterung von TĀ V 2,2 (ĀpŚS XV 1,2 usw.), die aber vielleicht am Ende des erhaltenen Textes (III 239a, und frgm. f. 357 b) nachgetragen ist. Selbst das Udvāsana ist nicht in KaṭhĀ II, sondern nach allerlei Einschüben (III 146-73) erst in KaṭhĀ III,3 in enger Anlehnung an das Soma-Opfer beschrieben und erläutert. (Ein Hinweis auf die Verbindung mit dem Soma-Opfer liegt aber vielleicht in KaṭhĀ II 137, im Mantra selbst vor: *sunvate* 'dem (Soma) Pressenden'.

27) man denke etwa nur an den Gebrauch des Perfekts als Erzähltempus, das m.W. in der Kaṭha-Schule nur in einigen Teilen des KaṭhB durchgedrungen ist, z.B. in dem Kaṭha-Abschnitt = TB III 10,11 (Nāciketas-Legende), dem Kūṣmāṇḍa-Br. (SB Wien 1898 p.77 ff.); das Alter einiger Abschnitte des KaṭhB ist aber unsicher, cf. Anm.37.

28) hier hat der Redaktor bzw. Verfasser des Textes häufig sogar das übliche bekräftigende *vái* nicht (mehr) für nötig erachtet; vgl. ferner die Identifikationen von TĀ V mit entsprechenden von KaṭhĀ II.

29) wörtliche Übernahme aus der Saṁhitā trotz veränderten (Sinn- u.) Ritualzusammenhangs; beide Male erscheint der Aśvin-Becher statt des in TĀ zu erwartenden Gharmatrunkes, wie dann etwa auch KaṭhĀ II 115 richtig erzählt.

30) z.B. die in dieser Form sonst unbelegte Legende II 100: Kurzfassung in III 225; vgl. II 115 gegenüber KS XXVII 4 : 143,8 (kontrastiere: TĀ/TS in Anm. 29!).

31) etwa II 115 zur Erläuterung des Mantra = KS XXIV 4:43,20; die Erläuterung der Ritualistenfrage *prāśyā3 ná prāśyā3* in II 143 = KS XXIX 2; III 177 und 233 *upagāyanam* ... bis ... *hnuvate* = KS XXXIV 2:37,2; III 198 *daśākṣarā* ...

bis zum Absatz = KS XXI 10, a.A.: 49,23 ff.; III 198 *kiṃ* ... bis ... •*-dīkṣayā* = KS XXIV 9 a.E. - Zum *araṇye 'nuvākyo gaṇaḥ* vgl. KS XXI 10. - Einen engen Bezug zu einem andern Kaṭha-Text, dem in TĀ I 5,2 erhaltenen Abschnitt des KaṭhB, zeigt III 207, wo KaṭhĀ offensichtlich auf KaṭhB zurückgreift; cf. auch III 207 mit TĀ V 10; - ferner: III 219 a.A. *araṇyam paretya* ... = KaṭhB (Svādhyāya-Br.) SB Wien 1898, p.64; - ein Rückbezug innerhalb des KaṭhĀ selbst liegt in III 170 : II 128 vor; vgl. auch die Stilisierung der Legende III 229 gegenüber der in II 76 u. 79.

32) II 123; vgl. schon die Anspielung auf den Pravargya im Zusammenhang mit der Regenzeit im 'Froschlied' des RV.

33) *svargākṛti-* in II 143; leider ist hier auch *saṁsthiti-* nicht ganz deutlich, cf. z.B. auch CALAND zu *saṁsthā-* in AO VI p.184 No.69 (lies dort: ĀpŚS VII 23,7!). Ist die Bedeutung jeweils 'strikte Regel'? - cf. den Gebrauch von *sthiti-*, *sthita-* in VādhS, AO II p. 155: diese bezeichnen den Siddhānta nach einer Diskussion: belegt auch schon ŚBK und KB. [In Anlehnung an TĀ V 8.2 **svagákṛti-* zu edieren?]

34) dort [III 229] ist allem Anschein nach bereits vom Pravargya-(text) als Upaniṣad die Rede (zu dieser, mehr ritualistischen Bedeutung von Upaniṣad, vgl. VādhS AO VI p.153 No.41: *upaniṣadādānam anvākhyānam*, und den Beleg in ŚB X, dem Agnirahasya); - auf den Charakter der 'Pravargya-Upaniṣad' als Geheimlehre deutet auch III 167; mehr zur 'philosophischen' Seite des Begriffs neigt die Aussage III 219 *ápa punarm]ṛtyúm jayati, yá eváṃ véda.*

35) so die häufige Warnung vor dem glühenden Kessel, der mit Sonne und Rudra identifiziert wird.

36) s. OLDENBERG, *Kl. Schriften*, *araṇyaka*; vgl. III 219 u. III 155: araṇye 'nuvākyo gaṇaḥ (KS XXI 10); cf. I 4.

36a) anders RENOU, *Ec. véd.* p.140f. über das Pravargya-Ritual an sich; andererseits nimmt er p.149 *eine* ursprüngliche Āraṇyaka-Komposition für den gesamten YV an (die ja dann relativ frühen Datums sein müßte!): wohl wegen der von ihm vertretenen Meinung, TĀ und KaṭhĀ seien sich sehr ähnlich (was für KaṭhĀ II recht zweifelhaft, für KaṭhĀ III sicher nicht richtig ist). - Ein Maitrāyaṇī-Ār., das Ec.véd. p.149 Anm.1 erschlossen ist, wird p.157 (für dessen Brāhmaṇa-Teil) als existent hingestellt, ist m.W. aber nicht aufgefunden (nicht zu verwechseln mit der manchmal, so von SĀTVALEKAR, als Ār. bezeichneten Maitr.Up.!)

37) solange noch nicht sicher ist, ob einige der von SCHROEDER (SB Wien 1898, z.B. p.57 o.) und CALAND (*Versl.* 1920) beigebrachten Fragmente des KaṭhB, die ebenfalls *vier*

Veden nennen, wirklich schon dem Brāhmaṇa angehören, ob sie spät interpoliert sind, oder ob Teile (oder alle bekannten Stücke) des KaṭhB in Wirklichkeit Texte sind, die den Brāhmaṇa-Partien des ŚŚS, BŚS und insbesondere den Anvākhāyānas des VādhS vergleichbar sind, d.h. vielleicht erst zum verlorenen KaṭhŚS gehörten. Vielleicht gehören in diesen Zusammenhang die in der Tradition als Kaṭha-Unterschulen erscheinenden *upagranthas* der Kaṭha? (cf. RENOU, *Ec. véd.* p. 130).

38) s. CALAND zu ĀpŚS VI 21; RENOU *op.cit.* p.177, TSUJI, *YV-Lit.* p.160 A.519, GARBE ed. ĀpŚS p. XVIII A.1 (vol.III).

39) AO IV p.162 f.

40) wenn man nicht entweder eine Verwendung beim Agnihotra (III 150, wo die rituelle Anwendung aber auch nicht recht deutlich ist) annehmen oder gar anhand der Mantras III 146 ff. und III 170 a.E.-172 ein neues Dadhigharma-Ritual konstruieren will. - Solange das KaṭhŚS nicht vorliegt, ist eine Entscheidung nur schwer zu treffen, wegen des oft unpräzisen Charakters der Mantras (s. schon LINDNER bei RENOU, *Ec.véd.* p. 138 Anm.1).

41) sonst auch beim Dadhigharma verwendet ist III 154! Hier gilt das in Anm. 40 Gesagte ebenso. Eine weitere Anwendung in KS XXI 10.

42) so BŚS IX 12:282,7 vor dem Zusammensetzen der beim Pravargya benutzten Geräte: vgl. CALAND zu ĀpŚS XV 17,4.

43) oder nach den Akṣararesten des Ms. vielleicht vom Udgātar gesungen; allerdings kann hier *udgātar-* auch als umfassende Bezeichnung für die Sāman-singenden Priester verwendet worden sein; dies wäre für einen YV-Text nicht ungewöhnlich, cf. etwa auch *adhvaryū* 'die beiden Adhvaryu' (d.h. Adhvaryu und Pratiprasthātar) in den RV-Brāhmaṇas zum Pravargya.

44) Dem Inhalt nach wäre eigentlich nach III 240 nicht mehr viel zu erwarten: Die Sühnespenden sind bereits erläutert, dazu noch ein Abschnitt über das zu Beginn von Kaṭha II nicht behandelte Zusammentragen der außer dem Pravargyakessel benötigten Opfergeräte nachgetragen und ganz zum Schluß noch auf den Beginn der eigentlichen Pravargya-Zeremonie in der Opferhütte hingewiesen worden; jedoch deutet die Markierung des Abschnittes vor den letzten gerade noch erhaltenen Wörtern an, daß hier noch ein mehr oder weniger langes Stück folgte. Nach dem Aussehen der Hs. könnten hier noch ein (oder noch mehr als ein) Blatt gefolgt sein (hierhin wohl das Fragment der zwei Zeilen von f.357b bzw. 358), da deren linke Hälfte als erste Blätter von Heft 10b von MaI 396 noch erhalten ist. Die letzten Blätter können aber ebenso gut, wie in Ṛcakas allgemein üblich, allerlei Disparates, wie

etwa einen der häufigen Purāṇa-Auszüge oder selbst Gedichte enthalten haben, oder, was auch vorkommt, einfach unbeschrieben gelassen worden sein.

45) Zwischen beiden Schulen gibt es auch sonst Berührungspunkte, s.o. Anm. 11, 39; weiter viell. die Stellung von KaṭhB und der Brāhmaṇa-Abschnitte (Anvākhyānas) der Vādhūlas innerhalb der Entwicklung der Ritualprosa-Texte beider Schulen, vgl. ferner Anm.34.

46) zu Beachten ist neben Sprachlichem (wie unbelegten Mantras, neuen Wörtern wie z.B. *ādhi-*, bisher unbelegten Verbformen wie *ṛghyāsam*, neuen Komposita wie in III 146 -149, phonetischen Besonderheiten wie 'ṛgvedischem' *-ḷ-* und den besonderen Sandhiformen) insbesondere die schon häufigere Makrokosmos-Mikrokosmos-Identifikation und der damit erfolgende Übergang zu den Upaniṣads, vgl. auch *pravargyopaniṣad-* in III 229, *punarmṛtyu-* in III 219.

47) unter der Bezeichnung 'Kaṭha-Āraṇyaka' erscheint der Text nicht in den Bibliographien; in SCHROEDERs Ed. verbirgt er sich zusammen mit den Fragmenten des KaṭhB, langen Inhaltsangaben von Ṛcakas usw. hinter dem Titel "Die Tübinger Kaṭha-Handschriften und ihre Beziehung zum Taittirīya-Āraṇyaka".

48) trotz der häufigen Hinweise CALANDs in seiner Übersetzung des ĀpŚS (und dort gerade im Pravargya-Praśna!) und des PB und etwa RENOUs deutlichem Hinweis, *Ec. véd.* p. 152 §141 ist KaṭhĀ z.B. nicht in SŪRYAKĀNTAs Kāṭhaka-saṃkalanam aufgenommen, nicht in BLOOMFIELD-EDGERTONs *Vedic Variants* verwertet (s. RENOU *Ec. véd.* p.152) und in die *Vedic Concordance* aufgenommen und auch in der einzigen Darstellung des Pravargya trotz der Bedeutung, welche die Vidhi-Elemente in den Brāhmaṇas zur Erklärung der Sūtren spielen (s. CALAND, Übers. ĀpŚS Vol. I p.3 f., TSUJI, *On the Relation*, p. 193, RENOU *Ec. véd.* p.142) nicht erwähnt worden: J.A.B. van BUITENEN, *The Pravargya*, Poona 1968, beruht ohnehin weitgehend nur auf den Sūtren; nur in der Einleitung sind Brāhmaṇas über den Pravargya (eben mit Ausnahme des KaṭhĀ) zur Deutung der Natur des Pravargya-Rituals herangezogen.

49) nichts im neuen *Catalogus Catalogorum* von RAGHAVAN u. RAJA und in den mir bekannten Ṛcakas und Kaṭha-Hs.; die Bemerkung Bhagavad DATTAs in seiner History of Vedic Literature (*Vaidik vāṅmay kā itihās*), Lahore 1927 p.26, es gäbe im Dayanand Anglo-Indian College eine Hs. (No. 173), die diesen Text enthalte, ist irrig, wie mir im VVRI Hoshiarpur gesagt wurde: Die Hss. des DAV-Colleges seien nach der Teilung Indiens vollständig nach Hoshiarpur überführt worden und die mit No. 175 bez. Hs. (jetzt No. 6445) enthalte den Kāṭhaka-Teil des TĀ, übrigens eine

der häufigeren Verwechslungen der in Südindien z.T. noch als eigenen Text gerechneten *aṣṭau kāṭhakāni* mit dem KaṭhĀ (vgl. auch AUFRECHT, *Cat. Cat.* p. 89 b).

50) hier: *oṁ śu[kriya]brā[hmaṇam],* offensichtlich die Bezeichnung für das gesamte, den Pravargya erläuternde Brāhmaṇa und wohl auch für das Mantra-Kapitel, cf. den Beginn von KaṭhĀ I und der Śāntis mit: *oṁ śukriyam rudrasya*; auch der Veda-Vrata, mit dem das Ār. gelernt wird, heißt bei den Kaṭhas *śukriyavrata*. - Die Randmarke ist auf den letzten drei Bll. abgebrochen.

51) trotz der fehlenden Seitenzählung auf den letzten drei Blättern ergibt sich deren Anordnung anhand des Inhalts.

52) Dieses Ṛcaka gelangte als erstes seiner Gattung nach Europa, konnte aber bis heute der Forschung kaum zugänglich gemacht werden, was umso bedauerlicher ist, als es sich hier um ein fast vollständig erhaltenes, noch immer im alten Ledereinband, so wie in Kashmir bei Bhūrjatexten üblich, befindliches, recht altes Ms. handelt: Zuerst von RIEU in den *Ind. Stud.* I p.70 angezeigt, wurde es dreißig Jahre lang WEBER *nicht* zugänglich gemacht (s. *Mon. Ber. d. Preuß. Akad.* Berlin 1879 p.201 Anm.1), dann von BÜHLER wenigstens kurz beschrieben (ebenda, p.200-202), von SCHROEDER in der Akzentuation des dort enthaltenen Kap. KS XXXV näher untersucht (*ZDMG* 45 p.432-438) und für ihm für die Ed. der KS (nur für XXXV!) benutzt. Der Rest des ca. 500 fol. starken Ms. ist nie untersucht worden. Bei einem Aufenthalt in Wien konnte ich vor Jahren nur wenige Notizen machen; die Herstellung eines Mikrofilmes wurde von der Verwaltung der Handschriftenabteilung der Nat. Bibl. 'wegen der Brüchigkeit des Beschreibstoffes' leider 'untersagt.' Ähnlich scheint es schon CALAND in den Zwanziger Jahren gegangen zu sein (s. ed. KGS p. IV, 2. Abs.). Auch von dem von L. v. SCHROEDER SB Wien 1895 als W_1 beschriebenen Ms. ließ sich aus dem o.a. Grund kein Film herstellen: Es handelt sich um ein gut erhaltenes Papier-Ms.

53) relativ häufig die Schreibung von *-o-* und *-au-* mit einer Kombination aus übergesetztem waagerechten und rechts neben den Akṣara gesetzten halblangen senkrechten Strich: im Ms. sind von 571 *-o/au-* nur 112 in der später allein üblich gewordenen, über den Akṣara gesetzten Schwalbenform (*o*⁀, *au*⁀ı) geschrieben, d.h. etwa ein Fünftel (19,61%) aller erhaltenen Fälle, - während der Rest die ältere o.a. Form (*o* ¯ı, *au* =ı) hat. Auffällig ist dabei, daß im ersten Brāhmaṇa-Abschnitt, dem Yuñjate-Br., von 258 Fällen nur 39 in Schwalbenform erscheinen (d.h. 15,12%), während es im Gharmājaṭharā-Br. bereits 73 von 313 (d.h. 23,32%) sind.

54) in Kaschmir werden häufig die Zahlen für das Jahrhundert der Saptarṣi (oder Laukika-) Ära nicht geschrieben, s. z.B. das HÜGELsche Ṛcaka bei BÜHLER (s.o. Anm.52).

55) wie mir auch Dr. B.K. DEAMBI bestätigte, der eine demnächst erscheinende, auf zahlreichen Manuskripten und Inschriften beruhende Paläographie der Śāradā verfaßt hat.

56) zu Schreibfehlern und 'dialektischem Einfluß' s. bes. SCHEFTELOWITZ, *WKZM* 21.

57) vgl. SCHROEDERs Vorwort zur Ed. der KS (über die Berechtigung von *ṁy, ṁv* zweifelnd); im vorliegenden Ms. finden sich: II 11 *yajñiyaṁ yad*, III 219 *rūpaṁ yajūṁṣi*, III 183a *enaṁ rudro*, III 207 a. E. *nainaṁ rudro*; *ṁv* ist hier, soweit ich sehe, nicht belegt, mir aber aus andern Texten, etwa dem Kūṣmāṇḍa -Br. -Abschnitt des KaṭhB geläufig.

58) diese Schreibung erscheint, zu *ṃyy, ṃvv* vereinfacht, z.B. in dem jüngeren Ms. Par. dév. 230; vgl. zu III 199. Dagegen schreiben der Kaschmirische RV und die RVKh, die SCHEFTELOWITZ benutzt hat, noch *ṁyy, ṁvv*, während sich im selben Ms. in den sich an die Khilāni anschließenden Partien von AĀ III schon *ṃyy, ṃvv* findet (s. SCHEFTELOWITZ p. 167 Ed. RVKh.). Die weitgehende Übereinstimmung der Schreibungen und damit wohl auch der zugrundeliegenden Aussprache in den Kaschmir-Mss, von RV, RVKh, AĀ, AVP und der Kaṭha-Texte hat ihren Grund sicher darin, daß die kaschmirischen Brahmanen (wie auch die Maitr.-Moḍhas) Caturvedins waren und ihre Aussprachegewohnheiten (vom Yajurveda) auf alle von ihnen studierten Texte übertrugen. Auch sonst findet sich gegenseitige Beeinflussung in Aussprache (und Wiedergabe von Akzenten) bei in derselben Gegend zusammenlebenden Schulen verschiedener Veden. - Der Sandhi von *-m l-* ist nur als *ṃl* bzw. *ṃll* belegt, so z.B. II 103, 108a, 109, III 179, 199.

59) Visarga ist bisweilen offensichtlich Zeichen für Pausa, so z.B. in I 42-47; häufiger ist er bzw. seine Varianten (ḫ, ẖ) auch weggelassen oder sie sind untereinander verwechselt worden (II 108a, Lesart 3); in den Hss. der MS erscheint übrigens auch der Sandhi *-ś ś-* , *-ṣ ṣ-*, *-s s-*, ist aber von SCHROEDER in der Edition nicht durchgeführt worden (s. Vorwort zur Ed. MS, Bd.I p.XLII).

60) s. SCHROEDER, MS Bd. I p.XLIII No.2.

61) so SCHROEDER im Vorwort zur KS; zu Ausnahmen von der Schreibung *śch* s. SCHEFTELOWITZ, WKZM p.120 und z.B. die Regelung der Mss. in I.II 41-47. Zur Literatur über *śch* s. TSUJI, *YV-Lit.* p.153 Anm.483.

62) weder in SCHROEDERs noch in SĀTVALEKARs Editionen; nicht in SCHROEDERs, CALANDs, SŪRYAKĀNTAs Sammlungen von Kaṭha-

Texten; auch nicht in CALANDs Ed. des KGS; lediglich in der Ed. des Laugākṣi-GS findet sich bisweilen -ḷ.-

63) wenn es auch wie viele der phonetischen Eigentümlichkeiten nicht mehr ganz durchgehalten ist: -ḷ- z.B. in II 100, III 213,215,219,233; -ḍ- z.B. in: III 198; -ḍh- in III, 233 a.E, 235; -ḷh- ist nicht belegt und scheint seltsamerweise auch nicht durch diakritisches Zeichen von -ḍh- differenziert, was ja nahe gelegen hätte, Zu -ḷ- in KpS s. Ed. RAGHU VIRA, repr.p.XXIII.

64) bei Kāṇvas, Jaiminīyas (wo meist dravid. Einfluß angenommen wird), und wohl auch bei Kāpiṣṭhalas (Anm.63).

65) *-a ṛ-* z.B. in II [9], 71, 97, III [181], 195, [234]; *-a r-* in II 9, 75 etc. Es scheint kein Unterschied in der Behandlung des Sandhi zwischen Mantras und Brāhmaṇa zu bestehen; - der übliche Sandhi von auslautendem und anlautendem *-r r-* liegt einmal, in III 158, vor: *ketū rātrī.*

66) SCHROEDER setzt in der Ed. allerdings auch andere Zeichen; zum Akzentuierungssystem der Kaṭhas vgl. SCHROEDER SB Wien 1898 p.3 usw.; das Ms. hält sich ausnahmslos an die Unterscheidung von echtem (unabhängigem) Svarita vor unbetonter Silbe (Zeichen:̑) und vor betonter Silbe (Zeichen:̭). Ausnahme ist eventuell aber *tanvàṁ* in II 13 (cf. Lesart). Ferner findet sich dreimal die von SCHROEDER im Ms. W_1 bemerkte Devanāgarī-Zwei (bzw. ein Zeichen, das zufällig diese Form hat!), also nicht etwa die Śāradā-Zwei (s. SB Wien 1895 p.29), davon zweimal ebenfalls zur Bezeichnung des unabhängigen Svarita vor betonter Silbe (II 101, Anm.2: *pravargye sáṅ•* ; II 101, Anm.3 aber zusammen mit dem Haken und über der Zeile: *•gyāṁ sáṅ•*). Der dritte Fall ist unklar, s. III 207, Lesart 12 (viell. nur zur Bezeichnung des abhängigen Svarita). - Einmal findet sich ein Zeichen, das einer Devanagarī-Drei ähnlich sieht: Hier (II 133, Lesart 3) liegt Abhinihita-Sandhi vor, nicht aber Svarita, sondern Udātta: Es handelt sich wohl nur um das Avagraha-Zeichen. - Eine Śāradā-Drei wird als Zeichen für die Pluṭi benutzt, s. II 143 *prāśyā3,* III 231 *jyotī3r.*

67) Der Terminus ist von K. HOFFMANN geprägt worden; die Ergänzungen sind hier natürlich mehr oder weniger sicher. Solche, die *nur* geraten sind, wurden in den Lesarten gekennzeichnet und sollten nur als Diskussionsvorschlag gewertet werden. Ein Beispiel mag genügen: In III 219 a. A. ergänzte ich zunächst, sogar aufgrund der in Par. dév. 230 enthaltenen Stelle aus dem KaṭhŚS: *grắmād adṛ́ṣṭo 'gnim prájvalayati*; eine Parallele in KaṭhB (Svādhyāya-Br., SB Wien 1898 p. 64) beginnt ebenfalls: *áraṇyam parétya śúcau bhūmyāvakāśé grā́mād acchadírdarśe* (s. dazu *pw*, Bd. II p.286b) *svādhyāyám eváinam adhīyánn* ... und legt deshalb eine entsprechende Ergänzung nahe: Die zuerst ge-

gebene Rekonstruktion hätte zwar auch in den Kontext gehört, aber das Brāhmaṇa drückt sich hier knapper aus als KaṭhŚS, und damit wäre die Ergänzung verfehlt gewesen.

68) erhalten sind nur die Anuvāka-Zahlen 1,2,3 und 7 des Yuñjate-Br., und lediglich 1 und 2 des Gharmājāṭharā-Br., (cf. aber noch Lesart 2 zu III 189); ferner eine größere Zahl von Unterabschnitten, die aber im Gegensatz zu den Anuvākas den Sandhi nicht auflösen. (Ähnliche Untergliederung auch in KS, ebenfalls unnummeriert, von SCHROEDER durch Doppel-Daṇḍa dargestellt.)

69) bemerkenswert der Unterschied in II 6 *ā́ devy* : I 6 *prá devy*.

70) die meisten Schreibfehler beruhen - von Einflüssen der lokalen Aussprache abgesehen (wie Wechsel *e/ī* usw.) - auf 'Schreiberhaplologie': II 19,35; III 229, Lesart 5 ist wohl der krasseste Fall; ferner Umstellungen von Silben bzw. Lauten: II 133 Lesart 7, 134 Lesart 2.

71) s.o. Anm.48 zur Bedeutung eines ständigen Vergleiches von Brāhmaṇa- und Sūtra-Texten.

72) *alle* abgebrochenen Stellen, auch wenn noch einige Buchstabenreste, insbesondere bei Beginn einer Seite, vorhanden waren, ließen sich selbstverständlich nicht ergänzen; oft ist ja auch das gemeinte Ritual an der betreffenden Stelle nicht auszumachen, am Häufigsten in KaṭhĀ III, wo es meist keine Möglichkeit zum Vergleich verwandter Br.-Texte gibt. - Daß nicht alle Ergänzungen das Richtige getroffen haben, ist demnach nur zu erwarten, cf. oben, Anm.67.

75) zu den Termini s. K. HOFFMANN, *IIJ* XI p.4.

74) III 229c-231 und 233-234 (*parisāmāni*).

75) Vieles Andere, was ich gerne noch kontrolliert hätte, ließ sich wegen der großen Lücken an Fachliteratur (insbesondere europäischer u. amerikanischer) in örtlichen Bibliotheken nicht mehr nachprüfen.

76) umfaßt neben dem vorliegenden Teildruck auch eine ausführliche Einleitung zu den Texten und der Geschichte der Kaṭha-Schule u.sw., und einen Kommentar zum gesamten Text. - Es ist vorgesehen, diese Teile als zweiten Band folgen zu lassen.

Vorbemerkung zu KaṭhĀ I

Dieser Teil des KaṭhĀ ist nur fragmentarisch teilweise mit, teilweise ohne Akzente, bisweilen mit Satzsandhi, bisweilen mit Pausa nach einem Mantra in den Paddhatis zum Śukriyavrata überliefert. Als Ganzes wird nur der erste Anuvāka (I 1-47) mit Bezeichnung als *prathamo 'nuvākaḥ* überliefert, sonst nur auch auf den Vrata Bezügliches. - Eine Übersetzung wurde hier nicht gegeben, da die Mantras entweder auch in II u. III oder im RV vorkommen.

atha
kāṭhake śatādhyayane brāhmaṇa
āraṇyakaṃ

| atha śukriyamantrāḥ |

[NOTE on the order of the existent sections of KaṭhĀ I

I 1-47 :	*prathamo 'nuvākaḥ*
I 198.1-10 :	*prathamaḥ pratīkānuvākaḥ*
I 198.11-198.39	*uttamaḥ pratīkānuvākaḥ*
I 198a-199.2	*pūrvakā śāntiḥ*
I 208-214	section I
I 58-63	section II
I 64-73	section III
I 98a-101h	section IV
I 219m-226a	section V
I 199b-206	section VI
I 207	section VII
I 216-217	section VIII
I 218-218b	section IX
I 218c	section X
I 218d	section XI
I 218e-218g	section XII
I 219-219c	section XIII
I 219d-219l	section XIV = *uttarā śāntiḥ*]

[atha prathamo 'nuvākaḥ]

< oṁ | śukriyaṃ rudrasya || >

1 **yuñjáte mána**[1] utá yuñjate dhíyo
víprā víprasya bṛható vipaścítaḥ[2] |
ví hótrā dadhe vayunāvíd[3] ékā[4] ín
mahī́[5] devásya[6] savitúḥ páriṣṭutiḥ ||

2 **devásya vas savitúḥ prasavè**[2] 'śvínor[3] bāhúbhyām[4]
pūṣṇó hástābhyām[5] ādadhe;[6] nā́rīs stha |

3 **úttiṣṭha**[1] **brahmaṇaspate**[2] devayántas tvemahe[3] |

4 **úpa práyantu**[1] **marútas**[2] **sudā́nava,**[3] índra[4] prāśū́r
bhavā sácā |

5 **práitu**[1] **bráhmaṇaspátiḥ**

6 **prá**[1] **devy**[2] **ètu**[2] **sūnṛ́tā** |

7 **áśchā**[1] **vīrám**[2] **náryaṃ paṅktírādhasaṃ**[3]
devā́ yajñáṃ[4] nayantu naḥ ||

8 **dévī**[1] **dyāvāpṛthivī devayájané**[2] **'nu mé maṁsāthām**[3]

9 **ṛtásya**[1] **ṛdhyāsam**[1] **adyá**[2] **makhásya śíro**[3], makhā́ya
tvā, makhásya tvā śīrṣṇé[4] |

10 **íyaty ágra āsīr**[1], ṛtásya ṛdhyāsam adyá[2] makhásya[3]
śíro, makhā́ya tvā, makhásya tvā śīrṣṇé |

11 **dévīr**[1] **vamriyo**[1] **'syá bhūtásya**[2] **prathamajā** ṛtá-
sya ṛdhyāsam adyá makhásya śíro, makhā́ya tvā,
makhásya tvā śīrṣṇé |

12 **índrasyáujo**[1] **'sy**, ṛtásya[2] ṛdhyāsam adyá[3] makhá-
sya śíro, makhā́ya tvā, makhásya tvā śīrṣṇé |

13 **prajā́pates**[1] **tanū́r**[2] **asy**, ṛtásya ṛdhyāsam adyá[3]
makhásya śíro, makhā́ya tvā, makhásya tvā śīrṣṇé || ||

14 **mádhu tvā mádhunā karotu.**

15 **makhásya śíro 'si.**

16 **yajñásya padé sthaḥ** |

17 **gāyatrò[1] 'si,**
18 **tráiṣṭubho[1] 'si,**
19 **jágato 'si,**
20 **makhò 'si,**
21 **makhásya rásnāsi, |**
22 **sū́ryasya hárasā śraya[1],**
23 **vŕ̥ṣṇo[1] niṣpád asi [2] prājāpatyám[2],**
24 **devā́nān tvā pátnīr[1] vŕ̥ṣṇo áśvasya niṣpádā dhū-**
payantv.
25 **arcíṣe tvā, śocíṣe[1] tvā, hárase tvā ||**
26 **mitrásya carṣaṇīdhŕ̥taś**
[1]śravo devásya sānasí |
dyumnáṃ citráśravastamam ||
27 **devás tvā savitódvapatu[1]**
supāṇis svaṅguriḥ[2] |
subāhur uta śaktyā ||
28 **ávyathamānaḥ[1] pr̥thivyā́m[2] ā́śā díśa ā́pr̥ṇa |**
29 **úttiṣṭha, br̥hán[1] bhavordhvás tiṣṭha, dhruvás[2]**
tvám |
30 **idám ahám amúm āmuṣyāyaṇám amúṣyāḥ putrán téjasā**
brahmavarcaséna sámardhayāmī-
31 **-dám ahám amúm āmuṣyāyaṇám amúṣyāḥ[1] putrán[2] té-**
jasā brahmayarcaséna vyàrdhayāmī-
32 **-dám ahám amúm āmuṣyāyaṇám amúṣyāḥ[1] putrám ójasā**
vīryèṇa sámardhayāmī-
33 **-dám ahám amúm āmuṣyāyaṇám amúṣyāḥ[1] putrám ójasā**
vīryèṇa vyàrdhayāmī-
34 **-dám ahám amúm āmuṣyāyaṇám amúṣyāḥ[1] putrám ūrjá**
paśúbhis sámardhayāmī-
35 **-dám ahám amúm āmuṣyāyaṇám amúṣyāḥ[1] putrám ūrjá**
paśúbhir vyàrdhayāmī-
36 **-dám ahám mā́n[1] téjasā brahmavarcasénáujasā vīr-**
yèṇa prajáyā paśúbhir annā́dyena sámardhayāmy.
37 **r̥jáve tvā, sādháve tvā, sukṣityái tvā.**

38 **sū́ryasya tvā cakṣuṣā́nvīkṣe ||**
39 **śchṛṇáttu[1] tvā vā́k.**
40 **śchṛṇáttu[1] tvórk.**
41 **śchṛṇáttu tvā páyaḥ.[2]**
42 **śchṛṇáttu tvā́ rásaḥ.**
43 **śchṛṇáttu tvā havíḥ.**
44 **śchṛṇáttu tvā sómaḥ.**
45 **śchṛṇáttu tvā yajñā́ḥ .**
46 **śchṛṇáttu tvā bráhma.[1]**
47 **śchṛṇáttu tvā prajā́patiḥ. | 1 |**

[iti prathamo 'nuvākas samāptaḥ]

Die folgenden Anuvākas wurden wohl von den in KaṭhĀ II und III enthaltenen Mantras 48-98, 101i-145, 146-154, 157-158, 167-197, 227-240a gebildet. Daran an schlossen sich wahrscheinlich der *prathamaḥ pratīkānuvākaḥ* (198.1-10), der *uttamaḥ pratīkānuvākaḥ* (198.11-39), die *pūrvakā śāntiḥ* (Teil I = 208-214, II = 58-63, III = 64-73, IV = 98a-101h, V = 219m-226a), und die *uttarā śāntiḥ* an (Teil VI = 199a-206, VII = 207 = 159-166b, VIII = 216-217, IX = 218-218b, X = 218c, XI = 218d = z.T. 215, XII = 218e-218g, XIII = 219-219c, XIV = 219d-219l). - Die hier nach den beiden *pratīkānuvākas* angeführten Vrata-Sprüche waren vielleicht in KaṭhĀ I an diese Stelle gesetzt; dies kann jedoch nicht mit Sicherheit festgestellt werden. Sie erscheinen in KaṭhĀ III zweimal, als 155-156 und in 198a-199.

[atha daśarcaḫ prathamaḫ pratīkānuvakaḥ]

< oṃ | śukriyaṃ rudrasya | >|
198.1 **úd u tyáñ jātávedasam**[1]
devám̐ vahanti ketávaḥ |
dṛśé víśvāya sū́ryam ||1||
198.2 imam ū ṣu[1] tvam asmabhyaṃ[2]
saniṅ gāyatraṃ[3] navīyāṃsam[4] |
agne[5] deveṣu pravocāt[6] ||2||
198.3 sám indra[1] no mánasā[2] néṣi[3] góbhis
sám sūribhir[4] harivas[4] sám̐ svastyā́ |
sám bráhmaṇā devákṛtaṃ[5] yád[6] ásti
sám̐[7] devā́nāṃ sumatyā́ yajñíyānām ||3||
198.4 sám̐ várcasā páyasā[1] sán tanū́bhir[2]
aganmahi mánasā sám̐[3] śivéna[3] |
tváṣṭā[4] sudátro vídadhātu rāyó[5]
'nu no mārṣṭu tanvò yád víliṣṭam ||4||
198.5 [1]anv agnir uṣasām agram[1] akhyad
anv ahāni prathamo jātavedāḥ |
anu sūryasya purutrā ca[2] raśmīn[3]
anu[4] dyāvāpṛthivī ātatantha ||5||
198.6 yā́ vā́ṅ[1] káśā mádhumaty[2]
áśvinā sunṛ́tāvatī |
táyā[3] yajñám̐[4] mimikṣatam[5] ||6||
198.7 dhātā́ dadhātu no rayím[1]
ī́śāno[2] jágatas[3] pátiḥ |
sá[4] naḫ[5] pūrṇéna vāvanat ||7||
198.8 dhātā́ prajā́nām[1] utá rāyá[2] īśiṣe[3]
dhā́tédaṃ víśvaṃ bhúvanam[4] jajāna |
sán dāśúṣe kirati bhū́ri[5] vāmám[6]
vayám̐ syāma[7] pátayo rayīṇā́m ||8||
198.9 trayastriṃśat[1] tantavo[2] yān vitanvata[3]
imaṃ yajñaṃ[4] svadhayā ye dadante[5] |

teṣāṃ[6] śchidraṃ[7] pratidadhmo[8] yad atra
svāhāyaṃ[9] yajño[10] apy etu devān ||9||
198.10 idáṃ víṣṇur vícakrāme[1]
tredhā́ nídadhe padám |
sámūḍham[2] asya pāṃsuré ||10||

[iti prathamaḫ pratīkānuvākas samāptaḥ]

[athaikonatriṃśadarca uttamaḫ pratīkānuvākaḥ]

198.11 < oṁ | śukriyaṃ rudrasya || >
mā́ no gharmó[2] vyathitó[9] vivyathó no[3]
mā́ naḫ [4]páram ádharam áhruto[4] naiḥ |
mò[5] ṣv asmā́ṁs[6] támasy antarā́dhā
mā́ rudríyāso abhíkurvato[8] naḥ ||1||
198.12 mā́ naẖ krátubhir īḷate[1] 'bhidvíṣo[2]
asmā́n súnīte mā́ párādāḥ |
mā́ no agnín[4] nírṛtin[5] mó[6] árātin[7]
mā́ no dyā́vāpṛthivī́ héḷate héḷayethām[9] ||2||
198.13 ánu[1] no[2] mitrā́váruṇā ihā́vatām
ánvādī́dhyānā[3] abhí nas sákhāyau[4] |
ādityā́nām[5] [6]prásṛtir[7] hetír[8] ugrā́[9]
śivā́ kā́ṣṭā[6] havíṣaḫ[10] pári no vṛṇaktu ||3||
198.14 vidhún dadrāṇáṃ[1] sámane[2] bahūnā́ṃ
yúvānaṃ[3] sántaṃ palitó jagāra |
devásya paśyá kā́vyam mahitvā́-
-dyā́m[4] mamā́ra sá hyás sámānaḥ ||4||
198.15 oṁ bhūs svāhā ||5||
198.16 oṁ bhuvas svāhā ||6||
198.17 oṁ svas svāhā ||7||
198.18 oṁ bhūr bhuvas svas svāhā ||8||
198.19 úd u tyáṃ[1] jātávedasaṃ[2]
deváṃ vahanti ketávaḥ |
dṛśé víśvāya sū́ryam ||9||

198.20 úd vayán támasas pári[1]
jyótiṣ[2] páśyanta[2] úttaram |
deván devatrā́ sū́ryam
áganma jyótir uttamám || 10 ||
198.21 úd u tiṣṭha svadharā́va[1] no devyā́[2] kṛpā́ |
dṛṣé ca bhāsā́ bṛhatā́ suśúkvabhir[3]
agné yāhi suśastíbhiḥ[4] ||11||
198.22 ūrdhvá ū ṣú ṇa ūtáye
tíṣṭha devó na savitā́ |
ūrdhvó vā́jasya[1] sánitā
yád añjíbhir vāghádbhir[2] vihváyāmahe[3] ||12||
198.23 púnar[1] ūrjā́[1] nívartasva[2]
púnar agna iṣā́yuṣā |
púnar naḫ pāhy áṁhasaḥ[3] ||13||
198.24 sahá rayyā́ nívartasvā-[1]
-gne pínvasva dhā́rayā |
viśvápsnyā viśvátas pári ||14||
198.25 dhātā́ dadhātu[1] no[2] rayím[2]
ī́śāno jágatas pátiḥ |
sá naḫ pūrṇéna vāvanat ||15||
198.26 dhātā́[1] prajā́nām[1] utá rāyā́[2] īśiṣe[3]
dhātédáṃ[4] víśvaṃ bhúvanaṃ jajāna |
sán[5] dāśúṣe[5] kirati[6] bhū́ri[7] vāmáṃ[7]
vayáṁ syāma pátayo rayīṇā́m ||16||
198.27 ágna ā́yūṃṣi[1] pavasa
ā́suvórjam íṣañ ca naḥ |
āré bādhasva duśchúnām ||17||
198.28 ágne[1] pávasva[1] svápā[2]
asmé várcas suvī́ryam[3] |
dádhad rayíṃ máyi póṣam ||18||
198.29 tvā́n[1] no[1] agne[1] váruṇasya vidvā́n
devásya héḷo 'váyāsisīṣṭhāḥ |
yájiṣṭho váhnitamaś śóśucāno[2]
víśvā dvéṣāṁṣi[3] prámumugdhy asmát ||19||

198.30 [1]sá[2] tván no agne[1] 'vāmó[3] bhavotī́
nédiṣṭho asyā́ uṣáso vyùṣṭau[4] |
ávayakṣva no váruṇaṁ[5] rárāṇo
vīhí mṛḍīkáṁ suhávo na edhi ||20||
198.31 vāyúr[1] agregā́[1] yajñaprī́s
sā́kaṅ[2] gan[2] mánasā yajñám
śivó niyúdbhiś śivā́bhiḥ || 21 ||
198.32 prá yā́bhir yā́si dāśvā́ṃsam[1] áschā
niyúdbhir vāya iṣṭáye[2] duroṇé[3] |[3]
ní nó[4] rayím subhójasaṃ[5] yuvasva[6]
ní[7] vīrā́ṅ gávyam áśvyañ[8] ca rā́dhaḥ ||22||
198.33 < [1]hiraṇyagarbha iti sapta[1] >
hiraṇyagarbhaḥ ||23||
198.34 yaḥ prāṇato ||24||
198.35 ya ojodā ||25||
198.36 yena dyaur ugrā ||26||
198.37 ya ime dyāvā ||27||
198.38 yasyeme viśve ||28||
198.39 yáṅ[1] krándasī ávasā[2] tastabhāné[3]
abhyáikṣetāṃ[4] mánasā[5] réjamāne |
yátrā́dhi sū́ra údito vibhā́ti
kásmai[6] devā́ya[7] havíṣā vidhema ||29||

[ity uttamaḥ pratīkānuvākas samāptaḥ]

198a **agne[1] vratapate[2]**, samrāḷ[3] asi, vratapā asi, vratabhṛd[4] asi, vratapatir asi, vratam ālabhe; [5]tat te prabravīmi,[5] tac[6] chakeyam, tena rdhyāsam.[7] ||
pṛthivī samit; tām[8] agnis[8] samindhe, tām ahaṃ samindhe;[9] sā mā samiddhā, suṣamiddhā[10] tejasā varcasā yaśasā brahmavarcasena[11] samindhyāt.[12] ||

198b **vāyo[1] vratapate**, samrāḷ asi, vratapā asi, vratabhṛd asi, vratapatir asi, vratam ālabhe; tat

te prabravīmi, tac chakeyam, tena ṛdhyāsam. ||
antarikṣaṃ[2] **samit**; tāṃ vāyus[3] samindhe, tām aham
samindhe;[4] sā mā samiddhā,[5] suṣamiddhā[6] tejasā
varcasā yaśasā brahmavarcasena samindhyāt.[7] ||

199 **sūrya**[1] **vratapate,**[1] samrāḷ asi, vratapā asi, vrata-
bhṛd asi, vratapatir asi, vratam ālabhe; tat te
prabravīmi, tac chakeyaṃ, tena ṛdhyāsam. ||
dyaus[1] **samit;**[1] tāṃ sūryaṃ samindhe, tām ahaṃ
samindhe;[2] sā mā samiddhā, suṣamiddhā[3] tejasā
varcasā brahmavarcasena[4] samindhyāt.[5] ||

199.1 dyaus samit ... [1] ... samindhyāt[2] ||
antarikṣaṃ[3] samit ... samindhyāt ||
pṛthivī[3] samit ... samindhyāt ||

199.2 sūrya vratapate, samrāḷ asi, vratapā asi, vrata-
bhṛd[1] asi,[1] vratapatir asi, vratam acāriṣam;[2]
tad aśakaṃ,[3] tat te prabrūmas, tan no gopāya.[4] ||
vāyo[4] vratapate[4] ... gopāya. ||
agne[4] vratapate[4] ... gopāya. ||

[atha pūrvakā śāntiḥ]

(I) < oṁ | śukriyaṃ rudrasya || >

208 [1]**<bhū́r bhúvas svàr>**[1] **námo vācé, námo vācáspá-
taye.**[2]

208b yā vāg uditā yā cānuditā, tasyai vāce namaḥ.[1] |

208c nama ṛṣibhyo mantrakṛdbhyo mantravidbhyo,

208d mā mām ṛṣayo mantrakṛto mantravidaḥ[1] parādur.

208e daivīṃ[1] vācam udyāsaṃ,

209 **śivā́m**[1] **ájasrām,**[1]

210 juṣṭām[1] devebhyas,[2]

211 **svadhā́vatīm**[1] **pitṛ́bhyaś,**[2]

212 **śuśruṣeṇyā́m**[1] **manuṣyèbhyas,**[2]

213 **tā́m**[1] **mā**[1] **devā́**[1] **avantu śobhā́yai, pitáro 'numa-
dantu.**[2]

214 **sucakṣā́[1] ahám akṣíbhyām̐, suvárcā múkhena, suśrút[2]**
kárṇābhyām[3] bhūyāsam;[4] bhūr[5] bhuvas svaḥ. || ||

(II)

58 **[1]prā́cyā tvā diśā́gnínā devátayā gāyatréṇa śchán-**
dasā[2] vasantám ṛtúm práviśāmi.[1,3]
59 **dakṣiṇā́yā tvā diśéndreṇa devátayā tráiṣṭubhena**
śchándasā grīṣmám ṛtúm práviśāmi.
60 **pratī́cyā[1] tvā diśā́ savitrā́[2] devátayā[3] jā́gatena[4]**
śchándasā[5] varṣā́ ṛtúm[6] práviśāmy.
61 **údīcyā[1] tvā diśā́[2] mitrā́váruṇābhyān[3] devátayā́nu-**
ṣṭubhena[4] śchándasā śarádam ṛtúm[5] práviśāmy.
62 **[1]ūrdhvā́yā tvā diśā́ bṛ́haspátinā[1] devátayā[2] pā́ṅk-**
tena śchándasā hemantám[3] ṛtúm práviśāmy.[4]
63 **anā́yā tvā diśā́[1] prajā́patinā[2] devátayānāptena[2]**
śchándasā śíśiram ṛtúm práviśāmi.[1] || ||

(III)

64 **gāyatrī́m chándah̭[1] prā́viśāmi.[2]**
65 **triṣṭúbham[1] chándah̭[1] prā́viśāmi.[2]**
66 **jā́gatīm[1] chándah̭[2] prā́viśāmi.**
67 **anuṣṭúbham[1] chándah̭[1] prā́viśāmi.**
67a **paṅktím[1] chándah̭[1] prā́viśāmi.[2]**
68 **átiśchandasam[1] chándah̭[2] prā́viśāmi.[2]**
69 **śchándāṁsi[1] prā́viśāmi.[1]**
70 **tā́ni[1] nah̭[1] pārayantu,[2] tā́ni no[3] 'vantu.[4]**
71 **tā́ni sá ṛśchatu, yò[1] 'smā́n dvéṣṭi, yā́ñ ca vayám[2]**
dviṣmáḥ.[3]
72 **ā́po[1] asmā́n[2] prā́viśantv,[3] ā́po[4] asmā́su[5] jāgṛta.[6]**
73 **ā́yur viśvā́yur[1] víśvam ā́yur[2] vyàśnavai; [3]sárvam**
ā́yur vyàśnavai.[3] || ||

(IV)

98a divyo[1] gandharvo bhuvanasya yas patir
ekāvyo manasā vikṣv īḍyaḥ[2] |
98c tan tvā yāmi brahmaṇā deva[3] daivyam[3]
99 namas te astu (99) **diví te sadhástham** |

100 **diví pṛṣṭó[1] yajatás[2] sūryatvág**
avayātā[3] haraso[4] divyasya |
ekāvyo manuṣyas suśevo[5]
mṛḷād gandharvo bhuvanasya yas patir ||
101 **anavadyā́bhis[1] sámajagmābhír[2]**
101a **apsarassv[1] api gandharva āsīt** |[2]
101b **samudrá āsā̃m[1] sádanaṃ va āhus**
101c tatas[1] sadhry[2] ā[2] ca[2] parā ca caranti[3] ||
101d abhriye[1] didhyun nakṣatriye[2]
101e yā[1] viśvāvasuṃ[2] gandharvaṃ[3] sasadhre[4] |
101f tābhyo namo[1] astu, tā no mṛḷayantu[2]
101g tā naś śarma[1] yaśchantu,[2] tā[3] yan[4] dviṣmo
101h yaś ca no dveṣṭi, tam āsāṃ[1] jambhe[2] da-
dhmaḥ || ||

(V)
219m āhus[1] te bhaga cakṣuṣī
[2]tābhyāṃ vipaśya mām abhi[2] |
220 [1]yad etat sāragham[2] madhu[3]
tena rūpam **anajmi te**[1] |
téna rūpám anagdhi[4] **me**[5] ||[5]

220a devasya tvā savituḥ[1] prasave[2] 'śvinor bāhubhyām pūṣṇo[3]
hastābhyām[4]
220b **devā́nāṃ krátubhir devābhyañjanáir** abhyàñje;[1]
bhágavan[1] **nā́māsi.**
221 **tásya[1] ta[1] ṛ́caś[1] ca yájūṁṣi[2] ca sā́māni ca.**
222 [1]**vā́g agnā́ anyác,[2] cákṣus sū́rye 'nyát; sū́rye 'n-
yád. [3]agnā́ anyád; agnā́ anyád, agnā́ anyád.**[3,1]
223 **bhágavān[1] bhūyāsam.**[2] |[2]
224 **airò[1] 'si,[1] cákṣur asi, śrótram asi, purándhir[2]
nā́ma[3] vā́g[4] asi.**[4]
225 **yéna śatákratur bhāgám upajuhvé,
téna tvópahvaye,[1] bhaga.**[2] ||[2]
226 **tád[1] vān[2] narā[3]** sanā́ye[2a] dáṃsa[4] ugrám[5]
āvíṣkṛṇomi tanyatúr[6] na[7] vṛṣṭím[8] |[8]
dadhyáṅ ha yán[9] mádhv ātharvaṇó[10] vām[11]
áśvasya[11] śīrṣṇā́ sumatím[12] ávocat[13] ||

226a agnír[1] īṣe[2] vasavyàsyā- [3]
-gnír mahás[4] sáubhagasya[5] |
tā́ny[5a] asmábhyam[5a] rāsate[6] ||

[iti prāvargikī pūrvakā śāntis samāptā]

[atha prāvargiky uttarā śāntiḥ]

(VI) < oṁ | śukriyaṃ rudrasya || >
199a āyurdā́[2] ā́yur me dehy. [1][ā́yuṣe naḫ púnar dehi.][1]
200 **prāṇadā́ḥ[1] prāṇám[2] me dehy.[3]** [ā́yuṣe naḫ púnar dehi.][3]
201 **vyānadā́[1] vyānám[2] me dehy.[3]** [ā́yuṣe naḫ púnar dehy.]
202 **apānadā́ apānám[1] me dehy.** [ā́yuṣe naḫ púnar dehi.]
203 **cakṣurdā́ś[1] cákṣur me dehy.** [ā́yuṣe naḫ púnar dehi.]
204 **śrotradā́ś śrótram[1] me dehy.** [ā́yuṣe naḫ púnar dehi.]
205 **varcodā́ várco me dehy.**
206 **ā́yuṣe naḫ púnar dehi.** || ||

(VII)
207 **námo[1] rudrā́ya[2] diviṣáde, yásya varṣám íṣavas; [2a] tásmai námas; téna mā́[2a] sámare; sá mā́ mā hiṁsīr.**
námo rudrā́yāntarikṣasáde, yásya vā́ta íṣavas; tásmai[4a] námas; téna mā́ sámare;[5] sá mā́ mā hiṁsīr.[6]
námo rudrā́ya pṛthivīṣáde, yásyā́nnam íṣavas; tásmai[6a] námas; téna[7] mā́ sámare;[8] sá mā́ mā hiṁsīḥ. || ||

(VIII)
216 **bráhmaṇa[1] upastáraṇam[1] asi, bráhmaṇe tvópastṛṇā-mī́-[3]**

217 -**ḷāyai**[4] **vástv**[5] **asi**; vāstumad[6] vāstumān[7] bhūyā-
sam.[8] avāstus[9] sa bhūyād, yo 'smān dveṣṭi,
[10]yañ ca vayaṃ dviṣmaḥ.[10] |
pratiṣṭhāsi; pratiṣṭhā me bhūyād.[11] aprati-
ṣṭhas[12] sa bhūyād, yo 'smān dveṣṭi, yaṃ[13] ca
vayaṃ[14] dviṣmaḥ.[15] || ||[15]

(IX)
218 **á vāta vāhi bheṣajám**
ví vāta vāhi yád rápaḥ[1] |
tvám hí visvábheṣajo[2]
devā́nān[3] dūtá īyase[4] ||
218a yád adó vāta te[1] gṛhè[1]
'mṛ́tasya[2] nidhír hitáḥ[3] |
táto[4] no dhehi jīváse
táto no ábhayaṅ kṛdhi ||
218b dyúbhir[1] aktúbhiḥ pári pātám asmā́n
áriṣṭebhir[2] aśvínā[3] sáubhāgebhiḥ
tán[4] no[4] mitró[5] váruṇo māmahantām
áditis[6] síndhuḥ pṛthivī́ utá dyáuḥ || ||

(X)
218c pṛthivī śāntir, antarikṣaṃ śāntir, dyauś śāntir,
diśaś śāntir, āpaś śāntir, oṣadhayaś śāntir,
vanaspatayaś śāntis. tayāhaṁ[1] śāntyā sarva-
śāntyā[2] mahyaṃ[3] dvipade catuṣpade śāntiṃ[4] karo-
mi.[5] śāntir no astu, śāntir asi. śāntiś śāntiś
śāntiḥ. || ||

(XI)
218d yā vāg uditā yā cānuditā
(215) **sivā́ naś śántamā bhava sumṛḷīká** |
(215) **sárasvati,**[1] mā te vyoma sandṛśe[2] ||

(XII)
218e mitrasya tvā cakṣuṣā prekṣe
mitrasya tvā cakṣuṣānvīkṣe |
sūryasya tvā cakṣuṣā prekṣe
sūryasya tvā cakṣuṣābhīkṣe ||

218f mitrásya carṣaṇīdhŕ̥taś
śrávo[1] devásya sānasí[2] |
dyumnáṃ[3] citráśravastamam ||
218g mitrásya carṣaṇīdhŕ̥taś[1]
śrávo devásya sānasí[2] |
satyáṃ[3] citráśravastamam ||

(XIII)
219 [1]**ápo hí ṣṭhá ma**yobhúvas[1]
tá na ūrjé dadhatana |
mahé ráṇāya cákṣase ||
219a yó vaś śivátamo rásas
tásya bhājayatehá naḥ |
uṣatī́r[1] iva mātáraḥ ||
219b tásmā áraṅ gamāma vo
yásya kṣáyāya jínvatha |
ápo[1] janáyathā ca naḥ ||
219c āpaḥ pṛṇītá[1] bheṣajáṃ
várūthan[2] tanvè[3] máma |
jyók ca sū́ryan dṛśé ||

(XIV)
219d[1] śán[2] no[2] devī́r[3] abhíṣṭaya
ápo bhavantu pītáye[5] |
śáṃ yyór[4] abhí sravantu naḥ ||
219e śán[1] no[1] mitrás śáṃ váruṇaś[2]
sán[3] no[3] bhavatv aryamá |
śán na índro bŕ̥haspátiś
śán no víṣṇur urūkramáḥ[4] ||
219f śán[1] no[1] mítrás śám váruṇaś[2]
śán no astv aryamá |
sán na índraś[3] cāgníś ca
śán no víṣṇur urūkramáḥ[4] ||
219g tyám ū ṣú vājínan[1] devájūtaṃ[2]
sahóvānan[3] tarutáraṃ ráthānām |

áriṣṭanemim[4] pṛtanā́jam[5] ā́śuṃ[6]
svastáye tā́rkṣyam[7] ihā́[8] huvema[9] ||

219h kā́yā[1] nás citrá ā́ bhuvad[2]
ūtī́ sadā́vṛdhas sákhā |
kā́yā śáciṣṭayā vṛtā́ ||

219i kás tvā[1] satyó mádānām[2]
máṁhiṣṭho[2] matsad ándhasaḥ[3] |
dṛdhā́ cid[4] ārúje[5] vásu ||

219j abhī́[1] ṣú[2] ṇas[3] sákhīnām
avitā́ jaritṝṇā́m[5] |
śatám[6] bhavāsy[4] ūtíbhiḥ ||

219k ya udagāt purastān[1] mahato arṇavād[2]
vibhrajāmānas[4] sarirasya madhye |
sa mā vṛṣabho[3] rohitākṣas sūryo
vipaścin manasā punātu ||

219l yad brahmāvādiṣma, tan mā mā hiṁsīt.[1] sūryāya
vibhrājāya vai namo namaḥ. || ||

[iti prāvargiky uttarā śāntis samāptā]

[iti prathamo 'dhyayas(?) samāptaḥ]

atha
śukriyabrāhmaṇam

fol. 337b
p. 92 < om̐ >

1 **yuñjáte mána**[1] ity [2]*āhavaníye juhoti. mánasā* vái
[prajā́]*p*atir yajñám ata*nuta*, *táto vācā́ tátaẖ*[2]
kármaṇā. mánasaiváitád yájamāno yajñáṃ vitátya,
2 táto [3]*vācā́*, *tátaẖ kármaṇā*[3] karoti. **devásya vas**
savitúḥ prasavá [1]íty *ábhrīr*[1] ā́datte. savitṛ́-
prasūta eváinā devátābhir ā́datte. cátasra ā́dat-
te.[2] [3]cátas[ro vái dí]*ś*o.[3] digbhyáḥ prava-

f.338a -rgyàs sámbhriyate.[4] digbhyá evá pravargyàm̐
sámbharati. vānaspatyā́ bhavanti. vánaspátibhir
vái pravargyàs sámbhriyate. vánaspátibhir evá
3 pravargyàm̐ sámbharaty. **úttiṣṭha brahmaṇaspata**
íty úttiṣṭhati. bṛ́haspátir vái bráhmaṇaspátir.
4 bṛ́haspátir evá bhūtvóttiṣṭhaty. **úpa práyantu**
marútas sudā́nava íti. sudā́navo vái marúta āraṇ-
yā́. áraṇye pravargyàs sámbhriyaté. 'raṇya evā́-
5 raṇyáṃ karoti. **práitu bráhmaṇaspátir** íti práti-
tiṣṭhati. bṛ́haspátir vái bráhmaṇaspátir. bṛ́has-
6 pátir evá bhūtvā́, prátitiṣṭhaty. **ā́** [1] **devy ètu**[2]
sūnṛ́téti. vā́g vái deví sūnṛ́tā. vācā́ pravargyàs
sámbhriyate. vācáivá pravargyàm̐ sámbharaty.
7 **áśchā vīráṃ náryaṃ paṅktírādhasam** íti. yajñó
vái vīró náryaḥ paṅktírādhā. devébhya evá yaj-
ñám̐ sámbharati ||

[1] (Mit dem Spruch) "Sie spannen das Denken an" opfert (der Adhvaryu die Savitar-Spenden) ins Āhavanīya(feuer). Mit Denken spannte sich Prajāpati das Opfer an, dann mit Rede, dann mit Tat. Hat der Opferherr das hier (behandelte) Opfer mit Denken angespannt, führt er es dann mit Rede, dann mit Tun aus. *[2]* (Mit dem Spruch) "Auf Geheiß des Gottes Savitar (ergreife) ich euch" nimmt (der Adhvaryu) die Schaufeln. Von Savitar angeregt nimmt er die (Schaufeln) mit den Gottheiten. Vier nimmt er. Die Himmelsrichtungen sind vier. Von den Himmelsrichtungen her wird der Pravargya(kessel) zusammengetragen. Nur von den Himmelsrichtungen her trägt man den Pravargya(kessel) zusammen. Vom Baum stammende (hölzerne) Schaufeln kommen zur Anwendung. Mit Bäumen wird der Pravargya(kessel) zusammengetragen, Nur mit Bäumen trägt man den Pravargya(kessel) zusammen. *[3]* (Auf den vom Adhvaryu gesprochenen Befehl hin) "Steh auf, Herr des Brahman!" steht (der Brahmane) auf. Der Herr des Brahman ist Bṛhaspati. Zu Bṛhaspati geworden steht der Brahmane auf. *[4]* (Der Adhvaryu murmelt:) "Herbeikommen sollen die gute Flüssigkeit besitzenden Marut!" Die zur Wildnis gehörigen Marut sind gute Flüssigkeit besitzende. In der Wildnis wird der Pravargya(kessel) zusammengetragen. In der Wildnis macht er ihn zu einem zur Wildnis gehörigen. *[5]* (Mit dem Spruch) "Voran gehen soll der Herr des Brahman!" nimmt (der Brahmane) festen Halt. Der Herr des Brahman ist Bṛhaspati. Zu Bṛhaspati geworden nimmt er festen Halt. *[6]* (Der Adhvaryu murmelt:) "Es soll herbeikommen die Göttin Lebenskraft!" Die Göttin Lebenskraft ist die Rede. Mit Rede wird der Pravargya(kessel) zusammengetragen. Nur mit Rede trägt man den Pravargya(kessel) zusammen. *[7]* (Der Adhvaryu murmelt:) "Um den Vīra(kessel) zu holen, den den Männern dienlichen, den fünffache Gaben enthaltenden." Der männliche, fünffache Gaben enthaltende Vīra(kessel) ist das Opfer. Für die Götter bringt er das Opfer zusammen. ||

8 **dévī**[1] **dyāvāpṛthivī devayájané**[2] **'nu me maṃsāthām**
ítīmé vái mahāvīrā́t[3] sámbhriyamāṇād[4] abibhī-
tām.[5] [6]téjasā nā úddhakṣyatī́ti.[6] sá bṛ́haspátir
abravīd: yuváyor bhāgadhéyam íti. táta enam
9 ánvamanyatām. [1]**ṛtásya ṛdhyāsam**[1] **adyá**[2] **makhásya**
p. 93 **śíra** íti sámbharati. yajñó vái makhó. yajñásyaivá śíras[3]
sámbharati.[3] trír harati. tríṣatyā hí devás. samantám
ábhrīḫ páriśrayati, rákṣasām párāṇuttyai. prajá-
pater vái prajā́s sísṛkṣamāṇasya tásya téjo yaj-
ñíyam ápākrāmat. tád imā́m prā́viśat. tád varāhó[4]
10 bhūtvā́nvavindad.[5] **íyaty á-**

f.338b **gra āsīr** íti. yád varāhávihatam[1] bhávaty,[2] asyā́[3]
11 evá téjo yajñíyaṁ sámbharati. **dévīr vamriyo 'sya**
bhūtásya prathamajā íti. vamríyo vā́ asyá bhū-
tásya prathamajā́s. tā́ vā́ etád vidur, yátrāsyā́
jīvā́ṃ yajñíyaṁ. yád valmīkavā́panāṁ sambháraty,
asyā́ evá jīvā́ṃ yajñíyaṁ sámbharatī́ndro vái yád
vṛtrám áhaṃs, tásyáujo vīryàm ápākrāmat. tád
12 óṣadhīḫ prā́viśat. té pūtī́kā abhavann. **índrasyáu-**
jo 'sīti. yát pūtī́kānāṁ sambháratī́ndrasyaiváujo
13 vīryàṁ sámbharati. **prajā́pates**[1] **tanū́r asīty.**
ajā́ṃ duhanti.[2] prajā́pater vā́ eṣā́ priyā́ tanū́r, yád[3]
ajā́.[3] yád ajā́ṃ dúhanti,[4] prajā́pater evá priyā́n[5]
tanvàṁ[6] sámbharati.

[8] (Der Adhvaryu murmelt:) "Ihr beiden göttlichen, Himmel und Erde, habt es mir auf dem Opferplatz erlaubt." Diese beiden (Welten, Himmel und Erde) fürchteten sich vor dem Mahāvīra(kessel), als er zusammengetragen wurde, (Sie liefen zu Bṛhaspati um Hilfe und sprachen:) "Mit seiner Glut wird er uns beide verbrennen." Bṛhaspati sprach: "Für euch beide gibt es einen Anteil." Da erlaubten sie es dem (Mahāvīra). [9] (Mit dem Spruch) "Heute möchte ich den Kopf Makhas, auf den ich gestoßen bin, erfolgreich vollenden" trägt er (den Ton für den Pravargyakessel) zusammen. Makha ist das Opfer. Den Kopf des Opfers trägt er zusammen. Dreimal nimmt er (die Schaufel voll). Drei Wahrheiten besitzend sind die Götter. Ringsherum legt er die Schaufeln: das dient zum Hinwegstoßen der Schädigungen. Die opferwürdige Glut Prajāpatis, der die Geschöpfe aus sich herauslassen (erschaffen) wollte, entwich. Sie drang in die Erde ein. Zum Eber geworden fand Prajāpati sie wieder. [10] (Der Adhvaryu murmelt) "So groß warst du zu Anfang." Wenn vom Eber aufgewühlte Erde verwendet wird, trägt man die opferwürdige Glut der Erde zusammen. [11] (Er murmelt) "Ihr göttlichen Ameisen, ihr Zuerstgeborene des Gewordenen." Die Ameisen sind die zuerstgeborenen dieses Gewordenen. Sie wußten dieses: wo sich die lebendige opferwürdige (Glut) der Erde befand. Wenn man den Ameisenhaufen zusammenträgt, trägt man die lebendige, opferwürdige (Glut) der Erde zusammen. Als Indra den Vṛtra erschlagen hatte, entwich seine Macht und seine männliche Kraft. Sie drangen in die Kräuter ein. Sie wurden zu den Pūtīka(pflanzen). [12] (Er murmelt) "Indras Kraft bist du." Wenn er von den Pūtīka(pflanzen) zusammenträgt, trägt er Indras Macht und männliche Kraft zusammen. [13] (Er murmelt) "Prajāpatis Leib bist du." (Die Gehilfen des Adhvaryu) melken eine Ziege. Die Ziege ist die liebliche Gestalt Prajāpatis. Wenn sie die Ziege melken, trägt (der Adhvaryu mit der Milch) die liebe Gestalt Prajāpatis zu-

14 **mádhu tvā mádhunā karotv** íty apá úpasr̥jati. ma-
dhu vā́ etán. mádhunā sáṃyauti.[1] madhavyò bhava-
15 ti. **makhásya śíro** 'síti, píṇḍam upā́datte. yajñó
16 vái makhó. yajñásyaivá śíraḫ karoti. **yajñásya
padé stha** íty, ávabādhate.[1] yajñásyaivá padé ka-
17 roti. **gāyatró**[1] 'síti prathamám ādhím ā́dadhāti.
téjo vái bráhma gāyatrī́. téja evá bráhma yája-
S.94 māne dadhāti **tráiṣṭubho**[1] 'síti dvitī́yam ādhím
ā́dadhāty. ójo[2] vái vīryàṃ triṣṭúb. ója evá vīr-
19 yàṃ yájamāne dadhāti. **jágato** 'síti tr̥tī́yam ā-
dhím ā́dadhāti. paśá[vo][1] vái[1] jágatī.[2] paśū́n evá yá-
20 jamāne dadhāti. **makhò** 'síti makhám eváinaṃ karo-
21 ti. **makhásya rā́snāsíti** rā́snāṃ karoti. yajñó vái
makhó. yajñā́yaiváinaṁ ka-

f.339a roti. prādeśamātró bhavaty. etā́vad vái múkhaṃ.
múkhaṃ devā́nām agnír. múkhena sámmita upáriṣṭāt-
pātro bhavati, devátānāṃ tŕ̥ptyai. tŕ̥pyati[1] pra-
jáyā paśúbhir. úpainaṁ somapīthó namati, yá eváṃ
22 véda. **sū́ryasya hárasā śrāyéty** ātápe nídadhāty.
amúṣyaiváinam ādityásya téjasā tapati. pū́rvam-
23 pūrvaṁ sādayatīmā́n evá lokā́n rohati. **vŕ̥ṣṇo niṣ-
pád asi prājāpatyám** íty aśvaśakā́ni[1] vyā́harati.
prājāpatyó vā́ áśvo. rūpéṇaiváinaṁ sámardhayati.

sammen. [14] (Mit dem Spruch) "Mit Süßigkeit soll es dich zur Süßigkeit machen" gießt er Wasser über (den Ton) aus. Dieses (Wasser) ist Süßigkeit. Mit Süßigkeit rührt er es vollständig (in den Ton) ein. Er wird ein für die Süßigkeit geeigneter. [15] (Mit dem Spruch) "Makhas Kopf bist du" nimmt er den (ersten Ton)kloß her. Makha ist das Opfer. Des Opfers Kopf verfertigt er. [16] (Mit dem Spruch) "Die beiden Fußspuren des Opfers seid ihr" drückt er (den Ton zweimal) nieder. Des Opfers Fußspuren macht er. [17] (Mit dem Spruch) "Von Gāyatrī-Art bist du" setzt er die erste Lage hin. Die Gāyatrī ist Glut und Brahman. Glut und Brahman setzt (der Adhvaryu) in den Opferherrn. [18] (Mit dem Spruch) "Von Triṣṭubh-Art bist du" setzt er die zweite Lage hin. Die Triṣṭubh ist Macht und Manneskraft. Macht und Manneskraft setzt er in den Opferherrn. [19] (Mit dem Spruch) "Von Jagatī-Art bist du" setzt er die dritte Lage hin. Die Jagatī ist Vieh. Vieh setzt er in den Opferherrn. [20] (Mit dem Spruch) "Makha bist du" macht (der Adhvaryu) den (Kessel) zu Makha. [21] (Mit dem Spruch) "Der Gurt Makhas bist du" macht er einen Gurt. Makha ist das Opfer. Für das Opfer macht er ihn. Es kommt ein eine Spanne hoher (Kessel) zur Anwendung. Ein Mund ist so groß. Agni ist der Mund der Götter. Es wird ein mit einem Mund gleich großer (Kessel), der oben eine Vorrichtung zum Trinken hat, angewendet: das dient zur Befriedigung der Gottheiten. Durch Nachkommenschaft und Vieh wird man zufrieden. Der Somatrunk wird dem zu eigen, der so weiß. [22] (Mit dem Spruch) "Durch der Sonne Glut werde gebacken" setzt er den (Kessel) in der Sonnenglut nieder. Durch die Glut jenes Āditya (der Sonne) brennt er ihn. Jeweils östlich setzt er (die drei Kessel) hin. Diese Welten ersteigt er. [23] (Mit dem Spruch) "Der Dung des Hengstes bist du, von Prajāpati stammend" breitet er Pferdemist aus. Das Pferd stammt von Prajāpati. Mit Hilfe der Gestalt (Prajāpatis) läßt er den (Opferherrn) vollständigen

24 **devā́nān tvā pátnīr**[1] **vŕ̥ṣṇo áśvasya niṣpádā dhū-**
payantv íty aśvaśakáir dhūpayati. prājāpatyó
25 v á [2] áśvo. yajñáḥ prajā́patis: sayonitvā́yā **rcíṣe**
tvā, śocíṣe tvā, hárase tvéti śamīśākhā́ abhyā́-
dadhāti. téjo vā́ agnís, téjaś śamīśākhā́s. téjasy
26 evá téjo dadhāti. **mitrásya carṣaṇīdhŕ̥ta** íty úpa-
27 tiṣṭhate mitrā́yaivā́inaṅ karoti. **devás tvā sa-**
28 **vitódvapatv**[1] íti. sāvitródvapati: prásūtyā. **ávya-**
S.95 **thamānaḥ pr̥thivyā́m ā́śā díśa ā́pr̥ṇéti.** tásmād
29 agnís sárvā díśo víbhāti. **úttiṣṭha bṛhán**[1] **bha-**
vordhvás tiṣṭha, dhruvás[2] **tvám** íti. dŕ̥m̐haty[3]
eváina-[4] || -m. [4]

30 **idám ahám amúm āmuṣyāyaṇám, amúṣyāḥ putrán, téjasā**
brahmavarcaséna sámardhayāmíti brāhmaṇám̥. téjo
vái bráhma gāyatrī́. téjasaivā́inam̥ brahmavarca-
31 séna sámardhayati. yády abhicáred: **idám ahám**
amúm āmuṣyāyaṇám amúṣyāḥ putrán téjasā brahma-
varcaséna vyàrdhayāmíti. téjo vái bráhma gāya-
32 trī́. téjasā brahmavarcaséna vyàrdhayatī**dám ahám**
amúm āmuṣyāyaṇám amúṣyāḥ putrám ójasā vīryèṇa
sámardhayāmíti rājanyàm. ójo

f.339b[1] vái vīryàm̥ triṣṭúb. ójasaivā́inam̥ vīryèṇa sámar-
33 dhayati. yády abhicáred: **idám ahám amúm āmuṣyā-**
yaṇám amúṣyāḥ putrám ójasā vīryèṇa vyàrdhayāmí-

Erfolg erlangen. [24] (Mit dem Spruch) "Die Frauen der Götter sollen dich mit dem Dung des Hengstes räuchern" räuchert er (den Kessel) mit Pferdemist. Das Pferd stammt von Prajāpati ab. Prajāpati ist das Opfer: das dient der Ursprungsgleichheit. [25] (Mit dem Spruch) "Für die Flamme dich, für die Glut dich, für die Hitze dich" legt er Śamī-zweige zu. Agni ist Glut. Die Śamī-Zweige sind Glut. In die Glut setzt er Glut. [26] (Mit dem Spruch) "Des völkererhaltenden Mitra" stellt er sich (ans Feuer). Für Mitra macht er ihn. [27] Mit dem auf Savitar bezüglichen (Spruch) "Der Gott Savitar soll dich herausholen" nimmt er (den Kessel) heraus: das dient dem Antrieb (durch Savitar). [28] (Er murmelt) "Nicht auf der Erde wankend erfülle die Weltgegenden und die Himmelsrichtungen." Deshalb bestrahlt das Feuer alle Himmelsrichtungen. [29] (Er murmelt) "Steh auf, werde hoch, steh aufrecht; du bist fest." Fest macht er den (Kessel). ||

[30] "Jetzt lasse ich den Soundso, aus dem Geschlechte des Soundso, den Sohn der Soundso, mit Glut und Brahmanenansehen vollständig zusammenkommen" (lautet) der auf einen Brahmanen bezügliche Spruch. Die Gāyatrī ist Glut und Brahman. Mit Glut und Brahmanenansehen läßt er den (Opferherrn) vollständig zusammenkommen. Wenn er zaubern sollte, (sagt er): [31] "Jetzt lasse ich den Soundso, aus dem Geschlechte des Soundso, den Sohn der Soundso, Glut und Brahmanenansehen verlieren." Die Gāyatrī ist Glut und Brahman. Glut und Brahmanenansehen läßt er ihn verlieren. [32] "Jetzt lasse ich den Soundso, aus dem Geschlechte des Soundso, den Sohn der Soundso, mit Macht und Manneskraft vollständig zusammenkommen" (lautet) der auf einen Adligen bezügliche Spruch. Die Triṣṭubh ist Macht und Manneskraft. Mit Macht und Manneskraft läßt er ihn vollständig zusammenkommen. Wenn er zaubern sollte, (sagt er): [33] "Jetzt lasse ich den Soundso, aus dem Geschlechte des Soundso, den Sohn der

ty. ójo vái vīryàṃ triṣṭúb. ójasaiváinaṃ vīryèṇa
34 vyàrdhayatīdám ahám amúm āmuṣyāyaṇám amúṣyāḥ pu-
trám ūrjā́ paśúbhis sámardhayāmī́ti váiśyam. paśá-
vo vái jágaty. ūrjáiváinam paśúbhis sámardhayati.
35 yády abhicáred: **idám ahám amúm āmuṣyāyaṇám amúṣ-**
yāḥ putrám ūrjā́ paśúbhir vyàrdhayāmī́ti. paśávo[1]
vái jágaty. ūrjáiváinam paśúbhir vyàrdhaya-[1] ||

36 -tī**dám ahám[2] mān[2] téjasā brahmavarcasénáujasā[3] vīr-**
yèṇa prajáyā paśúbhir annā́dyena sámardhayāmī́ty.
ātmā́ vái brahmavarcasy.[4] àtmā́nam evá tát téjasā
brahmavarcasénáujasā[5] vīryèṇa prajáyā paśúbhir
37 annā́dyena sámardhayaty. **ṛjáve tvā, sādháve tvā,**
sukṣityái tvéti. yathāyajúr áparamaparaṁ sādaya-
38 tīmā́n evá lokā́n pratyávarohati. **sū́ryasya tvā**
cákṣuṣā́nvīkṣa íty ávekṣate. yád vā́ idám manuṣ-
yàṇāṃ cákṣuṣā prékṣeta,[1] prádahec, cákṣur; andhā́ḥ
prajā́ jāyeran. sū́ryasyaiváinañ cákṣuṣā́nvīkṣate.
39 **śchṛṇáttu[1] tvā vā́g** íti, páyasā́śchṛṇatti, vā́g[2]
S.96 vái gāyatrī́, vācáiváinam ā́śchṛṇatti. **śchṛṇáttu[1]**
40 **tvórg** íty. ánnaṃ vā́ ū́rg. annā́dyenaiváinam ā́śchṛ-
41 ṇatti. **śchṛṇáttu tvā páya** íti. paśávo vái páyaḥ.
42 paśúbhir eváinam ā́śchṛṇatti.[1] **śchṛṇáttu[1] tvā**
44 **rásaḥ.[2] chṛṇáttu tvā havíḥ. chṛṇáttu tvā sómaḥ.**
47 **chṛṇáttu tvā yajñáḥ. chṛṇáttu tvā bráhma. chṛṇát-**
tu tvā prajā́patir íti yathāyajúḥ || 1 ||

Soundso, Macht und Manneskraft verlieren." Die Triṣṭubh ist Macht und Manneskraft. Macht und Manneskraft läßt er ihn verlieren. [34] "Jetzt lasse ich den Soundso, aus dem Geschlechte des Soundso, den Sohn der Soundso, mit Stärkung und Vieh vollständig zusammenkommen" ist der auf einen Vaiśya "bezügliche (Spruch). Die Jagatī ist Vieh. Mit Stärkung und Vieh läßt er ihn vollständig zusammenkommen. Wenn er zaubern sollte, (sagt er): [35] Jetzt lasse ich den Soundso, aus dem Geschlechte des Soundso, den Sohn der Soundso, Stärkung und Vieh verlieren." Die Jagatī ist Vieh. Stärkung und Vieh läßt er ihn verlieren. ||

[36] "Jetzt lasse ich mich mit Glut, Brahmanenansehen, Macht, Manneskraft, Vieh und Speise vollständig zusammenkommen" (sagt er) für sich selbst. Brahmanenansehen besitzend ist das Selbst. Sein Selbst läßt er mit Brahmanenansehen, Glut, Macht, Manneskraft, Nachkommenschaft, Vieh und Speise vollständig zusammenkommen. [37] (Mit dem Spruch) "Für das Gerade dich, für das Rechte dich, für das gute Wohnen dich" setzt er Spruch für Spruch einen (Kessel) nach dem andern hin. Zu diesen Welten steigt er herunter. [38] "Mit dem Auge der Sonne blicke ich auf dich" sagt er) und blickt auf (den Kessel). Wenn er auf ihn mit dem Auge der Menschen blickte, würde er das Auge wegbrennen; blind würde seine Nachkommenschaft geboren. Mit dem Auge der Sonne blickt er auf ihn. [39] (Mit dem Spruch) "Die Rede soll dich bespeien" bespeit er (den Kessel) mit Milch. Die Gāyatrī ist die Rede. Mit der Rede bespeit er ihn. [40] (Er murmelt) "Die Stärkung soll dich bespeien." Die Stärkung ist Speise. Mit Speise bespeit er ihn. [41] (Er murmelt) "Die Milch soll dich bespeien." Die Milch ist Vieh. Mit Vieh bespeit er ihn. [42] "Der Saft soll dich bespeien, die Opferspeise soll dich bespeien, das Opfer soll dich bespeien, das Brahman soll dich bespeien, Prajāpati soll dich bespeien!" (sagt er) Spruch auf Spruch. || 1 ||

48 **bráhman pravargyèṇa prácariṣyāma** íty, adhvaryúr
brahmā́ṇam ā́mantrayate. bráhmaṇi vā́ etárhi yaj-
49 ñás. tásmād enam āha. **yáju-**

f.340a **-ryuktam**[1] íti brahmā́.[2] yájuṣo vā́ eṣá rátho, yád
yajñás. [3]tám a[dhvaryúr adhvaré yuna]kti.[3] tád
adhvaryór adhvaryutvám.[4] adhvaryúr enam prā́ṇa-
yaty. adhvaryúr evā́sya [5]*sá*[rvasya praṇetā́dhva]r-
yúr[5] anyā́n ṛtvíjas[6] sámpréṣyatīdā́ṅ kurutedā́ṅ
50 kurutéty eváitád āha. [1]**sā́mabhi[r ā́ktakha]n**[1] **tvé-**
51 ti, sā́māny [2]evā́syābhítaś cakré.[2] **víśvābhir dhī-**
bhís sámbhṛtam[1] íti. sárvābhir *vái*[2] dhībhír yaj-
ñás [3]sámbhriyate. sárvābhir[3] evá dhībhír yája-
52 māno yajñám̐ sámbharati. **dákṣiṇābhiḥ prátatam**
pārayiṣṇúm íti.[1] vítatam pāragáṃ dákṣiṇābhir íty
54 eváitád āha. **stúbho vahantu sumanasyámānā** [1]íti.
hótrā[1] vái stúbhas. tā́ vā́ etárhi yajñáṃ vahanti.
56 **bhū́r bhúvas svàr; óm** íty. etád vái vācás satyáṃ.
yád[1] evá vācás satyán, ténainam̐ sahá prácaratī́**n-**
57 **dravantaḥ prácaratéti** sendratvā́ya ||[1]

58 **prā́cyā**[1] **tvā diśā́gnínā devátayā, gāyatréṇa śchán-**
S.97 **dasā,**[2] **vasantáṃ ṛtúm právíśāmíti.**[3] prā́cīñ[3] caivá
vasantā́ñ ca purástāt právíśanty,[4] apra-

[48] "Brahman, wir werden jetzt mit dem Pravargya beginnen" redet der Adhvaryu den Brahman an. Im Brahman ist jetzt das Opfer. Deshalb sagt er es zu ihm. *[49]* Der Brahman sagt: "Den mit Sprüchen angeschirrten." Das Opfer ist der Wagen des Opferspruches. Ihn [spannt der Adhvaryu beim Opfer (*adhvara*) an.] Das ist das Wesen der Bezeichnung 'Adhvaryu'. Der Adhvaryu führt ihn nach vorn. Der Adhvaryu [ist der Anführer des Ganzen.] Der Adhvaryu fordert die andern Priester auf: 'Tut dieses und jenes!' so sagt er dabei. *[50]* (Er sagt) "Dich, den durch Lieder mit geschmierten Radnaben versehenen." Die Lieder sind seine zwei Räder auf beiden Seiten. *[51]* (Er sagt) "Den mit allen Gedanken zusammengesetzten." Mit allen Gedanken wird das Opfer zusammengetragen. Mit allen Gedanken trägt der Opferherr das Opfer zusammen. *[52]* (Er sagt) "Den mit Opferbelohnungen ausgebreiteten, zum Ziele führenden." 'Den mit Opferbelohnungen auseinandergespannten (d.h. angespannten), zum Ziele führenden' sagt er damit. *[54]* (Er sagt) "(Den) sollen die wohlgesinnten Lobpreisungen ziehen!" Die Lobpreisungen sind die Rezitationen. Diese ziehen jetzt das Opfer. *[55]* (Er sagt) "*Bhūr, bhuvas, svar; oṁ.*" Das ist das Wahre der Rede. Was nun das Wahre der Rede ist, mit dem zusammen vollzieht er (das Opfer). *[57]* (Er sagt) "Vollzieht (den Pravargya-Ritus) als solche, die Indra (zum Freund) haben": das dient der Gemeinschaft mit Indra. ||

[58] "Im Osten dringe ich mit der Gottheit Agni, mit dem Versmaß Gāyatrī in dich, in die Frühlingszeit ein" (murmelt der Adhvaryu). Sowohl in die östliche (Himmelsrichtung) als auch in den Frühling dringen sie im Osten ein: um nicht verbrannt zu werden. *[59]* "Im Süden dringe ich mit der Gottheit Indra, mit dem Versmaß Triṣṭubh in dich, in die Sommerzeit ein" (murmelt er). Sowohl in die südliche (Himmelsrichtung) als auch in den Sommer dringen sie im Süden ein: um nicht verbrannt zu werden. *[60]* Im Westen dringe

59 -dāhāya. **dakṣiṇáyā tvā diśéndreṇa**[1] **devátayā, trái-**
ṣṭubhena śchándasā, grīṣmám ṛtúm práviśāmíti.
dakṣiṇāñ caivá grīṣmáñ[2] ca[2] dakṣiṇatáḫ̭ práviśanty,
60 ápradāhāya. **pratícyā**[1] **tvā diśá, savitrá**[2] **deváta-**
yā,[3] **jágatena**[4] **śchándasā,**[5] **varṣá ṛtúm**[6] **práviśāmí-**
ti. pratícīñ caivá varṣáś ca paścā́t práviśanty,
61 ápradāhāy**ódīcyā**[1] **tvā diśá,**[2] **mitrávárunābhyān de-**
vátayā́nuṣṭubhena śchándasā, śarádam ṛtúm[3] **prāvi-**
śāmíty.[3] údīcīñ caivá śarádañ cottarā́t práviśan-
ty, ápra-

f.340b [1][-dāhāy**ordhváyā tvā diśá, bṛ́]haspátinā**[1] **devátayā,**
62 **páṅktena śchándasā, hemantám**[2] **ṛtúm** [3]**pravi[śāmīty.**
ūrdhváñ caivá híma]ñ[3] copáriṣṭāt práviśanty,
63 ápradāhāyānáy**ā tvā diśá,** [1]**prajá[patinā devátayá-**
nā]ptena[1] **śchándasā, śíśiram ṛtúm práviśāmítīmáñ**[2]
caivá śíśira-[3][ñ cāsyáḫ̭ práviśa]nty,[3] ápradāhāya ||

64 **gāyatríṃ cháṇdaḫ̭**[1] **práviśāmíti.**[2] téjo vái bráhma
gāyatrí. téja evá tát práviśanty, ápradāhāya.
65 **triṣṭúbhaṃ cháṇdaḫ̭ práviśāmíty.**[1] ójo vái vīryàṃ
triṣṭúb. ója[2] evá tát práviśanty, ápradāhāya.
66 **jágatīṃ cháṇdaḫ̭**[1] **práviśāmíti.** paśávo [vái][2] já-
67 gatī. paśū́n evá tát práviśanty, ápradāhāy**ānuṣṭú-**
bhaṃ[1] **cháṇdaḫ̭**[1] **práviśāmíti.** vā́g vá anuṣṭúb. vá-
67a cam evá tát práviśanty, [2]ápradāhāya. **paṅktíṃ**
cháṇdaḫ̭ práviśāmíti. yajñó vái paṅktír.[3] yajñáṃ

ich mit der Gottheit Savitar, mit dem Versmaß Jagatī in dich, in die Regenzeit ein" (murmelt er). Sowohl in die westliche (Himmelsrichtung) als auch in die Regenzeit dringen sie im Westen ein: um nicht verbrannt zu werden. [61] "Im Norden dringe ich mit der Gottheit Mitra-Varuṇa, mit dem Versmaß Anuṣṭubh in dich, in die Herbstzeit ein" (murmelt er). Sowohl in die nördliche Himmelsrichtung als auch in den Herbst dringen sie im Norden ein: um nicht verbrannt zu werden. [62] "Im Zenith dringe ich mit der Gottheit Bṛhaspati, mit dem Versmaß Paṅkti in dich, in die Winterzeit ein" (murmelt er). Sowohl in (die Richtung) nach oben als auch in den Winter dringen sie oben ein: um nicht verbrannt zu werden. [63] "In dieser Richtung hier (d.h. nach unten) dringe ich mit der Gottheit Prajāpati, mit dem Anāpta-Versmaß in dich, in die Vorfrühlingszeit ein" (murmelt er). Sowohl in diese (Himmelsrichtung) hier (nach unten) als auch in den Vorfrühling dringen sie hier (d.h. in die Erde) ein; um nicht verbrannt zu werden. ||

[64] "In das Versmaß Gāyatrī dringe ich ein" (murmelt er). Die Gāyatrī ist Glut und Brahman. In die Glut dringen sie da ein: um nicht verbrannt zu werden. [65] "In das Versmaß Triṣṭubh dringe ich ein" (murmelt er). Die Triṣṭubh ist Macht und Manneskraft. In die Macht dringen sie da ein: um nicht verbrannt zu werden. [66] "In das Versmaß Jagatī dringe ich ein" (murmelt er). Die Jagatī ist Vieh. In das Vieh dringen sie da ein: um nicht verbrannt zu werden. [67] "In das Versmaß Anuṣṭubh dringe ich ein" (murmelt er). Die Anuṣṭubh ist die Rede. In die Rede dringen sie da ein: um nicht verbrannt zu werden. [67a] "In das Versmaß Paṅkti dringe ich ein" (murmelt er). Die Paṅkti ist das Opfer. In das Opfer dringen sie da ein: Um nicht verbrannt zu werden. [68] "In das Versmaß Aticchandas dringe ich ein" (murmelt er). Der Aticchandas ist (identisch mit den) Versmaßen. In die Versmaße dringen sie da ein: um nicht verbrannt zu wer-

68 tád právišanty,[2] ápradāhāy**átiśchandasaṃ**[1] **chán-**
dah̭[2] **právišāmí**ti.[2] śchándāṁsi[3] vā́ átiśchandāś.[4]
69 chándāṁsy evá tát právišanty, ápradāhāya. **śchán-**
dāṁsi[1] **právišāmíti.**[1] paśávo vái śchándāṁsi.[2] pa-
70 śū́n evá tát právišanty, ápradāhāya. **tā́ni nah̭ pā-**
rayantu,[1] **tā́ni no**[2] **'vantv** íty āśíṣam evā́śāste.[3]
71 **tā́ni sá ṛśchatu, yò**[1] **'smā́n dvéṣṭi, yā́ñ ca vayáṃ**
dviṣmá[2] íti. yám evá dvéṣṭi, tā́ṁ śucā́rpayaty.[3]
72 **ā́po asmā́n právišantv,**[1] **ā́po asmā́su jāgṛtéty.**[2]
ā́pas[2] sárvā devátā. devátā evá tát právišanty,
73 ápradāhāy**ā́yur višvā́yur**[1] **víśvam ā́yur**[2] **vyàśnavai;**
S.98 **sárvam ā́yur vyàśnavā** íty eváitád āha. sárvam
ā́yur eti, yá eváṃ védā́tho saṃvatsarā́ñ[5] caivá dí-
74 śaś ca sarváto várma kurute.[6] **yamā́ya tvā makhā́-**
ya tvéti mahāvīrā́m prókṣati.[1] yajño[1] vái makhó.
yajñā́yaivā́inam prokṣati.[2] || 2 ||

fol.341a [....

[3]prokṣitāni pratiprasthātā vyāyātayati[3]...

...

...

...

...

...

...

...

... ...]xy x x x*t* x xux x x x x x x

den. [69] "In die Versmaße dringe ich ein" (murmelt er). Die Versmaße sind Vieh. In das Vieh dringen sie da ein: um nicht verbrannt zu werden. [70] (Mit dem Spruch) "Die sollen uns beschützen, die sollen uns helfen" wünscht er einen Wunsch. [71] (Er murmelt) "An den (Versmaßen) soll sich der stoßen, der uns haßt und den wir hassen." Wen er haßt, den versieht er mit Schmerz. [72] (Er murmelt) "Die Wasser sollen in uns eindringen; o Wasser, seid wach in uns." Alle Gottheiten sind die Wasser. In die Gottheiten dringen sie da ein: um nicht verbrannt zu werden. [73] Er sagt so: "Lebensdauer, mit ganzer Lebensdauer versehene Lebensdauer will ich erlangen; die vollständige Lebensdauer will ich erlangen." Zur vollen Lebensdauer geht, wer so weiß. Jetzt macht er sich sowohl das Jahr als auch die Himmelsrichtungen auf allen Seiten zu seinem Schutz. [74] (Mit dem Spruch) "Dem Yama dich, dem Makha dich" besprengt er den Mahāvīra(kessel). Makha ist das Opfer. Für das Opfer besprengt er ihn. | 2 |

[...
Die besprengten (Opfergegenstände) stellt der Pratiprasthātar gesondert (jedes an seinen Platz).

geh]en

75 práca]ranti. **déva puraścara rghyása[ṃ]**[1] **tvā**
svárghyāsan[2] **tvéti**, vedéna mahāvīráṁ sámmārṣṭi.
[áthaivái]*n*aṃ[3] trís sámmārṣṭi. tríṣatyā hí
devā́s. sarvátas sámmārṣṭi. sarváta eváinam mé-
dhyaṃ yajñíyan téna karoti ||

76 **pṛthivyā́s saṃspṛ́śas**[1] **pāhī́ti**, rajatám adhástād
ádhikarṣatīmé vái lokā́ mahāvīrā́t pravṛjyámānād
abibhayus: sárvān no 'yán téjasóddhakṣyatī́ti.
prajā́patim úpādhāvan. sá prajā́patiḥ pṛthivī́m
abravīd: rajatā́ bhūtvā́, mahāvīrā́ṃ dhārayasvéty.
antárikṣam abravīd: vánaspátibhis tvāntár dhā-
syāmī́ti. dívam abravīd: dharitā́ bhūtvópáriṣṭān
mahāvīrám sahasvéti. tásmād rajatám adhástād[2]
77 ádhikarṣati,[2] pṛthivyā́ ápradāhāy**ārcír asi, śo-**
cír asíti. jválantam agníṁ haratas: satejastvā́-
78 **yāñjánti yám** íti, tásmin múkhyaṃ mahāvīrám prá-
yunakti. téjo vā́ agnís. téjo mahāvīrás. téjasy
evá téjo dadhāti || **3** ||

---

79 **prāṇáya sváhā, vyānáya sváhāpānáya sváhéti.**

f.341b [...

...

...

...

...

...

[vor]. *[75]* (Mit dem Spruch) "0 vorangehender Gott, ich möchte dir wert sein; als solcher möchte ich dir wert sein" reinigt er den Mahāvīra(kessel) mit dem Wisch. Er reinigt den [Mahāvīra(kessel) nun] dreimal. Drei Wahrheiten besitzend sind nämlich die Götter. Überall reinigt er. Überall macht er ihn dadurch opferrein und opferwürdig. ||

[76] (Mit dem Spruch) "Schütze vor der Berührung mit der Erde" zieht er die silberne (Platte) unter den (Kessel). Diese Räume fürchteten sich vor dem Mahāvīra(kessel), als er ans Feuer gesetzt wurde. (Sie sprachen:) "Er wird uns alle mit seiner Glut vollständig verbrennen." Sie liefen zu Prajāpati um Hilfe. Prajāpati sprach zur Erde: "Silbern geworden, trage den Mahāvīra!" Zum Luftraum sprach er: "Mit Bäumen werde ich dich schützen." Zum Himmel sprach er: "Golden geworden, überwältige den Mahāvīra von oben!" Deshalb zieht (der Adhvaryu) die silberne (Platte) unter den Kessel): das dient zum Nichtverbrennen der Erde. *[77]* (Mit dem Spruch) "Flamme bist du, Glut bist du" nehmen die beiden (Adhvaryu und Pratiprasthātar) das aufflammende Feuer: das dient dem Versehensein mit Glut. *[78]* (Wenn der Hotar den Vers rezitiert) "Den sie salben" verwendet (der Adhvaryu) dabei den mit einem Ausguß versehenen* Mahāvīra(kessel). Feuer ist Glut, der Mahāvīra ist Glut. Glut setzt er in die Glut. | **3** |

[79] (Der Adhvaryu murmelt) "Dem Einatmen, *svahā*! Dem Auseinanderatmen, *svāhā*! Dem Ausatmen, *svāhā*!"

[...

*oder: 'den Haupt-Mahāvīra', d.h.: nicht die Reservekessel

...

...

...

...

x mahāvī]rám̥[1] gharmyám práyunakti. díśo vái mahāvīrā́t pravr̥ktā́d abibhayus:[2] sárvā no 'yán téjasóddhakṣyatī́ti. tā́ḫ prajā́patim úpādhāvan. sá prajā́patir abravīt: prādeśā́mprādeśam̥[3] vaḫ prádahati. devátābhir[4] vo 'ntár dhāsyāmī́ti. tásmāt
S. 99 prādeśéna díśo mimīté.[5] ||[6]

80 **'nādhr̥ṣṭā purástād agnér ádhipatya** íty. agním
81 evá purástād antár dadhāty ápradāhāyá**yur**[1] **me dā**
82 íty ātmána eváitā́m āśíṣam ā́śāste. **putrávatī dakṣiṇatá índrasyádhipatya** ítī́ndram[1] evá[1] dakṣi-
83 ṇā́d antár dadhāty ápradāhāya. **prajā́m̥ me dā** íty.
84 ātmána eváitā́m āśíṣam ā́śāste. **suṣádā**[1] **paścā́d devásya savitúr ádhipatya** íti. savitā́ram[2] evá
85 paścā́d antár dadhāty[3] á[pradā]hāya.[3] **cákṣur me**
86 **dā** íty. ātmána eváitā́m āśíṣam ā́śāsta.[1] [1]**ā́śrutir ut[ta]rā́n mi[trāvá]ru[ṇa]yor ádhipatya**[1] íti. mitrā́váruṇā evóttarā́d antár dadhāty, ápradāhāya.
87 **śrótram̥ me dā**[1] íty. ātmána eváitā́m āśíṣam ā́śāste.
88 **vídhr̥tir upáriṣṭād bŕ̥haspáter**[1] **ádhipatya** íti.[2] bŕ̥haspátim evópáriṣṭād antár dadhā-

f.342a
89 [-ty, ápradāhāya. **vā́cam̥ me dā** íty ātmána eváitā́m

...

...]

verwendet er den für den Heißtrank geeigneten [Mahāvī]ra-(Kessel). Die Himmelsrichtungen fürchteten sich vor dem Mahāvīra(kessel), der ans Feuer gestellt worden war. (Sie sprachen:) "Er wird uns alle mit seiner Glut verbrennen." Sie liefen zu Prajāpati um Hilfe. Prajāpati sprach: "Spanne nach Spanne verbrennt er euch. Ich werde euch mit Gottheiten schützen." Deshalb 'mißt' (der Opferherr) mit der (zu einer) Spanne (ausgestreckten Hand) die Himmelrichtungen. ||

[80] "Unnahbar bist du im Osten unter Agnis Oberherrschaft" (murmelt er). Agni setzt er im Osten als Schutz zwischen (sich und den Mahāvīrakessel): um nicht verbrannt zu werden. *[81]* (Mit dem Spruch) "Gib mir Lebensdauer" wünscht er diesen Wunsch für sich selbst. *[82]* (Mit dem Spruch) "Reich an Söhnen bist du im Süden unter Indras Oberherrschaft" setzt er Indra im Süden als Schutz dazwischen: um nicht verbrannt zu werden. *[83]* (Mit dem Spruch) "Gib mir Nachkommenschaft" wünscht er diesen Wunsch für sich selbst. *[84]* (Mit dem Spruch) "Mit gutem Wohnsitz versehen bist du im Westen unter Savitars Oberherrschaft" setzt er Savitar im Westen als Schutz dazwischen: um nicht verbrannt zu werden. *[85]* (Mit dem Spruch) "Gib mir Augenlicht" wünscht er diesen Wunsch für sich selbst. *[86]* (Mit dem Spruch) "Hinhören bist du im Norden unter Mitras und Varuṇas Oberherrschaft" setzt er Mitra und Varuṇa im Norden als Schutz dazwischen: um nicht verbrannt zu werden. *[87]* (Mit dem Spruch) "Gib mir Gehör" wünscht er diesen Wunsch für sich selbst. *[88]* (Mit dem Spruch) "Trennung bist du im Zenith unter Bṛhaspatis Oberherrschaft" setzt er Bṛhaspati oben als Schutz dazwischen: [um nicht verbrannt zu werden. *[89]* (Mit dem Spruch) "Gib mir Rede" wünscht er diesen Wunsch

āśíṣam ā́śāste.[1]

...

...

...

...

...]

[2]xy t x s t x x [s]v[ā́héti, pariśra]*yato*. *'sáu*
vā́ ādity*ó* rudró mahāvīró. raśmáyo [vái] marúto.[2]
90 raśmíbhir eváinam páriśrayato. **'ntárikṣasyān-**
tardhír[1] asíty. upáriṣṭāt samídham ā́dadhāti.[2] vá-
91 naspátibhir evópáriṣṭād antár dadhāti. **divás**[1]
saṁspṛ́śas[2] **pāhíti.** háritenā́pidadhāti, divó 'pra-
92 dāhāy**árhan**[3] **bibharṣi sā́yakāni**[1] **dhánvā́rhan niṣ-**
S.100 **kā́ṃ yajatā́ṃ**[2] **viśvárūpam.**[3] - **árhann idā́ṃ dayase**
víśvam ábhvan. ná vā́ ójīyo[4] **rudra**[5] **tvád astíti.**
93 mahimā́nam evā́syaitád úddharṣayati. **gā́yatram**
asi,[1] **tráiṣṭubham asi, jā́gatam**[2] **asíti.** [prati]-
prasthātré[3] práyaśchati. hótrā vā́ ṛtvíjo. hó-
trābhya[4] eváinam [5]etá[t sa]mpráyaśchaty.[5] [6]ékam
agnídhe[6] [7]*pratiprasthātré* [pradakṣiṇá]m pári-
ya*nti*[7] ||[8]

94 **mádhu mádhu mádhv** íti[1] dhūnvanti.[2] mádhu sāra-
96 ghā́ṁ sā́mbhariṣyāmíty eváitad āha. **prāṇò**[1] **'si,**
vyānò[2] **'sy, apānò 'síti.**[3] prāṇā́ṃ vyānā́m apānā́n
97 tā́n evá yájamāne[4] dadhāti. **śrótram**[1] **asíti.** śró-
tram[2] evá yájamāne dadhāti. sárva ṛtvíjaḫ pári-

für sich selbst. ...

(Mit dem Spruch) "... ... *svāhā*" umge]ben die beiden (der Adhvaryu und der Pratiprasthātar den Mahāvīrakessel mit Hölzern). Rudra Mahāvīra ist [jener] Āditya (die Sonne), die Maruts sind (seine) Strahlen, mit Strahlen umgeben die beiden (Adhvaryu und Pratiprasthātar) den (Mahāvīra). *[* 90 *]* (Mit dem Spruch) "Du bist der Schutz des Luftraums" legt (der Adhvaryu) oben das (dreizehnte) Scheit hin. Mit 'Bäumen' schützt er oben den Luftraum. *[* 91 *]* (Indem er murmelt) "Schütze vor der Berührung mit dem Himmel" bedeckt er (den Kessel) mit der goldenen (Platte): das dient zum Nichtverbrennen des Himmels. *[* 92 *]* (Der Hotar rezitiert:) "Mit Fug und Recht trägst du Pfeile und Bogen, mit Fug und Recht den ehrwürdigen allfarbenen Goldschmuck. Mit Fug und Recht verfügst du über all diese Gewalt. Nicht gibt es ja etwas Stärkeres als du bist, Rudra."[6] Den mächtigen (Rudra) erfreut er damit. *[* 93 *]* (Indem der Adhvaryu murmelt) "Von Gāyatrī-Art bist du, von Triṣṭubh-Art bist du, von Jagatī-Art bist du" übergibt er (einen Fächer) dem Pratiprasthātar. Die Priester sind die Rezitationen. Mit Rezitationen übergibt er ihm den genannten (Fächer). Einen (dritten) übergibt er dem Agnīdh und dem Pratiprasthātar. Nach rechts gehen sie (fächelnd um den Mahāvīra) herum. ||

[94 *]* (Mit dem Spruch) "Süßes, Süßes, Süßes" befächeln sie (ihn). 'Das von den Bienen stammende Süße werde ich zusammentragen' sagt er damit. *[* 96 *]* (Mit dem Spruch) "Ausatmen bist du, Auseinanderatmen bist du, Einatmen bist du" setzt er Ausatmen, Auseinanderatmen, Einatmen in den Opferherrn. *[* 97 *]* (Mit dem Spruch) "Gehör bist du" setzt er Gehör in den Opferherrn. Alle Priester bedienen (den Mahāvīra). Die Priester sind die Rezitationen. Mit Rezitationen bringt er ihm dann vollständig dar. *[* 98 *]* (Er murmelt)

viśanti.[3] hótrā vā́ ṛtvíjo. hótrābhya eváinam
98 [4]etát samprā́yaśchaty.[4] **agníṣ ṭvā dhūnotv**[1] íty.
etábhir[2] eváinaṃ devátā-

f.342b [bhir dhūnoti. ...
...
[3]prajvalite rukmam apadatte.[3] ...
...
98a **divyo**[1] **gandharvo bhuvanasya yas patir...**
[2]ime vai lokā bhuvanaṃ. teṣām eṣo 'dhipatir,
yo rudraḥ.[2] ...
98b **ekāvyo manasā vikṣv īḍya ...**
98c [1]**tan tvā yāmi brahmaṇā deva dai**]**vyam** íti. yád
vā́ ena*m brahmáṇo*pacáreyur, hi*ṃ* syād *enam. bráhm*a
*ś*i*v*á *ṃ* śāntám.[1] bráhmaṇaiváinam[2] úpacarati.
99 **diví te sadhástham** [íti].[3] diví te gṛhám íty
100 eváitád āha. **diví pṛṣṭó**[1] **yajatás sūryatvág**
íti ||

devā́ vái rudrā́ṁ[2] svargáṃ lokáṃ gatáṃ na vyàjā-
nann[3] ādityávarṇaṃ cárantan. tè[4] 'bruvan: kò
S.101 'síty. aháṃ rudrò,[5] 'hám índro,[6] 'hám ādityò,
'háṃ sárvasyāvayā́ háraso divyáséti. tè 'bru-
van: nírbhajāmainam íti. tā́n ruvánn[7] abhyàva-
dat.[8] tā́n prā́*dh*raj*at*.[9] tè[9] 'bruvan: bhavā́n
sárvam íti. yád ruvánn[10] abhyávadat, tád ru-
drásya rudratváṃ. yád bhavā́n[11] íti, tád bhavásya

"Agni soll dich befächeln." Mit den genannten Gottheiten [befächelt er] ihn. [...

...

Wenn (das Feuer um den Kessel herum) aufgeflammt ist, nimmt er die goldene (Platte) weg.

...

[98a *]* "Der himmlische Gandharva, der der Herr der Welt ist" ... Die Welt, das sind diese beiden Räume; deren Oberherr ist Rudra. ...

[98b *]* "Er ist als Einziger nur Hilfe bietend, mit Denken verehrenswert in den Siedlungen" ... ...]

[98c *]* "[Um das Gött]liche [bitte ich dich, o Gott, als solch einen, mit einer magischen Formulierung]" (murmelt er.) Wenn man ihn mit einem Brahmanen verehrte (*brahmán*), würde er (Rudra) ihn verletzen; freundlich und beruhigt ist die magische Formulierung (*bráhman*). Mit einer magischen Formulierung verehrt er ihn. *[* 99 *]* (Wenn er murmelt) "Im Himmel ist dein Sitz" sagt er damit: 'Im Himmel ist dein Haus.' *[* 100 *]* (Er murmelt) "Den Himmel berührend, verehrungswürdig, sonnenhäutig." ||

Die Götter erkannten den in die Himmelswelt gekommenen, als sonnenfarbigen, einherschreitenden Rudra nicht. Sie sprachen: "Wer bist du?" - "Ich bin Rudra, ich bin Indra, ich bin Āditya (die Sonne), ich bin die Abwendung alles himmlischen Zornes." Die (Götter) sprachen: "Wir wollen ihn (von einem Anteil am Opfer) ausschließen." Brüllend schrie er sie an. Er drang auf sie ein. Sie sprachen: "Herr, du hast die gesamte Herrschaft." Weil er sie brüllend (*ruvan*) anschrie, ist das die Entstehung des Namens *'Rudra'*. Weil sie 'Herr' (*bhavān*) sagten, ist das die Entstehung des Namens *'Bhava'*. Weil sie 'die gesamte Herrschaft' (*sarvam*) sagten, ist das die Entstehung des Namens '*Śarva*'.

bhavatvám. yát sárvam íti, tác[12] charvásya śarvatvám̐. sá śivò[13] 'bhavat. tác chivásya śivatvám. tébhyo 'mṛḷata.[14] tán mṛḷásya[14] mṛḷatvám.[14] tám devā́ abruvan: bhavásya[15] bhūtásya bhávyasyā́dhipatyam íti. sárvasyā́dhipatyam[16]
101 yájamānam gamayaty. **anavadyā́bhis** [1]**sám *u* jagmābhír**[1] íti. hótrā vā́ anavadyā́s. tā́bhir vā́ eṣá pravargyè[2] sáṅgaśchate. tā́bhir evá pravargyàm̐[3]
101b sáṅgamayati. **samudrá āsām**[1] **sádanam va āhur** íti. védā vái samudrā́s. téṣu vā́ e-[2]

f.343a [váinam pravargyè sáṅgamayati. ...

101d **abhriye didyun nakṣatriye**

yā viśvāvasuṃ gandharvaṃ sacadhve

tābhyo namo astu, tā no mṛḷayantu

tā naś śarma yaśchantu, *taṃ*[1] yan dviṣmo, yaś ca no dveṣṭi, tam āsāṃ jambhe dadhmaḥ.

...

101i **ápaśyam gopā́m ánipadyamānam** íti. ... ...]
[1]x x x x x x x x x x x x x x x *ādityá*. eṣá
102 *lokānām goptā*. *náiṣá* rātrā́ ná divā́[1] sámviśaty.[2] **ā́ ca párā ca pathíbhiś cárantam** íti. tásmād eṣá sárvān pathó 'nusáñcarati,[1] yád dakṣiṇā́, yád
103 údaṅ. **sá sadhrī́cīs, sá**[1] **víṣūcīr vásāna** íti. cátasro[2] vā́ etásya díśas sadhrī́cīś, cátasro viṣūcīs. tā́ vā́[3] eṣá vásāna imā́m llokā́ms tejasā́-

Er wurde freundlich (*śiva*). Das ist die Entstehung des Namens *Śiva*. Er erbarmte (*amṛḷata*) sich ihrer. Das ist die Entstehung des Namens *Mṛḍa*. Die Götter sprachen zu ihm: "Dein ist die Oberherrschaft über das Seiende, das Gewordene, das Zukünftige." Zur Oberherrschaft über alles läßt er den Opferherrn gehen. [101] (Er murmelt) "Mit den tadelfreien ist er zusammengekommen." Die tadelfreien sind die Rezitationen. Mit diesen kommt er beim Pravargya zusammen. Mit diesen läßt er ihn beim Pravargya zusammenkommen. [101b] (Er murmelt) "Der Ozean ist deren Sitz, sagen sie euch." Die Ozeane sind die Veden. In diesen [läßt er ihn beim Pravargya zusammenkommen. ...

[101d] "Du aus der Wolke stammende, du blitzende, du sternenhafte, die ihr dem Gandharva Viśvāvasu folgt, als solchen sei ihnen Verehrung! Als so geartete sollen sie sich unser erbarmen! Sie sollen uns Schutz gewähren. - Wen wir hassen und wer uns haßt, - den setzen wir in ihre Fänge."

...

...

[101i] (Der Opferherr und die Priester rezitieren) "Ich sah den Hirten, der sich nicht niederlegt" ... ...] der Āditya. Jener (Āditya, die Sonne) ist der Beschützer der Welten. Nicht legt er sich bei Tag, nicht bei Nacht nieder.[2] [102] (Sie sprechen) "Den auf den Pfaden hin und her wandelnden." Deshalb wandelt jener Āditya (die Sonne) alle Pfade entlang, nach Süden und nach Norden. [103] (Sie sprechen) "Er, der die gleichgerichteten, der die auseinanderstrebenden anhat." Vier sind dessen gleichgerichtete Himmelsrichtungen, vier seine auseinanderstrebenden. Indem jener (Āditya) diese anhat, verhüllt er diese Welten mit seiner Glut.

104 vṛṇoty. **átra právīr mádhu mádhvībhyāṃ mádhu**
105 **mādhūcíbhyām**[1] íti. yádā **rucitó**[1] **gharmá** íti má-
S.102 dhu madhugháṁ sámbhariṣyāmíty, eváitád āha.
107 **sám agnír agnínāgata,**[1] **sáṃ devéna**[2] **savitrá, sáṁ**
sū́ryeṇa rocate sváhéty.[3] [4]átra vá[4] eṣá etárhy
108 agnír [5]agnínā sáṅgaśchate.[5] **sám agnís tápasā-**
gata,[1] **sáṃ devéna savitrá, sáṃ sū́ryeṇārukta.**[2] -
108a **dhartá divó rájaso víbhāti,**[1] **dhartóróг antári-**
kṣasya,[2] **dhartá pṛthivyá,**[3] **dhartá devó devánām**
ámartyas tapojá íty. asáu vá[4] ādityá imáṃ llo-
káṃs[5] téjasā dhārayati |[6]

109 **hṛdé** tvā, **mánase**[1] [**tvā**][1], **divé**[1] tvā, **sū́ryāya**
110 [2]**tvéty**, amúm[2] eváinaṃ[3] lokáṃ[4] gamayaty. **ūrdhvám**
imám adhvarám íti. yajñó vá adhvaró, yajñasyor-
111 dhvatváya.[5] **diví devéṣu hótrā yaśchéti.** hótrā-
bhi-[1]

f.343b [...

...

...

...

...

...

...

... ...]
112 ta. **gárbho devánām, pitá matīnám, pátiḥ prajánām**

[104 *]* (Sie sprechen) "Hilf dort dem Süßen für die das Süße liebenden, dem Süßen für die Honigfarbenen." *[* 105 *]* (Wenn der Adhvaryu sagt) "Der Gharma(kessel) hat aufgeleuchtet" so sagt er damit: 'Das Süßigkeiten strömen lassende Süße werde ich zusammentragen.' *[* 107 *]* (Sie sprechen) "Feuer ist gerade mit Feuer zusammengekommen, es leuchtet zusammen mit Gott Savitar, zusammen mit der Sonne, svāhā!" Dort (auf dem Opferplatz) kommt jetzt Feuer (*agni*, das Opferfeuer) mit Feuer (der Sonne) zusammen. *[* 108 *]* (Sie sprechen) "Gerade hat sich Feuer mit Hitze vereinigt, gerade zusammen mit Gott Savitar, zusammen mit der Sonne aufgeleuchtet. - Als Träger des Raumes des Himmels strahlt auseinander der Träger des weiten Luftraumes, der Träger der Erde, der Träger der Götter, der Gott, der Unsterbliche aus der Glut Geborene." Jener Āditya (die Sonne) erhält diese Welten mit seiner Glut. |

[109 *]* (Mit dem Spruch) "Dem Herzen dich, dem Denken [dich], dem Tage dich, der Sonne dich" läßt er ihn in jene Welt gehen. *[* 110 *]* "Aufrecht halte diese Ritualhandlung!" (sagt er). Die Ritualhandlung ist das Opfer: das dient dem Emporsteigen des Opfers (zum Himmel). *[* 111 *]* (Er murmelt) "Lenke die Opfergüsse in den Himmel zu den Göttern!" Mit Opfergüssen (oder: 'Rezitationen') [...

. . .]

[112 *]* (Er murmelt den Spruch) "Der Embryo der Götter, der Vater der Gedanken, der Herr der Geschöpfe.

S.103 [1]íti. *gárbho hy èṣá* devā́nām, pitā́ matīnā́m,[1] pátih̭
113 prajā́*nām*.[2] **āyurdā́s**[1] **tvám asmábhyaṃ gharmāsi,**
varcodā́h̭[2] **pitā́ no 'si, pitā́ no bodhíty** ātmána
114 eváitā́m aśíṣam ā́śāste. **námas te astu, mā́ mā**
115 **hiṃsīr** íty, ātmánó 'hiṃsāyai.[1] **tváṣṭṛmantas tvā**
sapeméty. áto hìmā́h̭ prajā́h̭ prajā́yante: prajána-
nāya ||[1]

yajñāsya vái śíro 'schidyata.[2] tā́ etárhy aśvínā ágharmapau bhiṣájau devā́nām āstāṃ. táu devā́ abruvan: bhiṣájau vái stha. idáṃ yajñásya śírah̭ prátidhattam íti. tā́ abrūtām: vā́ryaṃ vṛṇāvahā: āváyor evá pravargyò[3] bhavatv íti. táu devā́ abruvan: sárvaṃ[4] vái páryagṛhṇāthām,[5] ástu nó 'trápíti. tā́ abrūtām: āváyor ágre duhyatām, āváyor ágre hūyatām íti. tásmād etáyor evā́gre duhyaté, 'gre hūyate. vā́ryavṛtaṁ hy enayos. táu yajñásya śírah̭ prátyadhattān. táto yál lóhitam[6] samásravat,[6] táta udumbáras[7] sámabhavad.[8] yád áudumbarāṇi[9] pātrāṇi bhávanti, yajñá evórjaṃ dadhāti. yó rásas, té múñjās. tásmān mauñja[ṃ][10] vedáṃ kurvanti. pavítra-

f.344a [...

...

...

...

Dieser (das Feuer) ist nämlich der Embryo der Götter, der Vater der Gedanken, der Herr der Geschöpfe. *[113]* (Mit dem Spruch) "Lebensspender bist du für uns, o Glutkessel, du bist unser Vater, werde unser Vater!" wünscht er diesen Wunsch für sich selbst. *[114]* (Er murmelt) "Verehrung sei dir, verletze mich nicht!" Das dient zur Nichtverletzung seines Selbstes. *[115]* (Die Frau des Opferherrn murmelt) "Als mit Tvaṣṭar verbundene möchten wir uns dir widmen." Denn von hier (vom Penis) her wird die Nachkommenschaft erzeugt: das dient zur Erzeugung (von Nachkommenschaft). ||

Der Kopf des Opfers wurde abgeschnitten. Da waren die beiden Aśvin, die nicht am Gharmatrunk beteiligt waren, die Ärzte der Götter. Zu denen sprachen die Götter: "Ihr seid doch Ärzte. Setzt den Kopf des Opfers wieder an!" Die beiden sprachen: "Wir wollen uns etwas Wünschenswertes wählen: U n s e r soll der Pravargya(trank) werden!" Zu den beiden sprachen die Götter: "Ganz habt ihr den (Pravargyatrank) ergriffen. Es sei uns davon ein (Anteil)!" Die beiden (Aśvin) sprachen: "Für uns soll zu Beginn des (Pravargya-Opfers) gemolken werden, für uns soll zu Beginn geopfert werden!" Deshalb wird für die beiden zu Beginn (des Pravargya) gemolken, zu Beginn geopfert. Denn als Wünschenswertes gewünscht ist es von den beiden (Aśvin). Die beiden setzten den Kopf des Opfers (wieder) an. Das rote (Blut), das dann zusammenfloß, - daraus entstand der Udumbara(baum). Wenn (aus) Udumbara(holz gefertigte) Gefäße angewendet werden, setzt man ins Opfer Kraft. Der Saft (der vom Kopf des Opfers her zusammenfloß) - das sind die Muñja(gräser). Deshalb macht man einen Wisch aus Muñjagras. Ein Reinigungsmittel [...

...

...

...

...

... ...][11]x xv xv x x[u]
115a xcə'm r və'x *áhvayaty*: ***ásā ehī́ti***, divá eváinām[1] [1]
116 etád áhvayaty. **ásā ehíty**, antárikṣād eváinām
117 etád áhvayaty. **ásā ehíti**, pṛthivyā́ eváinām etád
áhvayati. bráhma vā́ etásyā vatsó, védās stánā.
devā́ vái bráhmaṇā vatséna vā́cam aduhran, paśū́ṃś
S.104 cāmṛ́tañ ca. yó vái védānāṃ gúhyāni nā́māni véda,
sárvam ā́yur éti, brahmavarcasī́[1] bhavati, práti-
tiṣṭhaty, ánnavān,[2] annādó bhavati. mayobhū́r
éko, vasuvíd ékas, sudátra éko, viśvapoṣy éka
íty. etā́ni vái védānāṃ gúhyāni nā́māni. sárvam
ā́yur eti, brahmavarcasī́ bhavati, prátitiṣṭhaty,
118 ánnavān annādó[3] bhavati, yá eváṃ véda. **yás te
stánaś śaśayó,**[1] **y ó**[2] **mayobhū́r,**[3] **yó ratnadhā́**[4] **va-
suvíd,**[5] **yás**[5] **sudátraḥ,**[5] **- yéna víśvā púṣyasi
vā́ryāṇi, sárasvati tám ihá dhā́tave kar**[6] íty,[6] ánu-
119 mantrayaté. **'dityā uṣṇī́ṣam asíty.** abhidhā́nyābhi-
dhā́ya[1] suvrátām[2] eváināṃ[3] karoti ||

120 **pūṣā́ tvéti**, vatsám upā́vasṛjati: satanūtvā́ya.
121 **gharmā́ya śinkṣvéty**, ápavartayati. gharmá evā́ṅ[1]
gha-[1]

...

...]

ruft er herbei. [115a] "Du, Soundso, komm!" (ruft der Adhvaryu). Vom Himmel her ruft er die (Kuh) herbei. [116] "Du, Soundso, komm!" (ruft der Adhvaryu). Vom Luftraum her ruft er die (Kuh) herbei. [117] "Du, Soundso, komm!" (ruft der Adhvaryu), Von der Erde her ruft er die (Kuh) herbei. Das Brahman ist deren Kalb, die Zitzen sind die Veden. Die Götter molken mit dem Brahman als Kalb die Rede, Vieh und Unsterblichkeit. Wer die geheimen Namen der Veden kennt, der geht zur vollständigen Lebensdauer, wird zu einem, der Brahmanenansehen besitzt, erlangt eine feste Lebensgrundlage als Nahrungbesitzender, wird zu einem Nahrungverzehrenden. Ein (Veda) ist 'Labung verschaffend' (*mayobhū*), einer 'Güter verschaffend' (*vasuvid*), einer 'gute Zuteilung besitzend' (*sudatra*), einer 'allgedeihend' (*viśvapoṣin*). Diese sind die geheimen Namen der Veden. Zur vollen Lebensdauer geht, zu einem Brahmanenansehen besitzenden wird, eine feste Lebensgrundlage erlangt, als Nahrungsbesitzender wird zu einem Nahrungsverzehrenden, wer so weiß. [118] (Der Adhvaryu murmelt den Vers) "Welche deine unversiegliche Zitze ist, die Labung verschaffende, die Reichtum verschaffende, die Güter verschaffende, die gute Zuteilung besitzende, durch die (Brust) du mit allen Wünschenswerten (Dingen) gedeihst, Sarasvatī, die mach hier zum Saugen (für das Kalb)." [119] Indem er (mit dem Spruch) "Die Stirnbinde der Aditi bist du" (die Kuh) mit dem Halfter festbindet, macht er sie gefügig. ||

[120] (Mit dem Spruch) "Pūṣan (soll) dich (hinzulassen) läßt er das Kalb ans Euter: das dient zur Gleichgestaltigkeit. [121] (Mit dem Spruch) "Lasse etwas für den Gharma(kessel) übrig" wendet er (das Kalb vom Euter) weg. Im(?) Gharma(kessel) ... so [...

f. 344b [... [1](*Kaṭhasūtre viśeṣah*:
... (śvaś cariṣyan pravargyeṇa, pūrvedyur
... (vatsavarkarau | apākuryāt tathā prātaḥ
... (sāyam votsṛjya dhenuke || nāśe gharma-
... (duho dhenvā vratadhenuṃ duhet tataḥ |
... (gharmayārddhavratā duhyād dvaudvau sta-
... (nau iha || gharmavrataduhor nāśe ājyena
... (pracared dvijaḥ | ajānāśe tu gavyenān-
... (yāṃ vā dhenum ānayet || sarvanāśe vṛtā-
... (dugdhaṃ payo vā dadhi vānayet ||[1]
gā́m du]-[2]hanti. hastyauṣṭhyá ev*ái*nāṃ du*há*ṅ,
g x x x x x x x x x x x x x [párā][2]-s*i*ñcan,[3]
yád ajā́ṃ duhánti. gharmá evá tád duhaty. [4]ū́rjaṃ
váiṣá t*á*t párāsiñcan, yád *ajā́ṃ*[4] duhánti. gharmá
122 evórjaṁ sámbharatas. tásmād āhus: **sahórjó [1]bhā-
gén*ópa me*híndrā́śvinā[1] mádhunas sāraghásya ghar-
máṃ pāta, vasavo; yájata; vá̄ḷ[2]** íti, mahāvīrá
ū́rjam ávanayato. gharmá evórjaṁ samā́nayatas.
123 **sū́ryasya tvā[1] raśmáye, vṛṣṭivánaye svā́hé**ty, ūrdhvám
útkrāntam ánumantrayate. yá̄ vá̄ itá ā́hutir udá-
yate, sā́múto vṛ́ṣṭiṃ cyāvayati. sváyaivā́hutyā
divó vṛ́ṣṭiṃ nínayati ||

S.105
124 **gāyatrò[1] 'si, tráiṣṭubho** 'síti śaphá ā́datte,
125 **jágato** 'síty, upayāmám chándobhir eváinam pári-
126 gṛhṇāti. **dyā́vāpṛthivíbhyān tvā párigṛhṇāmíti**,
śaphā́bhyām mahāvīrám párigṛhṇātīmé vái śaphá̄.
127 ābhyā́m eváinam párigṛhṇāty. **antárikṣeṇa tvópa-
yaśchāmí**ty, adhástād upayāména dhārayaty. átho

...]

melkt man. Wenn man sie nur in den Topf mit dem elefantenlippenförmigen Ausguß melkt, ... wegschüttend, wenn man die Ziege melkt. Nur in den Gharmakessel melkt man da. Kraft wegschüttend ist jener dann, wenn man die Ziege melkt. Im Gharmakessel nur tragen die beiden (Adhvaryu, d.h. Adhvaryu und Pratiprasthātar) Kraft zusammen. Deshalb sagt man: *[122]* "Komm zu mir heran mit einem Anteil an der Kraft; (du) Indra, und ihr Aśvin, trinkt den Heißtrank des von den Bienen stammenden Süßen, ihr guten: opfert! *vaṭ*!" Die beiden (Adhvaryu) gießen Kraft in den Mahāvīra(kessel) hinab; im Heißtrank bringen die beiden Kraft zusammen. *[123]* (Mit dem Spruch) "Dem regengewinnenden Strahl der Sonne dich, *svāhā*!" spricht er dem nach oben aufsteigenden (Dampf) nach. Der Opferguß, der von hier als Dampf aufsteigt, läßt von dort her Regen niederfallen. Durch seinen eigenen Opferguß gießt er vom Himmel her den Regen herunter. ||

[124] (Mit dem Spruch) "Von Gāyatrī-Art bist du, von Triṣṭubh-Art bist du" nimmt er die beiden 'Hufe' (der Zange, mit dem Spruch) *[125]* "Von Jagatī-Art bist du" den Untersatz. Mit den Versmaßen umfaßt er den Mahāvīra(kessel). *[126]* (Mit dem Spruch) "Mit Himmel und Erde umgreife ich dich" umgreift er den Mahāvīra(kessel) mit den beiden 'Hufen' (der Hebezange). Die beiden 'Hufe' sind die beiden (d.h. Himmel und Erde). Mit den beiden umgreift er ihn. *[127]* (Indem er murmelt) "Mit dem Luftraum halte ich dich unten" hält er (den Kessel) unten mit dem Untersatz. Der Untersatz ist jetzt der Luftraum. Im Luftraum hält er den (Kessel).

antárikṣaṃ vā́ upayāmò. 'ntarikṣa eváinan [1]dhā-
128 rayati. **devā́nān tvā**[1]
fol.345a **[pitṝṇā́m ánumato bhártuṁ śakeyam íti** ...

...

...

...

...

...

128a [1]x x x x x x x x x x x x x x [sa]***mudrā́ya tvā***,[1] **vā́-
tāya sváhéti** juhoti. *yathāyajúr*[2] yáj juhuyā́d,
rudrā́ya paśū́n ápidadhyād, apaśús syād. yajúr
evá vaded. rudrā́d evá paśū́n párivṛṇakti. sárvā
vā́ etárhy etásmin devátā ā́śaṁsante: máhyaṁ hoṣ-
yati, máhyaṁ hoṣyatī́ti. devátā eváinam abhi-
dhyā́yantīs. tā́ enam abhāgā́ īśvarā́ híṁstor. yád
129 áha**āgnáye tvā, vásumate sváhé**ti,[1] devátā evá bhā-
gínīḥ karoty: ātmáno 'hiṁsāyai. yájurbhājo[2]
[3]*'nyé devátā*,[3] áhutibhājo 'nyé. tā́n evóbháyān
prīṇāti ||[4]

130 **diví dhā imā́ṃ yajñā́m, imā́ṃ yajñā́ṃ diví dhā** ítī-
mé vái lokā́ díśaś ca gharmé 'pitvám aiśchanta.
131 yád áha: **diví dhā, dívaṃ gaśchāntárikṣaṃ gaśca,**
S.106 **pṛthivī́ṃ gaśca, páñca pradíśo gaśché**tīmā́n evá
132 lokā́n díśaś ca gharmé tarpayati. **devā́n gharma-
pā́n gaśchéti**. yá evá devā́ gharmapā́s, tā́n eváṃ

[128] (Der Adhvaryu murmelt:) "[Mit Zustimmung] der Götter [und der Väter möchte ich] dich [tragen können." ...

[128a] (Mit dem Spruch) "Dem Oz]ean dich, dem Winde dich!" opfert er. Wenn er Spruch für Spruch opfern würde, würde er ohne Vieh sein. Er soll nur den (zweiten, dritten usw.) Opferspruch laut sprechen. Vor Rudra verschont er das Vieh. Alle Gottheiten hoffen jetzt bei diesem Opfer: "Mir wird er opfern, mir wird er opfern." Die Gottheiten, die es auf ihn abgesehen haben, wären als Anteillose fähig, ihn zu verletzen. [129] Wenn er sagt: "Dem Reichtum besitzenden Agni dich!" macht er die Gottheiten anteilhaft: das dient zur Nichtverletzung seines Selbstes. Am Opferspruch teilhabend sind die [einen Gottheiten], an der Opferspeise teilhabend die anderen. Beide (Gruppen von Gottheiten) erfreut er. ||

[130] (Der Adhvaryu flüstert) "In den Himmel setze dieses Opfer, dieses Opfer setze in den Himmel!" Diese Welten und Himmelsrichtungen wünschten einen Anteil am Gharma(trunk). [131] Wenn er sagt: "Setze das Opfer in den Himmel, geh zum Himmel, geh zum Lufttraum, geh zur Erde, geh zu den fünf Himmelsrichtungen" befriedigt er diese Welten und die fünf Himmelsrichtungen hier beim Gharma(trunk). [132] (Er murmelt) "Geh zu den Heißtrank trinkenden Göttern!" Welche die Heißtrank trinkenden Götter sind, die ehrt er dann so beim Heißtrank.

133 tád gharmé tarpayati. **devébhyas tvā gharmapé-**
bhyas sváhéty, upayāména mahāvīré juhoti. yá evá
devá[1] gharmapās, tán evá tád gharmé tarpayati.
deváś ca vá ásurāś ca samávad evá pravargyè[2]
'kurvata. yád evá devá ákurvata, tád ásurā
akurvata. té[3] 'surā[3] upāṁśú pravargyèṇācaran.[4]
sá enān níradahad. uccáir[5] de-

f.345b [váḫ pravargyèṇācaran, té devá abhavan, té
'surāḫ párābhavan. ...

...

...

...

... ...]
[6]*g* hav rā x x x x x x x x x x x x x x x x x x x
x x [dvi]tī́yān[6] tád [7]evásy*ātmáne* *hutáṃ*.[7] vá-
133a ṣaṭkṛtam bhavati. [1]**gh*armám apātam aśvinéti*[1]**
yájamānas. tṛ́ptim evá tát pṛśchaty. átho váṣaṭ-
134 kṛtam bhavati. [1]**víśvā áśā dakṣiṇāsád**[2] íti,[2] brah-
má hutám ánumantrayate.[1] tád evásy*ātmáne*[3] hutám
135 bhavatīṣé **pinvasvorjé pinvasvétī́ṣam** evórjaṃ
136 yajñé dadhāty. **asmái bráhmaṇe pinvasvāsmái kṣa-**
tráya pinvasvāsyái viśé[1] **pinvasvéti**. brahmakṣatré
137 víśaṃ caivá bhāgínaḫ karoty. **asmái sunvaté**
yájamānāya pinvasvéti. yájamānāyaiváitám āśíṣam[1]
138 áśāste. **subhūtáya pinvasvéti**, bhūtim evópaiti.

[133] (Indem er flüstert) "Für die Heißtrank trinkenden Götter dich, *svāhā*!" opfert er mit (dem Inhalt des) Untersatzes in den Mahāvīra(kessel). Welche die Heißtrank trinkenden Götter sind, die befriedigt er da beim Heißtrank. - Die Götter und die Asuras unternamen (alles) beim Pravargya(ritual) gemeinsam. Was die Götter taten, das taten die Asuras. Die Asuras führten das Pravargya(ritual) leise aus. Der (glühende Pravargyakessel) verbrannte sie. Die Gö[tter führten das Pravargyaritual] mit lauter Stimme [aus. Die Götter gediehen, die Asuras gingen zugrunde. ...

... opfert er die zwei]te Spende. Für ihn selbst ist es dann geopfert. Der *Vaṣaṭ*-Ruf kommt zur Anwendung. [133a] "Habt ihr den Heißtrank getrunken, ihr Aśvin?" (fragt) der Opferherr. Zur Befriedigung (der Aśvin fragt er das. Nun kommt der Vaṣat-Ruf zur Anwendung. [134] "Alle Himmelsgegenden (hat) der südlich sitzende (geehrt)" spricht der Brahman dem geopferten (Heißtrank) hinterher. Damit wird er zu einem für ihn selbst geopferten. [135] (Mit dem Spruch) "Für den Saft schwill an, für die Kraft schwill an!" setzt er Saft und Kraft ins Opfer. [136] (Mit dem Spruch) "Für diesen Brahmanen schwill an, für diesen Adligen schwill an, für dieses Volk schwill an" macht er sowohl Priester- und Adelsstand als auch dasVolk anteilhaft. [137] (Mit dem Spruch) "Für diesen (Soma-)pressenden Opferherrn" wünscht er diesen Wunsch für den Opferherrn. [138] (Er murmelt) "Für den Wohlstand schwill an." Zu Wohlstand gelangt (der Opferherr).

139 **brahmavarcasáya pinvasvéti**, brahmavarcasí bha-
140 vati. **máhyam áyuṣe várcase jyáiṣṭhyāya rāyás-**
póṣāya suprajāstváya pinvasvéty. ātmána evái-
S.107 tám āśíṣam áśāste ||[1]

141 **tvíṣyai tvā, dyumnáya tvā, bhūtyái tvendriyáya**
tvéti pradakṣiṇám pátram práśrayati. díśa evá
142 bhāgínīḫ karoty, ātmánó[1] 'hiṃsāyai. **dhármāsi,**
sudhármemány asmai bráhmāṇi dhārayéti.

f.346a [...

...

...

...

...

... ...]

[2]x x x x x x x x x x x x x x x x x x x *kṣ* x x [ru]-
dró *vá* eṣá, yád agnír. yáthāgnáye[2] samavadyáty,
143 evám *eváitád*.[3] **bhúr, bhúvas, svàr; hutáṃ havír,**
mádhu havír, índratame[1] 'gnáu sváhéty agniho-
travidhíṃ juhoti. sáṃsthitir eváiṣá svargákṛ-
tir. átho ánantarhityai mánasā prājāpatyá ju-
hoti. mána iva vái prajápatiḥ. prājāpatyó yaj-
ñó.[2] yajñám evá sántanoti. práśyā3 ná práśyā3?
íti mīmāṁsante. yát prāśnīyát, prākárukas syād;
yán ná prāśnīyád, áhavis syād. ávajighred. ubhá-
yam evá karoti. yájamāna evá práśnāti. brahma-

[139] (Er murmelt) "Für das Brahmanenansehen schwill an!" Er wird zu einem, der Brahmanenansehen besitzt. [140] (Mit dem Spruch) "Für mich, für Lebensdauer, für Ansehen, für Vorrangstellung, für Gedeihen der Habe, für den Besitz an guter Nachkommenschaft schwill an!" wünscht er diesen Wunsch für sich selbst. ||

[141] (Mit den Sprüchen) "Der Energie dich, dem Glanz dich, dem Gedeihen dich, der Körperkraft dich.'" neigt er die Schale rechts herum. Er macht die Himmelsrichtungen anteilhaft; das dient zur Nichtverletzung seiner Selbst. [142] Halt bist du, einer der guten Halt hat; halte für ihn diese Brahma(formeln) fest!" (murmelt er). [...

... Ru]dra ist dieses Feuer. Als ob er (Holz) für das Feuer zerteilte und (die Holzstücke) sammelte, so ist das. [143] (Mit den Sprüchen) "*Bhūr, bhuvas, svar*! Geopfert ist die Opferspeise, in das Indra als Besten habende Feuer, *svāhā*!" opfert er nach der Regel des Agnihotra. Ein Abschluß ist diese Himmelsgestalt. Nun opfert er der Nichtverborgenheit mit Denken an Prajāpati. Prajāpati ist wie das Denken. Das Opfer ist prajāpatihaft. Das Opfer spannt er zusammen (d.h. beendet er). - Die Ritualisten überlegen: 'Soll man (von den Opferresten) essen, soll man nicht essen?' Wenn man äße, würde er verschwenderisch sein. Wenn er nicht äße, würde er ohne Opferspeise sein. Er soll daran riechen. Beides tut er (auf diese Weise: Genießen und Nichtgenießen). Nur der Opferherr genießt davon. Brahmanenansehen setzt er in sich.

144 varcasám evā́tmán dhatte. **saṁsādyámānāyā́nubrūhí-**
145 ty āha. prátiṣṭhāyā[2] **áhne tvā, sū́ryāya tvā;**
rā́tryai tvā, nákṣatrebhyas tvéty ahorātré sū́rya-
nákṣatrāṇi[1] caivá bhāgínaḥ karoti || 7 ||[2]

< yuñjatebrāhmaṇamantrā[3] samāptā > ||

<oṁ>[4]

146 **ghármājaṭharānnādám**[1] **māsmíñ jáne kurutam,**
S.108 **annnādò**[2]' **hám asmíñ jáne bhūyāsam** ítīndrāgní vái
devā́nāṃ gharmājaṭharā́u.[1] tā́ annā́dyasyeśāte.[4] tā́ asmā an-
nā́dyam práyaśchato. 'nnādó bhavati, yá evā́ṃ
147 véda. **kávīmātariśvānā,**[1] **pú́ṣṭivantaṃ māsmíñ jáne**
kurutam, pú́ṣṭivān ahám asmí-

f.346b [**-ñ jáne bhūyāsam** íti. ... ... vái devā́nāṃ
kavīmātariśvānā́u. tā́u puṣṭér īśāte. tā́ asmai
puṣṭím práyaśchataḥ. pú́ṣṭivān bhavati, yá evā́ṃ
147a védā́**rkāsadhasthā, cákṣuṣmantam(?) māsmíñ jáne**
kurutam. cákṣuṣmān(?) ahám asmíñ jáne bhūyāsam
íti. mitrā́váruṇā(?) vái devā́nām ar]*kā́sadhásthā.*
[tā́u cákṣuṣa(?) īśāte. tā́ asmai cákṣuḥ(?)
práyaśchataś. cákṣuṣmān(?) bhavati, yá]
148 evā́ṃ véda. **pítarāmātarā** [1]**śrótravantaṃ māsmíñ**
já[1][**ne kurutaṃ, śrótravān ahám asmíñ jáne**] **bhū-**
yāsam íti. dyā́vāpṛthiví vái devā́nāṃ pitárāmātá-
rau. tā́u śrótrasyeśāte. tā́ asmai śrótraṃ prá-

[144] (Der Adhvaryu spricht laut den Befehl:) "Sprich (den Vers) für das Zusammensetzen (des Pravargya)!" Das dient dem festen Stehen. *[145]* (Mit den Sprüchen) "Dem Tage dich, der Sonne dich; der Nacht dich, den Gestirnen dich!" macht er sowohl Tag und Nacht als auch Sonne und Sterne zu Teilhabenden. || 7 ||

< Der (mit dem Wort) *yuñjate* (beginnende) Brāhmaṇa- und Mantra-(Abschnitt) ist beendet. >

[146] "Ihr beiden, Gharma und Jaṭhara, macht mich in diesem Volke zu einem Nahrung Essenden; zu einem Nahrung Essenden möchte ich in diesem Volke werden!" (murmelt der Adhvaryu beim Hochheben des Pravargyakessels mit der Zange.)[3] Der Gharma ('die Hitze') und der Jaṭhara ('der Bauch') der Götter sind Indra und Agni. Die beiden herrschen über die Nahrung. Die beiden übergeben ihm Nahrung. Zu einem Nahrung Essenden wird, wer so weiß. *[147]* (Er murmelt) "Ihr beiden, Kavi und Mātariśvan, macht mich in diesem Volke zu einem Wohlhabenden, zu einem Wohlhabenden [möchte] ich in diese[m Volke werden!" ... und ... sind der Götter Kavi und Mātariśvan. Die beiden herrschen über den Wohlstand. Die beiden übergeben ihm Wohlstand. Wohlhabend wird, wer so weiß. *[147a]* "Ihr beiden, Arka und Sadhastha, macht mich in diesem Volke zu einem mit Gesicht(?) versehenen; Gesicht (?) möchte ich in diesem Volke haben!" (murmelt er). Mitra und Varuṇa(?) sind] Arka und Sadhastha [der Götter. Die beiden herrschen über den Gesichtssinn.(?) Die beiden übergeben ihm Gesicht.(?) Gesichtssinn erlangt, wer] so weiß. *[148]* (Er murmelt) "Ihr beiden, Vater und Mutter, macht mich in diesem Volke zu einem mit Gehör versehenen; ein mit Gehör versehener möchte ich in diesem Volke werden!" Himmel und Erde sind Vater und Mutter der Götter. Die beiden herrschen über das Gehör. Mit Gehör versehen wird, wer so weiß.

yaśchatas. śrótravān bhavati, yá evám̱ véda.
149 **yámāṅgirasā áyuṣmantaṃ māsmíñ jáne kurutam.**
áyuṣmān ahám asmíñ jáne bhūyāsam íti. yamáś
caivá váruṇaś ca devā́nāṃ yamā́ṅgirasau. tā́ áyu-
ṣa īśāte. tā́ asmā áyuḫ práyaśchata. áyuṣmān
bhavati, yá evám̱ vedā-[1] ||[2]

150 -**śyáma** te gharma mádhumataḫ pitumáto, **námas**[3]
te astu, mā́ mā hiṁsīr íty, ātmánó 'hiṃsāyai.
151 **jyótir asi, vánaspátīnāṃ rása** íti. mádhunā[1]
prathamám *pūrayati*.[2] vánaspátīnāṃ vā́ eṣá puṣ-
paphalā́nām ráso, yán mádhu. ténaiváinaṃ sámar-
dha*yati*.[3] tád āháyur vái mádhv. áyur agnáu[4]
152 prádadhyāt. pramā́yukas syād íti, yád áh**áyur**
máyi dhehíty, áyur[1] evātmán dhatta,[2] áyuṣmān
153 bhavati. **jyótir, bhā́ asy**[1] **apā́m**,[1] **óṣadhīnāṃ**
rása íti, ghṛténa dvitī́yam. etád vā́ etásya pri-
yáṃ dhā́-

f.347a [ma, ténaiváinaṁ sámardhayati, yád áha:
153a **cákṣur máyi dhehíti**, cákṣur evātmán dhatte,
cákṣuṣmān bhavati. ...

... ... íti dadhnā́ tṛtī́yam. etád vā́ etásya
S.109 priyáṃ dhā́ma. ténaiváinaṃ sámardhayati. yád
153b áh**órjam** [1]**máyi dhehít**]y ū́[rjam x x x x x x x x
154 evāt]*mán* dh*atta*. ū́rjasvān[1] bhavaty. **ugrā́ś ca**
dhúniś céty [1]*áraṇye 'nuvākyò*[1] gaṇáś: śā́ntyā.[2]

[149] (Er murmelt) "Ihr beiden, Yama und Aṅgiras, macht mich in diesem Volke zu einem Langlebigen; zu einem Langlebigen möchte ich in diesem Volke werden!" Sowohl Yama als auch Varuṇa sind die beiden Yama-Aṅgiras der Götter. Die beiden herrschen über die Lebensdauer. Die beiden übergeben ihm Lebensdauer. Zu einem Langlebigen wird, wer so weiß. ||

[150] (Er murmelt) "Wir möchten, o Heißtrank, von dir, dem Süßes Besitzenden, Speisereichen, genießen; Verehrung sei dir; verletze mich nicht!" Das dient zur Nichtverletzung seines Selbst. [151] (Mit dem Spruch) "Licht bist du, der Saft der Bäume" füllt er den ersten (Kessel) mit Honig. Honig ist der Saft der Blüten und Früchte der Bäume. Damit läßt er ihn gedeihen. Man sagt: 'Honig ist Lebensdauer.' Die Lebensdauer würde er ins Feuer setzen, er würde dem Untergang geweiht sein (wenn er den Honig opferte). [152] Wenn er (aber) sagt: "Setze Lebensdauer in mich!" setzt er Lebensdauer in sich, wird er zu einem Langlebigen. [153] (Mit dem Spruch) "Licht, Glanz bist du, der Saft der Wasser, der Kräuter" füllt er den zweiten (Kessel) mit flüssiger Butter. Die ist dessen liebe Stätte. [Mit seiner lieben Stätte läßt er ihn gedeihen. [153a] Wenn er sagt: "Gib mir Augenlicht!" setzt er Augenlicht in sich selbst, wird er zu einem, der Augenlicht besitzt. Mit dem Spruch: ...

füllt er den dritten Kessel mit Sauermilch. Das ist dessen liebe Stätte. Mit ihr läßt er ihn zusammenkommen. Wenn er sagt: [153b] "Gib mir Kraft!"] setzt er Kraft in sich selbst. Er wird einer, der Kraft besitzt. [154] (Der Adhvaryu murmelt) "Der Schreckliche und der Laute." Das ist die in der Wildnis zu sprechende Gruppe (von Sprüchen): (sie) dient zur Besänftigung (Rudras).

155 **ágne vratapate,**[1] **vā́yo vratapate, sū́rya**[2] **vratapa-**
ta íty eté vái devā́nāṃ vratápatayas. tébhya
156 evá prócyāvāntaradīkṣā́m[3] úpaiti. **pṛthiví samíd**
íti yathāyajúḥ || 1 ||

157 **áhaḫ kétunā juṣatāṃ sujyótir jyótiṣām svā́hét**i
rauhiṇā́ṃ juhoty asáu vā́ ādityó 'hnāṃ ketū́.
158 **rā́trī ketúnā juṣatāṁ sujyótir jyótiṣāṃ svā́hét**i
rauhiṇā́ṃ juhoti. candrámā vái rā́trīṇāṃ ketúś.
cákṣuṣī vā́ eté pravargyàsya, yát sūryācandra-
másau.[1] cákṣuṣī rauhiṇáu cákṣuṣor evá cákṣur
159 dadhāti. **námo rudrā́ya diviṣáde yásya varṣám**
íṣava íti. varṣā́ṃ vā́ eṣá iśūḫ[1] kṛtvā́ prajā́ hinas-
160 ti, yadógrā́ṃ vā́rṣati. **tásmai náma** íti varṣām[1]
161 evá[1] śivā́ṃ karoti. **téna mā́ sámara**[1] íti mā́ sam-
163 bādhé samā́gamāméty[2] eváitád[2] āha. [1]**námo rudrā́yān-**
tarikṣasáde,[1] **yásya vā́ta íṣava** íti. vā́taṃ vā́ eṣá
164 íṣūḫ[2] kṛtvā́ prajā́ hinasti, yadógrā́ṃ vā́ti. **tásmai**
165 **náma** íti vā́tam evá śivā́ṅ karoti. **téna mā́ sámara**[1]
166 íti mā́ sambādhé samā́gamāméty eváitád āha. **námo**
rudrā́ya[1] **pṛthivīṣáde yásyā́nnam íṣava** íty ánnaṃ[2]
vā́ eṣá íṣūḫ[3] kṛtvā́ prajā́[4] hina-
f.347b
166a [sti, yádógram ... **tásmai náma** íti ánnam
166b evá śivā́ṅ karoti. **téna mā́ sámara** íti mā́ sambādhé
samā́gamāméty eváitád āha. ...

[155] (Der Adhvaryu murmelt) "Agni, Herr der Observanz! Vāyu, Herr der Observanz! Sūrya, Herr der Observanz!" Diese sind die Observanzherren der Götter. Nachdem er diesen Göttern (seine zusätzliche Observanz) angekündigt hat, unterzieht er sich der Zwischenweihe. *[156]* (Die Sprüche) "Ein Scheit ist die Erde" (usw.) spricht er Opferspruch auf Opferspruch. || **1** ||

[157] (Mit dem Spruch) "Der Tag soll durch das Leuchtzeichen genießen, das helleuchtende der Lichter, *svāhā*" opfert er den (nördlichen) Rauhiṇa(kuchen). Jener Āditya (die Sonne) ist das Leuchtzeichen der Tage. *[158]* (Abends) opfert er den Rauhiṇa(kuchen mit dem Spruch) "Die Nacht soll durch das Leuchtzeichen genießen, das helleuchtende der Lichter, *svāhā*." Der Mond ist das Leuchtzeichen der Nächte. Sonne und Mond sind die beiden Augen des Pravargya. Die beiden Rauhiṇa(kuchen) sind die beiden Augen. In die beiden Augen setzt er Sehvermögen. *[159]* (Er murmelt) "Verehrung dem im Himmel sitzenden Rudra, dessen Pfeile der Regen sind." Indem er seine Pfeile zum Regen gemacht hat, verletzt er die Leute, wenn er heftig regnet. *[160]* (Mit dem Spruch) "Ihm sei Verehrung" macht er den Regen freundlich. *[161]* (Er murmelt) "Verhüte, daß ich damit zusammenstoße!" 'Verhüte, daß wir in Bedrängnis geraten' sagt er damit. *[163]* (Er murmelt) "Verehrung dem im Luftraum sitzenden Rudra, dessen Pfeile der Wind sind." Indem er seine Pfeile zum Wind gemacht hat, verletzt er die Leute, wenn er heftig stürmt. *[164]* (Mit dem Spruch) "Ihm sei Verehrung" macht er den Wind freundlich. *[165]* (Er murmelt) "Verhüte, daß ich damit zusammenstoße." 'Verhüte, daß wir in Bedrängnis geraten' sagt er damit. *[166]* (Er murmelt) "Verehrung dem auf der Erde sitzenden Rudra, dessen Pfeile die Speise sind." Indem er seine Pfeile zur Speise gemacht hat, verletzt er die Leute [wenn er heftig ... *[166a]* (Mit dem Spruch) "Ihm sei Verehrung!" macht er die

...

... ...[5] ṛ c o
yájūṁ]*ṣi sā́*[māni[5] ...

... ...]

167 stutíbhir [6]eváinaṁ xə'xə [stau]ti.[6] **yád bráhmaṇaś**
śṛṇávo, bhū́r íti brahmavarcasám evā́tmán dhatte.
tásmān nā́śrotriye[1] prā́vṛñjyān. ná vā́ eṣá tárhi
168 śrutábrahmā bhavaty. **átra bhūyiṣṭhabhā́ja ihá te**
syāméti védānām eváinaṃ bhāgínaṃ karoti. tás-
mād āhur: adhvaryúr vā́ adhvarā́ṃ védādhvaryúr
169 anyéṣām agraṇī́r bhavaty. **ácikradad[1] vṛ́ṣā hárir**
mahā́n mitró ná darśatá[2] íti yád vā́ eṣá várụṇo
S.110 bhūtvā́ prajā́ abhitápen, ná káñcanā́vaśiṁ syān.[3]
170 mitrá evá bhūtvā́ prajā́ abhitápati. **sáṃ[1] sū́ryeṇa[2]**
didyutad íti. sū́ryasyeva[3] vā́ eṣá etásya prakā́śo
bhavati, yásyaiṣā́[4] pravṛjyáte.[5] sárvā vā́ etárhy
etásmin devátā adhvaryór dadhigharmá āśaṁsante:
máhyaṃ grahīṣ*yati*,[6] *mahyaṅ*[6] grahīṣyatī́ti. devá-
tā[7] eváinam abhidhyā́yantīs tā́ [8]enam abhāgā́ [īś-
varā́[8] híṁstor.[9] yád etā́bhyāṃ sarvadevatyā̀bhyāṃ
172 gṛhṇā́ti: **yám índraṃ yā́vatī́ti**, devátā evá bhāgí-
nīḥ karoty: [1]ātmánó 'hiṃsāyai.[1] sárvam ā́yur eti,
yá eváṃ véda || 2 ||

173 **pūṣṇá ā́ghṛṇaye[1] sváhéti** páñcā́hutīr juhoti. pūṣā́
vái[2] rudró, rudrá ā́ghṛṇir. etā́ni vái[3] ru-

Speise freundlich.. (Er murmelt) [166b] "Verhüte, daß ich damit zusammenstoße!" 'Verhüte, daß wir in Bedrängnis geraten' sagt er damit. ...

... die Verse, die Opfersprüche, die Lieder ... ...

Mit Lobpreisungen [preist er ihn.] [167] (Mit dem Spruch) "Was du vom Brahman hören wirst, ist Gedeihen" setzt er Brahmanenansehen in sich selbst. Deshalb soll man bei einem Ungelehrten (der nicht den Veda studiert hat) den Pravargya nicht vollziehen. Nicht wird dieser (Ungelehrte) dann zu einem gelehrten Brahmanen. [168] (Mit dem Spruch) "Der du dort den größten Anteil hast, hier möchten wir dein sein" macht er ihn an den Veden anteilhaft. Deshalb sagt man: 'Der Adhvaryu kennt das Ritual; der Adhvaryu wird als der Andern Anführer verwendet.' [169] (Er singt) "Gerade gebrüllt hat der Bulle, der falbe, der große, gern gesehen wie Mitra (die Sonne)." Wenn dieser zu Varuṇa geworden auf die Nachkommenschaft brennen würde, würde er überhaupt niemanden übriglassen. Zu Mitra (d.h. zu einem Freund) geworden brennt er auf die Nachkommenschaft. [170] (Er singt) "Zusammen mit der Sonne läßt er hell aufleuchten." Wie (der Glanz der) Sonne wird dessen Glanz, von dem dieser (Kessel) ans Feuer gestellt wird. - Alle Gottheiten hoffen jetzt bei dem genannten Sauermilch-Heißtrank des Adhvaryu: 'Für mich wird er (davon) nehmen, für mich wird er (davon) nehmen.' Die Gottheiten, die es auf ihn abgesehen haben, wären als solche, die keinen Anteil haben, fähig ihn zu verletzen. Wenn er mit diesen beiden, zu allen Gottheiten gehörigen Spenden Sauermilch nimmt, (indem er) [172] "Welchen Indra als wie große" (murmelt), macht er die Gottheiten anteilhaft: das dient zu seiner eigenen Nichtverletzung. Zur vollen Lebensdauer geht, wer so weiß. || 2 ||

[173] (Mit dem Spruch) "Dem glühenden Pūṣan, *svāhā*" opfert er fünf (Butter)spenden. Pūṣan ist Rudra, der Glühende ist Rudra. Diese sind Ru[dras schreckliche Namen. ...

f.348a [-drásya ugrā́ṇi nā́māni ...
...
...
...
...
... ... udvāsaná-]
[4]-ṅ kariṣyán, sárvābhy*o* [devatā́bhya evá] *nirā́va-*
174 dayate. *sárvam ā́*yur [eti, yá evā́ṃ] véda.[4] **yā́ te**
gharma diví śúg, yā́ jā́gate śchándasi, yā́ sapta-
daśé stóme, yā́ havirdhā́ne, tā́n ta etád ávayaje,
tásyai sváhéty. amúṣyā eváinam etáj[1] jā́gatāc[1]
chándasas, saptadaśā́t stómād, dhavirdhā́nāc[2] ca
rudrā́ṃ[3] níravadayate. sárvam ā́yur eti, yá evā́ṃ
175 véda. **yā́ te gharmāntárikṣe śúg, yā́ tráiṣṭubhe**
śchándasi,[1] **yā́ pañcadaśé stóme, yā́gnīdhre, tā́n ta**
etád ávayaje, tásyai sváhéty. antárikṣād evái-
nam etát tráiṣṭubhāc[2] chándasaḥ,[2] pañcadaśā́t
stómād, ā́gnīdhrāc[3] ca rudrā́ṃ nirávadayate. sár-
vam ā́yur eti, yá evā́ṃ véda. [1]yā́ te gharma pṛthi-
176 vyā́ṃ śúg,[1] **yā́ gāyatré śchándasi, yā́ trivŕ̥ti stó-**
S.111 **me,** [**yā́**][2] **sádasi,** [1]**tā́n ta eténā́vayaje,**[1] **tásyai**
sváhéty. asyā́[3] eváinam etád gāyatrā́c[4] chándasas,
trivŕ̥tas stómāt, sádasaś ca rudrā́ṃ niráva[da]ya-
177 te.[5] sárvam ā́yur eti, yá evā́ṃ védā́nv **adyá no**
ánumata íti prátiṣṭhite juhotīyā́ṃ[1] vā́ ánumatir,

... wenn er die Entfer]nung (der Pravargyageschirre) ausführen will, findet er (ihn) von allen [Gottheiten] ab. Zur vollen Lebensdauer geht, wer so weiß. *[174]* (Er murmelt) "Welche, o Gharma, deine Glut im Himmel, welche im Jagatī-Versmaß, welche im Saptadaśa-Stoma, welche im Havirdhāna-Schuppen ist, die opfere ich so von dir weg; der (Glut) *svāhā*!" Von jener (Glut) im Himmel, vom Jagatī-Versmaß, vom Saptadaśa-Stoma, vom Havirdhāna-Schuppen, findet er Rudra so ab. Zur vollen Lebensdauer geht, wer so weiß. *[175]* (Er murmelt) "Welches, o Gharma, deine Glut im Luftraum, welche im Triṣṭubh-Versmaß, welche im Pañcadaśa-Stoma, welche im Āgnidhrā(zelt) ist, die opfere ich so von dir weg; der (Glut) *svāhā*!" Vom Luftraum, vom Triṣṭubh-Versmaß, vom Pañcadaśa-Stoma, vom Āgnidhrā(zelt) findet er Rudra so ab. Zur vollen Lebensdauer geht, wer so weiß. *[176]* (Er murmelt) "Welche, o Gharma, deine Glut auf der Erde ist, welche im Gāyatrī-Versmaß, welche im Trivṛt-Stoma, welche im Sadas(schuppen) ist, die opfere ich damit von dir weg; der (Glut) *svāhā*!" Von der Erde, vom Gāyatrī-Versmaß, vom Trivṛt-Stoma, vom Sadas(schuppen) findet er Rudra so ab. Zur vollen Lebensdauer geht, wer so weiß. *[177]* (Mit dem Spruch) "Heute [sollst du], Anumati, [unserm Opfer unter den Göttern zustimmen!]" opfert er, nachdem er festen Halt erlangt hat. Anumati ist die Erde; die Erde ist ein fester Halt. Auf ihr steht er so fest. ||

iyáṃ pratiṣṭhásyā́m eváṃ[2] prátitiṣṭhati ||

mádhunā prathamám pūrayaty. etád vā́ etásya priyā́ṃ dhā́ma. té-[3]

f.348b [-naiváinaṃ sámardhayati. ...

...

...

...

...

... ...]

[4]ta x x x x [í]ti *prā́ñcam abhyudā́nayanty. eṣá vái devalokó. devalokā́m eváinam*[4] abhyudā́nayanti.[5] pátnīm udā́nayanty, ásthūritvāya. vā́sasā pátnīṃ práśchādayati sarvadevatyàṃ vái vā́sas. sárvābhir eváinām̐[6] devátābhis sámardhayati. sā́ma[7] sampréṣyaty. upagā́yanam evásyaitád. átho
178 ny èvásmai hnuvate, 'bhiprá́yānti: **divás tvā**
paraspā́m antárikṣasya, tanvàm pāhi, pṛthivyā́s
tvā dhármaṇā vayám ánukrāmāma[1] **suvitā́ya návyasa**
180 ítīmā́ṃ llokā́n mā́ hiṁsīr[2] íty[2] eváitád āha. **prāṇā́m me pāhī́ty.** ātmána eváitā́m āśíṣam ā́śāste.
vyadhvé dvitī́yam úpayanty, abhiprá́yānti ||

181 **bráhmaṇas tvā paraspā́ṃ** [1]**kṣatrásya, tanvàṃ**[1] **pāhi, viśás tvā**[2] **dhármaṇā**[2] **vayám ánukrāmāma suvitā́ya návyasa** íti.[3] prajā́m mā́ hiṁsīr íty[2]
182 eváitád[2] āha. **vyānā́m me pāhī́ty** ātmána evái-

Mit Honig füllt er den ersten (Mahāvīrakessel). Das ist dessen liebe Stätte. Da[mit läßt er ihn zusammenkomnen.

(Mit dem Spruch: ... ...] führen sie (ihn) nach Osten gewendet hinauf. Die Götterwelt ist dieser (Osten). Zur Götterwelt führen sie ihn hinauf. Die Gattin (des Opferherrn) führen sie hinauf: das dient zur Nicht-Einspännigkeit. Mit einem Kleid verhüllt man die Gattin. Das Kleid ist zu allen Gottheiten gehörig. Mit allen Gottheiten läßt er sie zusammenkommen. (Der Adhvaryu) fordert zum Sāman auf. Das ist sein (des Pravargya-Rituals) gemeinsamer Gesang (d.h. mit Einstimmen aller Opferteilnehmer in das Schlußstück des Sāman). Jetzt nun leisten sie ihm Abbitte und gehen weiter (mit dem Spruch) *[178]* "Dir, dem Schutz des Himmels und des Luftraumes - schütze den Körper - dir wollen wir mit dem Halt der Erde folgen zum erneuten Fortgang." 'Verletze diese Welten nicht!' sagt er damit. *[180]* (Er murmelt) "Schütze mein Ausatmen!" Für sich selbst wünscht er diesen Wunsch. Auf halbem Wege stimmen sie in (das gemeinsame Sāman) zum zweiten Mal ein und gehen weiter. ||

[181] (Sie tun dies mit dem Spruch) "Dir, dem Schutz des Priesters und des Adels - schütze den Körper - dir wollen wir aufgrund des Haltes des Volkes folgen zu erneutem Fortgang." 'Schütze meine Nachkommenschaft' sagt er damit. *[182]* (Er murmelt) "Schütze mein Einatmen!" Für sich selbst wünscht er diesen Wunsch. (Dem Ziel[2]) genaht, stimmen sie in (das gemeinsame Sāman) zum dritten Mal ein und gehen weiter (mit dem Spruch) *[183]* "Dir, dem Schutze des Ausatmens und des Gesichtssinnes - schütze den Körper - dir

tā́m[1] āśíṣam ā́śāsta. upaprā́pya tṛtī́yam úpayanty,
183 abhiprā́yānti: **prāṇásya[1] tvā paraspā́ṃ[2] cákṣuṣas,
tanvàm pāhi, śrótrasya[3] tvā dhármaṇā vayám ánu-
krāmāma suvitā́ya návyasa** íti. prā-
f.349a
183a [ṇán mā́ hiṁsīr íty eváitád āhā**pānám me pāhí**ty.
ātmána eváitā́m āśíṣam ā́śāste. ...

...

...

...

... ve-]
[1]-*dā́* bh*a*v*an*ti. k*é*ś*ā*n *evái*[nān tát karot]y. *a*bhi-
t*a*ḫ kap*á*l*ā*n*i*. [kapā́lāny evá tá]t karoty.[1] abhí-
to rukmáu nídadhāty. cákṣuṣī evá tát karoti.
paścā́c[2] caruṣṭhālī́ nídadhāty. āsyàm[3] evá tát
karoti. paścā́t sruvā́ṃ[4] nídadhāty. grīvā́m evá
tát karoty. abhítaś śapháu nídadhāty. áṁsā[5] evá
S.112 tát karoti. srucáu[6] bāhū́ karoti, sāt*m*atvā́yābhí-
to[7] dhavítre bhavataḫ. pārśvé evá tát karoti.
mádhya upayāmó[8] rajjvóś[8] ca váiṇavāni[9] bhavan-
ty.[10] udáram evá tát karoti. paścā́d auṣṭhyáu[11]
nídadhāty. upástham evá tát karoty. abhíto ma-
yū́khā bhavanti. jáṅghe ūrū́ evá tát karoty. abhí-
to[12] dhṛ́ṣṭī[13] nídadhāti. pā́dā evá tát karoti.
mádhye dhavítram nídadhāti. nā́bhim evá tát ka-
roty. upáry āsandī́m[14] nídadhāty. úra evá tát

wollen wir mit dem Halt des Gehörs folgen zu erneutem Fortgang." 'Meine Le[bensfunktionen schütze!' sagt er damit. [183a] "Schütze mein Hinabatmen! " (murmelt er). Für sich selbst wünscht er diesen Wunsch. ... ...

... Grasbü]schel werden angewendet. Zum Haupthaar macht er sie damit. Auf beiden Seiten macht er die Schalen zu den Hirnschalen. Auf beiden Seiten setzt er die zwei Metallplatten nieder. Zu den beiden Augen macht er sie damit. Im Westen setzt er die zwei Milchtöpfe hin. Den Mund macht er so. Im Westen setzt er den Sruva-Löffel hin. Den Hals macht er so. Auf beiden Seiten setzt er die zwei 'Hufe' (der Hebezange) hin. Die beiden Schultern macht er so. Die beiden Sruc-Löffel macht er zu den Armen; das dient zum Versehensein mit dem Selbst. Auf beiden Seiten kommen zwei Fächer zur Anwendung. Die beiden Brustseiten macht er so. In der Mitte kommen der Untersatz und die Bambus(abschabsel) der beiden Stricke zur Anwendung. Den Bauch macht er so. Im Westen setzt er die beiden (mit einem Ausguß in Form einer Elefanten)lippe versehenen Gefäße nieder. Den Schoß macht er so. Auf beiden Seiten kommen Pflöcke zur Anwendung. Die beiden Unterschenkel und die beiden Oberschenkel macht er so. Auf beiden Seiten setzt er die beiden Schürhaken nieder. Die beiden Füße macht er so. In der Mitte setzt er den (dritten) Fächer nieder. Den Nabel macht er so. Obendrauf setzt er den Sessel hin. Die Brust macht er so. Mit dem Antilopenfell be-

karoti kṛṣṇājinéna práśchādayati. bráhmaṇo vā́
etád rūpám, yát kṛṣṇājinám. bráhmaṇaiváinam
práśchādayati. múñjaiḫ práśchādayaty. ū́rg vái
múñjā,[15] ūrjáiváinaṃ práśchādayati. dadhná sáṃ-
sṛjati, satejastvā́yāghātu*ká*[16] enaṁ rudró bhava-
ti ||

haṁsavat[17] karoty. asáu vā́ ādityó haṁsā́ e-[18]

f.349b [...

...

...

...

...

... ...]

[19]x x x x tri]ḫ páriṣiñc x x x x x x xux *pári-*
184 *ṣiñcan* pár*yeti*: ***valgúr asi***[19] **vayodhā́yā** íti.
185 váya [1]evā́syaitád ardhayati.[1] **śíśur jánadhāyā** íti.
rūpám evā́syaitán mahimā́naṃ vyā́caṣṭe. yádi[1] vā́yāṁ-
186 sy upā́sīran, gharmám etā́ḫ prajā́ úpāsiṣyanta íti
vidyāt. tásmād váyobhyaḫ páriraks̥etā́ **sṛṅmukho**,[1]
ví gā́ ivéti[2] dvā́bhyāṃ juhuyān. mṛtyúr vái yamás.
187 svénaiváinam[3] bhāgadhéyena śamayati. [1]**śā́ñ ca**
188 **vakṣi**,[1] **pári ca vakṣī́ty** āśī́ṣam evā́śāste. **sumitrā́**
na ā́pa íty apá útsiñcanti.[1] sumitrā́ eváināḫ ka-
189 roti. **durmitrā́s tásmai santv** íti [1]yásyām asya[1]
diśí dvéṣyas syā́t, tā́n díśam párāsiñced. durmi-

deckt er (die aus den Gerätschaften hergestellte Gestalt). Das Antilopenfell ist die Gestalt des Brahman. Mit dem Brahman bedeckt er (die Gestalt). Kraft sind die Muñja(gräser). Mit Kraft bedeckt er ihn (die Gestalt). Mit Sauermilch vermischt er (den Honig): das dient zum Versehensein mit Glut. Töten könnte ihn Rudra (wenn er nicht so täte). ||

Er macht (eine Figur, einen Altar?) in Gans-Gestalt (? d.h. Sonnengestalt?). Jener Āditya (die Sonne) ... ... Gänse ...

umgieß[... ...] umgießend geht er um (den Kessel herum (mit dem Spruch) *[184]* "Angenehm bist du; dem Spender der Kraft." Dessen Kraft läßt er da erlangen. *[185]* (Er murmelt) "Ein Kind, das Leute nährt." Seine Gestalt erklärt er damit als Größe. Wenn sich Vögel hinsetzen, soll er wissen: 'Diese Nachkommenschaft wird sich zum Kessel hinsetzen.' Deshalb soll er sich vor den Vögeln schützen (indem er mit den beiden Sprüchen) *[186]* "Als einer mit blutigem Mund" (und) "Die Kühe durchwandernd (?)" mit zwei (Löffeln flüssiger Butter) opfert. Yama ist der Tod. Mit seinem eigenen Anteil besänftigt er ihn. *[187]* (Mit dem Spruch) "Fahre das Glück herbei, fahre (es) herum," wünscht er einen Wunsch. *[188]* (Mit dem Spruch) "Freundlich sollen uns die Wasser sein" gießen sie Wasser aus. Freundlich macht er sie. *[189]* (Mit dem Spruch) "Feindlich sollen sie ihm sein" soll er in der Richtung, in der sich sein Feind befinden dürfte, (Wasser) weggießen. Feind-

trā́ eváinā̱ḥ karot- || -ty.[2]

190 **etát te gharmā́nnam, etát púrīṣam** íti. ghṛtáṃ vái
S.113 dádhi. mádhv íty etásyā́nnan.[1] ténaiváinaṁ sám-
192 ardhayati. **téna tváṃ vardhasvéty** annā́dyenaiváinaṁ
193 sámardhayati. **vardhiṣīmáhi ca vayám ā́ ca pyāyi-**
194 **ṣīmahíty** āśíṣam evā́śāste.[1] **rántir nā́māsíty.** etád
vái ru-

f.350a [-drasya śivó nā́ma. ...

...

...

...

...

...

...

... ... í-]

195 ty ātmána[1] ev*ā́i*tā́m[2] [3]āśíṣ*am ā́śā*sta.[3] **índur dák-**
195a **ṣaś śyenā́** [1]**ṛtā́[vā híraṇyapakṣas; so]mapīthā́nu**[1]
195b **mehy; édho 'sy, édhiṣīmahíti.**[1] rudrám evá [2]nir-
196 áva[dayante. náiváinaṁ śucā́r]payanti.[2] **samíd asi,**
197 **sámedhiṣīmahíty** āśíṣam [1]evā́ś[āste. **púnar té]jo**[1]
198 **máyi dhehíti** téja evā́tmán[2] dhatta. **úd u tyā́ñ**
jātávedasam íti dā́śā́hut*ī*r[1] juhoti. dā́śākṣarā
virā́ḍ, ánnaṃ virā́ḍ. virā́jy evā́nnā́dye[2] prátitiṣ-
ṭhati ||

kín dīkṣáyā spṛṇótíty āhu̱ḥ, kím avāntaradīkṣá-

lich macht er (die Wasser). ||

[190] (Er murmelt) "Dies, o Gharma, ist deine Speise, dies dein Kot." Die Sauermilch ist flüssige Butter. 'Süßes' heißt seine Speise. Mit ihr läßt er ihn zusammenkommen. [192] (Indem er sagt) "Gedeihe du damit" läßt er ihn damit zusammenkommen. [193] (Mit dem Spruch) "Wir möchten gedeihen und fett werden" wünscht er einen Wunsch." [194] (Er murmelt) "Ranti ('Gerne Verweilen') mit Namen bist du." Das ist Ru[dras freundlicher Name. ...

... sagt er).] Für sich selbst wünscht er einen Wunsch. [195] (Er murmelt) "Als geschickter Tropfen, der das Ṛta befolgende Falke, der goldgeflügelte; o Somatrank, komm zu mir; sein Brennholz möchten wir anzünden." Rudra fin[det er (so) ab. Nicht lassen sie ihn Schmerz erla]ngen. [196] (Mit dem Spruch) "Brennholz bist du, wir möchten dich anzünden" wünscht er einen Wunsch. [197] (Mit dem Spruch) "Setze [wieder Glut] in mich" setzt er Glut in sich selbst. [198] (Mit dem Spruch) "Hinauf (führen) diesen (Gott) Jātavedas" opfert er zehn (Butter)spenden. Die Virāj ist zehnsilbig; die Virāj ist Speise. In der Virāj] als Speise hat er festen Halt. ||

'Was rettet man mit der Weihe' sagt man, 'was mit der Zwi-

yéty. ātmánam evá dīkṣáyā spr̥ṇóti, prajā́m avān-
taradīkṣáyā. dvā́daśa vā́ eṣā́ varṣā́ṇi dīkṣitó
bhavati, yó brahmacārī́. tásya vā́ eṣā́ dīkṣā́ yád
avāntaradīkṣā́. mékhalām ā́badhnāte.[3] daṇḍám úpa-
yaśchati.[4] samídha ā́harati. púnar adhyā́haraty.
áudumbarīr bhavanty. ū́rg[5] vā́ udumbára. ū́rjam
evá brahmacāríṇi nídadhāti. parṇamáyīr bhavanti.
brahmavarcasáṃ vái parṇó. brahmavarcasám evá
brahmacāríṇi nídadhāti. śamīmáyīr bha-
f.350b [vanti téjo[6] vái śamī́. téja evá brahmacāríṇi
198a nídadhāty. **ágne vratapate; pr̥thiví samíd** íti
prathamā́ṁ samídham ā́dadhāty. agnír vái devā́nām
pr̥thivyā́yāṃ vratápatis. tásmā evá prócya vratā́ñ
198b carati. vrátyo bhavati. **vā́yo vratapate; antári-
kṣaṃ samíd** íti dvitī́yāṃ samídham ā́dadhāti. vā-
S.114 yúr vái devā́nām antárikṣe vratápatis. tásmā evá]
199 prócya[1] vratā́ñ carati. vrátyo bhavati. **sū́rya
vratapate; dyáus** [1]**samí[d** íti tr̥]tī́yāṃ[1] samídham
ā́dadhāti. sū́ryo vái devā́nām amúṣmiṃ lloké [vrá-
tápa]tis.[2] tásmā evá prócya[3] vratā́ñ carati. [4]vrá-
tyo bhavati.[4] nā́bhivyā́harati[5] [nā́]bhipré́kṣate.[6]
téja evā́tmán dhatte. párvaṇi tiṣṭhed divā́, āsīta
náktaṁ, satejastvā́yāgnínādityéna[7] ca śrītám aś-
nāti. havír vái dīkṣitó. havír evā́tti. sámāpté
'nvāha.[8] prá vā́ ítarebhyo lokébhyaś[9] cyavate[10]

schenweihe?' Sein Selbst rettet er mit der Weihe, die Nachkommenschaft mit der Zwischenweihe. Für zwölf Jahre wird zum Geweihten, wer ein Brahmanenschüler ist. Dessen Weihe ist die Zwischenweihe. Er bindet den Gürtel um. Er ergreift den Stab. Er bringt Brennholz herbei. Wieder bringt er (Brennholz) herbei (und ergänzt so täglich den Vorrat des Lehrers). Udumbara(hölzer) kommen zur Anwendung. Der Udumbara(baum) ist Kraft. Kraft setzt er in den Brahmanenschüler. Parṇamayi(hölzer) kommen zur Anwendung. Der Parṇamayi(baum) ist Brahmanenansehen. Brahmanenansehen setzt er in den Brahmanenschüler. Śamī(hölzer) kom[men zur Anwendung. Der Śamī(baum) ist Glut. Glut setzt er in den Brahmanenschüler. *[198a]* (Mit den Sprüchen) "Agni, Herr der Observanz; das Scheit ist die Erde" legt er das erste Scheit an. Agni ist der Observanzherr der Götter auf dieser Welt hier. Nachdem er es ihm angekündigt hat, hält er die Observanz ein. Er wird Teilnehmer an der Observanz. *[198b]* (Mit den Sprüchen) "Vāyu, Herr der Observanz; das Scheit ist der Luftraum" legt er das zweite Scheit an. Vāyu ist der Observanzherr der Götter im Luftraum. Nachdem er es ihm angekündigt hat, hält er die Observanz ein. Er wird Teilnehmer an der Observanz. *[199]* (Mit den Sprüchen) "Sūrya, Herr der Observanz; das Scheit ist der Himmel," zündet er] das drit[te Scheit an. Die Sonne ist] der Observanzherr [der Götter in jener Welt.] Nachdem er es ihr angekündigt hat, hält er die Observanz ein. Er wird Teilnehmer an der Observanz. - Nicht spricht er auf (etwas) hin, nicht blickt er auf (etwas) hin. Glut setzt er in sein Selbst. An einem Knotentag soll er tagsüber stehen, nicht sitzen: das dient dem Versehensein mit Glut. Mit (den Strahlen von) Feuer und Sonne Gekräftigtes ißt er. Der Geweihte ist Opferspeise. Opferspeise nur ißt er. Am Ende (der Nacht?) sagt er (die zur Observanz gehörigen Sprüche) auf. Von den andern Welten weg

yó brahmacārī́. yád itá ū́rdhvaṃ samídha ādádhāty, amúṣmiṃs téna loké prátitiṣṭhati. yád amúto 'rvā́ṅ pratyādádhāty,[11] asmíṃs téna loké [12]prátitiṣṭhati. yadā́ garmúto[12] viróhati, tadā́nubrūyād. dhāriṇo yadā́ yávam átti, tadā́nubrūyāt. sūkaró yadā́ bísam átti, tadā́nubrūyād.[13] rūpásamṛddhim evā́nvāha.[14] [15]téjasā[16] vā́ eṣá prajáyā paśúbhir brahmavarcasénānnā́dyena[17] ca vyṙddhyate[18] yó[19]

f.351a brahmacārī́. yán[20] nā́bhivyāhárati nā́bhipréksate, téjo[21] evā́tmán dhatte. yát kanyàm abhivyāhára-ty[22] abhipréksate, [23]prajā́m evā́tmán dhatte. yád vatsám abhivyāháraty,[24] abhipréksate,[25] paśū́n evā́tmán[26] dhatte.[27] yádādityám[28] abhivyāháraty abhipréksate, brahma-[23,29]-varcasám evā́tmán dhatte. [30]yát kṣīraudanám[30] abhivyāháraty abhipréksate, 'nnā́dyam evā́tmán [31]dhattè. 'tho[31] tejasvī́[32] prajā́vān paśumā́n brahmavarcasy ànūrādho[33] bhavati,[34] yá[35] eváṃ véda[35] ||[15]

[...

199a **āyurdā́**, **ā́yur me dehí**ty ā́yur evā́tmán dadhate. ...]
[1]x x x pravṛjyámāṇəxíx x xupadháya mārjayaty. axə'
200 x x x x x x x x tādevā́vyā́dhi **prāṇadā́ḥ prāṇā́ṃ me**
201 **dehí**ti prāṇā́m evā́tmán dadhate.[1] **vyānadā́ vyānā́ṃ**[1]
202 **me dehí**ti vyānā́m evā́tmán dadhate. **'pānadā́ apā-**

bewegt sich der Brahmanenschüler. Wenn er von hier weg die Scheite nach oben hin zulegt, hat er damit festen Halt in jener Welt. Wenn er von dort hierher gewandt in entgegengesetzter Richtung zulegt, hat er damit in dieser Welt festen Stand. Wenn eine Bohnenpflanze auseinanderwächst, soll er nachsprechen. Wenn eine Gazelle Gerste frißt, soll er nachsprechen. Wenn ein Eber einen Lotossproß frißt, soll er nachsprechen. In Übereinstimmung mit (deren jeweiliger) Gestalt spricht er nach. Um Glut, Nachkommenschaft, Vieh, Brahmanenansehen und Nahrung kommt der Brahmanenschüler (wenn er darauf hinspricht oder hinblickt). Wenn er nicht darauf hinspricht, nicht darauf hinblickt, setzt er Glut in sich. Wenn er zu einem Mädchen hin spricht, zu (ihm) hinblickt, setzt er Nachkommenschaft in sich. Wenn er zu einem Kalb hin spricht, zu (ihm) hinblickt, setzt er Vieh in sich. Wenn er zur Sonne hin spricht, auf (sie) hinblickt, setzt er Brahmanenansehen in sich. Wenn er auf einen Milchbrei hin spricht, auf (ihn) hinblickt, setzt er Speise in sich. Jetzt aber (nachdem ihn sein Lehrer auf ein Mädchen, ein Kalb, die Sonne, den Milchbrei hat hinsprechen und hinblicken lassen) wird der zu einem, der Glut, Nachkommenschaft, Vieh, Brahmanenansehen besitzt, zu einem Erfolgreichen, wer so weiß. ||

[...

[199a *]* (Mit dem Spruch) "Als Geber des Lebens, setze Leben in mich" setzen sie Lebensdauer in sich. ... ...] ... ans Feuer stellend ... zusetzend ... läßt er reinigen. ... (?) ... *[* 200 *]* (Mit dem Spruch) "Als Geber des Einatmens gib mir Einatmen" setzen sie Einatmen in sich selbst. *[* 201 *]* (Mit dem Spruch) "Als Geber des Auseinanderatmens gib mir Auseinanderatmen" setzen sie Auseinanderatmen in sich selbst. *[* 202 *]* (Mit dem Spruch) "Als Geber des Ausatmens gib mir Ausatmen" setzen sie Ausatmen in sich

203 **nám me dehíty** apānám evā́tmán dadhate. **cakṣur-
dā́ś[1] cákṣur me dehíti** cákṣur evā́tmán dadhate.
204 **śrotradā́ś[1] śrótram[1] me dehíti** śrótram[1] evā́tmán
205 dadhate. **varcodā́ várco me dehíti** várca evā́tmán
206 dadhata. **ā́yuṣe[1] naḥ púnar dehíty** ā́yur evā́tmán
207 dadhaté. 'tho 'visraṃsāyaivā́pradāhāya **námo ru-
drā́yéti** ||

rudrám[1] vái devā́ yajñā́n nírabhajan. sá dhánur avaṣṭábhyātiṣṭhat. tásyéndro[1] vamrirūpéṇa dhanurjyā́m aśchinat. sā́[3] ghṛṅṅ akarot. tásyā́rtiś śíra útpipeṣa. sá [4]pravargyò 'bhavad.[4] yán mahatī́r devátā vīryàvatīs, tásmān mahāvīró. yád
S.115 dhánur ghṛṅṅ ákarot, tásmād gharmó. yát pravṛjyáte, tásmāt pravargyàs. tásmād,[5] yás sápravargyeṇa yajñéna yájate, rudrásya śíra úpadadhāti. náinaṁ rudrá ā́ruko bhavati,[6]

f.351b [[7]yá eváṃ véda.[7] ...

...

...

...

...

...

...

... ...]

[8]x x x x [śú]*kriyāṇāṃ vā́* etáni śúkriyāṇi. tác

selbst. [203] (Mit dem Spruch) "Als Geber des Augenlichtes gib mir Augenlicht" setzen sie Augenlicht in sich selbst. [204] (Mit dem Spruch) "Als Geber des Gehörs gib mir Gehör" setzen sie Gehör in sich selbst. [205] (Mit dem Spruch) "Als Geber des Ansehens gib mir Ansehen" setzen sie Ansehen in sich selbst. [206] (Mit dem Spruch) "Dem Leben gib uns wieder" setzen sie Leben in sich selbst. Jetzt aber (sagt er) für das Nichtzerfallen (der Glieder) und für Nichtverbrennen (den Spruch) [207] "Verehrung dem Rudra." ||

Den Rudra schlossen die Götter vom Opfer aus. Auf seinen Bogen gestützt stellte er sich hin. Seine Bogensehne schnitt Indra in Gestalt einer Ameise ab. Die (Bogensehne) machte *'ghṛṅ'*. Sein Bogenende schmetterte (Rudras) Kopf empor. Der wurde zum Pravargya(kessel). Weil es sich um große, Manneskraft besitzende Gottheiten (*mahatīr vīryavatīḥ*) handelte, deshalb der (Name) 'großer Held' (*Mahāvīra*). Weil der Bogen *'ghṛṅ'* machte, deshalb der (Name) *'Gharma'* ('Heißtrank'). Weil der (Gharmakessel) ans Feuer gestellt wird (*pravṛjyate*), deshalb der (Name) 'Pravargya'. Deshalb setzt, wer mit einem Opfer für sich opfert, das mit der Pravargya(zeremonie) verbunden ist, den Kopf Rudras wieder an. Nicht wird Rudra zu einem den Angreifenden, [der so weiß. ...

...]

Von den leuchtenden (Sāman) [stammen] die besagten Śukriya-

chúkriyāṇāṃ śukri[yat]*vá*[ṃ tébhir de]*v*áḫ[8] pu-
rástād yajñásya právṛñjata. yát právṛñjata, tás-
māt právargyāṇi, tásmāt pravargyàs. tásmād, yás
sápravargyeṇa yajñéna yájate, múkhyo brahmavar-
casī́ bhavaty. eṣá vā́vá tárhi yajñá āsīd, yád
eṣá jyótiṣṭomas;[9] tád yáthā vā́ idám agnér jātā́d
agnáyo[10] 'nyé vihriyánta, evám asmād anyé yajña-
kratávaḫ prájāyante. tásmāj jyótiṣṭome právṛñ-
jyād, yajñásyordhvatvā́ya. nókthyè[11] právṛñjyāt.[12]
prajā́ vái paśáva ukthā́ni. yád ukthyè[13] pravṛñ-
jyā́t,[14] prajā́ñ cāsya paśū́ṃś ca[15] [16]nírdahet.
tásm[āt] pr[ajākámāya pa]śukā́māya[16] ná právṛñ-
jyād.[17] asáu vā́ ādityó rudró mahāvīró. rudrā́d
evá prajā́m paśū́n párivṛṇakti. tásmād vā́sasā pát-
nīm práśchādayati: prajā́yā ápradāhāya. sarváto-
208, pakramé právṛñjyād. **bhū́r bhúvas svàr; námo vācé,**
208a **námo vācaspátaya**[1] íti. vā́g vái sárasvatī.

f.352a [**yā vāg uditā yā cānuditā, tasyai vāce nama**
iti ...

208c **nama ṛṣibhyo mantrakṛdbhyo mantravidbhya** iti ...
...

208d **mā mām ṛṣayo mantrakṛto mantravidaḫ parādur**
iti ...

208e ... ... **daivīṃ vācam udyāsam** iti daivīm
209 eva vācaṃ vada]ti.[1] **śivá m**[2] **ájasrām**[2] íti śivā́m[3]

(Yajus?). Das ist die Herkunft des (Namens) 'Śukriya(yajus)'. Die Götter setzten (den Mahāvīrakessel) damit vor (dem Hauptteil)des (Soma)opfers ans Feuer. Weil sie ihn ans Feuer setzten (*prāvṛñjata*), daher der (Name) Pravargya-(Yajus?), daher der (Name) Pravargya. Deshalb wird derjenige, der mit einem Opfer für sich opfert, das mit dem Pravargya(ritus) verbunden ist, zu einem, der an der Spitze steht, zu einem mit Brahmanenansehen. Dieser Jyotiṣṭoma war damals nämlich das Opfer. Wie hier (auf dem Opferplatz!) aus dem entstandenen Feuer die anderen Feuer auseinandergenommen werden, so entstanden daraus (aus dem Jyotiṣṭoma) die andern Opferhandlungen (die abgewandelten Soma-Rituale). Deshalb soll man bei einem Jyotiṣṭoma den Pravargya vollziehen: das dient zur Erhöhung des Opfers. Nicht soll man ihn bei einem Ukthya vollziehen. Die Uktha-Preisungen sind Nachkommenschaft und Vieh. Wenn man den Pravargya bei einem Ukthya vollzöge, würde (der Pravargya) dessen Nachkommenschaft und Vieh [verbrennen. Deshalb soll er für einen, der Nachkommenschaft und Vieh] wünscht, den Pravargya (bei einem Ukthya) nicht vollziehen. Rudra Mahāvīra ist jener Āditya (die Sonne). Vor Rudra verschont er Nachkommenschaft und Vieh. Deshalb verhüllt man die Gattin (des Opferherrn) mit einem Gewand: das dient der Nachkommenschaft und dem Nichtverbrennen. Jedesmal soll man beim 'Herangehen' den Pravargya vollziehen (bei jeder Pressung?). *[208]* (Er murmelt) "*Bhūr, bhuvas, svar*, Verehrung der Rede, Verehrung dem Herrn der Rede." Sarasvatī ist die Rede. [(Er sagt die Sprüche:) *[208b]* "Welche Rede gesagt und welche ungesagt ist, dieser Rede Verehrung!" ...

[208c] "Den mantraverfassenden und den mantrawissenden Sehern Verehrung!" ...

[208d] "Nicht sollen mich die mantraverfassenden und die mantrawissenden Seher preisgeben!" ...

[208e] "Die göttliche Rede möchte ich sagen!" Die göttliche

210 eváinām ájasrāṃ karo[t]i.[4] [[1]**júṣṭāṃ devébhya**
211 í]ti[1] devébhya eváināṃ júṣṭāṃ karoti. **svadhá-**
vatīm pitŕ̥bhya [1]í[ti pitŕ̥bhya evái]nāṃ[1] svadhá-
212 vatīṅ karoti. **śuśrūṣeṇyáṃ manuṣyèbhya**[1] íti.[2]
213 manuṣyèbhya[1] *eváinaṃ*[3] *śuśrūṣeṇyáṅ*[3] karoti. [1]**tám**
mā devá[1] **avantu śobháyai, pitáró 'numadantv** íty
ánv enaṃ devá avanti śobháyai, pitáró 'numadan-
214 ti **sucakṣá ahám akṣíbhyāṃ, suvárcā múkhena,**
suśrút kárṇābhyāṃ bhūyāsam íti yathāyajúr. apa-
215 vargé 'pi mārjayante. **śivá naś śántamā bhava**
sumr̥ḷīká,[1] **sárasvatíti.**[1] vág vái sárasvatī. vā-
216 cáivá prayánti, vācódyanti. [1]**bráhmaṇa upastára-**
ṇam[1] **asi, bráhmaṇe tvópastr̥ṇāmíti**[2] prajáyā evá
217 paśūnám[3] upastáraṇaṃ karotíḷāyai **vástv**[1] **así**ti,
prátiṣṭhityā. **á vāta vāhi bheṣajáṃ, ví vāta**
218 **vāhi yád rápa** íti. prāṇó vái vāyúḥ. prāṇám evá-
219 sya bhúyiṣṭhaṃ karoty. **ápo hí ṣṭhá ma-**
f.352b [**yobhúva** íti ...

...

...

...

...

... xə'x *t*]

[1]x x x x x x x x x x x x x*ŕ̥*co yájūṁ ṣi sá*mā*ní[ti].
tád vái tredhāvi[hitó yád védaḥ. x x x x x kál-]

Rede spri]cht er. [209] (Indem er murmelt) "Die freundliche, nicht ermüdende (Rede)" macht er sie freundlich und nicht ermüdend. [210] (Indem er murmelt) "Die den Göttern angenehme" macht er sie den Göttern angenehm. [211] (Indem er murmelt) "Die für die Väter Labung enthaltende" macht er sie für die Väter Labung enthaltend. [212] (Indem er murmelt) "Die von den Menschen gern gehörte" macht er sie zur von den Menschen gern gehörten. [213] (Indem er murmelt) "Als solch einem sollen die Götter mir helfen zur Pracht, sollen die Väter sich mit (mir) freuen" helfen die Götter ihm weiter zur Pracht, freuen sich die Väter mit (ihm). [214] (Mit den Sprüchen) "Möchte ich gut sehend werden mit den Augen, wohlangesehen durch den Mund, guthörend mit den Ohren" (murmelt er) Spruch auf Spruch. Auch bei Beendigung (der Observanz) reinigen sie sich. [215] (Er murmelt den Spruch) "Werde uns, Sarasvatī, freundlich, ganz zum Heil, gut erbarmend." Sarasvatī ist die Rede. Mit der Rede gehen sie vor (beginnt man die Observanz), mit der Rede gehen sie hinauf (beendet man die Observanz). [216] (Mit dem Spruch) "Die Streu des Brahman bist du, dem Brahman streue ich dich hin" macht er der Nachkommenschaft und dem Vieh eine Streu. [217] (Er murmelt) "Der Platz für die Iḍā bist du": das dient dem fest Hinstellen. [218] (Er murmelt) "Wind, wehe Heilung herbei; weg wehe, Wind, was ein Gebrechen ist." Der Wind ist das Einatmen. Seinen Atem macht er zum Gedeihlichsten. [219] (Er murmelt) "Ihr Wasser seid nämlich er[quickend" ...

... ...] sind die Verse, Opfersprüche und Melodien. Dreifach geteilt [ist der Veda. Es gedei]ht ihm dreifach

(219) pate[1] 'smai tredhā́ yogakṣemā́ḫ prajā́yāḫ paśū-
[2][nā́ṃ viśā́ḥ. x x áthaiṣa vratā́ṃ cariṣ]yā́nn,[2]
áraṇyam parétya, śúcau bhūmyavakāśé [3]grā́mā[d
aśchadírdarśé 'dhyāpaya]ti.[3] mṛtyór vā́ eṣá
goṣṭhó yád grā́mó; 'thaiṣá devā́nāṃ yád [4]á[raṇ-
S.116 yam. ápa punarm]ṛtyúṃ[4] jayati,[5] yá eváṃ védódi-
ta ādityé pūrvāhṇé pūrvapakṣá udagáyané 'dhī-
yītaitád vái tríśukriyaṃ.[6] tríśukriyo[6] bhavati,
yá eváṃ véda ||

nā́bhreṣu,[7] ná samauhé, [8]*ná* gávām *án*te,[8] ná pár-vopaparváyor:[9] ātmánó 'hiṁsāyai. ná mṛtā́ṃ dvipā́dāñ cátuṣpadām práty: ātmánó 'hiṁsāyai. ná, mṛtā́ṃ dvipā́dāṃ[10] cátuṣpadāṃ,[11] māṁsám, ásthi, lóhitaṃ, caṇḍālám, áśuci vā dṛṣṭvā́medhyā́ni[12] vā́[13] etā́ni: medhyatvā́ya. ná, pūrvedyúr [14]māṁsám attvā́.[14] ná, pūrvedyúr[15] abrahmacaryā́m upétya. ná tád áhaḫ pūrvāhṇé[16] keśaśmaśrū́[17] lomanakhā́ni vāpayen, nā́valikhen, nā́ñjyān,[18] nā́bhyàñjyān, ná snāyāt: téjasó 'navabhraṁśāya. ná grāmyā́ṇām paśū́nāṁ[19] sandárśanenā́śāntikṛtas[20] sáṁsṛje-[21]

f.353a [-ta. ...

...

...

...

Umherziehen und friedliches Wohnen: für Nachkommenschaft, Vie[h und Volk(?). Um nun die Observanz einzu]halten, [lehr]t er, nachdem er in die Wildnis gegangen ist, auf einem reinen Stück freien Landes, das vom Dorf [aus nicht sichtbar ist]. Das Dorf ist die Kuhhürde des Todes, die Wildnis aber jetzt die der Götter. [Weg] siegt den [Wieder-t]od, wer so weiß. Wenn die Sonne aufgegangen ist, am Vormittag, in der ersten Monatshälfte, beim Gang der Sonne nach Norden (d.h. im Vorfrühling, Frühling und der heißen Jahreszeit allein) soll er lernen. Das ist dreifach glänzend. Durch dreifachen Glanz ausgezeichnet wird, wer so weiß. ||

Nicht (soll er lernen) unter (mit) Wolken (bedecktem Himmel), nicht bei einem Staubwirbel(?), nicht in der Nähe von Kühen, nicht an einem Knotentag und an dem einem Knotentag vorausgehenden oder folgenden Tag: das dient zur Nichtverletzung des Selbstes. Nicht angesichts eines Toten von Zweifüßlern (oder) von Vierfüßlern: das dient zur Nichtverletzung seines Selbstes. Nicht, wenn er einen Toten von Zweifüßlern (oder) Vierfüßlern, Fleisch, Knochen, Blut, einen Caṇḍāla oder Unreines gesehen hat, - diese sind unrein - das dient zur Opferwürdigkeit. Nicht, wenn er tags zuvor Fleisch gegessen hat. Nicht, wenn er eine Unkeuschheit begangen hat. Nicht soll er sich an diesem Tage, am Vormittag, Haupthaar und Bart, Körperhaare und Nägel scheren lassen, nicht soll er sich kratzen, nicht (den Körper) salben, nicht (die Augen) salben, nicht baden: das dient zum Nichtherabfallen der Glut. Nicht soll er sich auf das Anblicken von Dorfvieh einlassen, ohne die Beschwichtigung gemacht zu haben. [...

(219) ...

...

[22]x x x x x x x x x x x xt x x x *bhi*xr x x x
x x n[22] pátrāṇi kārayet. tápo vái dīkṣā́. tapa-
saivā́sya práyunakty. uttaratás[23] [tiṣṭhati].[23]
tásmin múkhyaṃ mahāvīráṃ práyunakty, anvahám
ítarau.[24] gāyatró vā́ [25]eté[ṣām pratha]más,[25]
tráiṣṭubho dvitī́yo, jā́gatas tṛtī́yo. 'nvahám evá
yathāpūrváṃ chándāṁsi yunakti. śíro vā́ [26]etád
yajñásya,[26] yát pravargyàs. tásya kapā́lāni kapā́-
lāni, kéśā vedáu,[27] dhavítre kárṇau, dhavitra-
daṇḍáu nā́sike, rukmáu cákṣuṣī: sáuvarṇo dákṣi-
ṇaṃ, rā́jata úttaraṃ. mahāvīrā́ḥ[28] kaṇṭhā́, āsyàñ
caruṣṭhālī́, hánū śaphā́, aniṣṭubdhī́[29] aṣṭhīván-
tau dáṁṣṭrā,[30] mayū́khā[30] dántā, yád gharmé nidá-
dhāti, jihvópayāmó rajjvóś[31] ca [32]váiṇavāni
snā́vāni, puroḷā́śo[32] mastíṣko. yád áṅgārair abhy-
ū́hati, tán māṁsáṃ, kéśā[33] vedā́,[34] ā́jyaṃ majjā́,
páyasī méda; ṛ́co rūpáṁ, yájūṁṣi prāṇā́s, sā́māni
S.117 jyótīṁṣi,[35] díśaś śrótram. eté ca vái yajñā́ś
śīrṣaṇváṃś.[36] chīrṣaṇyò múkhyo bhavati, yá eváṃ
védaitád[37] vā́ etác[38] chíro. nā́smád u[39]
f.353b [....
219m [1]āhus te bhaga cakṣuṣī, tābhyāṃ vipaśya mām
abhīti ...

...

...] soll er die Gefäße machen lassen. Die Weihe ist Glut (*tapas*). Mit dessen Glut verwendet er (die Gefäße). Nördlich [stellt er sie hin]. An dem (Tag) verwendet er den mit einem Ausguß* versehenen Mahāvīra(kessel), an den folgenden die beiden anderen. [Von ihnen ist der er]ste (Kessel) von Gāyatrī-Art, der zweite von Triṣṭubh-Art, der dritte von Jagatī-Art. Entsprechend den Tagen wendet er wie früher die Versmaße an. Der Kopf des Opfers ist der Pravargya(kessel). Dessen Schalen sind die Hirnschalen, die beiden Graswische die Kopfhaare, die beiden Fächer die Ohren, die beiden Fächerstücke die Nasenflügel, die beiden Metallstücke die Augen, - das südliche Auge ist das goldene (Metallstück), das nördliche das silberne (Metallstück), - die (beiden?) Mahāvīra(kessel) die Hals(knochen), der Caru(topf) der Mund, die beiden 'Hufe' (der Zange) die Kinnladen, die beiden nicht ausgehöhlten (Löffel) und die beiden 'Rund'(löffel) die Eckzähne, die Pflöcke die Zähne. Was er in den Gharma(kessel) niedersetzt, davon ist der Untersatz und die Bambus(abschabsel) der beiden Stricke die Zunge, der Puroḍāṣa(kuchen) das Gehirn. Was er mit Kohlen zudeckt, das ist das Fleisch, die zwei Grasbüschel die Haare, die geschmolzene Butter das Mark, die (Kuh- und die Ziegen)milch das Fett. Die Körpergestalt sind die Verse, die Lebensfunktionen die Opfersprüche, die 'Lichter' die Melodien, das Gehör die Himmelsrichtungen. Und (alle) diese genannten sind das einen Kopf besitzende Opfer. Am Kopf, an der Spitze befindlich wird, wer so weiß. Dies ist der erwähnte Kopf des Opfers. Nicht aber [... ...] von ihm [...

[219m] (Er murmelt) "Man sagt, Bhaga, diese sind deine

---

*oder: 'den Haupt-Mahāvīra' (d.h. nicht die Reservekessel)

...

[2]tasya sūryacandramāsāv eva cakṣuṣī.[2]

...

...

220 [1]x x x x x [**yád etát sāraghám mádh**]**u**, [**téna**
r]**ū**[**pám**] ***anajmi* te, *téna***[1] [2]**rūpám anagdhi ma**[2]
[3][íti rūpám evā́]syaitán[3] mahimā́naṃ vyā́caṣṭe.
220b **devā́nāṃ krátubhir**[1] **devābhyañjanáir** [2]**a**[**bhyàñje,**
bhága]**van**[2] **nā́māsíty.** etád vái [3][rudrásya pri-
yáṃ[3] nāmadhéyam. priyéṇaiváinaṃ nāmadhéyena de-
221 vābhyañjanáis sá*manakti*.[4] **tásya ta ṛ́caś ca**
yájūṁṣi [ca] **sā́māni** céty ṛ́co yájūṁṣi sā́mānı́ty eváı-
222 tad āha. **vā́g agnā́ anyác,**[1] **cákṣus sū́rye 'nyát;**
sū́rye 'nyád, agnā́ anyád; agnā́ anyád, agnā́ anyád
íti cákṣuṣī evā́syaitád úddharṣayati. andhó hí
223 bhágo. nā́syāndhā́ḥ prajā́ jāyante.[2] **bhágavān**[1] **bhū-**
224 **yāsam** íti cákṣur evā́tmán dhatta. **airò**[1] **'si,**
cákṣur asi, śrótram asi, purándhir[2] **nā́ma**[3] **vā́g**
asíti. śā́sty[4] eváinan.[4] tásmāc[5] chiṣṭā́ḥ prajā́
225 jāyante. **yéna śatákratur bhāgám upajuhvé, téna**
tvópahvaye,[1] **bhagéti**. rudrám vái devā́ nírabhajan.
sá devā́n ā́yatayābhiparyā́vartata. té devā́ eténa
nāmadheyéna[2] priyéṇa dhā́mnópahvayan, yát pra-
vargyàs. svénaiváinaṃ nāmadhéyena priyéṇa dhā́m-
226 nópahvayate. **tád vāṃ**[1] **na-**

Augen, mit denen blicke auf mich." ...

Dessen Augen sind Sonne und Mond. ...

[220] (Mit dem Spruch) "Was der von den Bienen stammende Honig ist, mit dem] salbe ich deine [Gestalt,] mit dem salbe ich meine Gestalt" tut er dessen Erhabenheit kund. [220a] (Er murmelt)" (Auf Geheiß des Gottes Savitar, mit den Armen der Aśvin, mit den Händen Pūṣans,) salbe ich mich mit den Kräften der Götter, mit den Göttersalbungen; ein glücklicher Name bist du." Dies ist [Rudras lie]be Benennung. Mit der lieben Benennung nur salbt er ihn mit Götter-Salbungen. [221] (Indem er sagt) "Ihm gehören die Verse, die Opfersprüche und die Melodien" nennt er damit nur die Verse, Opfersprüche und Melodien. [222] (Mit dem Spruch) "Das eine ist die Rede im Feuer, das andere das Auge in der Sonne; in der Sonne ist das eine, im Feuer das andere; im Feuer das eine, im Feuer das andere" erfreut er dessen Augen. Das Glück (*bhaga*) ist nämlich blind. Nicht wird dessen (des Opferherrn) Nachkommenschaft blind geboren. [223] (Mit dem Spruch) "Glückhaft möchte ich werden" setzt er Augenlicht in sich selbst. [224] (Mit dem Spruch) "Von der Irā stammend bist du, Gesicht bist du. Gehör bist du, die 'Fülle' genannte Rede bist du" belehrt er ihn (den Schüler). Deshalb werden gelehrte Nachkommen geboren. [225] (Er murmelt) "Womit der hundert Geisteskräfte besitzende einen Anteil hinzugerufen hat, mit dem, Bhaga, rufe ich dich herbei." Den Rudra schlossen die Götter vom Opfer aus. Er wandte sich den Göttern mit aufgelegtem (Pfeil) zu. Die Götter riefen ihn mit dieser Benennung, mit seiner lieben Stätte herbei, mit dem Pravargya(ritual). Mit seiner eigenen lieben Benennung, mit der lieben Stätte ruft man ihn herbei. [226] "Diese eure [gewaltige Meistertat, ihr Herren, künde ich, um belohnt zu werden, an wie der Donner den Regen, daß Dadhyañc, des Atharvan Sohn, es euch durch einen

f.354a [**rā sanáye dáṃsa ugrám āvíṣkṛṇomi tanyatúr ná
vṛṣṭím. dadhyáṅ ha yán mádhv ātharvaṇó vām áś-
vasya śīrṣṇá sumatím ávocat. - agnír īśe vāsav-
yàsyāgnír mahás sáubhagasya tány asmábhyaṃ rā-
sata** íti ...
... ...
agnír vái ru-]
[2]*drás*. sá vāsavyàs *sáubhaga*xy x x x x x x x x
x x x x x x x x x x x[2] devā́ś ca vā́ ásurāś ca
samā́vad evá [4][pravargyè 'kurvata. yád evá devā́
ákurvata, tád ásurā akurva]ta.[4] té devā́ etā́n
avakāśā́n [5]apaśyaṃs. tái[r etásmin yajñé gharmé
rucité 'vaikṣata. té devā́][5] ábhavan, párāsurā
abhavan. yát pravargyàm [6]etái[r avakāśáir avékṣa-
te, bhavati, prajā́vān paśumā́n madha]vyò[6] bhava-
227 ti. **dáśa prácīr dáśa bhāsi**[1] **dakṣiṇ***éti* x x x x x
x x x x x x x x x [diśā́m á]varuddhyai.[1] kó ha
tád veda, yā́vanta imé lokā́s. [2]sárvān [evá lokā́n
228 etáir avakāśáir ávarundhe. **dá**]**śa**[2] **prácīr dáśa
bhāsi dakṣiṇā́,**[1] **dáśa pratī́cīr**[2] **dáśa** [3]**bh**[**āsy**]
ú[**dīcīr, dáśordhvā́ bhāsi su**]**manasyámāna**[3] íti.
téjo vái bhā́s. téja evā́syaitád úddharṣayati.[4]
229 **sá naḥ** [1]**prajá**[**ṃ paśū́n pāhy áhṛṇi**]**yamāna**[1] íti:
prajā́yāḥ [2]paśūnā́ṅ gopīthā́ya.[2] [3]prajā́vān paśumā́n[3]
S.118 [4]bhavati, [yá eváṃ véda, yá]ḥ[4] [5]pravargyopaniṣá-
d*aṃ véda. de*vā́ vái[5] mahāvīrā́d rucitā́d[6] abibha-
yus:[6] [7]sárvān no ['yā́n téjasóddhakṣyatī́]ti.[7] té

Pferdekopf sagte, was die freundliche Süßigkeit ist. - Agni verfügt über einen Schatz, Agni über großes Glücksgut; diese soll er uns schenken."[3] ...

Agni ist Ru]dra. Er ist einer, der Güter und gute Anteile besitzt [...

...] Die Götter und die Asuras [taten beim Pravargya-Opfer] das Gleiche. [Was die Götter taten, das taten die Asuras.] Die Götter schauten diese (zum) Herabblicken (bestimmten Mantras). Mit ihnen [blickten sie auf den ans Feuer gesetzten Gharmakessel. Die Götter] gediehen, die Asura gingen zugrunde. Wenn man auf den Pravargya(kessel) mit diesen [Avakāśa-Mantras hinabblickt], gedeiht man, wird man [für den Süßtrank geeignet.] *[227]* (Der Opferherr(?) murmelt) "Zehn (Strahlen) strahlst du nach Osten, zehn nach Süden." [... ...]: das dient zur Gewinnung der [Himmelsrichtungen]. Wer weiß das, wie groß sind diese Welten? Alle [Welten erlangt er mit diesen Avakāśa-Mantras]. *[228]* (Er murmelt) "Zehn (Strahlen) strahlst du nach Osten, zehn nach Süden, zehn strahlst du nach Westen, zehn nach N[orden, zehn nach oben (zum Zenith) als wohl]gesinnter." Das Strahlen ist Glut. Seine Glut erfreut er so. *[229]* (Er murmelt) "Als so gearteter [schütze] unsere Nachkommen-[schaft und unser Vieh ohne zu] zürnen!" Das dient dem Schutz von Nachkommenschaft und Vieh. Nachkommen und Vieh besitzend wird, wer die Pravargya-Geheimlehre [kennt. Die Götter] fürchteten sich vor dem zum Glühen gebrachten Mahāvīra(kessel): "[Er wird] uns alle [verbrennen]" (sagten sie).

prajā́patim úpādhāvan sá prajā́patir [8]abravīd:
anyénainam[8] úpatiṣṭhata, [9]śivó *bhaviṣya*-[9]
f.354b [tī́ti
...
...
...
229a ... ... bhū́r bhúvas svàr íti ...
...
229b ... ... bhúvo 'dhyāyī́ti ...
...
...
... ...]
229c [1]x x x x x x x x x [**nṛmṇā́yi nṛmṇā́m** íti pra]jā́[1]
v*ái*[2] nṛm*ṇā́*,[3] paśávo nṛmṇā́m. prajā́bhyaś cai-[4]
[5][váinam etát paśúbhyaś ca rudrā́ṃ nirávadayate].[5]
230 [6]**n ídhāyy óvá nídhāyy óvéti**[6] vái [8]sā́mnó[dgāyati.
231 ténaivá nidháu prátiti]ṣṭhata. **é**[8] **svàr jyótī3r**
íty. asáu vā́ ādityá [9][etáj jyótis. ténaiváinaṃ
sámardhayat]y. *etā́*[9] vā́ etásya priyā́s tanvàs.
tā́bhir eváinaṁ [10]sáma[rdhayaty. etā́ vā́ etásyā́-
niru]*k*tās[10] stútayas. tā́bhir eváinam abhíṣṭu-
vanty. etā́ vā́ [11]etásyā́ni[ruktās stútayo, yát svàr
jyótis. tā́]*bhir* eváinam[11] abhivyā́haranty. etā́ni
vā́ etásyā́niruktāni nāma[dhéyā]*n*[i]:[12] bhúv*o*[13]
nṛmṇó nidhís svàr jyótis. tám evá pratyákṣam

Sie liefen zu Prajāpati um Hilfe. Prajāpati sprach: "Mit einem andern nähert euch ihm; er [wird] freundlich [werden."

... [229a] "*Bhūr, bhuvas, svar*" (singt der Adhvaryu)...
... [229b] "*Bhuvo 'dhāyi*" (singt der Adhvaryu) ...

... [229c] "Manneskraft ist in der Manneskraft" (singt er). Manneskraft ist Nach]kommenschaft. Manneskraft ist Vieh. Von Nachkommenschaft und [Vieh findet er Rudra so ab.] [230] [Er singt] mit einer Melodie: "Er ist niedergesetzt, *ovā*; er ist niedergesetzt, *ovā*." [Damit] stellt er sich [fest in einen Schatz.] [231] (Er singt) "*E*, das Licht ist die Sonne." [Das genannte Licht ist] jener Āditya (die Sonne). [Mit ihr läßt er ihn vollständig zusammenkommen.] Das sind dessen liebe Gestalten. Mit ihnen läßt er ihn vollständig [zusammenkommen. Das sind dessen nicht deutlich ausgesprochene] Lobpreisungen. Mit denen loben sie ihn. Das sind seine nicht deutlich ausge[sprochenen Lobpreisungen, was *svàr* und *jyótis* sind. Mit] denen reden sie ihn an. Das sind dessen nicht deutlich ausgesprochene Benen[nungen:] *bhuvó*, *nṛmṇó*, *nidhí*, *svàr* und *jyótis*. Ihn wollen sie vor aller Au-

ṛdhnuvanty. ayā́ṃ vái lóko gā́rhapatyo, 'sā́ āhava-
nī́yo.[13a] yā́nti vā́ etè [14]'s*mā́l lo*kā́d.[14] yá etā́ṃ
gā́rhapatye haviṣkṛ́tya,[15] prā́ñcam uddhṛ́tyaiténā-
havanī́ye[16] caranti. tá etā́m púnas saṁsthā́pya prá-
232 caranti. **tvā́m agne gṛhapata** íti gā́rhapatyam úpa-
tiṣṭhate. 'smínn evá loké prátitiṣṭhati ||

f.355a [...
...
...
...
...
...
...
... ...]
[1]-nta eṣā́ vā́ apā́ṃ yṓnis: *sayonitvā́ya*. yā́ṅ *kāmā́*-
yate: teja[svī́ bhūyāsam, brahmavarcasī́ bhūyāsa]m
íti,[1] tásyaitā́m udúhya mā́dhyandine sávane pra-
vargyèṇa careta.[2] [3][tējo vái brahmavarcasá]*m*[3]
pravargyàs. tḗja evá brahmavarcasā́m ávarundhe.
233 yádi [4]prayuñjy*ā́d* ***ā́nuṣṭubho 'sīti*** *cat*urthā́m[4]
píṇḍaṃ kuryād. vā́g vā́ anuṣṭúb. vā́cam evá yajña-
mukhé yunakti. dváidham pā́trāṇi kārayet. tā́ny
ā́ sutyā́yās tiṣṭheyur: ayātayāmatvā́yā́gnīdhre[1]
prā́vṛñjyād. ā́gnīdhre[1] rocyetā́gnīdhré[1] 'dhiśri-
yetā́gnīdhrāyatano[1] vā́ eṣá. etárhi svá evā́smā

gen fördern. Das Hausfeuer ist diese Welt, das Āhavanīya-Feuer jene. Sie gehen von dieser Welt (weg). Diejenigen, die ihn (den Agni) im Hausfeuer mit Opferspeise versehen haben, und ihn nach Osten herausgenommen haben, handeln mit ihm beim Āhavanīya-Feuer. Nachdem sie dies beendet haben, fangen sie wieder an. *[232]* (Mit dem Spruch) "Du Agni als Hausherr" nähert er sich dem Hausfeuer. In dieser Welt hat er festen Halt. ||

[...

...]en sie. Dieser ist der Ursprungsort der Wasser: das dient zum Versehensein mit gleichem Ursprung. Wenn er für sich wünschen sollte: 'Einer der Glut [besitzt, der Brahmanenansehen besitzt, möchte ich wer]den' soll er, nachdem er dessen genannten (Agni, das Feuer) herausgenommen hat, für sich bei der mittäglichen Pressung den Pravargya(ritus) vollziehen. [Glut und Ansehen ist die Anuṣṭubh]; Glut und Brahmanenansehen eignet er sich an. Wenn er (in diesem Fall den Pravargya) vollzieht, soll er einen [vier]ten (Lehm)kloß machen (mit dem Spruch) *[233]* "Von Anuṣṭubh-Art bist du." Die Anuṣṭubh ist die Rede. Die Rede spannt er bei Opferbeginn an. Doppelt soll er die Trinkgefäße machen lassen. Diese sollen bis zur Pressung stehenbleiben. Das dient zur Nichtverbrauchtheit. Im Āgnīdhra(zelt) soll er den Pravargya vollziehen. Im Āgnīdhra(zelt) soll er (den Kessel) für sich zum Leuchten bringen. Im Agnīdhra(zelt) soll er (den Kessel) für sich (ans Feuer) setzen. Einer, der das Agnīdhra(zelt) zur Stätte hat, ist dieser (Kessel). Jetzt setzt er ihm an

(233) āyátane[2] rúcaṃ dadhāty. auttaravediké juhoti.
svargó vái loká auttaravedikás: svargásya[3] loká-
sya sámaṣṭyā. etasmínn evá prā́g avabhṛthā́t[4] pā́-
trāṇi sáñcinoti. [5]*dakṣi*[ṇatá úpa hoha]ty[5] āhava-
nī́yam. pā́trāṇi sáṃcinoti. [6]pratyá*g* *ú*[pavapaty
āhavanī́yaṃ. gū́hati pā́trā]ṇy[6] ápi vā dvī́paṁ ha-
reyur. asáu vā́ ādityó [rudró mahāvīrás. tejasvī́
brahmavarcasī́] manuṣyèṣu bhavati. tā́d ahargaṇé[7]
[8]právṛñjyād. v x x x x x x x x x x x x x x[8]
f.355b [...
...
...
...
...
...
...
... ...]
x x x x x x x x x x [9]na pravargyàsya x x x cə'g v
brahma*varcasám* ávarundhe, *vai*[śvadevéṣu x x xāh-
ṇi]kaṃ[9] varuṇapraghāséṣv áparāhṇikaṃ,[10] mahā́haviṣi
[11]paurvā*hṇika*ṁ, śunāsīryà[11] áparāhṇikam.[12] etás-
S.119 minn evá prā́g avabhṛthā́t[13] pā́trāṇi sáñcinoti. da-
kṣiṇatá úpa hohaty āhavanī́yam. pā́trāṇi sáñcinoti.
pratyág úpavapaty [14]āhavanī́yam. *gū́*hati[14] pā́trāṇy
ápi vā dvī́paṃ hareyur. asáu vā́ ādityó rudró [15]ma-

seiner eigenen Stätte Glanz. In das auf der Uttaravedi befindliche (Feuer) opfert er - das Uttaravedi(feuer) ist die Himmelswelt - das dient zur Erlangung der Himmelswelt. Vor dem (Hinabsteigen ins) Reinigungsbad schichtet er die Gefäße zusammen. Nach Sü[den schiebt] er sie [hin] zum Āhavanīya(feuer). Er schichtet die Gefäße zusammen. Nach West[en bedeckt er das Āhavanīya(feuer). Er versteckt die Gefä]ße oder man soll sie auf eine Insel bringen. Die Sonne [ist Rudra Mahāvīra. Mit Glut und Brahmanenansehen versehen] wird er unter den Menschen. Dann [soll er] an einer Reihe von Tagen den Pra[vargya vollziehen. ...

....] des Pravargya ... ... Brahmanenansehen gewinnt er. Bei den Vai[śvadeva-Opfern den vor(?)-] mittäglichen (Pravargya), bei den Varuṇapraghāsa-Opfern den nachmittäglichen, beim Mahāhavis-Opfer (des Sākamedha-Opfers) den vormittäglichen, beim Śunāsīrya-Opfer den nachmittäglichen. Dabei schichtet er vor dem (Hinabsteigen ins) Reinigungsbad die Gefäße zusammen. Nach Süden schichtet er sie hin zum Āhavanīya(feuer). Er schichtet die Gefäße zusammen. Nach Westen bedeckt er das Āhavanīya(feuer). Er versteckt die Gefäße, oder man soll sie auf eine Insel bringen. [Glanz ist] Rudra Mahāvīra als jener Āditya (die Sonne). [Brahmanenanse-

(233) hāvī[ró várco. brahmavarcasám] ávarundhe.[15] tád āhur: ánavaruddhaṃ vā́ asomayajinó [16]*brahma*va[rcasám. sápravargyaṃ jyótiṣṭomam][16] kuryāt, svá evá yónau brahmavarcasáṃ dadhāti. [17]brahma-[varcasī́ bhavati. ||

gā́yat]y *udgā*t[aitā́ni][17] párisāmāni. pravargyàsya[18] vā́ etā́ni sā́mṛddhyai [19][gāyati. śārgám bhavat]i. [t]*ád aj*[yá]m[ā]ne *gā*yati. *té*jo *vái* śārgán. *té*jasaiváinaṁ sáma[rdhayati. śukracandré bhavatas. té][19] jātarūpáyor gāyatīyáṃ[20] vái śukrám, asáu [21]candrá[n. tā́bhyām eváinaṃ sámardhayati. gha]rmásya[21] tanvàu[22] bhavatas. té[23] abhīdhyámāne gāyati. sváyai-

f.356a [-vá tanvàinaṁ sámardhayati. ...

...

...

...

...

...

...

... ...]

vratapakṣáu bhavatas. té [24]adhihriyámāṇ*e* gā*y*at*i*. rákṣāṃsi vā́ etárhi *sá*[rvaṃ gharmáṃ ca]mitóḫ.[24] prāmadó vájro vratapakṣáu: [rákṣa]sām[25] ápahatyā. aśvínau[26] vraté bhavatas. té huté[27] *gā*[yati].[27]

hen] gewinnt er. Man sagt: 'Nichterlangt ist das Brahmanenansehen eines, der kein Soma-Opfer ausführt.' [Zu einem mit dem Pravargya-Ritus versehenen] soll er (das Soma-Opfer) machen. An seine eigene Geburtsstelle setzt er das Brahmanenansehen. Brahmanen[ansehen besitzend wird er.] ||

Der Udgāt[ar(?) singt] die 'Herumgesänge'. [Er singt] sie zum guten Gelingen desPravargya(rituals). [Das Śārga-Sāman kommt zur Anwendung.] Beim Salben (des Gharmakessels) singt er es. Das Śārga ist Glut. Mit seiner Glut [läßt er] ihn voll[ständig zusammenkommen. Die beiden, das Śukra- und das Candra-Sāman, kommen zur Anwendung. Die] singt er auf die beiden entstandenen Gestalten. Das Śukra ist die Erde, das Candra ist jener (Āditya, die Sonne). [Mit beiden läßt er ihn zusammenkommen. Die beiden] Gharmasya Tanvau ('die Gestalten des Glutkessels') -Sāmans werden angewendet. (Der Udgātar)(?) singt sie beim Anlegen (der Scheite). Mit seiner eigenen [Gestalt läßt er ihn zusammenkommen. ...

... Das Gharmarocana-Sāman wird angewendet. ...
... Das Dhenu-Sāman wird angewendet. ...
... Das Payas-Sāman wird angewendet. ...
... Das Sindhu-Sāman wird angewendet. ...
... Die beiden Vasiṣṭha-Śaphau-Sāmans werden angewendet.
... ...]

Die beiden, das Vrata- und das Pakṣa-Sāman werden angewendet, Er singt sie beim Hinbringen (des Glutkessels zum Āhanantya-feuer). Die Schädigungen könnten den ganzen [Gharma auflekken]. Die beiden, das Vrata- und das Pakṣa-Sāman, sind eine erfreuliche(?) Keule: das dient zum Wegschlagen der Schädigungen. Die beiden Aśvinavrata-Sāmans werden angewendet. Die beiden singt er, nachdem (der Gharmatrank) geopfert ist. Er

svadáyaty. upagā́yanam evā́syaitád. átho ny èvā́s-
mai hnuvate. rājanarauhiṇé bhavatas. *té*[28] puro-
ḷā́śayor[29] gāyati. cákṣuṣī vā́ eté[30] pravargyàsya
yát sūryācandramásau; cákṣuṣī rājanarauhiṇé.
cákṣuṣor evá cákṣur dadhāty. āṅgirasám[31] bha-
vati. tát [32]parigharmyá āropyámāṇe[32] gāyaty.
áṅgiraso vā́ itás svargáṃ lokám āyaṃs. tá eténa
sā́mnordhvā́s svargáṃ lokám āyan. yád āṅgirasám
bhávaty, - ā́rūḍhavat[33] sá[33] svargó lokás - [34]svar-
gásya lókasya[34] sámaṣṭyai. [35]tá*d* [āhur:[35] [1]**ṛ]ṅ-**
(234) **m*á*yo yajurmáyas sāmamáyo *ghar*má** íti yásyaiṣá
pravṛ[jyámānaḫ pravargyà]ḫ.[1] pravṛñjánti sárvam
eváinaṃ sávīryaṁ[2] sáyoniṁ sátanūm: ṛ́ddhyai.[3]
sá[3] [4][ṛ́ddhiṃ yájamāna árśchaty].[4] āyuṣā vā́ eṣá
vīryèṇa ṛdhyate.[5] yásya mahāvīró bhidyát*e*,[6]
235 [1][**yá ṛté cid abhiśrí**] **ṣa**[1] íti karmaṇyàyā[2] mṛdā́
dṛḍhīkáraṇena [3]vā́śr*eṣava*[tābhíśriṣyet.] x x x[3]
f.356b [...

235a ... [1](198.11: **mā́ no gharmó vyathitáḥ**)[1]

...

...

...

...

... [2]yásya mahāvīráḫ pravṛjyámānas skándet. prā́-
235b kāruko yájamāṇas syād. **áskān dyáuḫ [3]pṛthivím**

würzt (den Pravargya). Einfallen in den Gesang ist das (s.o. M.177). Jetzt nun leisten sie ihm Abbitte. Die beiden, das Rājana- und das Rauhiṇa-Sāman, kommen zur Anwendung. Er singt sie bei (der Darbringung der) beiden Puroḍāśa(kuchen). Die beiden Augen des Pravargya sind Sonne und Mond. Das Rājana- und das Rauhiṇa-Sāman sind die beiden Augen. In die beiden Augen setzt er Sehvermögen. Das Āṅgirasa-Sāman kommt zur Anwendung. Er singt es beim Hinaufsetzen der (goldenen) Platte. Die Aṅgiras gingen von hier in die Himmelswelt. Sie gingen mit diesem Sāman nach oben in die Himmelswelt hinauf. Wenn das Āṅgirasa-Sāman zur Anwendung kommt, - die Himmelswelt ist das Ārūḍhavat-Sāman - dient das zur Erlangung der Himmelswelt. *[234]* Man [sagt]: "Ṛg-haft, Yajus-haft, Sāmanhaft ist der Gharma" desjenigen, für den dieser [Pravargyakessel] ans Feuer ge[stellt wird.] Sie stellen (den Pravargyakessel) ans Feuer als einen vollständigen, Manneskraft besitzenden, mit einer Heimstätte versehenen, mit Körpergestalt versehenen: das dient dem Erfolg. [Zum Erfolg gerät] der [Opferherr]. Mit Lebensdauer und Manneskraft gedeiht (der Opferherr). - Wessen Mahāvīra(kessel) zerbricht, (dessen Kessel klebt er mit dem Spruch) *[235]* ["Wer auch ohne Verband zusammenfü]gt" mit zum Werk tauglichen Lehm oder mit einem als Binde(mittel) dienenden (Stoff) zum Festmachen (wieder zusammen). [...

... (Verhüte, daß unser Gharma(kessel) als Schwankender ins Schwanken gerät ...)

... dessen Mahāvīra(kessel), wenn er ans Feuer gestellt wird, überläuft. Verschüttend würde der Opferherr sein. Mit dem Spruch: *[235b]* "Es hat der Himmel die Erde besprun-

íti dvā́bhyām̐ juhuyād: á]nabhih*o*māya.[2] *sárvam*
*ā́*yur *e*ti. *sáivá tátra* prā́y*aści*[tti]*r* [á]pa[3]
vā́ etásya vaidyutáḫ pravargyàḫ[4] krandate, yás-
ya mahāvīré pravṛjyámāne [5]stanáya[ti. s]ā́[5] śúg
236 yájamānam ṛśchati. **yád ákrandó; 'krandad agnír**
íti dvā́bhyām̐ juhuyād. agnír [1]vái [kránda]s.
svénaiváinam[1] bhāgadhéyena śamayati. sárvam
ā́yur eti. sáivá tátra [2]prā́yaścitti*r*. vájre*ṇ*a[2]
vā́ etásya pravargyò 'bhíhanyate, yásya mahāvīré
pravṛjyámāne várṣati. sá pramā́yuko[3] yájamāno
237 bhavati. **parjányāya prágāyatedám̐ vácaḫ parján-**
yāyéti [1][dvā́bhyām̐] j*u*huyād. ā́po[1] vái parjányas.
svénaiváinam bhāgadhéyena śamayati. sárvam [2]ā́-
yur eti]. *sáivá*[2] tátra prā́yaścittis. támo vā́
S.120 [3]etásya yajñám̐ yuvate,[3] yásya [4]mahāvī[ré pra-
vṛjyámāne sū́ryò 'stam é]ti. sá[4] ā́rti*m̐*[5] yájamā-
238 na ā́rśchaty.[6] [1]**úd u tyám̐ jātáveda**[**sam̐; citrám̐**
devā́nām údagād íti dvā́]bhyām̐ juhuyād.[1] asáu vā́
ādityó rudró[2] [3]mahāvīrá[s. svénaiváinam bhāga-
dhéyena śamaya]ti.[3] sárvam ā́yur eti. sáiva tá-
tra [4]prā́yaścitti- ||[4]

---

f.357a [...

...

...

...

gen" soll er mit zwei (Opfergüssen flüssiger Butter) opfern: das dient zur 'Nicht]begießung'. Zur vollen Lebensdauer geht er. Das ist hier die Sühnehandlung. - Es brüllt ihn dessen mit einem Blitz versehener Pravargya an, bei dessen Mahāvīra(kessel), wenn er ans Feuer gesetzt wird, es donnert. Leid befällt den Opferherrn. *[236]* (Mit den beiden Sprüchen) "Als du brülltest; Agni brüllte" soll er mit zwei (Opfergüssen) opfern. Agni ist [das Brüllen]. Mit seinem eigenen Anteil beruhigt er ihn. Zur vollen Lebensdauer geht er. Das ist hier die Sühne. - Mit einer Keule wird auf dessen Pravargya geschlagen, bei dessen Mahāvīra(kessel), wenn er ans Feuer gesetzt wird, es regnet. Der Opferherr wird einer, der dem Untergang verfallen ist. *[237]* (Mit dem Spruch) "Für Parjanya singe dieses Wort, für Parjanya" soll er mit [zwei (Opfergüssen)] opfern. Parjanya ist Wasser. Mit seinem eigenen Anteil beruhigt er ihn. Zur vollen Leb[ensdauer geht er.] Das ist hier die Sühne. - Finsternis verbindet sich mit dessen Opfer, bei dessen Mahāvī[ra, wenn er ans Feuer gesetzt wird, die Sonne unterge]ht. Ins Unglück gelangt der Opferherr. *[238]* (Mit den Sprüchen) "Hinauf (fahren) ihn, den Jātavedas" und "Das schimmernde (Antlitz) der Götter ist aufgegangen" soll er mit zwei (Opfergüssen) opfern. Rudra Mahāvīra ist jener Āditya (die Sonne). [Mit seinem eigenen Anteil beruhigt er ihn.] Zur vollen Lebensdauer geht er. Das ist hier die Sühne. ||

...

...

...

...

...

... sáivá tátra prā́yaścittī. rudró vā́ etásya]
paśū́n abhímanyate,[5] yásya mahāvīré[6] pravṛjyámāne[6]
239 gharmadhū́ṅ niṣī́dati. [7]tā́xə'x x x[7] **yásmād bhīṣā́**
niṣī́dasi,[1] **táto no ábhayaṅ kṛdhi.** |[2] **ábhayan naḫ**
paśúbhyo; námo rudrā́ya[3] **mīḍhúṣa** íti dvā́bhyāṃ
juhuyād. agnír vái rudrás.[3] svénaiváinam[4] bhāga-
dhéyena [5]*praśáta*•(?) *śama*[yati].[5] sárvam ā́yur eti.
sáivá tátra prā́yaścittir. mṛtyúr vā́ etásya prajā́
[6]a[bh]í[manyate, yásya ma]hā*v*īré pravṛjyá*mān*e
239a *váyāṃ*si[6] śvā́padāni [7]vāpidhā́va*ntá*[**sṛṅmukho; ví gā́**
ivéti dvā́bhyāṃ juhuyān. mṛtyúr vái yamás.[7] své-
naiváinam bhāgadhéyena [1]pra[śata•(?) śamayati] x
x x x x x x x x x x x x x[1] [2]ātmánó 'hiṁ*sāy*ai.[2]
[3]x x x x x x x x x x x x x [pravargyèṇa praca-]
riṣyā́n dīkṣitásya x x x x x x x x x x x x x x x
[prava]rgyàṁ sámbharaty. ajíne sámbharaty. agnír
vā́ x x x x x x x x x x x x x x [sámbha]rati, śár-
karābhir dhṛ́tyā, ármyaiḫ kapā́lai[r] x x x x x x x
x x x x x x x x x x[3]

f.357b [...

... Das ist hier die Sühne.] Auf das Vieh [desjenigen hat es Rudra] abgesehen, bei dessen Mahāvīra, wenn er ans Feuer gesetzt wird, die Gharmakuh sich niedersetzt. ... ... *[239]* (Mit dem Spruch) "Wovor du dich aus Furcht niedersetzst, davon schaffe uns Furchtlosigkeit, Furchtlosigkeit für uns und das Vieh! Verehrung dem mildtätigen Rudra!" soll er mit zwei (Güssen flüssiger Butter) opfern. Rudra ist Agni. Mit seinem eigenen Anteil beruhigt er ihn. Zur vollen Lebensdauer geht er. Das ist hier die Sühne. - Der Tod hat es auf dessen Nachkommenschaft [abgesehen, bei dessen Ma]hāvīra, wenn er ans Feuer gestellt wird, Vögel oder reissende Tiere hinzulaufen. *[239a]* (Mit den Sprüchen) ["Als einer mit blutigem Mund" und "Die Kühe durchwandernd"(?) soll er mit zwei (Opfergüssen) opfern. Yama ist der Tod.] Mit seinem eigenen Anteil be[ruhigt(?) er ihn. ... ...] das dient zur Nichtverletzung seines Selbst. [... ... Wenn er im Begriff steht, mit dem Pravargya zu be]ginnen, ...
für einen Geweihten [... ...]
trägt er den Pravargya zusammen. Mit einem Ziegenfell trägt er (die benötigten Utensilien) zusammen. [... ...] ist Agni. [... ...] trägt er zusammen, mit Kieseln: das dient zum Halten, mit Schuttscherben, [...

...

...

...

...

...

...

...

...

... ... áudumbarāsandī́ bha-]
[4]v*a*ty. ū́rdhvā[4] udúmbara ūrjáiváinān̥[5] dādhāra.
m*au*ñjā́vivānā[6] bhavaty. [7]ū́r*g* [vái múñjā́. ūrjái-]
váinām̥[7] dādhāra. prādeśamātrā́pādā bhavaty. etā́-
240(?) vad dhīme. [1]**ví prāṇá** x *ta*x x x x x x*áinān*[1] dā-
dhāra. kr̥ṣṇājinám ástr̥ṇāti. kr̥ṣṇājinéna[2] prá-
śchādayati. [bráhma vā́ e]tád rūpám̥[3] yát kr̥ṣṇā-
jinám. [4]bráhmaṇaiváinām̥ dā[dhāra. prā́g úda]g
gā́rhapa*ty*[āt kharám̥ karoty, údañcau][4] [5]paráu
kharáu[5] karoty. ayám̥ vái [6]lo[kó gā́rhapatyo, 'sā́
āhavanī́yo. gā́rhapa]tye[6] hutám̐ svargám̥[7] lokám̥
[8]gama[yati] x x x x x x x x x x x x x x x x x x
x x xə'ti. tád bahí[ṣṭāt] x x x x x x x x x x x x x
x x x x x x x x x x x *dv*ārā́ṇy apidhā́ya pravar-
gy[èṇa prácarati]. x x x x x x x x ṇayátho[8]
pāpavasīyasásya[9] vyāvŕ̥tyai ||

[10]x x x x x x x x x x x [as]áu[10] vā́ ādityó rudró

... Ein Sessel aus Udumbara(holz) kommt zur Anwend]ung. Nach oben hält der Udumbara(baum) ihn mit Kraft. Aus Muñja(gras) verfertigtes Flechtwerk (für die Sitzfläche des Sessels) kommt zur Anwendung. [Das Muñja(gras) ist] Kraft. [In der Kraft] hält er ihn. Ein Fuß (des Sessels) von Spannengröße kommt zur Anwendung. So groß sind diese beiden Welten. *[240?]* (Mit dem Spruch?) "Auseinander (streben?) die Lebensfunktionen(?)" [... ...] hält er den (Sessel?). Er breitet das Antilopenfell aus. Mit dem Antilopenfell bedeckt er ihn (den Sessel). [Das Bráhman ist je]ne Gestalt, welche das Antilopenfell ist. Mit dem Bráhman [hält er] ihn. - [Im Nordost]en des Gārhapatya(feuers) [macht er den einen Abfallhaufen, im Norden] die beiden anderen Abfallhaufen. [Das Gārhapatya(feuer) ist] diese Wel[t, das Āhavanīya(feuer) ist jene. Den ins Gārhapatya]feuer geopferten [läßt] er in die Himmelswelt gehen. [... ... ...]t er. Das ... draußen [... ... ...] nachdem er die beiden Tor(flügel) (der Opferhütte) geschlossen hat, [beginnt er(?)] mit dem Pravargya(ritual). [... ...] Das dient jetzt zur Abwendung des Schlechten und des Guten. ||

[... ...] Rudra Mahāvīra ist

[11]mahāvīrá x x [11]

f.358a [...[12] ... ...]

[iti gharmājaṭharābrāhmaṇaṃ samāptam]
[iti śukriyabrāhmaṇaṃ samāptam]

---

fragm. f.357b(?)

... [dvā]bhyāṃ dī[kṣitásya] ...
...[dvā́]bhyāṃ nirúpya[...

jener Āditya (die Sonne). [...

......

[Das Gharmājaṭharā-Brāhmaṇa ist beendet]

[Das Śukriya-Brāhmaṇa ist beendet]

... opfert er mit] zwei (Opfergüssen) für einen Ge[weihten ...
...] nachdem er mit zwei ... ... hinzugestreut hat [...

Lesarten zum Mantra-Kapitel (KaṭhĀ I)

KaṭhĀ I

1-47, der **erste Anuvāka**, ist belegt in den Handschriften: **t1**, fol. 280b: nur I 1-5; **P** p. 312a-313a; **P2** mit Akentresten (Svaritapunkte) p. 10 ff.; z.T., meist in Pratīka-Form, in KaṭhĀ II, III: **T**, was durch Fettdruck [im ursprünglichen Teildruck durch Unterstreichung] hervorgehoben ist; - Akzente nach **T**, **t1**, **P2**

1 (1) manạ P2 (2) vịpaścitaḥ P2 (3) vayənavídh t1 (4) eka P, P2 (5) mam̈āhí (d.h. das zweite *ma* ist sec. manu getilgt) t1 (6) •savituḥ P, •sya savituḥ t1

2 (1) getilgt (2) prạsavyẹ P2 (3) śvinọr P2 (4) bāhubhyạm P2 (5) hastạbhyām P2 (6) ādạde P2

3 (1)utiṣṭha P2 (2) brāhmaṇaspate P2 (3) temahe P2

4 (1) prayanto P2 (2) marutạs P2 (5) sudānạva P2 (4) indrạ P2

5 (1) prái[... : Ende von f. 280b: der Text bricht hier ab, da die folgenden Bll., verloren sind: t1

6 (1) pra P, P2 (2) devy atu P, devy ạtu P2, devy àtu T

[Note that BŚS 9.2.3: 269: 20 and VādhS read *ā devy*]

7 (1) aśchạ P2 (2) vīran P2, viraṃn P (3) •rādhasan P2, •rādasan P (4) yajña P2, yajñaṃn P

8 (l) devīr P (2) devayajané T (3) māṃsātham P, maṃsāthām P2

9 (1) ṛtasyavyāsam P (2) adhya P (3) śirọ P2 (4) śīrṣṇe | evaṃ | P2 um anzudeuten, daβ der gesamte M. 9 in den M. 10-13 stets wiederholt wird

10 (1) āsīṃn P2 prima manu, āsīr P2 sec.m. (2) adya || P2 um Wiederholung von M.9 anzudeuten; adhya P

(3) makhasya P pr.m., makhasi P sec.m.

11 (1) deve[va]mmriyo (*va* sec.m. über der Zeile) P2, devī vamriyo P (2) bhūta pr.m., bhūtasya sec.m. P (3) prathamajā rṛtasya || P mit Abkürzung des Mantra

12 (1) indrosyaujọ P2 (2) ṛtasya | P2 m. Abkürzung (3) adhya P

13 (1) prajāpatis P (2) tanūr ạsy P2 (5) adya || P2 mit Abkürzung; adhya P; [14: read: **madhulā?*]

15 fehlt ganz in P, P2

17 gāyatró T

18 tráiṣṭu*bho* T

22 śroya oder śrayo P2

23 (1) viṣṇo P2 (2) asi | [prajā]patyan P2, •tyan P

24 (1) patnī T, patnīr P2, patnī P

25 (1) śociṣe [tvā] P2, suciṣe tvā P

26-29 = KS XVI 6 (mit Ūha zu fem. in letzten Spruch)

26 (1) śravọ devasya sānasi | dyumnaṃ citra [... = Ende der Seite, nächstes Blatt fehlt: P2; śravo devasya sānasi | dyumnañ citraśravastamam | P; Akzente nach KaṭhĀ I 218f; - NB. Ende des ersten Anuvāka in P2

27 (1) savitudvāpatu pr.m., savitudvapatu sec.m. P (2) svāṅguririḥ pr.m., svaṅguliriḥ sec.m. P

28 (1) ávyathamānāḥ T, avyathamānā P; wahrscheinlich angeglichen an KS XVI 6, wo •mānā; danach corr. S, aber in KS fem., hier mask. •mānaḥ, scil. pravargyàḥ! (2) pṛthivīvyām pr.m., pṛthivyām sec.m. P

29 (1) bṛhád T, P; wohl angeglichen an KS XVI 6: bṛhatī, wo fem. (2) pūrvás S, verlesen; dhruvás T

30 (1) amuṣyaḥ P (hier und im Folgenden stets so: I 30-35) (2) putram P ;

36 (1) ahamān P

39 (1) chṛṇatu P (auch in in den folgenden Mantras I 40-47)

40 (1) śchṛṇáttu T, cchṛṇáttu S

41 (2) hier u. in den Mantras 41-45 dient Visarga wohl

zur Bezeichnung der Pausa; kein Daṇḍa in P

46 (1) brahmaḥ pr.m., brahmā sec.m. P

----

198. Die Bezeichnung der zehn Verse 198.1-10 als *prathamaḥ pratīkānuvākaḥ* erscheint in den Paddhatis zum Pravargyavrata, cf. LGS II p. 64; wahrscheinlich waren einige dieser Verse in KaṭhĀ I nur als Pratīka enthalten, cf. etwa die Parallele in MS IV 9,11:132,11 f.; viele der Verse sind tatsächlich schon in KS enthalten; wegen der gewöhnlichen Ausführlichkeit der Ṛcakas läßt sich aber nicht entscheiden wo hier Pratīka- und wo kompletter Vers gemeint waren.

Die Verse sind belegt in: **P** p. 311a -311b, (ohne Verszahlen); **P2** p.14a,b mit Akzentresten (Svaritapunkte); LGS II p. 64-69, mit Kommentar des Devapāla; nicht erhalten in **t1**, da fol.280-281a verloren sind; akzentuiert nach den Akz. Resten in P2 und nach Parallelen in KS. - LGS folgt weitgehend moderner Orthographie; deren Abweichungen von der Schreibweise der Mss. sind hier nicht verzeichnet.

198.1 (1) jātavedasaṃ || P mit Abkürzung des Mantra, Akzente nach KaṭhĀ I 198.19

198.2 (1) ṣa P (2) asmabhyạṃ P2 (3) gạyatraṃ P2 (4) navīyāṃsaṃ | P2 (5) agnẹ P2 (6) pravocaḥ P, P2; pravocat LGS - cf. RV I 27,4, TĀ IV 11.8; beide mit Varianten (*pravocaḥ*)

198.3 (1) indro P2 (2) manạsā P2 (3) neśi P (4) sūribhi harirvas P, sūribhir harivās P2 (5) devākṛtam P, devakṛtaṃ P2 (6) yyad P, P2 (7) san P - akzentuiert nach KS IV 12

198.4 (1) payạsā P2 (2) tanūbhir | P m. Abkürzung (3) *saṃ* xavəna | P2 (Rand der Seite hier abgerissen) (4) taṣṭā P2 (5) rāya pr.m., rāyo sec.m. P2; -

Akzente nach KS IV 12

198.5 (1) *a*xəxəruṣasəxəgram P2; •graṃm P2 (2) cạ P2 (3) raśmin P, rax x P2 (4) ə*n*ə P2; - auch in KS XVI 2, aber dort ohne Akz. (nur Ms. Ch.)

198.6 (1) vaṅ P, P2; vāṃ L (2) madhụmaty P2 (3) x x P2 (4) yajñim P, P2 (5) •tām P, P2; •tam L; - Akzente nach KS IV 2

198.7 (1) rayiṃ || P m. Abkürzung (2) īśạno P2 (3) jagạtas P2 (4) *sa* P2 (5) naḥ P2 (ḥ wohl sec.m.); - Akzente nach KaṭhĀ I 198.25

198.8 (1) prajānāṃm P, prajānạm P2 (2) rāye P2; rāya L, P - cf. KaṭhĀ I 198.26 (3) īṣe pr.m., īśiṣe | sec.m. P m. Abkürzung īśiṣe | : P2 kürzt so ab (4) bhuvana P, bhuvaxə*ṃ* P2 (5) bhūrị P2 (6) vāsaṃ L (7) syạma P2; - Akz. n. 198.26

198.9 (1) x x trəśat P2 (2) tantạvo P2 (3) vitanvatạ P2 (4) yyajñam P, P2 (5) dadanti P (6) teṣạṃ P2 (7) chidram P2 (8) pratix x P2 (9) svāhā | yaṃ P (10) yyajño P, P2; - auch KS XXXIV 19, o. Akz.

198.10 (1) vicakkrame P (2) sammūḍham P; - Akz. n. KS II 10

198.11-39 Dieser Anuvāka gehört wohl an diese Stelle, cf. die Parallele in MS IV 9,12; eine andere Möglichkeit wäre, ihn in Anlehnung an TĀ IV 20 zu den Prāyaścittas (III 235-39a) zu rechnen; in jedem Fall dürfte er vor den beiden Śāntis gestanden haben. - Die Bezeichnung *uttamaḥ pratīkānuvākaḥ* folgt den Paddh. und LGS II p. 69. - Belegt in: t1 fol. 282a-283a (1. Bl. von Heft 8 von t1); auch transkribiert von SCHROEDER, SB Wien 1898 p. 81 f. (nur: 198.11-14!): **S**; **P2** p. 12a-12b, beginnt erst mit 198.32 *duroṇe*, da die vorausgehenden Bll. verloren sind, Akzentreste (Svaritapunkte); **P** p. 313b-314b, ohne Nummerierung der Verse; LGS Vol. II p. 69-76, mit Komm. Devapālas

198.11 (1) ma P (2) gharmó P; gharmo P; gharma L: also wohl Nom. gegen MS, TĀ (3) na pr.m., no sec.m. P

(4) paramadhamomāhruto t_1, S (SB Wien 1898 p. 81): páramadhamo máhūto (statt Lesung t_1!); paramadhāmomāhruto P; paramadhāmāhruto L; - zu korrigieren: páram ádharam; offensichtl. Verlesung von •dhạrạ• > •dhā• [illegible] > [illegible]; *-moma-* wohl aus verbessertem *-möma-* (d.h.: *mā*): [illegible] [illegible] eingedrungen; auch sonst häufig dieselben Lesungen in T, t_1, u. P. - (5) mó S (6) asmāṃs P (7) mā t_1 (8) abhíkúrvato t_1; abhí kúrvatā S; abhikurvata P (9) vyáthito t_1

198.12 īḍate S (2) •dviṣa pr.m; •dviṣo sec.m. t_1 (3) •dhāḥ | L; •daḥ | P (4) agmán pr.m., -gni- über der Zeile sec.m. t_1; agman P; agnír S (5) nírṛtir S (6) fehlt LGS (7) árātir S, arātiṃ L, aratīn P, árātam pr.m., árātim sec.m. t_1 (8) héḍate S, héḷate t_1, heḷate L, hīḷite P (9) t_1, L; héḍaṣethām || S; hīḷayethām P

198.13 (1) ā S (-nu anscheinend durch Spalte im Blatt verdeckt); ano pr.m., anu sec. m. P (2) nu pr.m., no sec.m. P (3) anvā• t_1, S, P; anudī• L (4) sákhəyau t_1, śákhayau S (5) ādityánām t_1; ādityánām S (6) abgebrochen in t_1, aber wohl über der Zeile zu erkennen: *pa* sec.m., wohl als Verbesserung für kāṣṭā gemeint: t_1; pāṣṭā L; paṣṭā pr.m., kāṣṭā sec. manu P; nichts bei S; ...]pə'[... t_1 (7) prasitir P (8) hṛtir L (9) udrā pr.m., ugrā sec.m. P (10) haviṃsaḥ pr.m., havisaḥ sec.m. P

198.14 (1) datrāṇām S, dadhrāṇām t_1, dadhrāṇam P (2) samāne P (3) t_1, yuvānaṃ L, yyuvānaṃ P (4) zu lesen •adyā "heute"?

198.15-18 ohne Akzente in t_1; Nummern der Sprüche fehlen mit Ausnahme von ||8|| in t_1; S fälschlich: 'oṁ bhūs svāhā; vier mal so, ohne Accente'

198.19 (1) tyan P (2) jātavedasaṃ || P m. Abkürzung des Mantra; - belegt auch KS IV 9, aber mit anderen darauf folgenden Versen; cf. I 198.1 u. III 198, 238

198.20 (1) pari || P m. Abkürzung (2) KS XXXVIII 5, ohne Akzente, mit umgekehrter Stellung: paśyanta jyotir

198.21 KS XVI 4, o. Akz., liest: •āvā; (2) divyā t_1; divyā P (3) suṣukvabhir P (4) •bheḥ pr.m., •bhiḥ sec. manu P

198.22 (1) vāja(sya) t_1 (2) vāgadbhir P (3) •hai P

unakzentuiert auch in KS XVI 4

198.23 (1) puna dṛrjā pr.m., punar ūrjā sec.m. P (2) ní(varta)sva t_1 (3) aṃhasā P; - o.Akz. auch KS VIII 14

198.24 (1) níva(rta)*sva* t_1; •sva• L; - o. Akz. KS VIII 14

198.25 (1) dadhātu || P m. Abkürzung (2) (no ra)yím t_1, akzentuiert auch KS XIII 16 a.E.; als Yajus in L.

198.26 (1) dhā́(tā pra)jā́nām t_1 (2) raya L, P; rayá oder rayé (undeutlich) t_1 (3) īṣe P (4) dhātedaṃ t_1 (Udātta über •daṃ vielleicht überklebt) (5) sandā(śuṣ)e t_1; saṃ dāśuṣe L (6) kirate pr.m., kirati sec.m. t_1 (7) bhūrivāṃsaṃ L

198.27 (1) agna ayūṃṣi• | : so kürzt ab L; agna āyuṃ || P kürzt ab; á(gna a)yūṁsi t_1; - akzentuiert KS IV 11

198.28 (1) agne pavasva• | L kürzt so ab; (2) svapā | P kürzt so ab; (3) so wohl t_1: undeutliches Zeichen über *-rya-*; akzentuiert auch KS VII 16

198.29 (1) tvan no agne• | L kürzt ab; •agne || P kürzt so ab (2) śúśucāno t_1 (5) dvíṣāṁsi t_1; - o. Akz. auch in KS XXXIV 19, a.E.

198.30 (1) sa tvam no agne• | L, •agne || P : beide kürzen ab (2) sa t_1 (3) vamó t_1 (4) vyuṣṭau t_1 mit richtigem Svaritazeichen (5) hier Anunāsika, vgl. Einleitung, Anm.57; - o. Akz. auch KS XXXIV 19 a. E.

198.31 (1) vāyur agre gā• | L: kürzt ab; Devapāla zu 198. 25-31: 'ete sapta mantrāḥ(!) vyākhyātāḥ LGS (2) sākaṅ ghan pr.m.; sākaṅ gan sec.m. P; - o. Akz. auch in KS X 12

198.32 (1) dāśvaṃsam P (2) vistaye L, (3) hier Beginn des Fragmentes in P_2: p.12a duroṇe | (4) no P_2 (5) •jasvam P_2 (6) yyuvasvi pr.m., yyuvasva sec.m. P (7) niṃ pr.m., sec.m.: nī P (5) aśvaṃ P, aśvañ P_2 ohne Akzente auch in KS X 12

198.33 (1) t_1, P, P_2; fehlt L; KS XII 1 enthält diesen und die folgenden Verse (198.33-38) mit Akzenten

198.34-38 fehlen als Pratīkas in t_1; yaḫ prāṇadā || ya ojodā• || yena dyaur ugrā• || ye ime dyāvā || yasya me viśva• || L : Devapāla: 'ete ṣaṭ(!) vyākhyātāḥ' LGS; yaḥ prāṇatoḥ || ya ojodāḥ || yena dyau | ya ime dyāvā | yasyeme viśva (pr.m., •viśve sec.m.) || P yaḥ prāṇa || ya ojo || yena dyau || ya ime || yasyame || P_2

198.39 (1) yaṅ krandasīti saptamī | oṁ yáṅ t_1 (2) apasā L, avapasā (cf. 198.11, Anm.4 über Korr. des Schreibers) P, avasā P_2 (3) tástabhānḗ t_1, tastabhāne P_2 (4) •tā t_1 (5) manasā P_2 (6) kasmai P_2 (7) devā || P kürzt so ab; devāya P_2; - cf. RV X 121,6; TS IV 1,8,5 etc.

198a-199 sind belegt in: **t_1**, fol. 280b-281a; **P** p. 311a; **P_2** p. 12a; L LGS Vol. II p. 62 f.; überall ohne Akzente; die Reihenfolge in den Mss. weicht von der hier befolgten, sich an das Brāhmaṇa (KaṭhĀ III 155,156 u. 199) anlehnenden ab; diese ist: pṛthivī samit ..., antarikṣam ..., dyaus ...; agne vratapate ..., vāyo ..., sūrya ...; im Gegensatz zum Zeugnis der Mss. aber hat L: agne, vāyo, sūrya; pṛthivī, antarikṣaṃ, sūrya (cf. aber KaṭhĀ III 155,156!)

198a (1) hier und im Folgenden stets Beginn mit: oṁ; oṁ agnə t_1 (2) vratapatə t_1 (3) samrāḍ L (4) •bhṛd P_2 aber sec.m. über der Zeile: *ta* (5) t xt xr xr xīmi t_1 (6) taś P_2, P, t_1 (7) rdhyāsamama pr.m., rdhyāsam sec.m. P (8) tā^{magni} P_2 (*magni* über der Zeile) (9) saxəndhe P_2 (10) suṣamiddha sec.m. über der Zeile P_2; suṣaniddhā pr.m., suṣamiddhā sec. m. P (11) brahmavarcasena | P (12) samindhyāt 1 | P_2, t_1

198b (1) evam vāyo vratapate || sūrya vratapate || P_2; vāyo vratapate samrāḷ a || sūrya vratapate samrāḷ asi || P; evaṃ vāyo vratapate | oṁ sūrya vratapate | t_1; vāyo vratapate• || sūrya vratapate• | | L: stets abgekürzt. (2) oṁ antarikṣam P, antarikṣaṃ samit ... aham• || L kürzt ab; (5) vāyu P_2 (4) samindhe || P kürzt ab (5) samiddhā auch sec.m. über der Zeile hinzugefügt P_2 (6) suṣamiddhā sec.m. über der Zeile P_2 (7) samindhyāt 2 | P_2, t_1

199 (1) siehe Art der Abkürzung in 198b, Anm. 1 (2) samindhe || P kürzt ab; dyauḥ ... aham• || L kürzt ab; (3) suṣaximiddhā über der Zeile P_2, (4) x x x x sena t_1 (5) samindhyāt |3| P_2; •dyāt mit Virama t_1

192.1-2 sind belegt in: **t_1** fol. 293a; **P** p. 314b; **P_2** p.12a; **L** p. 64 Vol. II; - stets ohne Akzente

199.1 (1) samrāḍ L (2) yaśasā + samindhyāt | t_1: am unteren Seitenrand hinzugefügt: brahmavarcasena + t_1 (3) evam antarikṣam | pṛthivī samit tām | t_1; evam | antarikṣaṃ samit tām || pṛthivī samit tām || P_2; antarikṣaṃ samit tāṃ vāyus samindhe || pṛthivī samit tām agnis samindhe || || P

199.2 (1) vratabhṛd asya P_2; vratabhṛt asi P (2) ācariṣaṃ t_1 (3) aśake pr.m., aśakam sec.m. P (4) gopāya | evam vāyo vrata | agne vratapate vratam acāriṣaṃ || t_1 gopāya || evaṃ vāyo vratapate || agne vratapate || P_2 gopāya || vāyo vratapate || sū (gestrichen) agne vratapate || P; gopāya || vāyo vratapate• || agne vratapate• || L

Prāvargikī pūrvā śāntiḥ: Die beiden Śāntis dürften den Schluß des Mantra-Kapitels gebildet haben; sie werden hier in der Reihenfolge der Mss. von KaṭhĀ I, aber mit Nummerierung der Mantras nach KaṭhĀ II, III gegeben, zusätzlich aber nach Ausweis der Mss. von KaṭhĀ I (Markierungen von Anuvākas u. weiteren Unterabteilungen) mit römischen Zahlen abschnittsweise durchnummeriert, was dem leichteren Auffinden bei Zitaten dienen dürfte, z.B. KaṭhĀ I 58 (II) u. dgl.

Die *purvā śānti* ist belegt in: **t1** fol. 278, ohne Akz., sehr zerstört; **P** p. 3o8-309b; **P2** p. 14a (erst ab IV 101); **L** LGS Vol. II p. 52 sqq. mit Komm. Devapālas; **T** (II, III)

I

208 (1) bhū́r bhuvás svàr, nur in T; in den andern Mss. am Ende des Anuvāka (214) (2) •pátaye S; T wohl: •pataye, dabei ist das *-e* wohl ausradiert (wegen folgenden íti)

208b (1) namaḥ | P, namaḥ t1; námaḥ L (ohne Satzzeichen)

208e (1) daivaṃ pr.m., daivīṃ sec.m. t1

208d (1) mantravidaḥ ~| P

209 (1) śivam ajasraṃ S, •ajasraṃ P

210 (1) juṣṭan P, juṣṭān t1 (2) devebhyaḥ | P; devebhyaḥ L

211 (1) svadhāvatīm t1 (2) pitṛbhyaḥ P

212 (1) śvaśrūṣenyām P; •ṣeṇyām t1 (2) manuṣyabhyas P, manuṣyebhyaḥ(!) t1; manuṣyébhya (íti) T,S

213 (1) tásmād evá S, corr.: tásmād devā́; taṃ māṃ devā L (2) tamadantu (viell.: umadantu) P

214 (1) sucakṣām P (2) suśrūt P (3) karṇābhyāṃ P, •bhyāṃ t1 (4) bhūyāsam P (5) oṁ bhūr• L , oṁ fehlt P, t1

II

58 (1) prāśyā• P, *prācā* (folgt Lücke von ca. 7 Akṣaras, ohne Grund, viell. Astloch) tvā diśā xi (folgen 5 Akṣ., die auf dem Film nicht lesbar sind; Birkenrindenstreifen umgeknickt) x x x xe x x chandasā vasanx (wieder Lücke)

mpraviśā (zwei Akṣ. umgeknickt) x[... (Rest abgeblättert bis Anfang M.59) t_1 (2) cchándasā S (hier und im Folgenden stets cch•, ebenso L) (3) právix x T (4) hier u. in den folg. Fällen Daṇḍa (|) nach jedem Spruch in L, P; kein Zeichen in t_1

59 vollständig abgebrochen in t_1, bis: *d*evatayā[...

60 vollständig zerstört in t_1; (1) pratīśya T (2) savitrá̄ T (3) devatayā | P, devá• B (4) já̄ga(tena) T (5) śchándasā T (6) ṛtvam P, ṛtvám T

61 vollständig zerstört in t_1, (1) udīśyā P, •odīśyā (mit Sandhi, da Brāhmaṇatext vorausgeht!) T (2) diśā T (3) •varuṇābhyāṃ P (4) devatayā | nuṣṭu• P (5) ṛ(túm prá)vi• T

62 (1) ūrdhvayā... bṛ] abgebrochen in T, Akzente ergänzt (2) devatayā | P (3) ha(m)antám T (4) pravix x T; - in t_1 M. 62 vollkommen zerstört bis: ...]my

63 vollkommen abgebrochen in t_1 bis ...]śāmi | t_1, (2) prajá̄ x x x x ptana T; prajá̄ -------- S; •tinā anāptena L

III

64-68 stets Daṇḍa nach jedem Spruch in L, nicht aber P, t_1

64 (1) śchandah̭ P, śchandah̭ t_1, cch• L (2) pravi(śā)míty T (mit +íti wegen Br.Text);

65 (1) •schandaḥ P, triṣṭu(bhaṃ ś)chandah̭ t_1 (2) prá(viś)āmíty (mit +íti wegen Br. Text) T

66 (1) jāgataṃ pr.m., jāgatīm sec.m. über der Zeile t_1, (2) śchandah̭ P, t_1

67 (1) •śchandah̭ P, t_1; anuṣṭú(bhaṃ chán)daḥ T

67a (1) śchandah̭ P (2) pra(viśā)mi t_1; - 67a fehlt ganz S

68 (1) •sāṃ P, atichandasam t_1; (2) chá(ndah̭ prá)vi• T, śch• P

69 (1) chandāṃsi• t_1; śchándāṁsi prá)vi• T

70 (1) t(āni no) t_1 (2) pā(rayantu) T (3) ne (viell.: no) P (4) vantva t_1

71 (1) -o sec.m. P (2) vayan P (3) dviṣmaḥ | t_1, (dviṣmá) T

72 (1) ein oder zwei unleserliche Akṣara vor *āpo* t_1, aber zwischen *dviṣmaḥ* | in M.71 und *āpo* M.72 dürfte nichts stehen! (2) 'smān L (3) praviśa(ntv) t_1, praviśanty S (4) (ā)po t_1, āpa pr.m., āpo sec.m. P (5) 'smāsu L (6) jāgṛt(éty) T, jāgrata L

73 (1) viśvāyu P (2) ā(yur) T (3) da dieser Teil von M.75 sowohl in P, t_1 als auch in der mod. Ed. L folgt, dürfte auch in KaṭhĀ II 73 dieser Teil zum Mantra gehören, nicht also Br.-Erläuterung sein wie II 52, 94 usw. nahelegen.

IV

98a-101h sind in KaṭhĀ I wohl als Yajus behandelt; nur L druckt diese Mantras als Verse; einzige YV-Parallele von AVŚ II 2, AVP I 7, aber mit anderem Schluβ.

98a (1) d(i)vyo t_1, (2) aḍya pr.m., īḍya sec.m. t_1 (3) dev(a daiv)ya(m) t_1, •daivī L

99 (1) sadhastam t_1 mit Virāma zur Kennzeichnung der Pausa

100 (1) -ṣṭ- und -ṣṭh- haben *ein* Śāradā-Zeichen gemeinsam; pṛṣṭhó S (2) yajata L (3) avayāto L (4) h(aras)o t_1 (5) suśevaḥ t_1 (Zeichen für Pausa); suśevaḥ | L

101 (1) avadyābhis pr.m., a^{na}vadyābhis sec.m. P, anavadyā(bhis) t_1 (2) sám u jagmābhír wohl T, aber -u- nicht deutlich; S liest: sáma•

101a ...]ssu. Beginn von **P_2** p.14b (2) āsīt | P_2, āsīt (mit Virāma) t_1; L macht hier keine Pausa sondern druckt fortlaufend

101b (1) āsāṃ P, āsā́ṃ S, āsāṃ T, āsāṃ P_2

101c (1) tataḥ P, ta(tas) t_1, (2) (sadhry)• t_1, sadhry x x x x (viell.: sadhry x ca x x) P (3) caranty t_1, L, P, wohl auch P_2 (hier zerstört)

101d (1) xbhriye P_2 (2) nakṣatraye P_2

101e (1) yāḥ t_1, P; yā pr.m., yāḥ sec.m. P_2 (2) viśvāvasaṃ P (3) nach *gandharvaṃ* folgt in P eine Ergänzung sec. m. von ca. 3 Akṣ., aber wieder gestr., unleserlich (4) sasadhre P, t_1, sacadhve AV, AVP; wohl: sasaśre, (viell.: •dre) P_2; cf. Einfluß von *sadhry* in 101c

101f (1) (na)mo t_1 (2) mṛḷayanta pr.m., *tu* sec.m. über der Zeile; mṛḍayantu L; mṛḷaxəta P_2

101g (1) śarmā P (2) yaśchata P_2, t_1 (dort *-ntu* sec.m. über der Zeile) (3) tā t_1,P, P_2,L; ob *taṃ* zu lesen ist? (4) yaṃ t_1

101h (1) asañ P, āsā(ṃ) t_1 (2) (jam)bhe t_1

V

219m (1) āx x P_2, (2) P fügt noch einmal hinzu: tābhyāṃd vipaśya (sec.m. noch mal: am Rand: *vi*) mām abhi P, •mā(m a)bhi t_1; dieser Pāda auch in t_1, P_2 noch einmal hinzugefügt, aber in P_2 sec.m. wieder gestrichen.

220 (1) x xə̩x xə̣x x x x xu̩x x xū̩x xə̣*n*ə*j*m*i*ta+ ^{tə}nạ T (2) sāraghaṃ̩ t_1, abgerieben̩ in P_2̩ (3) madhu abgebrochen P_2 (4) amagdhi pr.m., anagdhi sec.m. P (5) me | P_2, t_1

220a (1) sa(v)i(tu)ḫ t_1 (2) prasavi pr.m., prasave sec.m. P (3) abgebrochen P_2 (4) hastābhyāṃ P, dann Daṇḍa sec.m.; hastābhyām (mit Virāma) P, hastābhyāṃ t_1

220b (1) •(bhaga)van t_1; abhyañjai• P; ax x x x ván T, a-------ván S, •bhagavān P_2

221 (1) tax x x caś P_2; tasya ca• P (2) yajūṃṣi P, P_2

222 (1) L lediglich: vāg agnā anyac, cakṣuḥ sūrye 'nyad, agnā anyad (2) anyaś P, anyáś T, anyaś P_2 (3) das dritte *agnā anyad* fehlt in P, t_1; agnā a̲x x gnā anyad P_2 (d.h. auch hier fehlt das dritte Mal: agnā anyad)

223 (1) bhaga...vān (mit Lücke von einem Akṣara) T (2) bhūyāsam (mit Virāma) | t_1, P_2; bhūyāsam || L

224 (1) airosi L, airo si pr.m., sec.m.: über der Zeile: ḷo t_1; airó si T, S (2) púranzir T (3) nā́ma T; S aber liest: *asi*, wohl wegen des folgenden *asi* (4) vāg asi | L

225 (1) •hvaye T, •hūye S (2) bhaga | t_1, bhaga || P_2

226 (1) ab hier akzentuiert in t_1 (2) vā P, vā S, aber wohl: váṃ T (der Rest von M.226 u. 226a fehlt in T, da abgebrochen) (2a) sanax P_2 (3) naras P (4) daṃsā P, dáṃsá t_1

(5) ụgram t_1 (6) tányatur t_1 (7) na t_1 (8) vṛṣṭím (mit Virāma) t_1, •m | P_2 (9) yaṅ P (10) ātharvaṇor P (11) vām xəsya P_2 (12) sumátim t_1, P_2; •tir L, P (13) avocat | t_1, avocat | P_2

226a (1) oṁ agnír t_1 (2) īśa P, īśo L (3) vasavyaisyā• (m.richtigem Svaritazeichen) t_1, vāsavyai• P_2 (4) mahās P_2 māhas P (5) sobhagasya | P_2 (5a) t x smabhyaṃ P_2; asmabhyaṃ P (6) rāsati P, L, t_1, (7) P_2, t_1; iti prāgvargeke (sec.m.: prāvargike) pūrveke śānti||ḥ|| P

Prāvargiky uttarā śāntiḥ: Diese Śānti ist belegt in: **t_1**, fol.283b-284a, akzentuiert davon: 218-219j, mit Ausnahme von 218c-e; **P** p.308a-310b; **P_2** p.12a-12b; **L** LGS vol. II p. 76 ff.; Pausa erscheint in t_1 nur bei Versen; in P_2 dagegen werden auch die einzelnen Yajus durch Daṇḍas voneinander getrennt.

VI

199a fehlt ganz in T: abgebrochen; - (1) fehlt t_1, P, P2, L; - aber Devapāla: *etāni sapta yajūṃṣi | saptānām api ca "āyuṣe naḥ punar dehi" iti sādhāraṇo 'nuṣaṅgaḥ*. - Dieser Satz auch in P_2 und t_1 (2) āyurā pr.m., āyurdā sec.m. P, āyurdhā pr.m., •dā sec.m. P_2

200 (1) prāṇadā P, prāṇadā pr.m., •dāḥ (!) sec.m. t_1 (2) prāṇaṃ P (3) āyuṣe naḥ punar dehi; fehlt auch hier und in den folg. Mantras in allen Mss.

201 (1) vyānadā P (2) vyānaṃ t_1, vyánáṃ T (3) dehi pr.m. dehy sec.m. P, dehi L

202 (1) apānaṃ t_1

203 (1) cakṣurdā P, cakṣurdā pr.m., cakṣurdāḥ (!) sec.m. t_1, cakṣurdác T

204 (1) śrotraṃ t_1

205 (1) dehi pr.m., dehy sec.m. P

206 āyuṣe T (2) na pr.m., naḥ sec.m. P (3) dehe P

VII

207 (1) vgl. KaṭhĀ II 159-166 zu diesen Sprüchen; T in II 207 hat deshalb nur: námo rudrā́yéti

(2) rudrā(ya) t_1 (2a) tasmai namas te namaḥ L (3) sámara íti oder sámana íti T (4) hiṃsiḥ P, hiṃsīḥ P_2 (4a) tasmai• L (kürzt ab) (5) såmanạ T, sámaga S (+íti) (6) hiṃsiḥ P, hiṃsīḥ P_2 (6a) tasmai• L (kürzt) (7) te(na) t_1 (8) samarə t_1

VIII

216-217 Sandhi zwischen beiden Mantras in den Mss. durchgeführt; - (1) brəhməxə *u* t_1; brá(hmaṇa upa)stáraṇam T (2) entfällt (3) tvépa• T (4) •mīḷāyai P (5) vấstvam S (6) fehlt P_2; vāstamad pr.m., vāstu• sec.m. P, vāstumad t_1 (7) vāstumār pr.m., vāstumān sec.m. P_2 (8) bhūyā L (9) vāstus L (10) yañ ca• P, t_1; yaṃ dviṣmaḥ | P_2, •dviṣmaḥ || || t_1 (hier zur Zeilenfüllung angewandte Pausa-Markierungen) (11) bhūyā pr.m, bhūyāḥ (!) sec. m. t_1: hier läge die ältere Form vor, wenn nicht schematisch korrigiert ist (12) apratiṣṭhās P_2 (13) yañ ca P (14) vayan P (15) dviṣmaḥ || t_1

IX

218 ab hier akzentuiert überliefert in t_1; (1) rapaḥ P, t_1; rapaḥ | P_2 (2) viśvábh• t_1, viśvabh• P, P_2; viśvasya bh• L ; •bhiṣa• pr.m., •bheṣa• sec.m. P_2, (3) devānāṃn P, devấnāṃ t_1; devānạṃ P_2 (4) ${}^{\text{I}}$yase (ī über der Zeile) P_2

218a (1) té gṛhé t_1 (2) mṛtạsya P_2, nihitasya P, nihitasya L (3) hịtaḥ t_1, hitaḥ | P_2;, nidhitaḥ L (4) tạta pr.m., tatạ sec.m. P_2

218b (1) dyubhịr P_2 (2) ariṣṭibhir P (3) aśvinạ P_2 (4) (•tan)nọ P_2 (5) mitromi (d.h. das zweite *mi* ist gestr.) P_2 (6) adi ∧ || P (es fehlen 4 Wörter, die nicht nachgetragen sind; adịtis P_2

218c (1) tayāhaṃ P, P_2; tvayāham L (2) sarvaṃ śāntyām pr. m., •tyā sec.m. P_2 (3) mahyan P (4) śāntiṅ P (5) karāmi pr.m., karomi sec.m. P_2 (6) asi pr.m., asīti sec.m. P; -- cf. III 215; hier o. Akz. in t_1

218d sāsvatī pr.m., sārasvatī sec.m. P; (sára)svatíti T (2) sandṛśi pr.m., sandṛśe sec.m. P; sandṛśe | t_1; sandṛśe P_2

218e ohne Akz. in t_1; (1) sec.m. hinzugefügt; sūryasya tvā cakṣuṣābhivīkṣe | P; •bhivīkṣe P_2 (2) •nvīkṣe | t_1, P_2

218f (1) śravọ P_2 (2) sānasya P_2 (3) dyumnañ P; - akz. t_1

218g (1) •dhṛtaḥ P (2) sānasya P_2 (3) satyañ P (4) •śravastam P_2

219 (1) •mayobhuvaḥ || P_2: das Weitere fehlt hier bis: 219b; āpo P_2; •ma[yobhuvaḥ etc. abgebrochen in T; L lediglich: āpo hi ṣṭhā ity ādayas tisraḥ (es fehlt 219-b)

219a (1) úśatī́r t_1

219b (1) āpọ janayācane ity aṃntam (sec.m. antam) P_2

219c (1) praṇīta P, pṛṇīta L, t_1, pṛṇīta P_2 (2) varūthaṃ P, t_1, (3) tanvo L, tanva P, tanve P_2, t_1

219d (1) śaṃ no devīr abhiṣṭaya iti vyākhyāta L (2) śaṃ na pr.m., śaṃ no sec.m. P; •no t_1, śan nọ P (3) divīr pr.m., devīr sec.m. P (Rest von d fehlt hier) (4) śaṃ yyor P_2; śáṃ yyór t_1 (5) pītaye P_2 (statt des *-ī-* ist sec.m. *-e-* geschrieben, aber wieder gestrichen)

219e (1) śan nọ P_2 (2) varụṇaś P_2 (3) śán no t_1 (4) urukramaḥ | P, P_2; - in P ist *śan na indro* zunächst ausgefallen, dann aber unten auf der Seite sec.m. nachgetragen (bis *aryamā*)

219f (1) śañ nọ P_2 (2) varụṇaś P_2 (3) indrạś P_2 (4) urukramaḥ P, P_2

219g (1) vājinạn P_2 (2) devájūtaṃ t_1; devajūtaṃ L, P, P_2 (3) sahovānan P, P_2, L; sahóvānan t_1, (4) •nemim t_1; •nemiṃ pr.m., •nemi sec.m. P_2 (5) pṛtanājạm P_2 (6) āṁsūṃ oder āśūṃ P, āśúṃ t_1; (7) tārkṣam P, tārkṣyạm P_2 (8) ihā pr.m., ihāvā sec.m. P; ivaṃ pr.m., iva sec.m. P_2 (9) ruhema P_2

219h (1) kāya P (2) bhūva || P (kürzt ab) (3) sadhāvṛ̣dhās pr.m., sadāvṛdhas sec.m. P_2

219i (1) tvạ̄ P_2 (2) madānāmaṃhiṣṭo P, mádānāṁmáṃ• t_1; madạnāṃmaṃ• pr.m., madạnāmaṃ• sec.m. P_2 (3) aṃhasaḥ L (4) cịd P_2 (5) āruji P

219j (1) abhí t_1; abhī P, L; abhi P_2 (2) ṣu P (3) ṇas P, ṇas t_1, P_2 (4) bhavasy P_2 (5) jaritrīṇām P, jarítṛṇām t_1 (6) śatám t_1

219k (1) purastāt P_2 (2) 'rṇavād L (3) mṛṣabho P, P_2 (4) vibhr· L, t_1, P_2; bibhṛ· wohl P, - dieser Mantra o. Akz. in t_1, ebenso wie der folgende:

219l (1) hiṃsīs P (2) iti prāvargikī uttarā śānti || || t_1,P; - o. Akz. in t_1

....

Lesarten
zum
Śukriya-Brāhmaṇam
(KaṭhĀ II, III)

Vorbemerkung: Lesarten aus dem Mantra-Kapitel (KaṭhĀ I) sind hier, wo es sinnvoll erschien, wiederholt worden. Abweichende Lesungen L. von SCHROEDERs sind, obwohl meist ohne textkritischen Wert, unter der Sigle S aufgeführt. Die Angabe von Lücken durch ihn ist aber nicht korrekt sondern folgt drucktechnischen Notwendigkeiten. Die Markierung durch Striche --- bei S ist deshalb hier nur durch Punkte ... angedeutet.

fol.337b Der Text beginnt mit der stark zerstörten, viertletzten Zeile dieser Seite; voraus gehen Paddhati-Texte über Ajasthāpana und Godāna; - zu den M. 1-47 siehe auch KaṭhĀ I 1-47

1 (1) T, yañjáte S; yuñjate P, P_2 (2) ·*b*ạxáxīxexəxəxetəmə́{nạsāv*e*}x x x x x x x x x x (Zeilenende) *dannaná*xəxexəxə́xə́tạḫ T nach der Lesung des Films; das mit { } bezeichnete Stück ist als loses Bruchstück mitverfilmt worden (fehlt bei S); bei der Kontrolle des Original-Ms. in Tübingen im Juli 1972 war durch Abheben übereinandergeschobener Fragmente folgende Lesung möglich: āha*vān*íxẹxəx*eti*má{nạsāv*e*}x x x śa(?)tiryaxñámạta (Zeilen-

ende) *nu tatə̀xexəxə̀xə̀taḫ* T: das Ganze fehlt bei S (3) vəcátətəḫkəmạxə T; vacá... S

2 (1) íty ə̀xīr T, ítya..īr S (2) ā́da... S; ā́datte T (3) cáta... S; śátasx x xə̀śo T

fol.338a

(4) •ta T, •té S

6 (1) pra P, P_2; ā́ T (2) àtu T, ètu corr. S; atu P, àtu P_2: hier ist noch der unabhängige Svarita geschrieben!

8 (1) devīr P (2) devayajané T, S, •yajanẹ P_2 (3) mahāvīrāt S (4) sambhriyāṇād S (5) abibhrītāṃ T, abibhītaṃ | S stillschweigend (6) téjamānā tád vakṣyatī́ti S

9 (1) ṛtasyavyāsam P (2) adya S, adhya P (3) śíras sámbharati T (Zeile gespalten), ... S (4) varāhó T, varāho S (5) •dar T, •dad S stillschweigend

fol.338b

10 (1) varāhavihatam S (2) bhavaty S (3) asyā S

13 (1) prajāpatis P (2) ruhanti S (3) fehlt S (4) ruhánti S (5) T; piyā́n S in Lesart (6) tanvàm̐ S corr., liest: tanvas; in T ist die Stelle wohl recht verschrieben, ebenso wie das darunter in der folg. Zeile Stehende:
{ priyā́n tanvās sámbharati } statt: {priyā́n tanvạm sám•}
{mádhunā saṃyáuti } {mádhuṇāsáṃyạuti }

14 (1) saṃyauti T, sáṃyauti S stillschweigend

15 fehlt ganz in P_2

16 (1) ávadhāvate S, ávabh• T

17 (1) gāyatró T

18 (1) tráiṣṭubho T? (2) ojo T, ójo S stillschweigend

19 (1) paśávài T, paśávo vái S stillschweigend, cf. II 35 (2) jágatī T, jágatī S stillschweigend

fol.339a

21 (1) tṛpyati S

23 (1) aśvaśakān T, S

24 (1) patnī T, patnīr P, patnī P_2 (2) vá T, vā́ S

25 (1) śuciṣe P

26 (1) von P_2 wird der gesamte Vers gegeben (cf. I 218f)

27 (1) savitud• P

28 (1) ávyathamānāḫ T, ávyathamānā corr. S, s. aber I 28

29 (1) bṛhád T, S; cf. I 29 (2) dhruvás ध्रु व स° T, aber pūrvás S (verlesen: dhru• > pū• ध्रु > पू व स°): altes -r- in T (3) dṛm̊hati S (4) eváina टट m• T, || fehlt S

fol.339b (1) 329 T (Schreibfehler)

35 (1) paśá₊vái T (am Rande sec.m.: vọ)

36 (1) so die Trennung in T; || fehlt bei S (2) ahamān P (3) •sénójasā T, •sénáujasā S (4) •varca*sy*àtmánam T, S (5) •sénójasa T, •sénáujasā S

38 (1) prékṣet T, S

39 (1) cchṛṇattu T, S; chṛṇatu P (P stets nur ch• im Folgenden bis M. 47) (2) *vấg* T

40 (1) cchṛṇáttu S, śch*ṛ*ṇáttu T

41 (1) ấśchṛṇatti T, ácchṛṇatti S

42 (1) śchṛṇattu T, cch• S (2) der ungewöhnliche Sandhi von -ḥ ch- hier und in den folg. Mantras soll wohl Pausa ausdrücken.

fol.340a

49 (1) yájuryuktam T (*-ryo-* über der Zeile wohl sec.m., angedeutet durch einen kleinen Kreis unter *-yu-*)

(2) brahm(a yá)juṣo T (3) tắmạx x x x x x x x kti T, táma...kti S (4) (adhvaryut)vám T (5) *sắ*xạx x x x x x ryúr T, ...yur S; ist hier zu ergänzen: sá[rvasyāgraṇī́r a]dhvaryúr...? cf. III 168 (6) ṛtví(jas sam)-preṣya• T

50 (1) sắmạbhịx x x n T (2) ẹ(vắsy̦)ābhítạśçạkrẹ T, evásyābhitaścakre S

51 (1) sambhṛ́tam T, S (2) fehlt S, *ve* T

52 (1) (ítí) T

54 (1) í(ti h)ótrā T

56 (1) (yá)d T

57 (1) (|) T

58 prāśyā P (2) cchándasā S (so auch im Folg. stets wieder; T und P schreiben śch•, LGS druckt cch• (3) •í(ti pr)ā́cīn T (4) práviśaty S

59 1) •śéndre(ṇa) T (2) •(ñca) T

60 (1) pratī́śyā T (2) savi*trā́* T (3) *d*evá• T (4) jā́ga(tena) T (5) *śchánd*asā T (6) ṛtvám T, P

61 (1) ápra(dāh)āyódīśyā T; •ódīcyā S; •udīśyām P (2) diśā́ T (3) ṛ(túm prá)viśāmī́ty T

fol.**340b**

62 (1) ápra x x x x x x x x haspátinā T, ápradāhāya...bṛ́haspátinā S; •ūrdhvayā tvā diśā bṛhaspatinā P (2) he(ma)ntám T (3) ergänzt nach der Zwangsläufigkeit : právix x x x x x x x ñ T; praví... S

63 (1) prajā́x x x x x pt*a*na T, prajā́...na S; prajāpatinā devatayānaptena P, prajāpatinā devatayā anāptena t_1, LGS (2) •ī́(tīm)ā́ñ T (3) ergänzt nach der Zwangsläufigkeit: x x x x x x x nty T, ...ty S

64 (1) śch• P (2) právi(śā)mī́ty T

65 (1) prá(viś)āmī́ty T (2) oja T, ója S stillschweigend

66 (1) śch• P (2) vái fehlt in T; frei ergänzt: vgl. II 35 und 19; *vái* scheint aber bisweilen nicht benutzt

67 (1) •ṣṭú(bhaṃ chá)ndaḥ T, ápradāhāyānuṣṭúbhaṃ chándaḥ S (2) fehlt ganz bei S ('Schreiberhaplologie')

67a (3) p(aṅktí)r (durch Falte im Blatt verdeckt) T

68 (1) atiśchandasām P (2) chá(ndaḥ prá)viśāmī́ti T, śch• P (3) chándāṁsi T (4) (vā́ áti)śchandā́ś T

69 (1) śchándāṁ(si prá)viśāmī́ti T (2) (śchándāṁ)si T

70 (1) pā(rayantu) T (2) ne P (3) (evā́)śāste T

71 (1) yo (das *-o-* sec.m.) P (2) (dviṣmá) T (3) śuc(árpa)yati T

72 (1) práviśanty S (2) jāgṛt(éty ā́pa) T, jāgrata L

73 (1) viśvāyu P (2) ā́(yur) T (3,4) entfallen (5) saṃ(vatsa)rā́ñ T (6) ku(ru)te T; - zur Form d. Mantra cf. I 73

74 (1) pró(kṣa)t(i) T; - hier **endet T MaI 396, Heft 10a**

fol.341a Hier **beginnt Mal 396, Heft 10b** mit den Blättern, bei denen das obere Drittel oder mehr abgebrochen ist, d.h. jeweils 4 oder 5 Zeilen.
Hier sind etwa 5 Zeilen abgebrochen, von der fünften ist noch zu lesen: ...xy x xəxtəxəxuxəx x x x x x (2) prókṣa(ti) T (3) ergänzt nach ĀpŚS XV 6,4.5

75 (1) rghyāsa S (2) svarghyāsa S: "zu vermuten *saghyásaṃ tvā saghyásam tvéti*"; die authentische Form der Kaṭhas ist die des Textes; die originale dürfte ... **sá *rghyásaṃ tvā* gelautet haben; in T vor: *svàrghyāsan tvèti* eine Lücke von ca. 2 Akṣaras (3) x x x naṃ T, ...raṃ S; Ergänzung nicht sicher, viell. *úrdhva eváinam* (cf. ĀpŚS XV 7,2)

76 saṃspŕśas T, sampŕcas S (cf. II 100) (2) a... S, aber lesbar in T

fol.341b

(1) vor: x fehlen ca. 5 Zeilen; keine Akṣarareste ausser zu Beginn der Zeile: x x x x x x x xəxəxrəx x xtə T (2) a*dh*ibhayus ? T (3) prādeśám prādeśam S (4) davatābhir T (5) (m)i(mī)te T (6) hier finden sich ausnahmsweise die üblichen Daṇḍas (|| ||) statt der Śāradā-Form ([Śāradā]), dargestellt hier als: || T,S

81 (1) ápradāhā(yấyur) T

82 (1) ítī(ndram e)vá T

84 (1) (suṣá)dā | T, ...S (aber durch die überklebte Stelle hindurch lesbar) (2) sax x x x vitāraṃ T (3) (dadhāty a)x x haya T, dadhā...hāya S

85 (1) T, ấśāste S

86 (1) ấśrutirutzə{rànmi} xəx rux yoràdhipatya T; das mit { } bezeichnete Fragment war als loses Bruchstück auf dem Rand der Seite mitgefilmt; ā...dhipatya S

87 (1) (dā) T

88 (1) bŕhaspáter, mit alter Schreibweise des *-e-* (*pṛṣṭhamātrā*): [Śāradā] T; cf. III 162, 233: deutet auf eine

recht alte Vorlage für T, da *pṛṣṭhamātrā* bereits im 15. Jht. obsolet geworden waren; S ohne Bemerkung (2) *íti* T

fol.342a es fehlen ca. 4 Zeilen, abgebrochen

89 (1) ergänzt nach der Zwangsläufigkeit und Mantra nach MS (2) xy *t* xə̣ *s t* x xə̣xv x x x x x x *y* tə̣s *və* ạdịxya-x drāmạhāvīróraśmáy x mạrúto T, yo marúto S

90 (1) antar(dh)i(ra)sṛ́ty T (2) ā́(da)dhāti T

91 (1) di(vás) T (2) sampṛ́cas S, cf. II 76, aber auch II 100 diví pṛṣṭó (3) alte Form des *-r-* in pra• T

92 (1) sā́ya(kāni) T (2) yajataṃ T (3) अपम •rūpam (mit Virāma: RV-Vers); •rū́pam | S (4) ọjīyo T, ójīyo S (5) (ru)dra T (6) RV-Übers. Geldners

93 (1) asi T (2) (jā́)gatam T (3) prasthātré T, S (4) *h*ótrābhya T (5) etá₊m práyaś(chaty é)kam T: die mit + angedeutete Stelle ist aber nicht ergänzt worden; ...práyacchaty ékam S (6) agnídho S (7) pra*ti*xr x*th* xə́x x x xə̣x mpáriyati T; pra...m páriyati S; Ergänzung nach ĀpŚS; viell. zu lesen: *pratiprasthātá [tríḥ pradakṣiṇá]ṃ páryeti* (8) hier wieder Daṇḍas T

94 (1) í(ti) T (2) (dhu)nvanti T

96 (1) prāṇô si T, prāṇọ si S (2) vyāno T, vyānọ S (3) sí(ti) T (4) yá(ja)māne S

97 (1) śrótram T: mit altem *-r-* : śro श्रो, aber: (2) *-r-* स्रु T (3) pa₊ viśanti : sec.m. über der Zeile: *ri* (4) etá(t sá)mprayaśchaty T

98 (1) dhūnūtv T, S (kaschm. Aussprache: ū/o!) (2) etábhin T (3) nach ĀpŚS XV 8,10 : nur eine Möglichkeit!

fol.342b es fehlen ca. 4 Zeilen; keine Akṣ. Reste

98a (1) cf. KaṭhĀ I 98a etc. (2) = Zitat in LGS, Vol. II, p. 56, aus der Śruti: '*śrūyate*'

98c (1) vyạm*i*t*i*yadvaẹnax x ṇạpacarạyurh*i*syạdənəbrəxma*n*āśạ-vaśāntam T, fehlt ganz bei S (2) bráhmaṇ*a*iváinam T

99 (1) frei ergänzt; cf. II 52, 94

100 (1) pṛṣṭhó S; *-ṣṭ-* und *-ṣṭh-* haben die gleiche Form! - die authentische Form des Mantra wohl *pṛṣṭó*, cf. aber II 91, 76: *saṁspṛ́śas*; cf. auch AVP 1.7 (2) altes *-r-* in *-dr-* T (3) vyajānann T, S (4) té S, te T (5) T (6) índrò T, índro S (7) ruván T, S (8) abhyàvadat T, abhyavadan S (9) právrajete + té bruvan T (*té* sec.m. über der Zelle; viell. zu lesen: prárdhrajetetē); právrajete té bruvan S (10) ruvád T, S: diese Stelle kommt dem langgesuchten Kāṭhaka-Zitat bei Yāska nahe: Nirukta X 5,8: *yad arudat tac rudrasya rudratvam iti kāṭhakam*; cf. aber KS XXV 1:103,1 = KS XXXVIII 4: *yat samarujat tat rudrasya rudratvam* (11) S, bhṛván T (12) tác S (13) śivo S, śivō T (14) mṛdāta, ebenso mit *-ḍ-* : mṛḍásya, mṛḍatvám S, obwohl deutlich *-ḷ-* geschrieben ist (15) bhavásya T, S: "Dein, o Bhava, ist die Oberherrschaft über das Gewordene und Zukünftige" (16) sárvasyādhípatyam T, sárvasyádhipatyam S stillschw.

101 (1) sámajagmyābhír S, *ma/mu* sind sich recht ähnlich, म : मु hier aber wohl *mu*मु; die anderen Hss. (KaṭhĀ I): *-ma-* L, P, auch Devapāla kommentiert *diesen* Text: *samajagmābhiḥ samaṃ kṛtvā agniṃ yatantībhiḥ* (scil. *āhutībhiḥ*); in T wohl zu lesen: *sámujagmā*· मभुरःग्य, wobei die 'Devanāgarī-Zwei' zu *pravargyàṁ* in der Zeile darunter gehören dürfte (s. Lesart 3, vgl. auch Lesart 2); die authentische Lesung wohl *samajagmābhir*, die originale Form aber wie AV (Ś, P) *sám u jagma ābhir*, während die Kaschmir-Tradition des AVP ebenfalls die Kaṭhaform *samajagmābhir* zeigt.

(2) pravargye T, d.h. pravargyè: hier liegt wohl die seltene Schreibung mit Dev.-Zwei für Svarita vor, vgl. Einl., Anm. 66 und die folg. Lesart: (3) pravargyàṁ T

101b (1) āsā́m S, āsāṃ T (2) e T

fol.343a abgebrochen ca. 4 Zeilen, ergänzt nach KaṭhĀ I

101d (1) ta tı, P, L

101i x x x x x x x x x x x x x x x xə ạxịxyə eṣalạkánạgāptánaṣarạtrānadịvā T (2) s. SIEG, Der Nachtweg der Sonne; vgl. CALAND, AO VI p. 146 f.

102 (1) nu sáñcarati S

103 (1) S, sáṃ T (2) S, cátasró T (3) corr. S, vá T

104 (1) mādhūtíbhyām T, mādhutíbhyām S

105 (1) ruc*i*to T, ...tó S

107 (1) agnínā́gata T, S (2) (d)evéna T (3) svāhéty T (vorausgehend aber: rocate); sváhéty S stillschweigend (4) s. Lesart 2, II 108 (5) agnínā́ saṅgaścha(te śa)m T, agnínā sáṅgacchate S

108 (1) tápasā́gata T, S (2) S, sū́ryéṇārukta T; - zwischen *sū́* und *ryé* ist *tre* über der Zeile eingefügt; dies könnte auch zu *svāhétya* *tre* *trạ* (M.107) gehörig aufgefaßt werden, viell. *svā́héty átraivá* gemeint?

108a (1) víbhā(ti) T (2) S, *akṣ*árikṣasya T (3) pṛthivyā́ḥ T, S (4) (vā́) T (5) (l)lo(k)ā́ṃs T (6) || S

109 (1) mánasa dị⁺ vé T (Akzent über *-i-* gestrichen?): hier sollte wohl das nach Zeugnis der verwandten Texte fehlende *tvā* eingefügt werden: viell. steht es auf dem überklebten Rand der Seite: Dann ist *mánasā* nur Schreibfehler für **mánase*. (2) tvé(ty amú)m T (3) eváina S. (4) so in T (5) yajñásy(ordhvatvā́)ya T

111 (1) hótrạbhị T; cf. MS IV 5,3: 66,6 ff., ŚB III 9,3,4 ff.

fol.343b es fehlen ca. 4 Zeilen, cf. TĀ IV 7,3

112 (1) *gəxbhạhyạṣədạvānạmp*ị*tāmạ*tṛnām T, ... devā́nām pitā́ matīnā́m S (2) prajā́m T, S (S druckt: prajā́máyurdā́stvām asmábhyam!)

113 (1) ā́yurdā́s T, S (vgl. II 112) (2) vacaródā́ḥ T, S: "vacanó dā́ḥ (!), viell. vṛcanó; die Correcturen liegen nahe prajā́nām āyurdā́ḥ und varcodā́ḥ" [SCHROEDER]

114 (1) S, hiṃsāyái T

115 (1) || || S (2) śchidya T, cchidyata konjiziert S (3) pravargyo T, S (4) sárve T, S (5) páryagṛhṇathām T, S

(6) T, lóhitam ásravat S (7) S, udumbháras T (8) S, sámābhavad T (9) konjiziert S; ấdumbarāṇi T (10) mauñjá S, T

fol.344a es fehlen ca. 4 Zeilen; am Ende der vierten Zeille: ...xv xvə̣x xu̥ T

115 (11) xc mə̣rə̣v x hvə̣yə̣xy x x x x tịdịvaẹvenāṃ T; divá eváinām S

117 (1) bra(hma)varcasī́ T (2) wohl: átravātr•, oder: ánnavānn T; ánnavān S (3) atrādó T, annādó S

118 (1) śaśáyo T (2) fehlt T; yó stillschweigend S, cf. folg. Anm. (5) über *māyobhūr* eingefügt: *yo* (über *-ma-*) T, máyobhū́r S (4) ratnadhā́ T, va• S (5) vasuvíd *yas* sudátraḥ T, v• sudátraḥ S; Sandhi nicht durchgeführt weil RV-Vers (6) kaḥ | íty S, ka íty T, über dem *-i-* ist kleingeschrieben sec.m. eingefügt:

ri, etwas verwischt, deshalb ähnelnd einem *tri*; hier lag lediglich Schreibfehler (Auslassung des Akṣara *ri*), keine Reinterpretation (*ka* > *kaḥ* "wer?") vor.

119 (1) apidhā́nyāpidhā́tya T, •dhā́ya S (2) sruvátām S (3) evainām T, eváinām S

121 (1) evā́ṅ ghạ T, oder: evā́*d* ghạ? T, evá... S

fol.344b es fehlen ca. 4 Zeilen

(1) KaṭhŚS = Paraphrase, s. SŪRYAKĀNTA, Kāṭhakasaṃkalanam, Śr.Saṃk., p.36 (2) hanti hastyạuṣṭyā̀ ẹvenạ̄du̥*h*əxgə̣x xə̣x x x x x x x x x x x x x x T, fehlt bei S; Satztrennung unsicher; vielleicht ist zu ergänzen: ... ū́rjam vái párāsiñcan, yád gā́ṃ du]hánti. hastyauṣṭhyá eváinām duhed. g[ór ū́rjam evá hastyauṣṭhyé sámbharata. ū́rjaṃ vái párā]siñcan, yád ajā́ṃ duhánti. gharmá evá tád duhaty. ū́rjaṃ náiváitát párāsiñcan, yád ajā́ṃ duhánti. gharmá evórjam sámbharatas. tásmād... (3) sạñcan T, S (4) *ū*rj*a*və*v*ətəpərạ̄s*iñc*ạnyədə*jā* T, ū́rja... S

122 (1) S, bhāgénáhī́ndrā́śvinā T, Lesart S (2) T, vāḍ

123 (1) tvā T

124 (1) gāyatro T, gāyatro S

127-128 unter der letzten Zeile rechts pr.m. hinzugefügt: ti devā́nān tvā T

fol.345a es fehlen ca. 5 Zeilen

128a (1) x xəxəx x x x x x x x x x x x x xuxr yəxvə T, ... S (2) yathəyəjúr T

129 (1) svohéti S (2) yájurzājo T (3) xəx xexe T, ... S (4) || || S

133 (1) dévá T, devá S (2) pravargyẹ S, pravargye T (3) té ʒsurā T (= Avagraha, wohl nicht Zeichen für Svarita, da kein Abhinihita-Svarita vorliegt), •te surā S (4) pravargyeṇā T, S (5) uśċair T (d.h. mit lauterer Stimme als die *yājyā*!)

fol. 345b es fehlen ca. 5 Zeilen

(6) *gəhav rā* x xəx x x x x təx x x x x x x x x x x x x x x tíyān T, ...tíṣān S (7) téna S, evasyatē x (Lücke von ca. 3 Akṣaras) x na T: derselbe Schreibfehler wie in II 134, Lesart 2 ? = *evā́syātménа?

133a (1) ghaxməməpātaməśvinəti T, ... S

134 (1) sá• links von der Zeile T; der Mantra auch KaṭhŚS SŪRYAKĀNTA, Kāth.saṃk. p. 36 (2) evā́syatménaT, S

135 Mantra auch KaṭhŚS, s. II 134 Anm.1

136 (1) diśé S

137 (1) āśíṣam T

140 (1) || || S

141 (1) S, ātmā́no T

fol.346a es fehlen ca. 3 Zeilen

142 (2) x x x x x x x x x x x x x x x x x x kṣ xəx x drāvā́eṣəyadagnīryatha• T, ...S (3) əvətad T, ... S

143 (1) •ndra•: alte Schreibung des *-r-* : ꣴ T (2) yajñó am Rande nachgetragen, an der ausgel. Stelle durch + markiert ; S ohne Bemerkung

144 (1) -brū- alte Schreibung des *-r-* : ꣴ (2) prátiṣṭhā-

tyā T, S: "prátiṣṭhātyā (!)"

145 (1) sū́rya ná• S (2) || 7 || S (3) yuñjatībrāhmaṇa-*mənzrā* T, yuñjatī brāhmaṇa... S (4) S: o

----

KaṭhĀ III

146 (1) -ṭh- S zweifelnd, jedoch deutlich lesbar (2) annadà T, annadọ S (3) cf. AO IV p.162 f. (4) •śạtẹ T

147 (1) kávī mātariśvāna S (2) hier wäre analog AO IV p. 163 ein mit *arkāsadhasthā* beginnender Spruch zu erwarten: viell. an der Stelle von 147a.

fol.346b es fehlen ca. 4 Zeilen; von der vierten noch zu lesen: xạx x *k* xạ*dh th* x xạ, dann ganz abgebrochen; die hier gegebene Ergänzung ist nur geraten; vgl. II 100

148 (1) śrótrạvantamạsmixjə xạx x x x xrạx x *m* xạx xjəxạ T, śrótravanta S

149/150 (1) veda T (2) || || S (3) rásas S

151 (1) mádhunā T, mádhu mā S (2) pūsarati T, prásarati S (verlesen: pū > pra), vgl. III 177 (3) sámardhati T, S (4) ágnáu T

152 (1) ạyur T, ā́yur S (2) dhatta T, dhatte (Sandhi!) S

153 (1) ạsyạm T, S; verbessert nach MS IV 9,10 a.A.

fol.347a es fehlen ca. 3 Zeilen

153b (1) x x xạxyū x x x x x x x x x xạx xm xdhạxtạxūrjạsvān S, ...rjasvān S; vielleicht ein Satz vom Typ: *ū́rg vái...* zwischen *dehī́ty* und *ū́rjam* zu ergänzen

154 (1) ára...ktró S, áraxye xuxəktró T (2) cā́ntyā S, śā́ntyā T

156 (1) ursprünglich wohl *vratapạté* akzentuiert; jetzt verwischt und zu lesen: vratapatẹ (2) sū́rya T (3) prośyā̆• T

158 (1) sū́rya• T, cf. III 233

159 (1) íśūn S (verlesen), íśūḫ T

160 (1) vạxə*me* T, varṣám evá S

161 (1) oder: sámana? T, sámana S, wegen > *rạ* > *na* leicht

zu verlesen (2) samágamāmetyẹ• T: ऱ्ॆ altes -e- !, S ohne Bemerkung

163 (1) namə̣rụdrâyạ̄ntarikṣasâdə T, ... S (2) íṣūn S

165 (1) sȧmanạ T, sámaga S

166 (1) auf *rudrāya* folgt eine Lücke von einem Akṣara, da -*ṅka*- (*śiváṅ karoti*) aus der Zeile darüber hereinragt (2) ȧnnȧṃ T, ánnaṃ S (3) íṣūn S (4) prajấm S, prajấ T

fol.347b es fehlen ca. 4 Zeilen, am Anfang der vierten ist noch zu lesen:

(5) x x sịs T, danach abgebrochen; Ergänzung hypothetisch; vgl. III 219, 221, 234 (6) evȧinạṁ x x x tị T, eváinam ...ti S; zu ergänzen: *sámardhayati* ?

167 (1) -*śro*- in alter Schreibweise श्रो aber *śrutabrahmā* wenig weiter:श्रु•

169 (1) altes -*r*- (2) darśata T, S (3) káñcanấvaśiṣyān T, kañcanấvaśiṣṭān S (verlesen: *ṣya*ष्य> *ṣṭā*ष्टा)

170 (1) sáṃ T, sá S (2) sūryəṇa T, sū́ryeṇā• S (3) •syevá T, •syeva corr. S (4) yesyaiṣá S (5) pravṛjyate T, pravṛjyáte corr. S (6) grahīxyəxịxə̇hyə̣ṅ S; grahī... S ; (7) devatā T (8) enabhə̣gȧ T, ena... S; cf. II 128a; danach ergänzt: *īśvarā́* (9) T, hiṁstor S

172 (1) ạ̄tmȧnọ hiṁsāyai T

173 (1) āghṛ́ṇaye T, ấgh• corr. S (2) ve T, (aber: pụṣȧ ve rụdrȯ) T, vái S (3) T, vá S

fol.348a es fehlen ca. 3 Zeilen

(4) ṅkạrịṣyansarvạ̄bhə *ev* xə̣xy x x xə̣rəvə̣*dayat*ạ*sarv*ạ-məyụr x x x x vedạ T, fehlt ganz bei S

174 (1) etáj jấgatāś (mit Ligatur aus *jā*+*jā*) S (2) dhānāś T (3) rudró T, S

175 (1) chándasi T, cf. aber III 177; chrándasi S (2) •bhāc chándasā S, •bhāś ch• T (3) •dhrāś T, •dhrāc S

176 (1) über eine durch ein Astloch unebene Stelle geschrieben! Häufig wird sonst so eine Stelle frei ge-

lassen (2) fehlt T, S; ergänzt nach der Zwangsläufigkeit (3) asyā T, aber Akzentuierung: etąsyā ęvai• T (4) gāyatrā́s T (5) nịrā́vạyatẹ T, nirávadayate corr. S

177 (1) juhótīyám T,S (2) evá S (3) té T, te S

fol.348b es fehlen ca. 3 Zeilen

(4) tạx x x x tịprāñcạmabhyụdā́nayantyạṣ v xạx x k ḍə-vəlạ̄kāmạvenạṃ T, ...m S (5) aty• S (6) eváinam T, S (7)máma T, S

178 (1) *ma* links am Rande T (2) hiṃsīríty T

181 (1) kṣatrá(sya ta)nvàṃ T (2) schwer lesbar, da auf Astloch geschrieben T (3) í(ti) T

182 (1) evái(tā́m) T (2) cf. ĀpŚS XV 13,10 u. 14,1 und CALAND) zur Stelle

183 (1) prā(ṇá)sya T (2) paraspā́ T, •pā́m S (mit Fehllesung eines Svaritapunktes aus der Zeile darüber!) (3) altes *-r-* in *-śro-*स्रT (4) prą T

fol. 349a es fehlen ca. 3 Zeilen

183a (1) dābhạvatịkəśạ̄nạv x x x xyạbhitạḥkapālānix x x x x tkạroty T, ...roty S (2) paścā́ś T (3) āsyám T, S (4) mit altem *-r-* (5) ásā T, S (6) srúcáu T (aber ohne vorausgehenden Anudātta) (7) sātmatváyābhíto T, sātra• S corr., sātadvā• liest S (Ms. hier sehr wellig! (8) upayā́mo rajvóś T, S (9) wohl: vā́iṇạvā́nị+ zu lesen; das durch Auslassungszeichen Markierte ist am Rand, quergeschrieben, sec.m. ergänzt; snā́vạni+ T, S liest: vái...vāni; snāvāni fehlt S (10) bhávaty T, S (11) ạu--ṣṭhyā́u T: Lücke wegen Astloch; cf. *abhíto* in der folg. Anm.; oṣṭhyáu S (12) ą---bhíto̧ (Lücke wegen Astloch) T (13) vṛ́ṣṭī T, S (14) āsandī́ T, S (15) múñjā T, muñja S (16) •ghātu T, •ghātuká corr. S (17) haṁsā́vát T, haṁsavát corr. S (18) e T

fol.349b es fehlen ca. 3 Zeilen

(19) x x x x x pərịṣiñc x x x x x x xux pərịṣiñc xpə-ryətixəxzu x si T, ...si S

184 evásyaitá ŕddhyati (oder: •tád áddha•) T, emend. zu •úddhayati, liest: ŕddh• S

185 (1) yedi S

186 (1) páriraksetásṛṅmukhé T, pariraksatásṛṅmukhó S (2) viell. ist der Mantra *ví gá indréti* gemeint (TĀ IV 28,1) (3) svénaiváina T

187 (1) śa(ñ ca vakṣi) T

188 (1) (útsi)ñcanti T

189 (1) (yásyām asyá) T (2) (karo)ty T, aber trotz Überklebung zu erkennen: karo | | ty T; zwischen den Pausamarkierungen steht evtl. eine Zahl (viell.: 5)

191 (1) ẹtásy(ā)nnạ(ṃ) T

193 (1) ẹváśạxtẹ T

fol.350a es fehlen ca. 4 Zeilen

194 (1) S, atmana T (2) S, ev*a*tām T (3) ạśixəx *śəs*ta T, āśi... S

195 (1) ṛtáxəx x x x x T, ṛtá... S; ergänzt nach MS (2) nirávạx x x x x pạyanti T, niráva... S

195b (1) edhiṣīmahíti T, S, cf. III 193, 196: Akz. wegen Satzanfang bzw. Mantra-Anfang (= Satzbeginn)

196 (1) eváśạ*s* x x x jọ, eváśáste ... S (2) evátman T, evátman S stillschweigend

198 (1) dáśāhu*tīr* T, dáśāhu... S (2) enánnádye T, evá• S stillschweigend (3) ábadhnāte: verbessert zu •ti? T, •ti S (4) T, úpagacchati S (5) T wohl úrv oder úrdh, úrg S (6) śamīśākhás = téjas in II 25!

fol.350b es fehlen ca. 4 Zeilen; von Zeile 4 einige kaum identifizierbare Reste, etwa: x x x x x x x x tixəx x*u*x x x x x x xəx*s*əxəx*r*, x x x ; der ergänzte Text dürfte etwa 3 1/2 bis 4 Zeilen ausgemacht haben

198a zu diesen Mantras cf. KaṭhĀ I

198b (1) próśya T, prócya S

199 (1) samix x x *tīy*āṃ T, samí...ṣāṃ S (2) x x x *tis* T, ... S; in T scheint das -*s* nachträglich über das *t*-

des folgenden Wortes gesetzt zu sein (3) prośya T (4) vrấtyố bhạvati T, vrátyo bhavati S stillschweigend (5) •haratẹ T, S (6) x bhị• T, ...bhi• S (7) •āgnírādityéna S (8) S, tvāha T (9) lokábhyaś S (10) śyavate T, cyavate S (11) pratyấdadhāti T, S (12) prátitiṣṭhati *yadấ* garmúto T, •tiṣṭhati ya...múto S (13) tạddxụxrəyād T, ta...yād S (14) S, evấtvāha T (15) (Dieses Stück **auch in Ms. Bibl. Nat. Paris, dév. 230 fol. 287a**, ohne Akzente (hier, wo nötig ergänzt), nur für diesen Abschnitt bezeichnet mit **P**; der Sandhi -*ṃ vv-* ist eigentümlich für dieses Ms., aber vgl. die Mss. von KaṭhĀ I (und Einl. p. IX m. Anm. 58) (16)

oṁ tejasā P (17) brahmávarcasénā• T, •varcasenannādyena P (18) nyṛddhyate P (19) ye

fol.351a es fehlen ca. 4 Zeilen; hierher Gehöriges jedoch z.T. am unteren Rande, sec.m. nachgetragen (= 23, im Text); von der letzten Zeile, die abgebrochen ist (vierte Zeile), sind nur erhalten: ... xạxrạx x xạ ... (20) yān P (21) tejā P (22) abhivyāharety P (23) in T fol. 351a unter der letzten Zeile und dann quer geschrieben am rechten Rand hinzugefügt, sec.m.; fehlt ganz bei S; endet mit *brahma+* (24) abhivyāharabhū P, abhitvāhāraty T (25) atiprekṣate P (26) anevātman P, aivấtmán T (27) dhattẹ T (hier Svarita durch _ ausgedrückt?) (28) yádādityám S, yadādityam P (29) brahma+ T (30) yad xīraudanam P (31) dhety atho P (32) tejasvīṃ P (33) anurādo P (34) tavati P (35) evaṃ vveda ~ || ~ || P

199a hier beginnt Zeile 6 oder 5 von T; der Text muß sich ohne große Einschübe an die Rekonstruktion angeschlossen haben, behandelt nun aber etwas anderes: zu lesen ist: xạx xprạxrxy mạxạxixạx xupạdhấyạmārjayatyạx x x x x x x x x *tā* ' T, fehlt ganz bei S; - zu ergänzen: pravṛjyámāne síkatām/híraṇyam/samídham? Schluß ganz unklar: viell. ...ru]drād evā́vyadhī? Ist etwas ausgefallen?

200 (1) dadhata T

201 (1) vyā́nā́ṃ T

203 (1) cakṣurdā́c T

204 (1) -*śro-* mit altem -*r-* T

206 (1) ā́yuṣè T

207 (1) altes -*r-* in -*dr-* T (2) entfällt (3) sá T, S (4) *pravargyā̂* bhavad T, pravargyò bhavad S stillschw. (5) tasmā́d T (6) bhavati T; in der nächsten Zeile der Nachtrag sec.m. (s.o. Lesart 23)

fol.351b es fehlen ca. 4 Zeilen

(7) ergänzt nach TĀ I 5,2 = aṣṭau kāṭhakāni! (8) x x x x x *kriyāṇāvāętā́niśukriyəxitā́śchúkriyānāśukrixə-xvəx* x x*əvāḥ*. T, fehlt bei S: ...s; wegen des Akzents und der erhaltenen Akṣ. Reste ist wohl auszuschließen: śu]krávarṇau vá́ bzw. śu]krávanti vá́; cf. TĀ V 10 (9) jyotiṣṭomás T, S (10) agnáye T, S (11) nókyè T, nókthyè corr. S (12) wohl: pravṛñjyāt T: unter dem -*r-* eine Devanagārī-Zwei mit untergesetztem normalen, hier aber falschen Anudātta-Zeichen, cf. Anm. 15 (13) ukthyá T (-*y-* wohl sec.m.) (14) pravṛñyyāt oder pravṛñjyād (dann mit Doppelbez. des -*ā*-!) T, Lücke wegen Astloch (15) cạ T, über dem Akṣ. die in Lesart 12 genannte 'Zwei'; ca S (16) xi xəx xməx*pr* x x x x *śukạ*mā́yo T; hierher gehört ein Fragment, das sich erst bei Kontrolle des Original-Ms. im Juli 1972 viel weiter hinten im Ms. fand; es bestätigte die schon emendierte Lesung: n*i*rdahẹt tā́smə T; - mit Beginn dieser, der viertletzten Zeile des Blattes, stehen am Rande der letzten vier Zeilen jeweils zwei Daṇḍas; - S liest lediglich: ...yó (17) prā́vṛñjyạd T, pravṛñjyā́d S

208a (1) •pátaye S, T wohl: •pataye, wobei das -*e-* ausradiert zu sein scheint

208e (1) *ti* fehlt bei S: ... S

209 (2) sívam ájasram S (3) śrivā́m (mit alter Schreibung des *-r-*) T, śivā́m S (4) karoti S, karoxi T

210 (1) x x x x x x T, ...S

211 (1) íx x x x x x• S, íti...• S

212 (1) manuṣyébhya T, S (2) iti S (3) evanạxuśrūṣeṇyā́ṅ T, evá...śuśrūṣeṇyā́ṅ S (mit altem *-r-*)

213 (1) tásmād devā́ corr. S., er liest; tásmād evā́

215 (1) sumṛḷ(īkā́ sára)svatī́ti T, •sárasvatī́ti S; Akzente wegen Versanfang: sárasvati, s. KaṭhĀ I 218d (XI)

216 (1) brá(hmaṇa upa)stáraṇam T, brahma...stáraṇam S (2) S, tvé• T (3) (paśūnā́)m T

217 (1) vā́stvam S

219 Ende fol. 352a: mạ T

fol.352b es fehlen ca. 3 Zeilen; die letzten drei Akṣ. der dritten Zeile wohl: x x *t* (?) (1) x x x x x x x x x x x x cọyā́jụṣịsā́*m* ənī₊ tadvetrạ-dhāvix x x x x x x x x x xpạte T, ...yájuṣi sā́... S; nach *sā́mānī́*₊ fehlte wohl ein: •*ti*, nicht nachgetragen; vgl. III 221 (2) paśụ̄x x x x x x x x x x xyənn T, paśū...nn S; Ergänzung unsicher, vgl. aber Ms. Par. 230, fol. 310b, auch zum Folgenden (3) grā́mạ̄x x x x x x x *y* ti T; grā́mā... S; Ergänzung nach KaṭhB (SCHROEDER, SB Wien 1898 p. 64), vgl. Einl. Anm. 67 (4) axạxạxạxạx*u*xạxṛtyụ̄ṃ T, á... S, cf. KaṭhB p. 61 (5) jạyạtī T, jayati S (6) altes *-r-* in *-kri-* T; tríśukriya- 'drei Veden kennend' (RENOU, Ec. véd. p. 17 Anm. 1): 'dreifachen Glanz habend' (7) nā́kreṣu S, cf. KaṭhB p. 60f., KGS 9,12 (8) gávāte T, S (cf. KGS) (9) pạrvopạ[pa] ₊rvā́yor T (*pa* über der Zeile hinzugefügt) (10) dvipā́dam T, S (11) cátuṣpadaṃ T, S (12) dṛṣṭvā́-médhyā́ni T, dṛṣṭvā́ médhyāni emend. S (liest: dṛṣṭvā́-médhyā́ni) (13) vā́ über der Zeile nachgetragen, durch + angezeigt; deshalb fehlt unter •*médhyā́ni* der

Svarita bzw. Anudātta (14) māsaṃmatvá T, má sá matvá S (15) pûrvedyúr T, pūrvedyúr S stillschweigend (16) pūrvāhṇí T, S (17) keśaśmaśrū T, •rû S stillsch. (18) fehlt ganz bei S (19) paś*ch*anâm? T, paśūnám S (20) sándárśanenâśântikṛtas T (21) saṃsṛję T

fol.353a es fehlen ca. 3 Zeilen

(22) fehlt bei S; zu ergänzen ein Akk.Pl.m.? dīkṣitáṃ? dváidhaṃ: cf. III 233, II 115 a.A.; T liest: xəx x x x x x x x x x x xt x x x bhixrəxəxəx x x n (23) uttarạtəs x x x T, antá... S (24) itaráu (mit Fehllesung eines Anudātta-Punktes aus der Zeile darüber) S (25) ẹtèx x x más S, e...más T (26) ẹtá-+dyạ jñásya (*dya* über der Zeile pr.m.) T (27) védó T, védáu liest S, corr. zu: vedáu (28) statt: *mahā-vīráu*? angeglichen an *kaṇṭhá*? T liest: •rā (29) anuṣṭu...í S, anuṣṭubví meine erste Lesung, zu lesen ist aber: *anuṣṭubdhí: bdhī [illegible] / [illegible] bvī, [illegible] T (30) dáṁ(strā mā)yûkhā T (31) rajjváś T, S (32) vàiṇạ(vàni) snàvạni *pa*rọlàśo T, vái... S (33) kéś(ā) T (34) (védā) T (35) (j)y(ótiṁ)ṣi T, vgl. III 231; sámāni = jyótiṣ (36) śīrṣaṇváś T, śīrṣaṇvác S (37) S, védetád S (38) etáś T (39) u T

219m (1) nach KaṭhĀ I 219m (V) (2) nach dem Śruti-Zitat in LGS II p.59

fol.353b es fehlen ca. 5 Zeilen

220 (1) x x x x x x xəx xəx x x x xu x xūx x*ənəjm ita*+ tə nạ T, fehlt bei S (2) fehlt bei S (3) x x x x xəx syaitán T, ...syaitán S

220b (1) altes *-r-* in *-kra-* T (2) a...ván S, ax x x x ván T (3) nach: *vái* ist der Rest der Zeile unbeschrieben (15 Akṣara etwa), dann fehlen ca. 4 abgebrochene Akṣ.: x x x x yáṃ T, ...yaṃ S (4) sà*mənə*kti T

222 (1) anyáś T (2) jạya ndhe ntę (ndhe: über der Zeile sec.m. hinzugefügt) T

223 (1) bhaga..vān T (Lücke von einem Akṣara)

224 (1) airó T, S; (2) puránzir T (3) nā́ma T, fehlt S, liest stattdessen: asi (4) sā́syaiváinan S (5) tásmā́ś T

225 (1) •hvāye T, •hūye S (2) •dheye[na] T (*na* über derZeile)

226 (1) vo? eher: vám̥, mit Störung der Lesung durch das darüberstehende: dhāmno • ... T, vā S

fol.354a es fehlen ca. 5 Zeilen ; ergänzt nach KaṭhĀ I

(2) *drassavəsavyasassəbhə*x xy xəx xə T, fehlt bei S; der Rest der Zeile (ca. 20 Akṣ) abgebrochen (3) Übersetzung GELDNERs (4) x x x x x x x x x x x x x x x x x x x x x x ta T, ... S (5) apaśyam̥s táix x x x x S x x x x x x x x x x x x x T, apaśyam̥s tái S (6) etaix x x x x x x x x x x x x x x x xvyo T, etá S

227 (1) dakṣiṇexix x x x x x x x x x x x x x x x vạruddhyai T, dakṣi...varudbhai S (2) s(árva)nəx*y* xəx x x x x x x x x śā T, sárvā... S

228 (1) (dáśā) dakṣiṇā́ (d.h.: *dáśa* ist pr.m. gestrichen) T, S läßt es aus, ohne Bemerkung (2) pra(tī́cīr dá)śa T (3) bhaxux x x x x x x x manasyámāṇa T, bha...mana• S (4) (úddharṣay)ati T

229 (1) prajāx x x x x x yamāna T, S (2) paśūnāxəpīthāya T (3) pra(jāvān p)aśumān T (4) bhavatix x x x x x ḥ T, bhavati ... S (5) •ṣādovāvāi T, •ṣado vā́ vái S: 'Schreiberhaplologie': cf. auch: II 35, Lesart 1; II 19, Lesart 1: besonders häufig bei *-v-v-*! (6) rucitā*d*(əx x x)s T, fehlt bei S: ra... (7) sárvān *no* ˌyán x x x x x x x ti T, fehlt bei S (Avagraha vor: *yán*!) (8) abravī(s anyénaina)m T, abravīd corr. S (9) *śivā bhavi*x T, fehlt bei S

fol.354b es fehlen ca. 5 Zeilen; lediglich noch einige

Akzentreste in der 5. Zeile erkennbar: xəx x xəx xəx xə

229c (1) x x x x x x x x x x x x x x x x jā T, S

(2) *va* T, va S (viell.: *n a*? *rạ* nicht mögl.: र) (3) viell. nṛmṇám नृम्णां, da Anusvāra-Punkt abgebrochen sein kann (4) cạ̄i T (5) fehlt bei S; unsichere Ergänzung, cf. III 174 ff.; der letzte halb abgebrochene Akṣara (vor *nídhāyy*) viell.: (n)ā ; T

230 (6) nidhā́yyó vā́ nídhāyyó véti S; x x x x x x x x x x

(231) x x x x x x nịdhā· T[*] (7) entfällt (8) sā̀mnọx x x x x x x x x x x x x ṣṭhatạ ẹ̀ T, sā́mno ... S; zu ergänzen: sā̀mnọ[dgātā̀ gāyati]? oder: oder: sā̀mnọ[rdhvā̀s (III 233!) ténaivá...prátiti[ṣṭhata ? - sā̀mnọ[pạgāyanam...] wohl auszuschließen. (9) ẹx x x x x x x x x x x xyə-*tā* T, e... S (10) sámax x x x x x x x x *k*th*əs* T, sáma... S (11) ẹtā̀syā̀nịx x x x x x x *bh tə*rẹvā̀inam T, etásyā́ni...váinam S; PARPOLA (briefl.) verbessert meine ursprüngliche Ergänzung: ...yád adhá nṛmṇám zu: ...yád nṛmṇá nṛmṇám; - wegen des Pl. im Verbum denke ich jetzt eher an eine sich an III 231 (Nidhana) anschließende Ergänzung: yád svàr jyótis. (12) nāma...S, nāmạx x*ən*ị T (13) bhuvọ T, bhúvo S (13a) āha*v*əxīyọ T, āhavanī́yo S (14) szə̀-x*le*kā̀d T, ...kā́d S (15) haviṣkṛ́tyam S, T (16) uddhṛ́tyai ténā· T, S

fol.355a es fehlen ca. 4 Zeilen

232 (1) ntaẹṣā̀vāạp*ā̀yāniss* x x x x*əyə*ṅkāmayạ̄t t jạx x x x x x mịtị T, ...míti S (2) carè S, care*tə* T (3) ax x x x x x x x x*əm* T, fehlt bei S; Ergänzung geraten; T hier wohl: ·m pravạrg·, evtl.: ·p prạv·

233 (4) prayuñjyā*d*ạxuṣṭubh*ạsītị*xəxụrthā̀m T, prayuñjyá... S (1) *-dhre-* mit alter Form des *-r-* ध्रे T (2) alte Schreibung des *-e-*: ऋध्र्यायतने ạyā̀tanẹ T, keine Bemerkung S (3) svargásyə T, svargásya S (4) avabhṛyát S (5) *da*xix x x x x x ty T, ...ty S (6) pratyá*gú*x x x x x x x x x x x x x x ṇy T, pratya...ṇy S (7) ahargaṇe S

---

* die im Text gegebene Interpretation aufgrund des Vorschlags von PARPOLA (briefl.). Ich war mir zunächst nicht

(8) prá... S, pravṛñjyādvəx x x x x x x x x x x x x x T

fol.**355b** es fehlen ca. 4 Zeilen

(9)ṇapravạrgyạxy *xj*ə̣xc g v *br*ạhm v x*cə̣s* mávạrunddhev*a* x x x x x kaṃ T, fehlt bei S (10) ápar̀āhnikam S, aber •āhni• T (11) paurvạxṇə*k*əx*śun sīry*ə̣ T, paurvā... S (12) T, áparāhṇikam S (13) T, avabhṛyát S, cf. KaṭhB, SB Wien 1898 p.63 (14) *ā*haxəx*īy*aṃgə̀h*a*t*i* T, āhavanī́yam... S (15) mahāxīx x x x x x x xə̀varundhe T, mahāvī...varundhe S (16) *b h v* x x x x x x x xəxə̀m (*ṃ* • oder Udātta ꞌ : hier Udātta, weil *kụryāt* folgt); ...S (17) brahmax x x x x x x xa (oder: *yu*) *gə̣təni* T, brahma ... S; die Akṣarareste legen die Ergänzung nahe, die im Text gegeben wird (18) S, pravarxə̀sya T (19) x x x x x x xixə̀dəjzə̀*m* ə*n*eg*ā*yatitèjováiśārgántejọsaivaixəm̊ samax x x x x x x x x x x T, fehlt bei S (20) entfällt (21) cạndráx x x x x x x x x x rmásya T, candrá... sya S (22) tanvò S (23) tè bhī• T, S und PARPOLA, Übers. LŚS/DŚS Vol. I 2, p.101, cf. aber Dual richtig geschrieben in fol. 356a (S. 98, Zeile 22): té adhihriyámāne; in T ist das Svaritazeichen vielleicht sec.m.

fol.356a es fehlen ca. 4 Zeilen

(24) ádhịhṛiyámạṇəgəyətəráksāṃsivàetárhịsax x x x x mị- tó T, adhihriyámā...mi táu S; Ergänzung ganz unsicher; zu erwarten: *cámitoḫ, viell. eine Zeile ausgefallen? : ...*sárvāṇi gharmáṃ jighāṁsanti. prácyutam itó 'prā(p-tam amútrainam purástād dharanti. náiváinam īśvarā́ cámitoḫ pra)madó*... o.dgl.; zu *pramad(á-)* vgl. *Caland* AO VI p. 146; MS III 9,7; s. v. *dīrghajihvī* JB [1.161; PB 13.6.9].

---

sicher ob nicht Zweifelsfrage (wie II 143 *prásyá*3) vorliegt (Akzente!): dies könnte zumindesten für den Br.-Autor gegolten haben, der ja ohnehin den Text hier in seiner Weise versteht (*nídhāyi/nidháu/nidhíḥ*, etc.). PARPOLA verweist auf die Parallele RV X 10,3 : *ní* te máno mánasi *dhāyi* :: *ní-* nṛmṇā́yi (= nṛmṇé) nṛmṇám *-dhāyi*

(233) (25) so schon PARPOLA, loc. cit.; sạm T, sām S: 'Schreiberhaplologie' (26) aśvíno T, aśvínau S (27) huta... S, hụtəgəx x T (28) *ta* T, ta S (29) puroḷā́śayor T, puroḍā́śayor S (30) ẹvā̀tè T, S; verbessert schon durch PARPOLA, loc. cit., cf. III 158 (31) aṅgirasā́m T, S (32) parighármyáropyámāṇe T, S, cf. II 76, 92, 98; VādhS AO IV p. 203 (33) ā́rūḍhavat sá T, á... S (34) svargá(sya loká)sya T (36) tā̀*d* x x T

234 (1) das Folgende durch Riß im Blatt gespalten und deshalb von SCHROEDER ausgelassen, aber lesbar: xn̆mə̀yọyajụrmə̀yạssāmā̀mayọ*gh*ərmā̀ iti yā̀syạiṣā̀pravṛx x x x x x x x x ḥ T (2) sarvá... S, sàvīryạṁ T (3) ṛ... S, ṛddhyạiṣa T (4) x x x x x x x x x T, ... S (5) ṛ́ddhyate T, S (6) bhịdyā̀t*e* T, fehlt bei S

235 (1) x x x x x x x ṣạ T, ...ṣa S (2) T, karmaṇyā̀yā S (3) vā̀śrẹṣa*va*x x x x x x x x x T, vā́śrepa... S

fol.356b es fehlen ca. 4 Zeilen, ohne Akz.Reste

235a (1) hier einzufügen? cf. SCHROEDER SB Wien 1898, p. 81 f. und KaṭhĀ I 198.11 (2) frei ergänzt wegen: á]nabhihomāya, in Anlehnung an die umgebenden Passagen (3) x x x x x x x x x nạbhiha*ā*m*ā*yạsəx*v*ạ*m*əyụrətịsəvə*tə*-*tr*əprāyạ*ś*cəxə*r*əpạ T, fehlt bei S (4) pravargyà S, T (5) stạnā̀yạx xa T, stanáya... S

236 (1) vā̀ix x *ss*vè̀naịvā̀inạm T, vái...naiváinam S (2) prā̀yạścitị*rvaj*rəṇa T, práyaścittir vájreṇa S; zum Folgenden cf. KaṭhB, SB Wien 1898, p. 60 f. (3) mit altem -*r*-

237 (1) x x *jə*huyā*dā*pọ, fehlt bei S (2) ā̀x x *se*vā̀ T, á...sáivá S (3) etā̀*sy*ạyajñā̀ṃyụvətẹ T, etá...te S (in gespaltener Zeile) (4) ṃahāvīx x x x x x x x x x tị-sā̀ T, mahāvī... S (5) ā̀rtị T, (-ṃ wohl abgebrochen), ārtiṃ S (6) T wohl: ār*ch*áty; árcchaty S stillschw.

238 (1) ụdutyā̀ṃjātā̀vẹda x x x x x x x x x x x x *bh*yāṃjuhuyād T, úd u tyáṃ jātáveda...juhuyād S; ergänzt nach

ĀpŚS XV 17,12 und KS IV 9, KaṭhB, SB Wien 1898, p. 63 (2) mit altem -r- (3) mahāvīrāx x x x x x x x x x x x ti T, mahāvīra... S ; (4) prāyaścitti || T, prā́yaścittiḥ || || S

fol.357a es fehlen ca. 5 Zeilen

(5) T, •manmate S (6) mahā*vī*rə*pra*vṛjyamāne T, mahāvāré pravṛjyámāne S (7) ta *su/mu/a k*thə*v*əx T (hier *mu/su/a*- zu lesen?), tá. .. S

239 (1) T, niṣī́dati S (cf. KGS, p. 228, Anm. 1, Mantra 1: yasmād bhīṣā nyasadas ...) (2) hier ein echter Daṇḍa von halber Akṣaralänge, da es sich um einen Vers handelt, T; || S (5) altes -*r*- T (4) svenaivainam T, svénaiváinam S stillschweigend (5) *pra*ś*a*t*a*śamax x T, ... S (6) axix x x x x x hāvīxepəv*ṛ*jə*m* ā*n*exəxəṃsi T, ... S (7) vāpidhāvantəx x x x x x x x x (Zeilenende) x x x x x x x x x x x s T, vāpidhāva... S; zur Ergänzung vgl. III 186

239a (1) prəx x x x x x x x x x (Zeilenende) x x x x x x x x x x T, pra... S (2) ātmānó hiṃsaxaixə T, ātmánó hiṃsāyai S (3) fehlt ganz bei S; T aber liest: xəx x x x x x x x x {x xəxy x x*r* x *r*iṣyandīkṣi*t*əxyə*v*ə} ({} = **Fragm.** c, Beginn; der Akzent *v*ə aus der Zeile darüber in Fragm. a; Fragm. c wegen des linken Schreibrandes an dieser Stelle leicht zu lokalisieren) x x x x x x x x x x x x x x x x x x x (Zeilenende) rgyaṃsambharatyajenasambharatyagnignirv*a*x x x x x x x x x x x x x x x x (Zeilenende; *g*ṅ*i* = getilgt!) ratiśarkarābhirdhṛtyā ārmyaiḥkapālaix x x x x x x x x x x x x x x x x (Zeilen- u. Seitenende)

fol.357b es fehlen etwa 5 Zeilen

(4) v*a*tyūrdhvā T, ...ty ūrdhvá S; im Folgenden stets die Āsandī gemeint, deshalb alles im Fem. (5) T, •áinan S (6) m*ā*ñjavivānā T, māñjávivārā S (7) ūrg*ze*-x x x x• T, ū...váinaṃ S; cf. III 183

240 (1) vípraṇáxutəx x x x x x xénan T, ví prāṇá S (2) hierher gehört **Fragm. b**, im Folgenden gekennzeichnet durch { }; auf dem Film auf dem Blatt links unten lose mitverfilmt; schließt sich genau dem letzten Akṣara von **Fragm. a** an: kṛ·: k{ṛṣṇājiné}*n*apráśchādayati (Zeilenende) x x x x x tád T; fehlt bei S; cf. III 183 (3) altes *-r-* in *-drū-* S (4) bráh*m*aṇaivāinaṃda x x xəggārhapa*t*y x (Zeilenende) x x x x x x x T, bráhmaṇai... S; vielleicht also ... udák prā́g gārhap· zu ergänzen? (5) paráu kharáu T, paroparó S (6) *le*x x x x x x x x x x x x tye T, ... tye S (7) *s*vargá T, svargáṃ S (8) gamax x x x x x x x x x (Zeilenende) x x x x x x x x x x x x x x xə*t*itádbahì x x x x x x x x x x x (Zeilenende) x x x x x x x x x x x x x x x x x *dv*āráṇyapidh*á*yaprava*v*agyə x x x x (Zeilenende) x x x x x x x x x x ṇayátho T, gama...yátho S (9) S, pāpavasīya+ sá syą T (*sá* über der Zeile hinzugefügt) (10)x x x x x x x x x x x x x x x xáu T, fehlt S (11) mahāvīrā́ṃ S, mahāvīráxəx (Zeilenende) T

Fragment fol. 357b (?)

Dieses kleine, nicht mitgefilmte Bruchstück scheint aus dem unteren Teil einer Seite zu stammen, da unter den wenigen Akṣaras der beiden erhaltenen Zeilen ein größerer Raum freigeblieben ist. Der Farbe nach (dunkle Birkenrinde wie in f. 357b) könnte es zu dieser letzten erhaltenen Seite gehören, paßt sich [aber] dort in den letzten beiden Zeilen dem Kontext nach nicht recht ein. Vielleicht ist es ein Bruchstück einer folgenden Seite, vgl. Einleitung, Anm. 44: Vielleicht der einzigen, die hier noch fehlte.

Erste Zeile: ...]*bhy*ādīk*ṣ*ə [...

Zweite Zeile: ...]x x bhyānirupy[...

Das Fragm. fehlt bei S.

===

Faksimile

der einzigen fortlaufenden Hs.
von KaṭhĀ II.III

Tübingen, Universitätsbibliothek
MaI 396 Heft 10a,b
fol. 337b-357b

Vorbemerkung: Das Faksimile wurde mit Hilfe von Fotos hergestellt, die von einem im Frühjahr 1969 aufgenommenen Negativ-Film gemacht wurden. Es zeigt das Ms. in dem Zustand, in dem es 1898 von R. v. ROTH und L. v. SCHROEDER belassen worden war (vorläufige 'Restauration' durch Überkleben mit relativ undurchsichtigem Klebstreifen). Inzwischen dürfte das Ms. auf von vom Verf. ausgehende Anregung hin restauriert worden sein. Da bei derartigen Operationen aber stets kleine Bruchstücke falsch plaziert werden bzw. ganz verloren gehen bzw. das Ms. sogar weiterhin geringfügig beschädigt werden kann, erschien es sinnvoll, hier den Zustand von 1969 zu dokumentieren, zurnal die überklebten, im Original aber lesbaren Stellen auch zusätzlich durch L. v. SCHROEDERs Lesung von 1898 abgesichert sind und so auch in den Lesarten innerhalb runder Klammern angegeben sind; außerdem wurden diese Stellen vom Verf. im Juli 1972 wiederum kontrolliert.

150

Paddhati zum Godāna, Ajasthāpana

KaṭhĀ II 1

2

f.[33]7b

MaI 396, Univ. Bibl. Tübingen

frg.zu I 1

10
11
12
13
14
15
16
17
18
19
20

f.338b 21

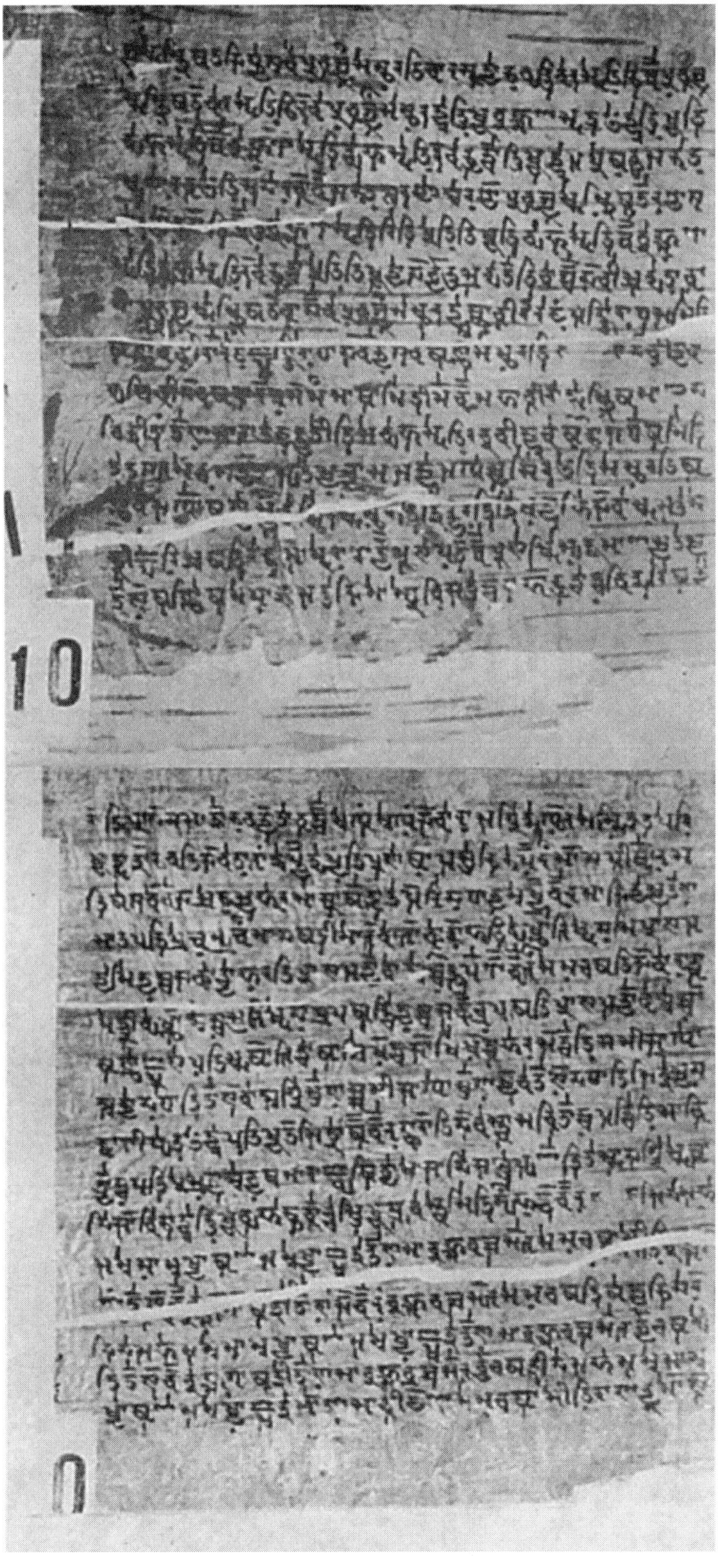

3
4
5
6
7
8
9
10 f.338a

22
23
24
25
26
27
28
29
30
31
32 f.339a

33
34
35
36
37
38
39
4o
42
46
48
f.339b 49

62
63
64
65
66
67
67a
68
69
7o
71
72
73
f.34ob 74

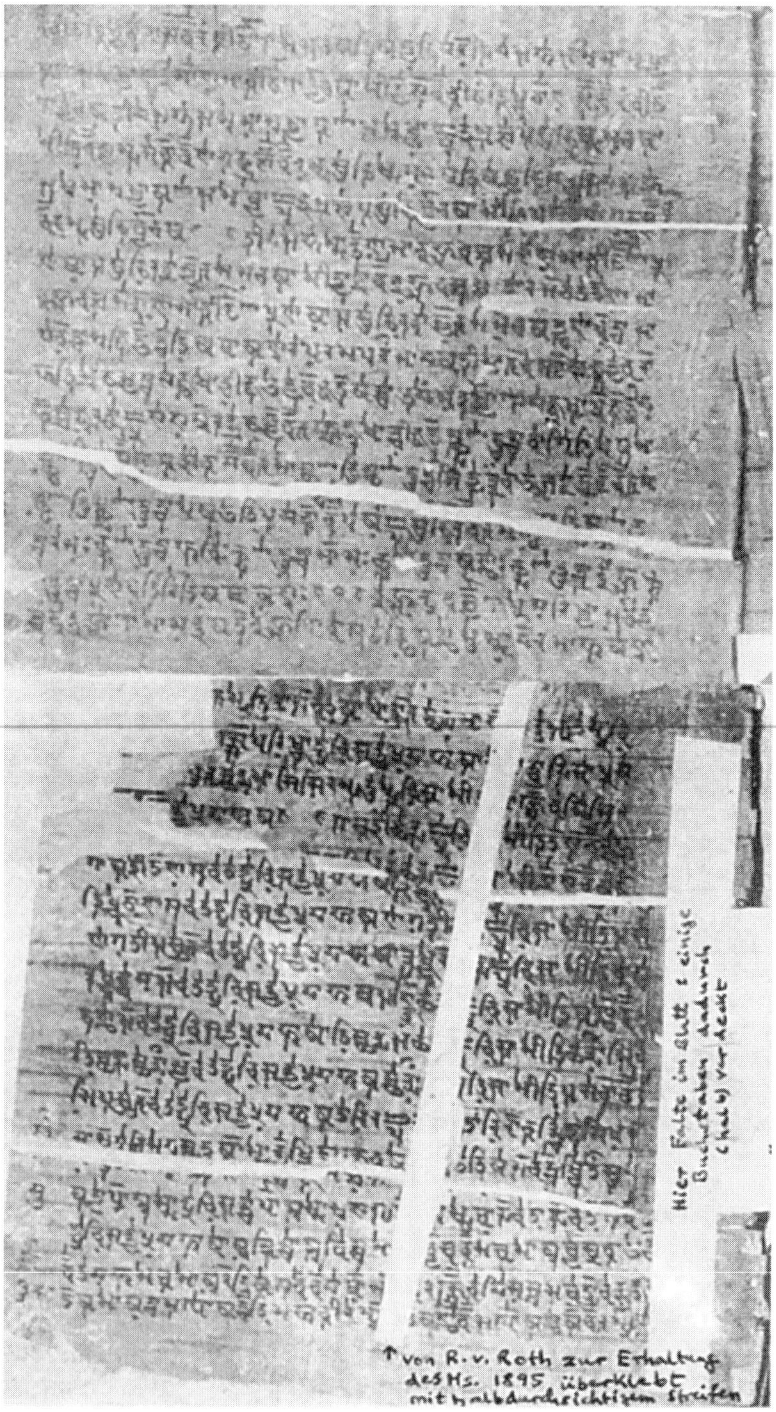

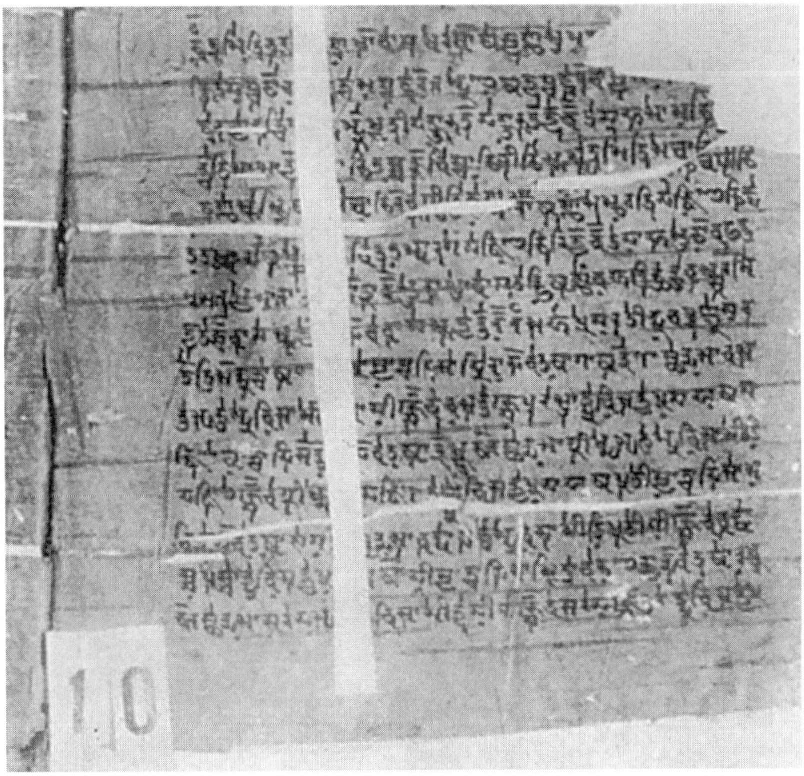

49

5o

51

52

54

55

57

58
59

6o

61

f.34oa

Ende von Ms. Tübingen,
Universitäts-
bibliothek No. MaI 396
Heft 1o a.

Es folgt Heft 1ob mit
noch weiter zerstörten
Blättern, den letzten
erhaltenen von MaI 396

75

76

77

f.341a

90
91
92

93

94
95
97
f.342a

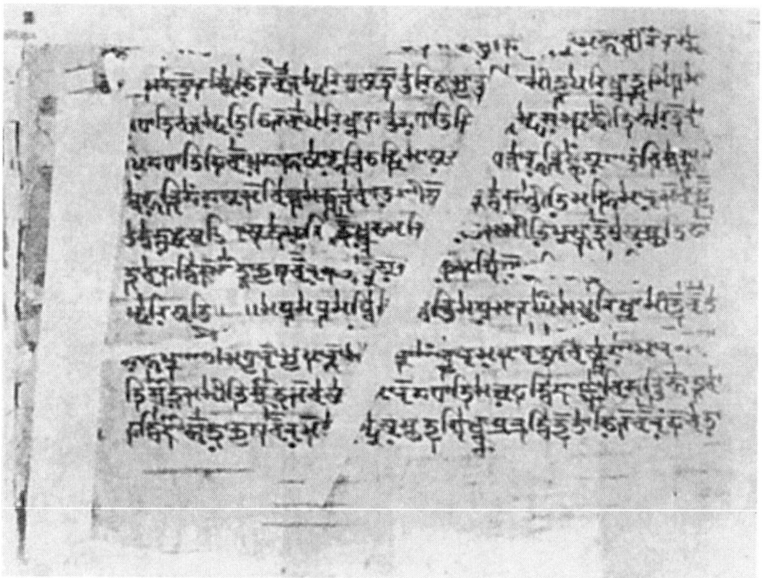

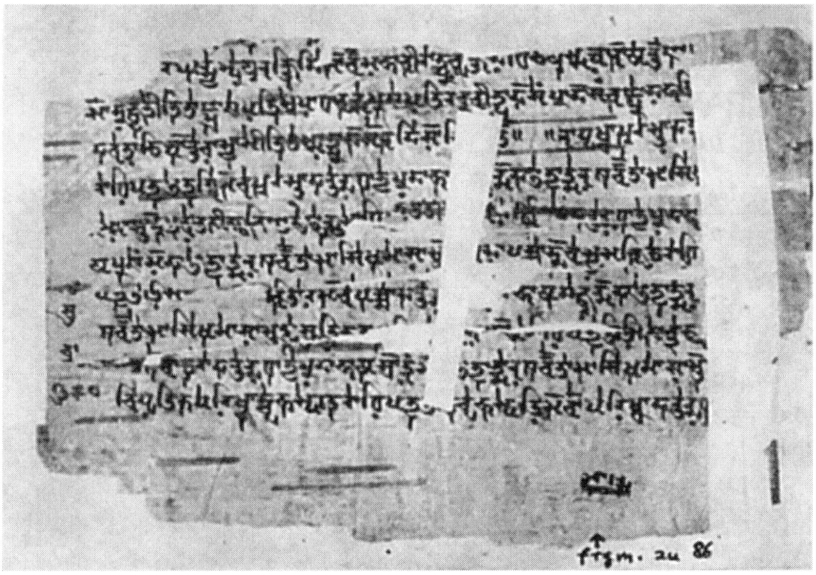

80
81
82
83
85
86
87
88
f.341b

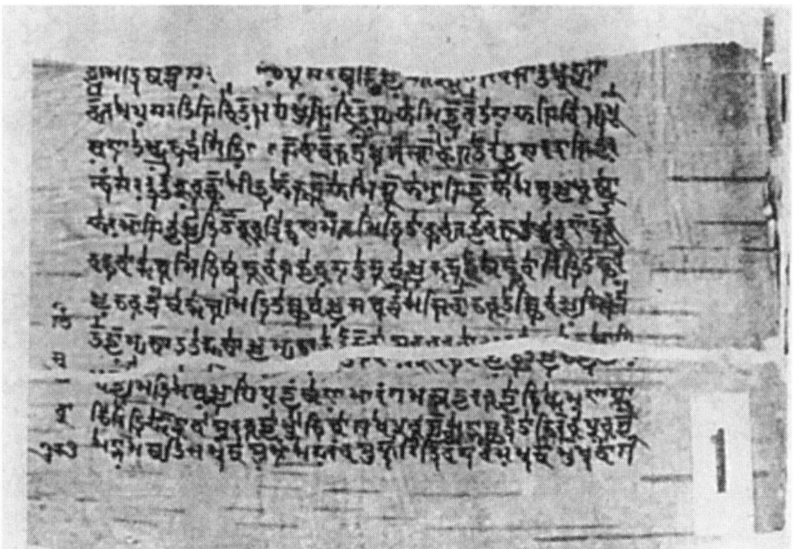

98c
99
100
101
01b
f.342b

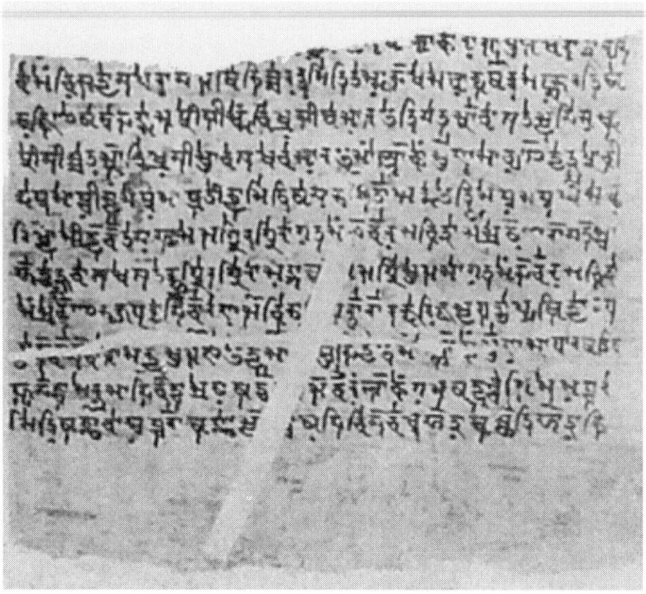

1o2
1o3
1o4
1o5
1o7
1o8
1o8a
1o9
f.343a 111

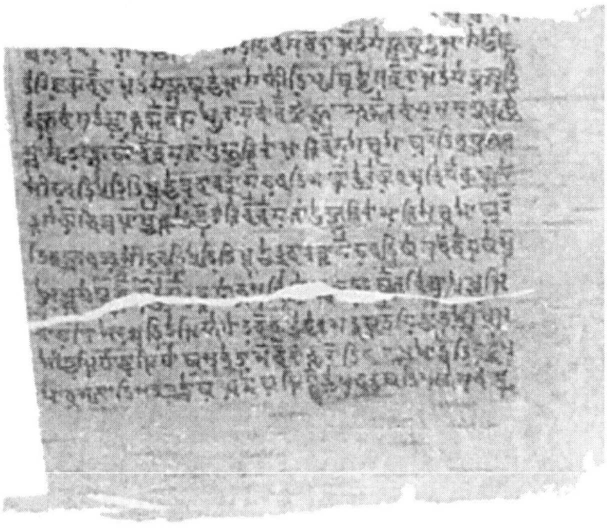

115a
117
118
119
12o
f.344a 121

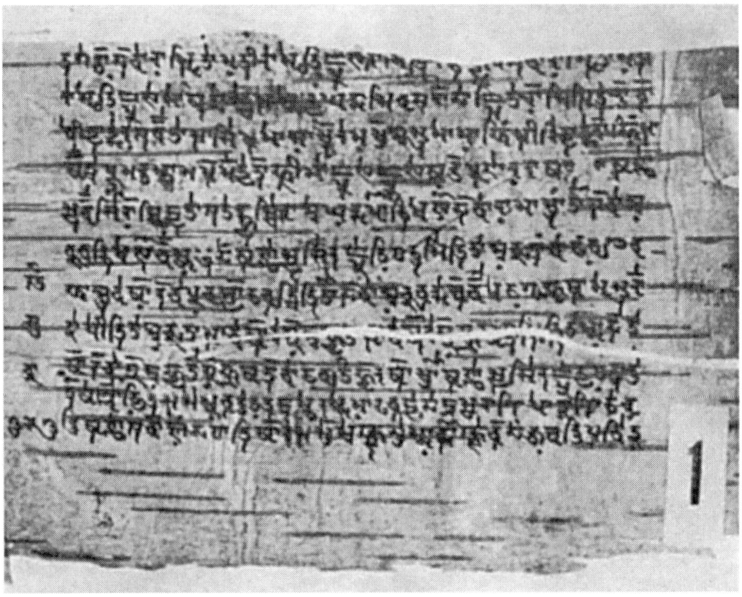

112
113
114
115

f.343b

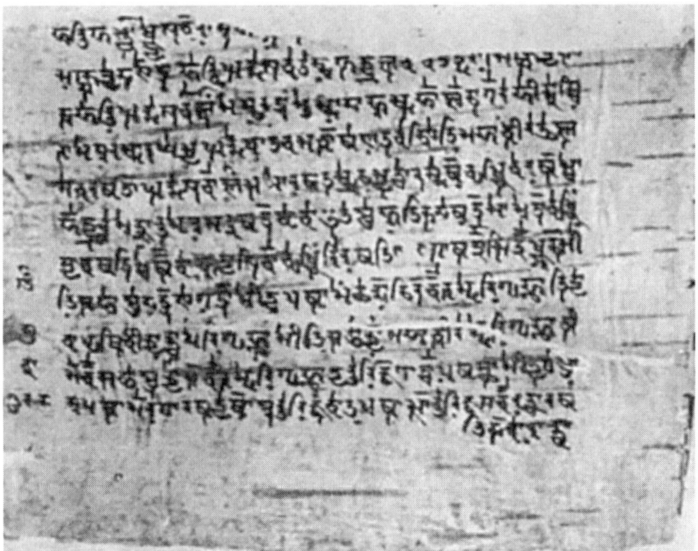

122
123
124
125
126
127
128 f.344b

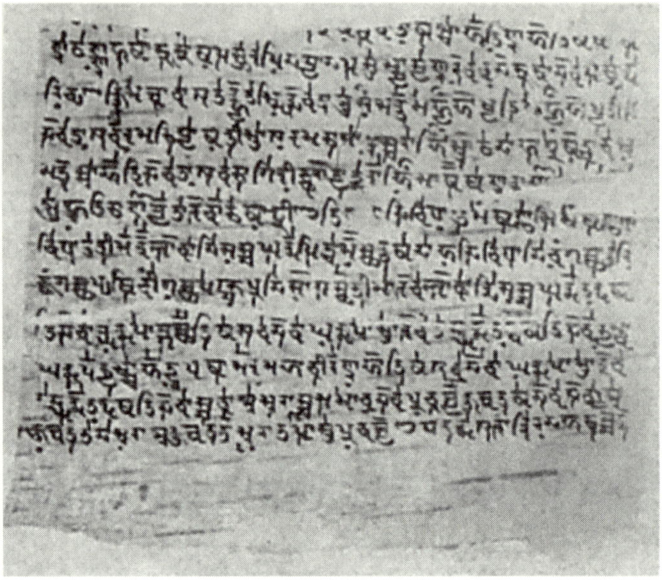

129

130
131

132
133

f.345a

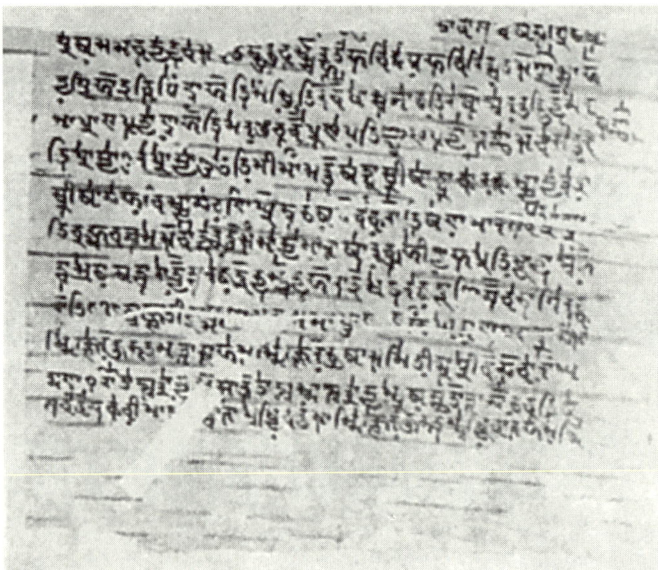

143

144
145

Kaṭhā III 146

147
f.346a

133a
134
135
136
137
138
14o
141

f.345b

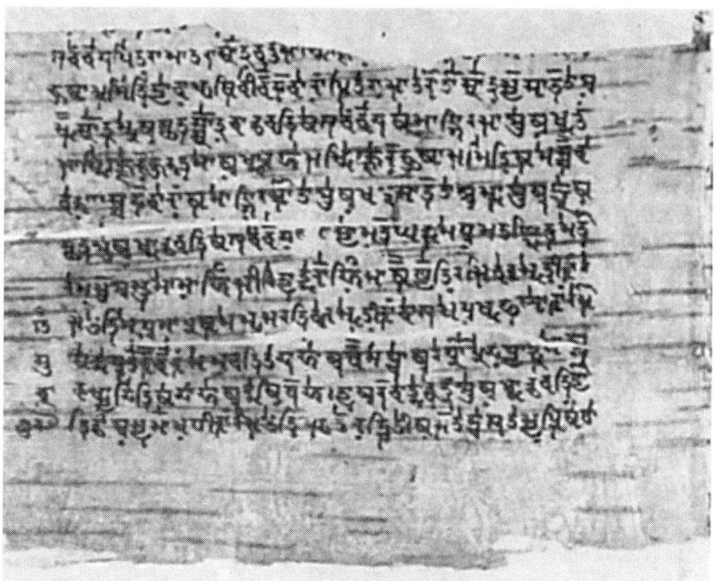

148
149
15o
151
152
153
f.346b

154
155
156
157
158
159
160
161
163
164
165
f.347a

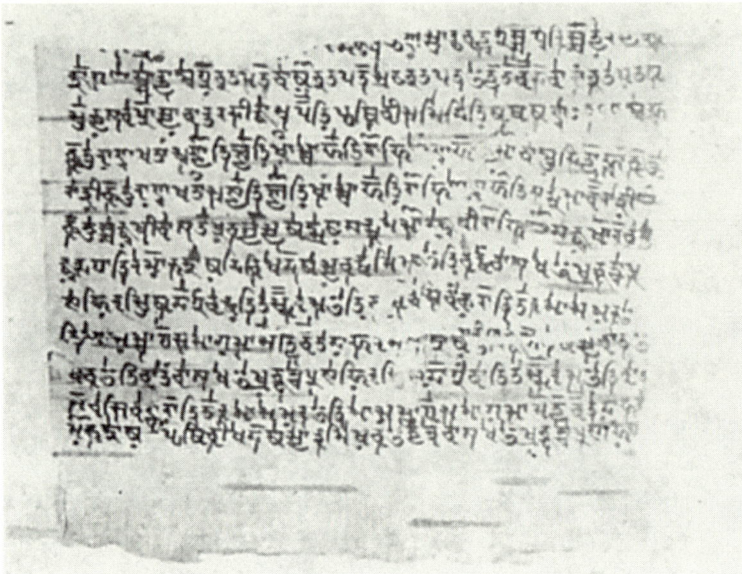

174
175
176
177
f.348a

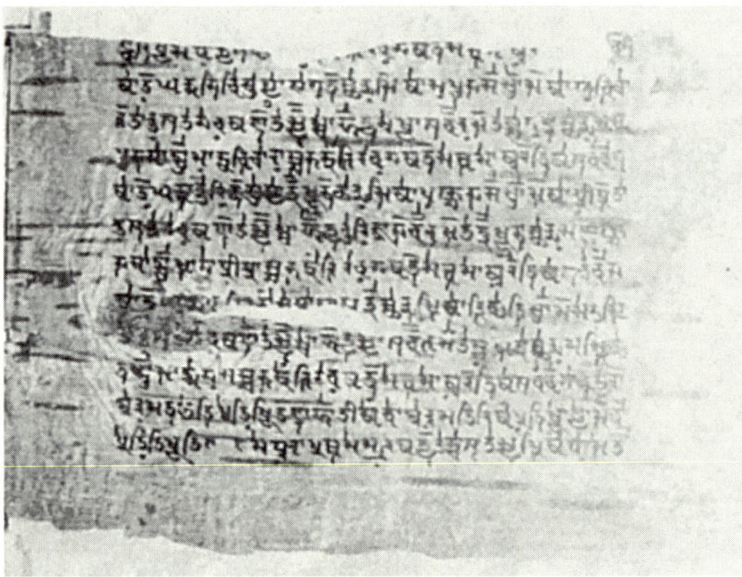

167

168

169

170

172

173

f.347b

178

180

181

182

183

f.348b

(183a)

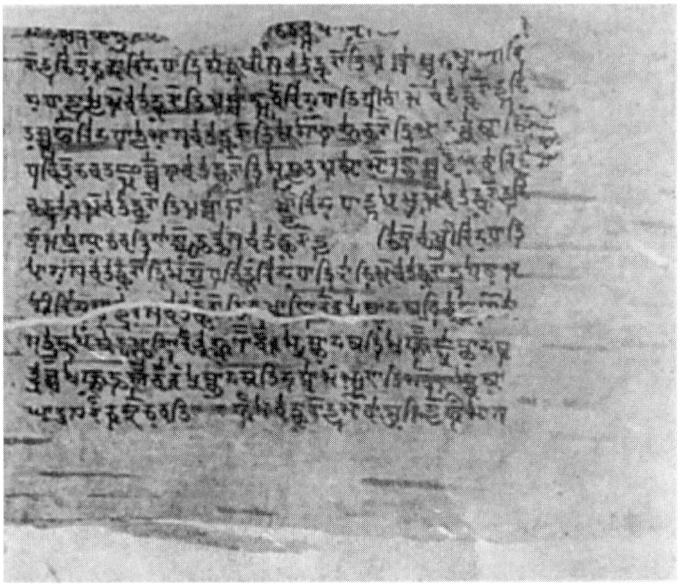

f.349a

195a

196
197
198

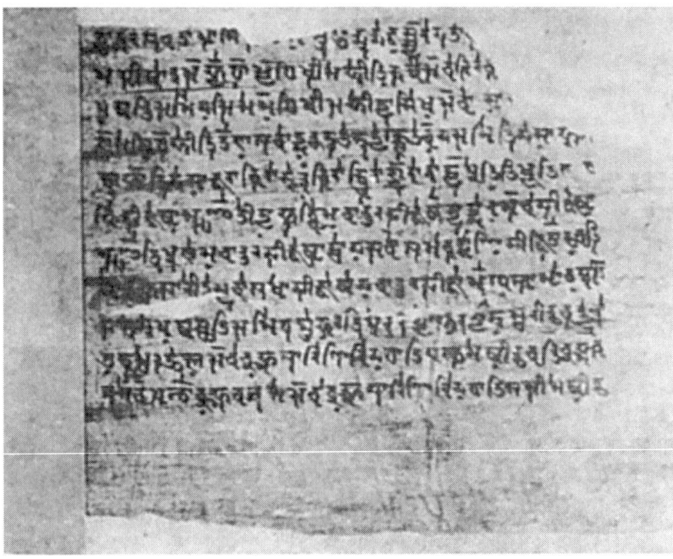

f.350a

184
185
186
187
188
189
190
192
193
194 f.349b

198a
199

f.350b

200
202
204
205
206
207

f.351a

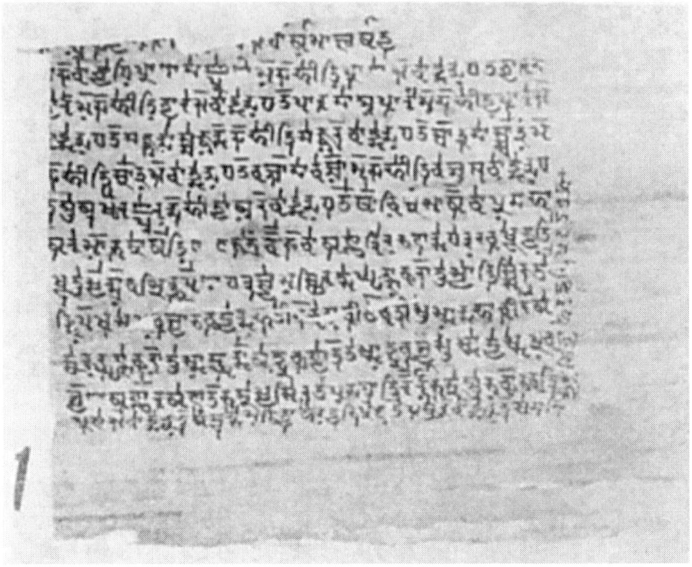

209
211
212
213
214
215
216
217
218
f.352a 219

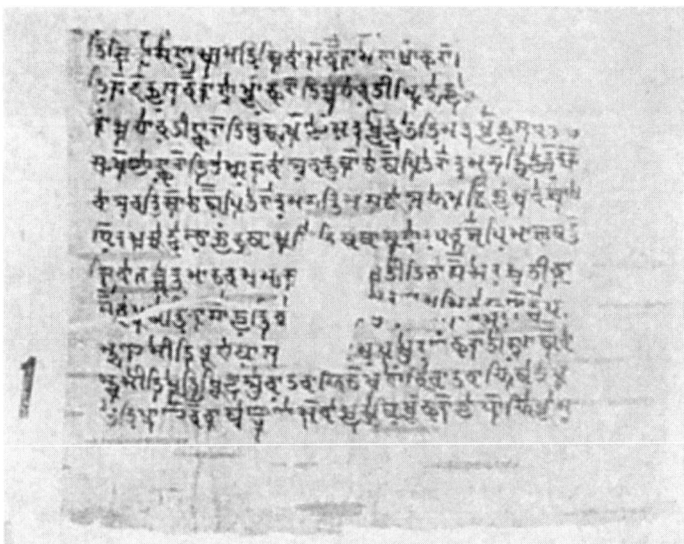

(207)

208

f.351b

(219)

f.352b

(219)

f.353a

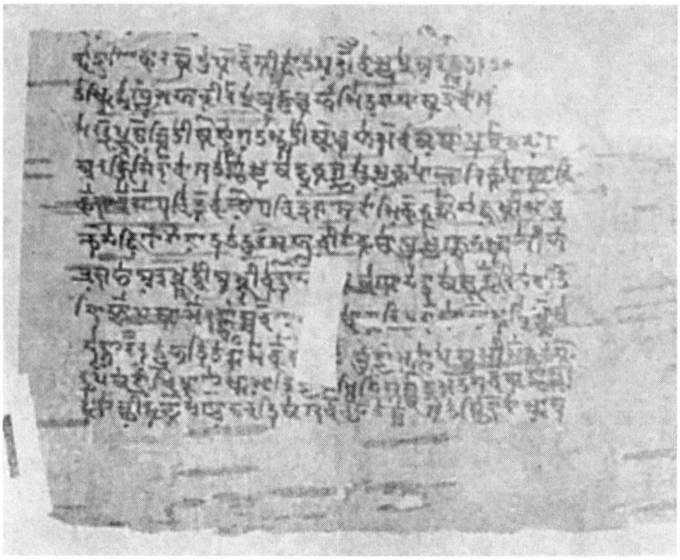

(226)

227

228

229

f.354a

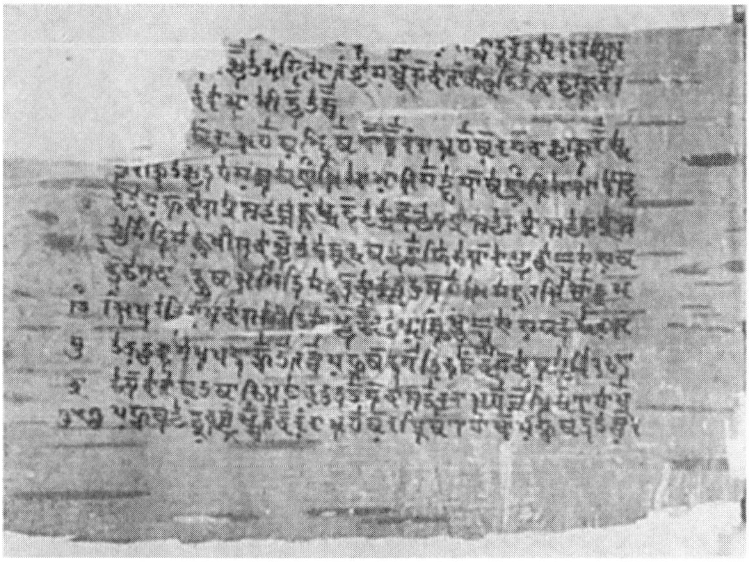

220
220a
221
222
223
224
225
226 f.353b

(229c)
230
231
232 f.354b

233

f.355a

234

235

f.356a

(233)

f.355b

(235b)

236

237

238

f.356b

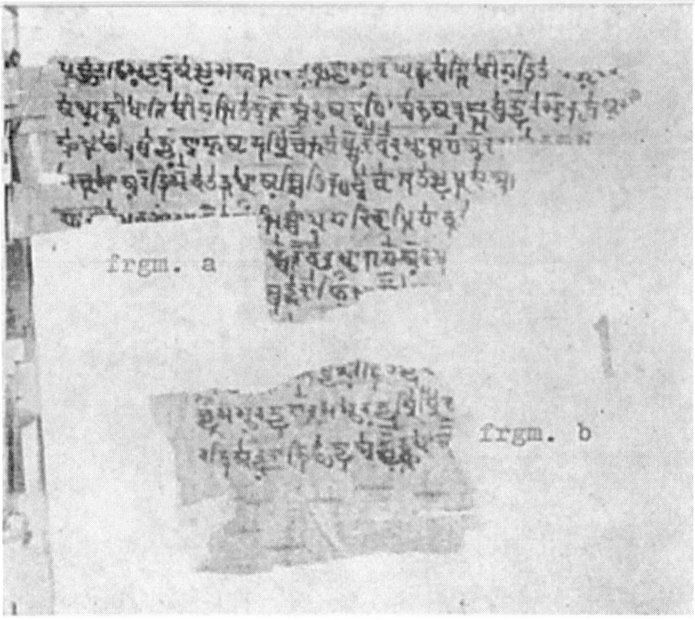

239

239a

f.357a

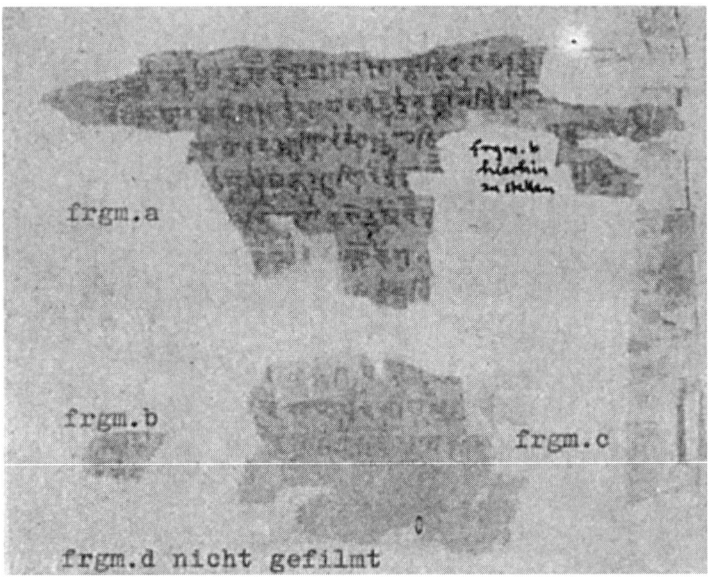

24o

f.357b

fol.357b Photokopie, Juli 1972. Hier ist auch das Fragment d, das evtl. nicht hierhin gehört, mit aufgenommen. Wegen des dunklen Untergrundes der Birkenrinde ist nicht viel zu erkennen, zeigt aber wohl doch auf, daß frgm. d vom Innenrand der Seite zu stammen scheint. Das auf dem Film getrennt mitgefilmte Fragm.b ist hier an die zugehörige Stelle gesetzt worden.

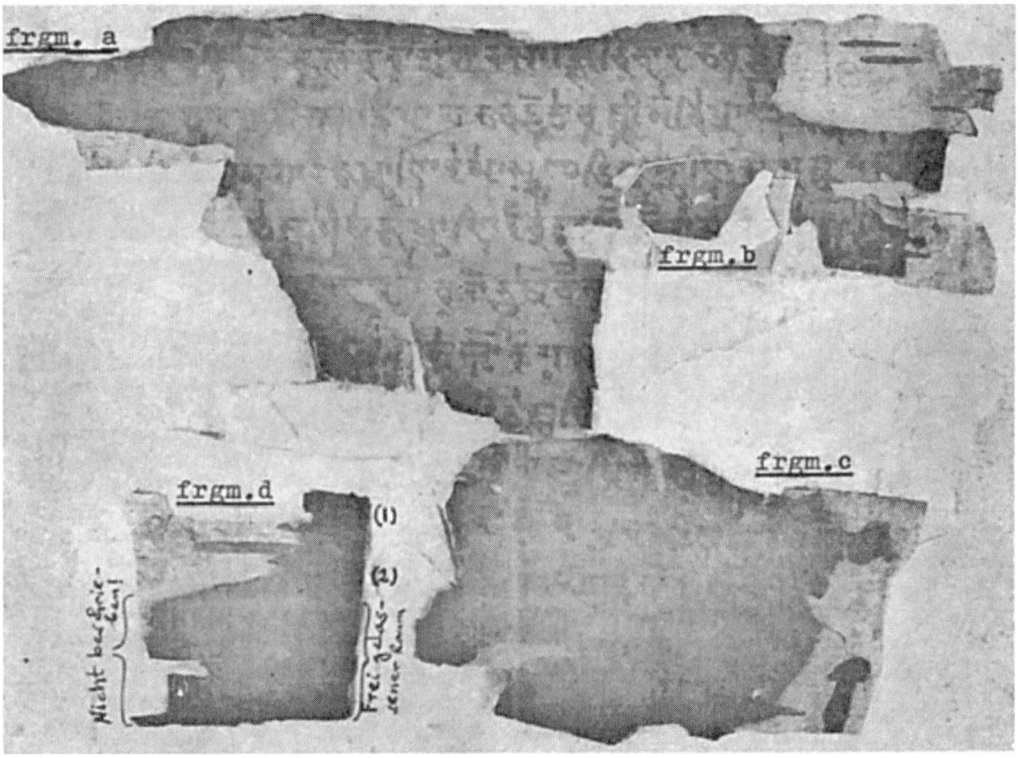

Fotografie, hergestellt von einem Negativ-Film der Bibl. Nationale, Paris, Ms. Dév. 227 (b): Ein Teil der Paddhati zum Pravargyavrata

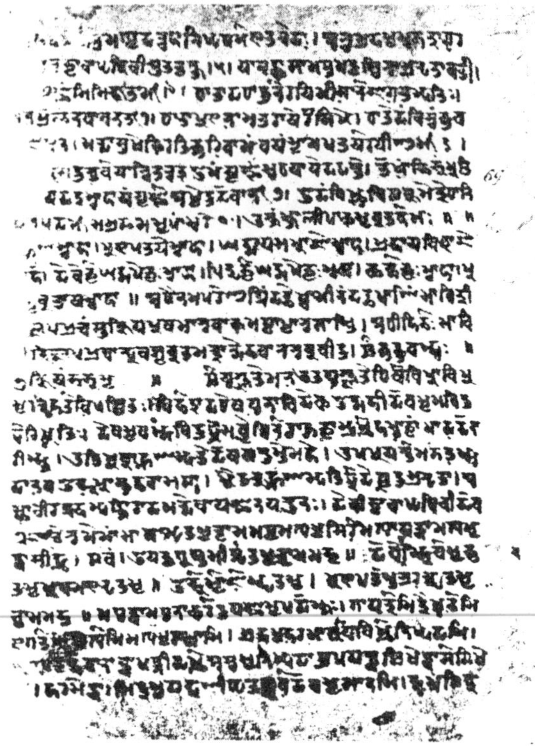

Prath.prat.anuv.: I 198.5

Opferspr. beim Vrata

Paddh. über das Lehren der Prav.Mantras

KaṭhĀ I 1-47 = 'prathamānuvākya'

NB: z.T. noch prim.u. sek. Svaritabez. erhalten: Punkte bzw. Haken

Vorbemerkung zum Prātīka-Index

Im folgenden Verzeichnis werden ganze Verse, Versanfänge, Mantras und auch Sinnabschnitte von kompletten Mantras aufgeführt, da ein derart detaillierter Index insbesondere bei dem fragmentarischen Zustand des Kanons der Kaṭha-Schule in der Identifizierung eines Mantra in KGS-Kommentaren, Ṛcakas usw. weiterhelfen kann. - In eckigen Klammern Aufgeführtes [ ] ist im Text ergänzter Mantra. Die Orthographie der Mss. ist auch hier befolgt worden, die besonderen Schreibungen allerdings an der gewohnten alphabetischen Stelle aufgeführt d.h. *śch* als *cch*, *-ḷ-* als *-ḍ-*, *ḥ̂*, *ḫ* als *ḥ* u. dgl.

APPENDIX

1. Specimen of the NRC edition (1976/77)
2. Specimen of the Maharishi University edition
3. Plan of the sacrificial ground (from Houben 1991)
4. Facsimile of the restored MS MaI 396

अथ शुक्रियमन्त्राः

[अथ प्रथमोऽनुवाकः]

ॐ । शुक्रियँ रुद्रस्य ॥

1 युञ्जते मन[१] उत युञ्जते धियो
विप्रा विप्रस्य बृहतो विपश्चितः[२] ।
वि होत्रा दधे वयुनाविदेका[३] इन्-
मही[४] देवस्य[५] सवितुꣳ[५] परिष्टुतिः ।

2 देवस्य वस्सवितुꣳ प्रसवे ऽश्विनोर्बाहुभ्याम्पूष्णो[६] हस्ताभ्यामादधे[७] ᵛ
नारीस्स्थ ।

3 उत्तिष्ठ[८] ब्रह्मणस्पते[९] देवयन्तस्त्वेमहे[१०] ।

4 उपप्रयन्तु[११] मरुतस्सुदानव[१२] ᵛ इन्द्र[१३] प्राशूर्भवा सचा ।

5 प्रैतु[१४] ब्रह्मणस्पतिꣳ

6 प्र[१५] देव्येतु[१६] सूनृता

1–47: मातृकासु प्रथमेऽनुवाके केवलं १–४७ मन्त्रा लभ्यन्ते ।

t_1 : २८० ख पृ. केवलं I. 1–5 मन्त्रा लभ्यन्ते ।

P : ३१२क पृ.–३१३क पृ. पर्यन्तमेव लभ्यते ।

P_2 : स्वरचिह्नेषु स्वरितमात्रं प्रयुक्तम्; कठ. आ. I.1–26 मन्त्रा एव लभ्यन्ते ।

T : ब्राह्मणभागे (द्र. कठ. आ. II–III) लभ्यमानानां मन्त्राणां प्रतीकान्यत्र भिन्नाक्षरैर्मुद्रितानि । स्वरचिह्नानि च T, t_1, P_2 मातृकानुसारीणि ।

१. मन् P_2 २. विपश्चितः P_2 ३. वयनविधेका t_1; °देक PP_2 ४. ममहि द्वितीयो मकारोऽत्रानावश्यकः; भवेदयं लिपिकरप्रमादः । ५. °सवितुः P; °स्य सवितुꣳ t_1 ६. प्रसव्येश्निोर्बाहुभ्या° ७. हस्ताभ्यामाददे P_2 ८. उतिष्ठ P_2 ९. ब्राह्मणस्पते P_2 १०. °तेमहे P_2 ११. °प्रयन्तो P_2 १२. मरुतस्सुदानव P_2 १३. इन्द्र P_2 १४. प्रै[···· 'प्रै' इति पर्यन्तमेव पाठो लभ्यते । अतः परं पत्राण्यपि नष्टानि । t_1 १५. प्र P, P_2; आ T १६. देव्यतु P; देव्यतु T P_2

7 अश्छा[१] वीरन्नर्यम्पङ्क्तिराघसन्[२] –
देवा यज्ञन्नयन्तु[३] नः ।।

8,9 देवी[४] द्यावापृथिवी[४] देवयजने[५] ऽनु मे मँसाथामृतस्यघ्र्यासमद्य[६]
मखस्य शिरो[७] v **मखाय त्वा** v **मखस्य त्वा शीर्ष्णे**[८] ।

10 इयत्यग्र आसीरृ**तस्यघ्र्यासमद्य**[९] **मखस्य**[१०] **शिरो** v **मखाय त्वा** v
मखस्य त्वा शीर्ष्णे ।

11 देवीर्वम्रियो[११] ऽस्य भूतस्य[१२] प्रथमजा **ऋतस्यघ्र्यासमद्य**[१३] **मखस्य
शिरो** v **मखाय त्वा** v **मखस्य त्वा शीर्ष्णे** ।

12 इन्द्रस्यौजो[१४] ऽस्यृ**तस्यघ्र्यासमद्य**[१५] **मखस्य शिरो** v **मखाय त्वा** v
मखस्य त्वा शीर्ष्णे ।

13 प्रजापतेस्तनूरस्यृ**तस्यघ्र्यासमद्य**[१६] **मखस्य शिरो** v **मखाय त्वा** v **मखस्य
त्वा शीर्ष्णे ।। ।।**

14 मधु त्वा मधुना करोतु v

15 [१७]मखस्य शिरो ऽसि v

16 यज्ञस्य पदे स्थः ।

17 गायत्रो[१८] ऽसि v

---

१. **अश्छा** P_2; २. **वीरन्न**° P_2 ; **वीरंन्नर्यम्पङ्क्तिरादस**° P ३. **यज्ञन**° P_2 **यज्ञंन्न**°P
४. **देवीर्द्या**° P ५. **देवयजने** T ६. **मांसाथामृतस्यव्या**° **मध्य** P; **मंसाथा**° P_2 ७. **शिरो** P_2
८. **शीर्ष्णे । एवं ।** P_2 'एवम्' इत्यनेनास्य मन्त्रस्याग्रेऽपि 10–13 मन्त्रेषु पुनरावृत्तिः कर्तव्येति सूच्यते । ९. **आसीनतस्य**° मू.पा.; **आसीरृ**° संशो.पा. P_2 °**मद्य ।।** नवमो मन्त्रोऽत्रावर्त्यत इति दण्डाभ्यां सूच्यते । १०. **मखस्य** मू.पा., **मखसि** संशो.पा. P
११. **देवेवम्म्रियो** द्वितीयो वकारोऽत्र संशोधकेन पङ्क्त्युपरि लिखितः । P_2 ; **देवीवमम्रियो** P
१२. **भूत** मू. पा., **भूतस्य** संशो. पा. P. १३. **रृतस्य ।।** P एवं संक्षिप्तः । १४. **इन्द्रोस्यौजो**° P_2.
१५. °**रृतस्य ।** P_2 एवं संक्षिप्तः । ; °**मध्य** P. १६. **प्रजापति**° °**मध्य** P; °**तनूरस्यृ**° °**मद्य ।।** P_2 एवं संक्षिप्तः । १७. संपूर्णमन्त्रोऽयं P P_2 मातृकयोः न लभ्यते । १८. **गायत्रो** T

18 त्रैष्टुभो[१] ऽसि [v].

19 जागतोऽ सि[v]

20 मखो ऽसि[v]

21 मखस्य रास्नासि[v]

22 सूर्यस्य हरसाश्रय[२] [v]

23 वृष्णो[३] निष्पदसि[४] प्राजापत्यन्[५]-

24–25 -देवानान्त्वा[५] पत्नीवृष्णो[६] अश्वस्य निष्पदा धूपयन्त्वर्चिषे
त्वा [v] शोचिषे[७] त्वा[७][v] हरसे त्वा ।।

26 [८]मित्रस्य चर्षणीधृतश्–
[९]श्रवो देवस्य सानसि ।
द्युम्नश्चित्रश्रवस्तमम्[९] ।।

27 देवस्त्वा सवितोद्वपतु[१०]
सुपाणिस्स्वङ्गुरिः[११] ।।
सुबाहुरुत शक्त्या ।।

28 अव्यथमानऽ[१२] पृथिव्यामाशा[१३] दिश आपृण ।

29 उत्तिष्ठ बृहन्भवोर्ध्वस्तिष्ठ[१४] [v] ध्रुवस्त्वम्[१५] ।

---

१. त्रैष्टुभो T २. श्रोय अथवा श्रयो P_2 ३. विष्णो P_2. ४. °दसि । P_2 ५. [प्रजा]पत्यन्दे° P_2 ६. पत्नीवृ° T, P; पत्नीवृ॑° P_2 ७. शोचिषे [त्वा] P_2 ; सुचिषे त्वा P ८. 26–28 मन्त्राः कठ. सं. १६.६ विद्यन्ते; कठ. आ. I.28 इत्यत्रोहितः । ९. श्रवो देवस्य सानसि। द्युम्नंचित्र[··· पाठोऽत्रावसितः, अतः परं पत्राण्यपि नष्टानि । P_2; श्रवो देवस्य सानसि । द्युम्नश्चित्रश्रवस्तमम् । P; स्वराङ्कनं कठ. आ. I. 218 अनुसारि; P_2 मातृकायामत्र प्रथमेऽनुवाकेऽन्त्यमेति । १०. °तुद्वापतु मू.पा., °तुद्वपतु संशो.पा. P ११. स्वाङ्गुरिरिः मू.पा., स्वङ्गुलिरिः संशो.पा. P १२. अव्यथमानाऽ T; अव्यथमाना P; °माना S; द्र० कठ. सं. १६. ६: °माना १३. पृथिवीव्याम° मू.पा., पृथिव्याम° संशो.पा. P १४. बृहद्° T, P; द्र० कठ. सं. १६. ६: बृहती १५. पूर्व° S; ध्रुव T

30 इदमहममुमामुष्यायणममुष्याꣳ[1] पुत्रन्तेजसा[2] ब्रह्मवर्चसेन समर्धयामी-

31 -दमहममुमामुष्यायणममुष्याꣳ[1] पुत्रन्तेजसा ब्रह्मवर्चसेन व्यर्धयामी-

32 -दमहममुमामुष्यायणममुष्याꣳ[1] पुत्रमोजसा वीर्येण समर्धयामी-

33 -दमहममुमामुष्यायणममुष्याꣳ[1] पुत्रमोजसा वीर्येण व्यर्धयामी-

34 -दमहममुमामुष्यायणममुष्याꣳ[1] पुत्रमूर्जा पशुभिस्समर्धयामी-

35 -दमहममुमामुष्यायणममुष्याꣳ[1] पुत्रमूर्जा पशुभिर्व्यर्धयामी-

36 -दमहम्मान्तेजसा[3] ब्रह्मवर्चसेनौजसा वीर्येण प्रजया पशुभिरन्नाद्येन समर्धयाम्यृ-

37 -जवे त्वा v साधवे त्वा v सुक्षित्यै त्वा v

38 सूर्यस्य त्वा चक्षुषान्वीक्षे ॥

39 श्छृणत्तु[4] त्वा वाक् v [5]

40 श्छृणत्तु[4,6] त्वोर्क् v [5]

41 श्छृणत्तु[4] त्वा पयः v [5]

42 श्छृणत्तु[4] त्वा रसः v [5]

43 श्छृणत्तु[4] त्वा हविः v [5]

44 श्छृणत्तु[4] त्वा सोमः[5]

45 श्छृणत्तु[4] त्वा यज्ञः v [5]

46 श्छृणत्तु[4] त्वा ब्रह्म v [5,7]

47 श्छृणत्तु[4] त्वा प्रजापतिः

[इति प्रथमोऽनुवाकस्समाप्तः]

---

१. अमुष्यः P, अतः परं I 30–35 मन्त्रास्तथैव । २. पुत्रं° P ३. °महमान्ते° P

४, छृणतु P अग्रे 39–47 मन्त्रेष्वपि तथैव । ५. एतेषां वाक्यानामन्ते सन्धिच्छेदः कृतः ।

६. श्छृणत्तु T; च्छृणत्त S; छृणतु P ७. ब्रह्मः मू.पा. ब्रह्मा संशो.पा. P.

[अथ दशर्चꣳ प्रथमꣳ प्रतीकानुवाकः]

ॐ। शुक्रियँ रुद्रस्य ।।
198.1 उद उ त्यञ्जातवेदसन्[1]-
देवँ वहन्ति केतवः ।
दृशे विश्वाय सूर्यम् ।। १ ।।
198.2 इममू षु[2] त्वमस्मभ्यँ[3]
सनिङ्गायत्रन्नवीयाँस[4]- ।
-मग्ने[5] देवेषु प्रवोचात्[6] ।। २ ।।
198.3 समिन्द्र[7] नो मनसा[8] नेषि[9] गोभिस्-
सँ सूरिभिर्हरिवस्सँ[10] स्वस्त्या ।
सँ ब्रह्मणा देवकृतँ[11] यदस्ति[12]
सन्देवानाँ[13] सुमत्या यज्ञियानाम् ।। ३ ।।

प्रवर्ग्यपद्धतिष्विमे 198.1–10 मन्त्राः प्रथमे प्रतीकेऽन्तर्गताः (द्र०लौ. गृ. सू. २, ६४ पृ.) । एतेपु केचन मन्त्राः कठारण्यके प्रतीकरूपेण प्रयुक्ताः स्युः (द्र० अपि च मैत्रा. सं. ४.६.११: १३२. ११. इत्यादि) ।

P : (३११ क पृ.–३११ख पृ.) मन्त्राश्चेमे सङ्ख्यारहिताः ।

P_2: (१४ क, ख पृ.) अत्र स्वरचिह्नेषु स्वरितमात्रं दृश्यते ।

t_1 : पत्राणि (२८० पृ.–२८१ क पृ.) नष्टानि ।

अत्र लभ्यमानानां मन्त्राणां स्वरितमपहाय स्वरचिह्नानि कठसंहितातः सङ्गृहीतानि; स्वरितचिह्नं तु P_2 मातृकातः ।

१. जतवेदसम् ।। P एवं संक्षिप्तः; स्वरचिह्नानि कठ. आ. I. 198. 19 अनुसारीणि । **२. ष** P **३. °भ्यं°** P_2 **४. °गायत्रंनवीयांसं** P_2 **५. अग्ने** P_2 **६. °चः** P, P_2; **°चात्** L द्र० ऋ. सं. १. २७. ४; तै. आ. ४, २, ८ **७. °न्द्रो** P_2 स्वरचिह्नानि कठ. सं. ४. १२ अनुसारीणि । **८. मनसा** P_2 **९. नेशि** P **१०. सूरभिहरिर्वास्°** P; **सूरिभिर्हरिवास्°** P_2 **११. देवाकृतं** P; **देवकृतं** P_2 **१२. य्यद°** P, P_2 **१३. सन्दे°**P

198.4[१] सँ वर्चसा पयसा[२] सन्तनूभि[३]-
-रगन्महि मनसा सँ[४] शिवेन[४] ।
त्वष्टा[५] सुदत्रो विदधातु रायो[६]
ऽनु नो मार्ष्टु तन्वो यद्विलिष्टम् ।। ४ ।।

198.5 [७]अन्वग्निरुषसामग्रमख्य–[७]
-दन्वहानि प्रथमो जातवेदाः ।
अनु सूर्यस्य पुरुत्रा च[८] रश्मी-[९]
-ननु[९] द्यावापृथिवी आततन्थ ।। ५ ।।

198.6[१०] या वाङ्कशा[११] मधुम-[१२]
-त्यश्विना[१२] सुनृतावती ।
तया[१३] यज्ञँ[१४] मिमिक्षतम्[१५] ।। ६ ।।

198.7[१६] धाता दधातु नो रयि-[१७]
-मीशानो[१८] जगतस्पतिः[१९] ।
स[२०] नꣳ[२१] पूर्णेन वावनत् ।। ७ ।।

198.8[२२] धाता प्रजानामुत[२३] राय[२४] ईशिषे[२५]

---

१. स्वरचिह्नानि कठ. सं ४. १२ अनुसारीणि । २. पयसा P_2 ३. °तनूभिर् । P एवं संक्षिप्तः ४. सं×वेन। P_2 ५. तष्टा P_2 ६. राय मू.पा., रायो संशो.पा. P_2 ७. अ×× रुषस×ग्रम° P_2; °ग्रंम° P द्र. कठ. सं. १६.२ ८. च P_2 ९. रश्मिन° P; र××न P_2 १०. 198.6 स्वरचिह्नानि कठ. सं ४. २ अनुसारीणि । ११. वङ्क P, P_2; वा° L १२. मधु° P_2 १३. त्रुटितम् P_2 १४. यज्ञिम° P, P_2 १५. °ताम् P, P_2; °तम् L १६. 198.7 स्वरचिह्नानि कठ. आ. I. 198. 25 अनुसारीणि । १७. रयिं ।। एवं संक्षिप्तः P १८. ईशानो P_2 १९. जगत° P_2 २० स P_2 २१. नꣳ P_2 २२. 198.8 स्वरचिह्नानि 198.26 अनुसारीणि । २३. प्रजानांमु° P; प्रजानामु° P_2 २४. राये P_2; राय L, P. द्र० कठ. आ. I 198.26 २५. ईषे मू.पा., ईशिषे । संशो. पा. एवं संक्षिप्तः P; ईशिषे । एवं संक्षिप्तः P_2

धातेदँ विश्वम्भुवनञ्जजान[1] ।
सन्दाशुषे किरति भूरि[2] वामँ[3]
वयँ स्याम[4] पतयो रयीणाम् ।। ८ ।।

198.9[5] त्रयस्त्रिँशत्तन्तवो[6] यान्वितन्वत
इमँ यज्ञँ[7] स्वधया ये ददन्ते[8] ।
तेषाँ[9] श्छिद्रम्प्रतिदध्मो[10] यदत्र
स्वाहायँ[11] यज्ञो[12] अप्येतु देवान् ।। ९ ।।

198.10[13] इदँ विष्णुर्विचक्रामे[14]
त्रेधा निदधे पदम् ।
समूढमस्य[15] पाँसुरे ।। १० ।।

[इति प्रथमः प्रतीकानुवाकस्समाप्तः]

१. ˚भुवन˚; P ˚भुव×˚ P २. भूरि P₂ ३. वासं L ४. स्याम P₂ ५. १९८.९ द्र० कठ. सं. ३०.४ अपि स्वरचिह्नेन रहितः ६. ××त्रशत्तन्तवोतन्वत P₂ ७. य्यज्ञँ P, P₂ ८. ददन्ति P ९. तेषां P₂ १०. छिद्रम्प्रति×× P₂ ११. स्वाहा । यं P १२. य्यज्ञो P, P₂ द्र०कठ. सं. ३४.१९ १३. १९८.१० स्वरचिह्नानि कठ. सं. २.१० अनुसारीणि १४. विचक्क्रमे P १५. समूढम˚

कठारण्यक

युञ्जते ब्राह्मण

युञ्जते मन इत्याहवनीये जुहोति । मनसा वै प्रजापतिर्यज्ञमतनुत । ततो
वाचा ततः कर्मणा । मनसैवैतद्यजमानो यज्ञं वितत्य । ततो वाचा । ततः
कर्मणा करोति १ देवस्य वस्सवितुः प्रसव इत्यभ्रीरादत्ते । सवितृप्रसूत
एवैना देवताभिरादत्ते । चतस्र आदत्ते । चतस्रो वै दिशो । दिग्भ्यः
प्रवर्ग्यस्सम्भ्रियते । दिग्भ्य एव प्रवर्ग्यँ सम्भरति । वानस्पत्या भवन्ति ।
वनस्पतिभिर्वै प्रवर्ग्यस्सम्भ्रियते । वनस्पतिभिरेव प्रवर्ग्यँ सम्भरति २ उत्तिष्ठ
ब्रह्मणस्पत इत्युत्तिष्ठति । बृहस्पतिर्वै ब्रह्मणस्पतिर् । बृहस्पतिरेव भूत्वो-
त्तिष्ठति ३ उपप्रयन्तु मरुतस्सुदानव इति । सुदानवो वै मरुत आरण्या ।
अरण्ये प्रवर्ग्यस्सम्भ्रियते । अरण्य एवारण्यं करोति ४ प्रैतु ब्रह्मणस्पतिरिति
प्रतितिष्ठति । बृहस्पतिर्वै ब्रह्मणस्पतिर् । बृहस्पतिरेव भूत्वा । प्रतितिष्ठति
५ आ देव्येतु सूनृतेति । वाग्वै देवी सूनृता । वाचा प्रवर्ग्यस्सम्भ्रियते ।
वाचैव प्रवर्ग्यँ सम्भरति ६ अश्छा वीरं नर्यं पङ्क्तिराधसमिति । यज्ञो वै
वीरो नर्यः पङ्क्तिराधा । देवेभ्य एव यज्ञँ सम्भरति ७ देवी द्यावापृथिवी
देवयजनेऽनु मे मंसाथामितीमे वै महावीरात् सम्भ्रियमाणादबिभीताम् ।
तेजसा ना उद्धक्ष्यतीति । स बृहस्पतिरब्रवीद् । युवयोर्भागधेयमिति ।
तत एनमन्वमन्यताम् ८ ऋतस्य ध्र्यासमद्य मखस्य शिर इति सम्भरति ।
यज्ञस्यैव शिरस्सम्भरति । त्रिर्हरति । त्रिषत्या हि देवास् । समन्तमभ्रीः
परिश्रयति । रक्षसाम्पराणुत्त्यै । प्रजापतेर्वै प्रजास्सिसृक्षमाणस्य तस्य तेजो
यज्ञियमपाक्रामत् । तदिमाम्प्राविशत् । तद्वराहो भूत्वान्वविन्दद् ९ इत्यत्यग्र
आसीरिति । यद्वराहविहतम्भवत्यस्या एव तेजो यज्ञियँ सम्भरति १०
देवीर्वम्रियोऽस्य भूतस्य प्रथमजा इति । वम्रियो वा अस्य भूतस्य प्रथमजास्
। ता वा एतद्विदुर्यत्रास्या जीवं यज्ञियं । यद्वल्मीकवापनाँ सम्भरत्यस्या एव
जीवं यज्ञियँ सम्भरतीन्द्रो वै यद्वृत्रमहंस्तस्यौजो वीर्यमपाक्रामत् । तदोषधीः
प्राविशत् । ते पूतीका अभवन्न् ११ इन्द्रस्यौजोऽसीति । यत्पूतीकानाँ
सम्भरतीन्द्रस्यैवौजो वीर्यँ सम्भरति १२ प्रजापतेस्तनूरसीत्यजां दुहन्ति ।
प्रजापतेर्वा एषा प्रिया तनूर्यदजा । यदजां दुहन्ति । प्रजापतेरेव प्रियान्तन्वँ

1 (१)

वसीयसस्य व्यावृत्यै --- असौ वा आदित्यो रुद्रो महावीर ---

इति घर्माजठराब्राह्मणं समाप्तम्

इति शुक्रियब्राह्मणं समाप्तम् २४०

Credits

Source: Das Kaṭha Āraṇyaka. *Textkritische Edition mit Uebersetzung und Kommentar,* Teildruck. Diss. erlangen 1972.

Typescript: Preliminary edition prepared by Michael Witzel, Harvard
Conversion to Devanagari using Vedapad Software by Ralph Bunker

Formatted for Maharishi University of Management Vedic Literature Collection

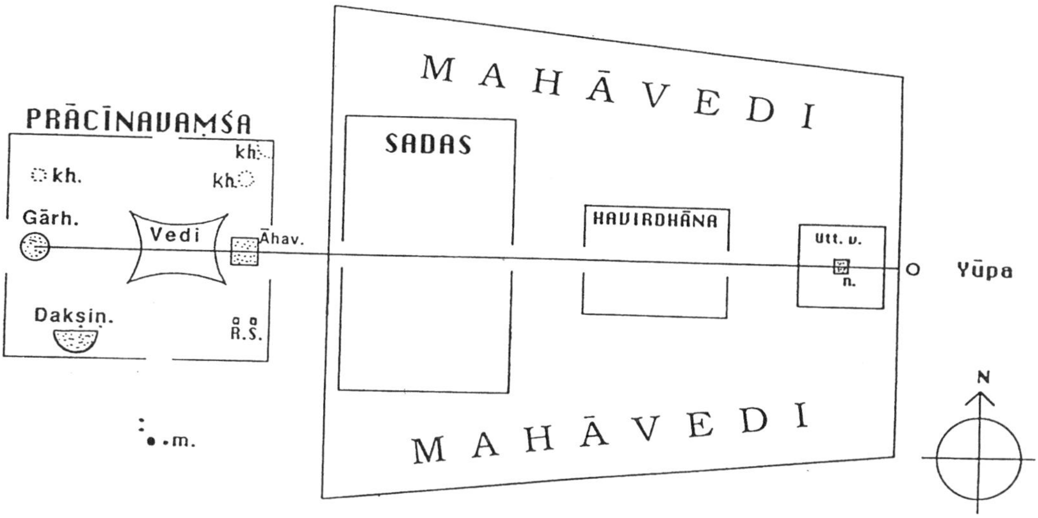

Gārh.	Gārhapatya or Domestic Fire.
Āhav.	Āhavanīya or Offering Fire.
Dakṣiṇ.	Dakṣiṇāgni or Southern Fire.
R.	Rājāsandī, the King's Throne for the Soma stalks.
S.	Saṃrāḍ-āsandī, the Emperor's Throne for the Pravargya vessels.
m.	*methī* and *mayūkha*-s, the peg and pins for the cow, the calf, the she-goat, and the lamb.
kh.	*khara*-s, the mounds.
Utt. v.	Uttaravedi.
n.	nābhi.

(The plan and the additional information are mainly based on: Planche IV of Caland-Henry, *Agniṣṭoma* (at the end of vol.1); BŚS 11, 6, 8-16; ĀpŚS 15, 6, 10-22; HirŚS 24, 2, 10-11; van Buitenen, *Pravargya*, Plate 2 (opp. to p. 12); Staal, *Agni* 1:376-377, Plate 60B.)

Facsimile of the restored MS MaI 396

Paddhati zum Godāna, Ajasthāpana

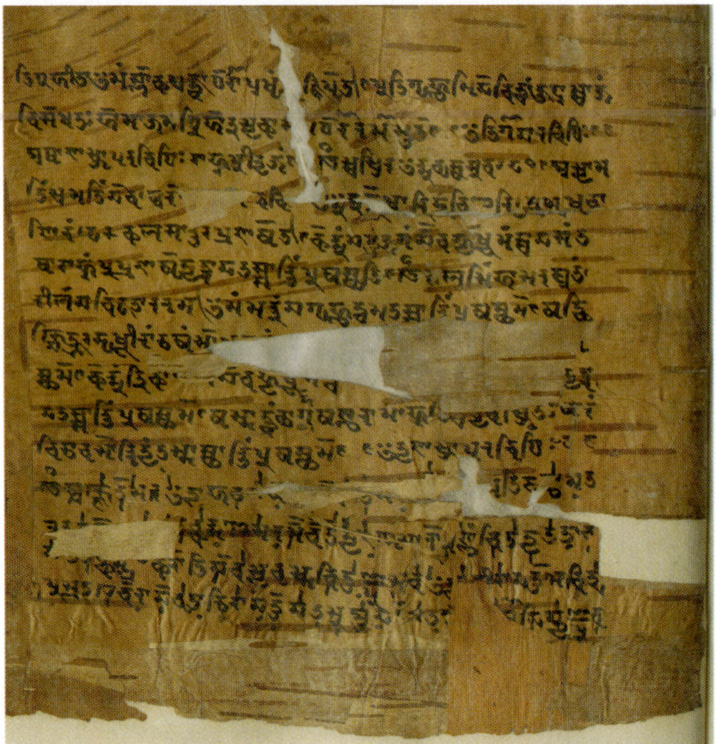

KaṭhĀ II 1

2

f.[33]7b

MaI 396, Univ. Bibl. Tübingen

frg.zu I 1

10

11

12

13

14

15

16

17

18

19

20

f.338b 21

3 4 5 6 7 8 9 10 f.338a

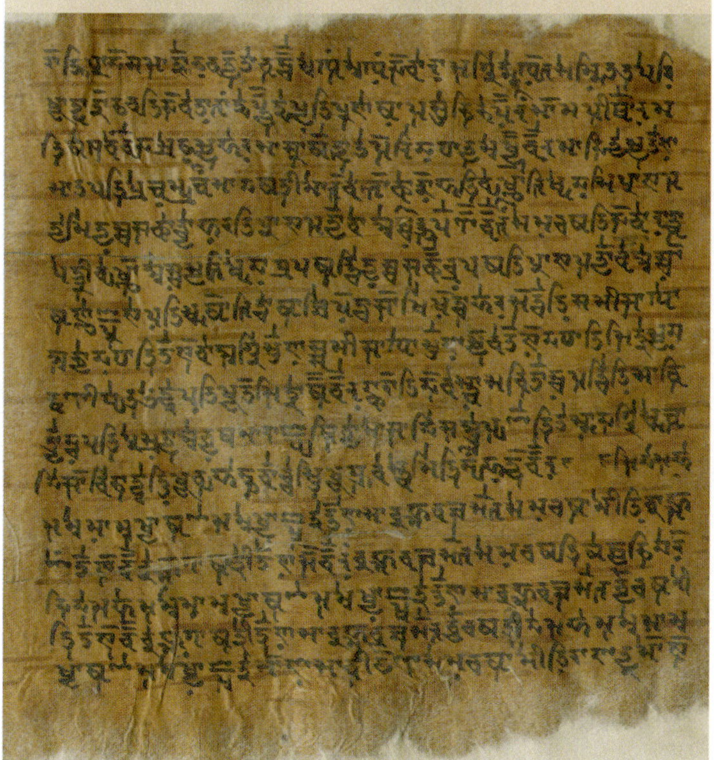

22 23 24 25 26 27 28 29 30 31 32 f.339a

33
34
35
36
37
38
39
4o
42
46
48
f.339b 49

62
63
64
65
66
67
67a
68
69
7o
71
72
73
f.340a 74

49
5o
51
52
54
55
57
58
59
6o
61
f.34oa

Ende von Ms. Tübingen,
Universitäts-
bibliothek No. MaI 396
Heft 1o a.

Es folgt Heft 1ob mit
noch weiter zerstörten
Blättern, den letzten
erhaltenen von MaI 396

75

76

77

f.341a

9o

91

92

93

94

95

97

f.342a

80
81
82
83
85
86
87
88
f.341b

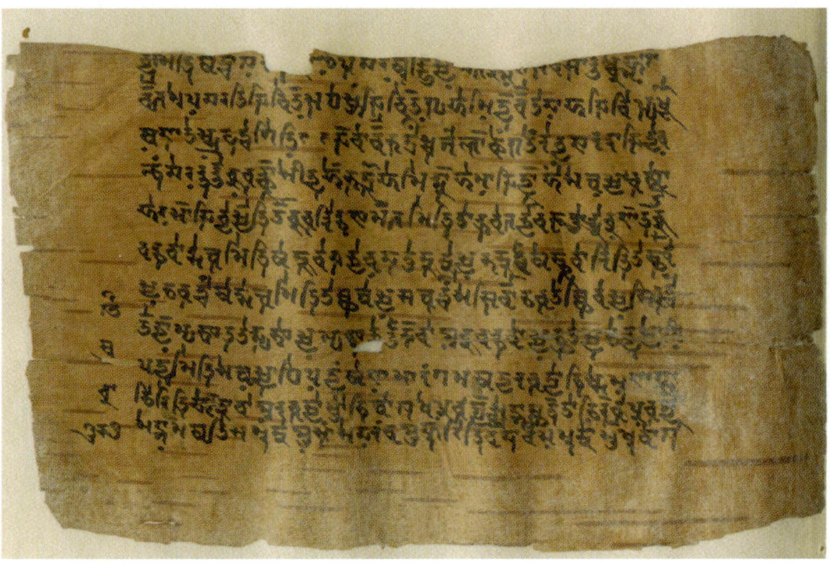

98c
99
100
01
c1b
f.342b

1o2
1o3
1o4
1o5
1o7
1o8
1o8a
1o9
f.343a 111

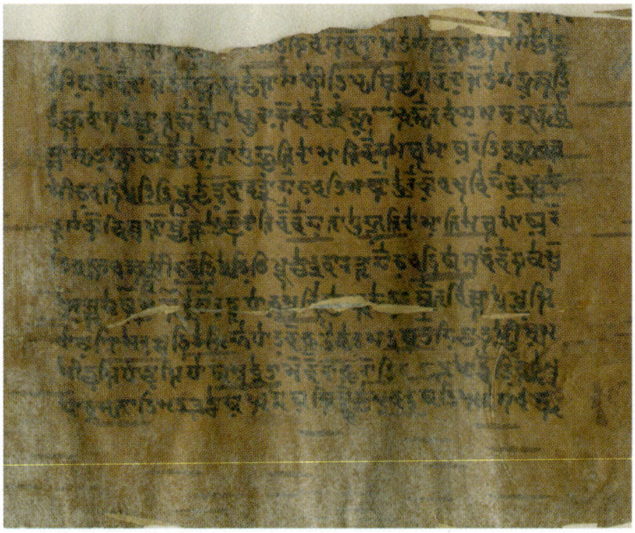

115a
117
118
119
12o
f.344a 121

112
113
114
115

f.343b

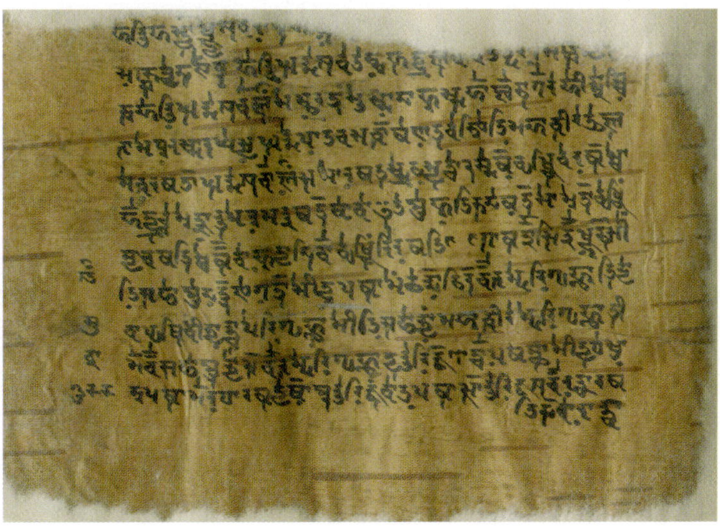

122
123
124
125
126
127
128

f.344b

129

130
131

132
133

f.345a

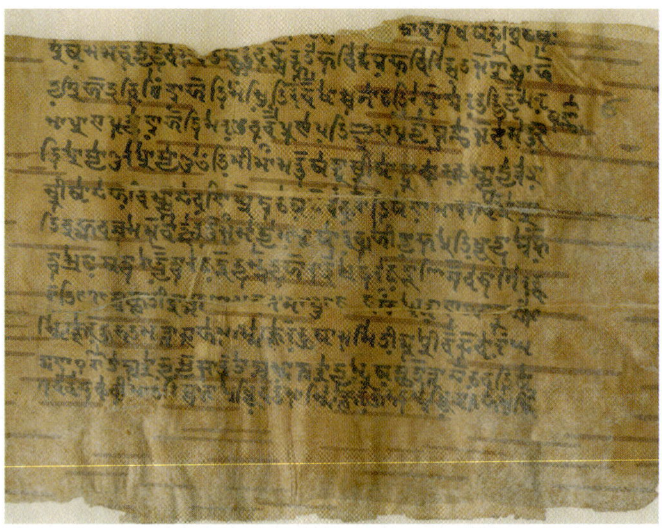

143

144
145
Kaṭhā III 146

147
f.346a

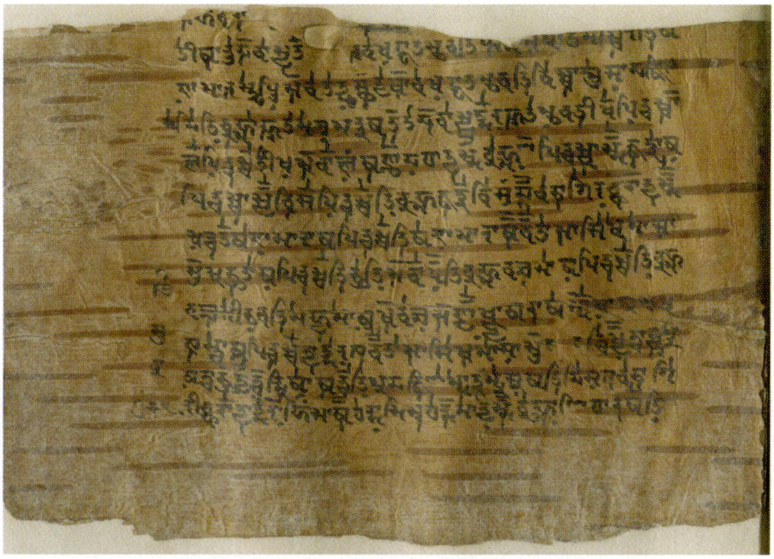

133a
134
135
136
137
138
140
141

f.345b

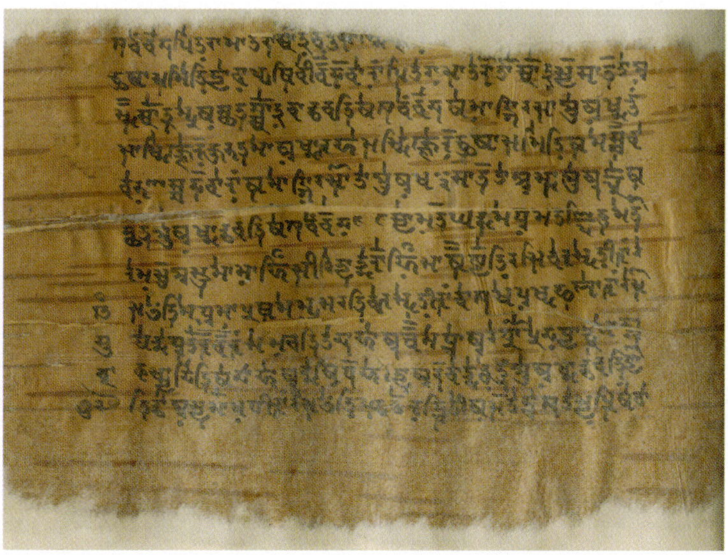

148
149
150
151
152
153
f.346b

154
155
156
157

158

159
160
161
163
164
165
f.347a

174

175

176

177

f.348a

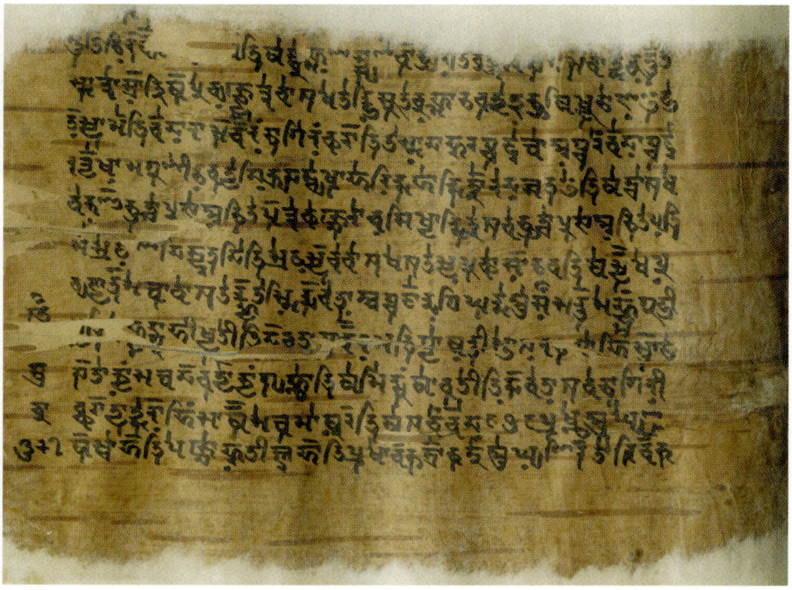

167
168
169
170
172
173
f.347b

178
180
181
182
183
f.348b

(183a)

f.349a

195a

196
197
198

f.350a

184
185
186
187
188
189
190
192
193
194

f.349b

198a
199

f.350b

200
202
204
205
206
207

f.351a

209
211
212
213
214

215
216
217
218
f.352a 219

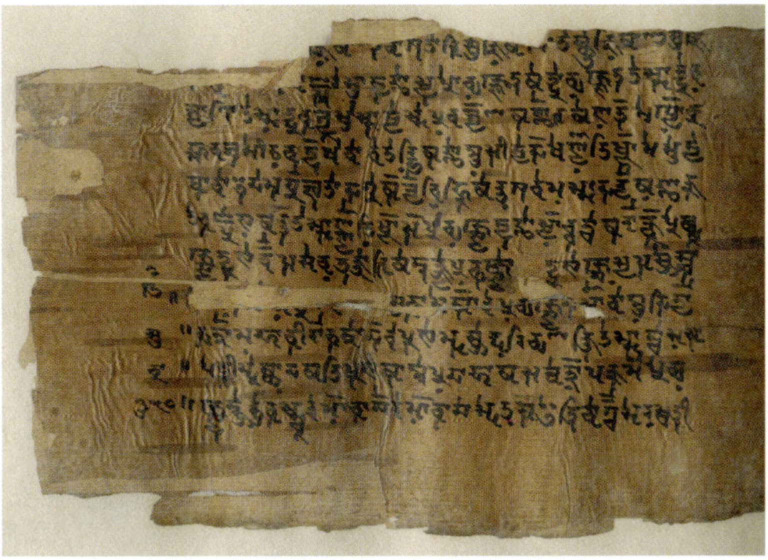

(207)

208 f.351b

(219)

f.352b

(219)

f.353a

(226)

227

228

229

.354a

220
220a
221
222
223
224
225
226 f.353b

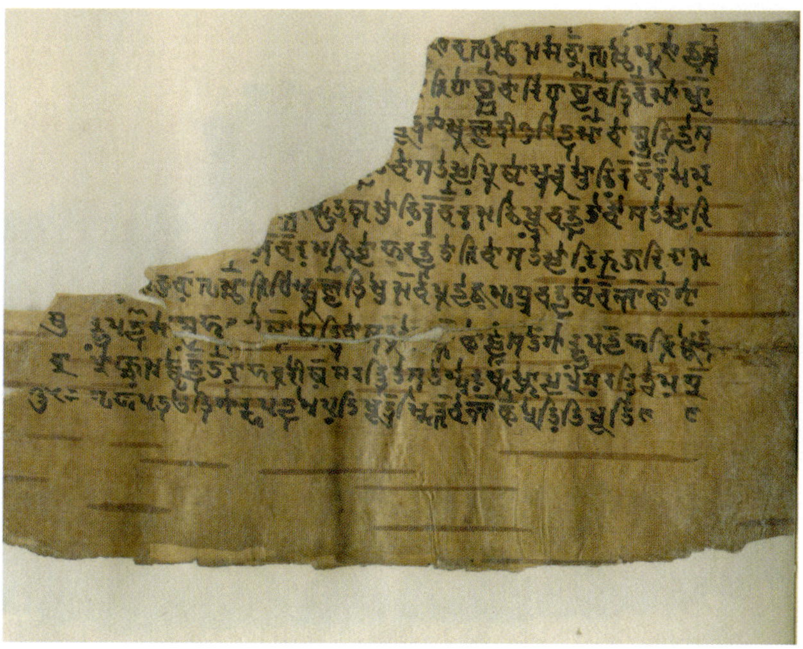

(229c)
230
231
232 f.354b

233

f.355a

234

235

f.356a

(233)

f.355b

(235b)

236

237

238

f.356b

239

239a

f.357a

240

f.357b